A MAN'S

An

ROGER

LIFE

Autobiography

WILKINS

A TOUCHSTONE BOOK
Published by Simon & Schuster, Inc.
New York

First Touchstone Edition, 1984
Published by Simon & Schuster, Inc.
Simon & Schuster Building
Rockefeller Center
1230 Avenue of the Americas
New York, New York 10020
TOUCHSTONE and colophon are registered trademarks
of Simon & Schuster, Inc.

Designed by Karolina Harris

Manufactured in the United States of America

10 9 8 7 6 5 4 3 2
10 9 8 7 6 5 4 3 2 1 Pbk.

Library of Congress Cataloging in Publication Data

Wilkins, Roger W., [date]
    A man's life.
    1. Wilkins, Roger W., [date]. 2. Afro-Americans—
Civil rights. 3. Afro-Americans—Biography. I. Title.
E185.97.W687A35   973.91′092′4 [B]   82-686
                                            AACR2

ISBN 0-671-22673-8
ISBN 0-671-49268-3 Pbk.

FOR AMY AND DAVID

I

1 Perhaps because we live in different cities, conversation does not flow easily between my children and me—particularly between my son and me. When my daughter's interest is engaged, she talks. Otherwise, there's silence, but a not-uneasy silence. With my son, it's different. He is eleven, and there is a boundless admiration for a distant and mysterious father who writes in Greenwich Village and earns a living at *The New York Times.* Our closeness causes distance, and our silences are filled with searchings for the next thing to say. Conversation comes in short, quick bursts.

One day during one of my visits to them in Washington, David and I were driving to pick up Amy at some house where she had been attending a party. "Yuh know, Dad," he said, breaking a silence, "I can't decide what I want to be when I grow up. A writer or a football player." I looked at him quizzically. "Well," he asked, "what do you think?"

What indeed did I think? I thought at that moment almost everything I had ever known and felt. My son wanted me to help him to choose an occupation by which he could define himself. And his question showed how completely he believed all that his world had told him, especially that he could be whatever he wanted to be. How could I help him? What of value could I tell him? Or Amy either, for that matter. At fifteen she was rapidly becoming more adult than child, her dark and brooding face filled with questions—"Who are you? . . . And what is that to me? . . . Where am I going? . . . How will it be?"

There is no answer in a sentence or in a paragraph to such questions—rather, there is everything that I can remember and all

9

that I have learned, beginning with the day my father began telling me what it meant to be a black in America. It was Kansas City, Missouri, where I was born, and it must have been about 1936, when I was four. I loved to watch the "streamlined trains"—the ones where gleaming, steel-encased power roared under our viaduct on its way to some mysterious Western place called Santa Fe. He'd often take me on Sunday night to stand on the viaduct to wait for the rumble and the tremor that was the sure signal that my train was on its way.

One of those Sunday nights, I told him that I wanted to drive a train like that when I grew up. He didn't say anything, so I repeated my words. His face grew somber. To me he was a commanding and somewhat mysterious man. He had been sick and away at a sanitarium for tuberculosis patients for as long as I could remember and had just returned home. Did his silence mean disapproval? Had I made him angry? I was growing uneasy. When he finally spoke, he said—in a very gentle voice—"You can't do that, Peter." (He had suggested to my mother that they name me Roger after a character in a book he liked but when it came time to talk to me, he always called me Peter.)

"Why not?" I wanted to know. Why was he being mean?

"There are white people and Negro people in the world," he answered. "And the white people make the rules. One of the rules is that Negro people can work on the trains, but they can't drive them."

"What?" I asked, incredulous and uncomprehending. "What?"

"That's one of the rules," he continued. "There are many more."

"But that's not fair," I protested.

"That's right," he said. "It's not fair, and you must fight against that all your life."

I promised him I would.

Two years before that, when he was in the tuberculosis sanitarium, he had written me a letter, which I obviously couldn't read, but which tells a lot about how he planned to raise his Negro son in America and something about his hopes for me. It read:

Friday, March 22, 1934

Dear Roger—

Let me congratulate you upon having reached your second birthday. Your infancy is now past and it is now that you should begin to turn your thoughts upon those achievements which are expected of a brilliant young gentleman well on his way to manhood.

During the next year, you should learn the alphabet; you should learn certain French and English idioms which are a part of every cultivated person's vocabulary; you should gain complete control of those natural functions which, uncontrolled, are a source of worry and embarrassment to even the best of grandmothers; you should learn how to handle table silver so that you will be able to eat gracefully and conventionally; and you should learn the fundamental rules of social living—politeness, courtesy, consideration for others, and the rest.

This should not be difficult for you. You have the best and most patient of mothers in your sterling grandmother and your excellent mother. Great things are expected of you. Never, never forget that.

Love,

YOUR FATHER

That was his approach to raising a black child in America, and as a beginning it was enough. But he never lived long enough to face the tougher and substantially more complex kind of challenge his grandchildren have put to me. Whether Amy actually decides to continue writing poetry, and whether David chooses football, writing or neither, I hope that their occupations will never define them. I want them to be evolving creative forces in the worlds they come to inhabit. I have no answers on how they are to get there—only lessons learned in experiencing life as a black man in America at a complicated time. And the most valuable things I can give my black children, I suppose, are the stories of my own broken illusions—and my continuing growth from the struggle.

In the beginning, it was warm and empty in Kansas City, Missouri. There was a neat little stucco house on a hill in a small Negro section called Roundtop during the depths of the Depression. There was always food, and there was always clothing. I had no sense of being poor or any anxiety about money. If my mother ever worried about money, she never let on to me. At our house, not only was there food and furniture and all the rest, there was even a baby grand piano that my mother would play sometimes. My father had bought it for her for an anniversary. And there was a cleaning lady, Mrs. Turner, who came every week. She was very religious and would not tell lies. Once when the phone rang and my mother didn't feel like being bothered, she told Mrs. Turner, "If it's for me, tell her I'm not here." So she told the caller, "Mrs. Wilkins does not feel like being molested." We called her Saint Turner.

In addition to the furniture and the cleaning lady, the house harbored, but barely contained, an enormously vigorous woman whom I
called Gram. She was my mother's mother. She took care of me when
my mother was at work and did the woman's work around the house.
My father's tuberculosis kept him away. It was lonesome without him.

My father was not a big man. He stood five foot nine and weighed
140 at most. He was very neat and well-groomed, and his mind,
according to those who knew him well, was as fastidious as his ward-
robe. He had been business manager of a black weekly newspaper in
Kansas City, the *Kansas City Call*, until he was stricken—when he
was twenty-eight and I was one. He entered the state tuberculosis
sanitarium at Springfield, about a hundred miles south of Kansas
City. Occasionally during those three years when he was away, my
grandfather would drive us down to see him.

My grandfather was a preacher. He pastored an African Methodist
Episcopal church in Kansas City, Kansas, across a viaduct over the
stockyards from which there emanated an incredible stench. He was
taller than my father and shorter than my uncle Roy—maybe about
five ten. He had a large stomach and wore a key chain across his vest
with a big cross hanging from it. He gave me dollars on my birthday
equaling my age. I recall that my father disliked him very much.

As far as I can tell, my grandfather was born in Holly Springs,
Mississippi. In later years that fact was to be of some small comfort
to me when street blacks would challenge the validity of my blackness. I could always summon up my "old country" connection as some
token of authenticity. My grandfather's father was a man named
Asberry Wilkins. He must have been born in slavery or close to it.
Anyway, he was wise enough to have become in the 1890s somebody
who was respected—in the ways that blacks were then respected by
whites in such Mississippi towns. The town fathers gave him the only
honorific title bestowed on blacks in those days. They called him
"Uncle Asberry."

Grandpa was about twenty near the turn of the century when
lynching blacks was not an uncommon occurrence in Mississippi. He
was walking down a road one day when a white man came along
driving a wagon. As was the custom in that place then, the white man
demanded that Grandpa get off the road. For some reason, Grandpa
didn't feel like getting off the road and he didn't. So the white man hit
him with his horsewhip. Grandpa grabbed the whip, pulled the white
man off the wagon and beat the shit out of him.

As a result of that, the town fathers of Holly Springs went to my great grandfather and said to him:

"Uncle Asberry, you're a good nigger and we like you. But your boy Willie is a crazy nigger and if it wasn't for you, we'd have killed him by now. If you don't get him out of town by sundown, we will." By sundown, the man who was to become the Reverend William De Witt Wilkins was on his way to St. Louis, Missouri, where he was to marry a woman named "Sweetie" Mayfield Edmonson. In the years between 1901 and 1905, bad Willie and his wife Sweetie had three children, a son Roy, a daughter Armeda and a son Earl.

Soon after the birth of my father, Earl, in 1905, Sweetie Wilkins died, and her sister Elizabeth came down from St. Paul, Minnesota, for the funeral and took all three of the children back home, where she and her husband, Sam Williams, a sleeping-car porter, raised them and sent them all to the University of Minnesota. Men who worked on the railroad in those days were the backbone of the black middle class. Sam Williams provided the Wilkins children with a modest, but stable and wholesome childhood. When the boys became old enough, they too went to work serving white people on the railroad. It was good employment for black youngsters in those days.

Roy and Earl finished the University of Minnesota—Roy in 1923 and Earl in 1926. Their sister, Armeda, who had become a Christian Scientist somewhere along the way, contracted pneumonia and died while she was still in college. When Roy finished Minnesota, he went to Kansas City to work for the *Call*, and when his little brother finished college a few years later, Roy had prepared a job in the business department of the paper for him. Roy was six feet tall and Earl was smaller. They were jaunty, well dressed, and adored each other. Their wives laughed at their devotion and called them "big Jesus and little Jesus."

The *Call* was not the only place where Roy had made a place for Earl. While he was in college, Roy began dating a Minnesota coed from Minneapolis named Marvel Jackson. The daughter of another railroad man, Madison Jackson—a dining-car waiter on the Northern Pacific—Marvel was light-skinned, had dark flashing eyes, a warm generous personality and quick, supple mind. It was heavy romance and neither doubted that it would lead to marriage. Sometime after his courtship with Marvel had become serious, Roy took his little brother on the long streetcar ride from Nicollet Avenue in St. Paul over to 2003 S. Franklin in Minneapolis. There, in the bosom of the

Jackson family was another light-skinned, dark-eyed and brilliant girl named Helen Jackson.

The Jacksons thought well of themselves and their station. Or at least Amy Wood Jackson, the mistress of 2003 S. Franklin, did. She had been born the eleventh of thirteen children of a pair of former slaves just ten years "after surrender," as the old people used to say. She was a small, extremely pretty caramel-colored woman with long, soft hair and the flashing eyes that all of her daughters would someday inherit. Farm life in rural Virginia held few attractions for her, and she set out on an independent journey that was to include the friendship of the great black intellectual W.E.B. DuBois. Dr. DuBois has described the shock of intuition he felt when he came upon her as an eighteen-year-old servant in the house of some white people in Connecticut. She was beautiful, so he talked to her and found out that she had a splendid mind. In time he asked her to marry him, but she rejected his proposal because she thought he was too old for her. Later in a book called *Dusk of Dawn*, DuBois wrote that it was a tragedy that such a fine person should have to spend her life serving white people. She finally settled down as a teacher with an eighth-grade education in a school for native American children in the Dakota country.

It was there in South Dakota that she met Madison Jackson, who was then both "running on the road" and also reading law between the meals he served to travelers in the dining cars on the trains of the Great Northwest. After reading for the bar in South Dakota, he took the examination and became the first black to be admitted to the bar there. But then, as I once told George McGovern, he was dismayed to find that there was no pool of potential clients for him there. (McGovern didn't laugh, but then, McGovern wasn't laughing at very much in 1973.) So, Madison Jackson kept on serving white people on the train, and when he married Amy Wood, they moved to Minneapolis, where there was a great state university and he could educate his children inexpensively.

Though he was a very idealistic man, Madison Jackson had a quite practical side to his nature. When he moved to Minneapolis, he wanted a good solid house that would be sturdy over the years as his family grew. The one he found back then before 1905 in Minneapolis was on the south side of town in an otherwise all-white neighborhood. Though Madison Jackson and his family were light-skinned Negroes, the neighbors were discomforted by this new family, but they were not rude people. So they would ask broad questions of Madison Jackson, testing his inclination to sell and move away. Grandpa Jackson was a patient man, but finally the persistence of the questioners got to him, so he mused aloud one day that maybe he would sell out and move away. And the next Sunday, he had a succession of the biggest and the blackest men he knew walk slowly and appraisingly back and forth in front of his house. None of his neighbors ever asked those questions again.

His wife was a rigid Victorian who declined to tell her three daughters, Marvel, Helen and Zelma, anything about menstruation until it happened to them. Her husband's job, the physical distance of the Jackson family from more ordinary black people, and the brains the family displayed, all served to confirm for Amy Jackson the very special and exalted quality of her family.

The Jackson girls were anomalies in their all-white schools. Nobody at first knew quite what to make of them. And sometimes, they didn't quite know what to make of themselves. Helen didn't know that she was different from the blue-eyed, blond-haired descendants of Scandinavia with whom she played and studied. So she was overwhelmed with chagrin and grief when she learned that a friend had described her as "the girl with the dark eyes and the dark, dark face." Though quite benign as such things go, my mother's first encounter with race left her limp with tears and sadness.

The parental response to such affronts to their daughters' dignity was to assure them of their human worth, to remind them of their superiority, to deride with logic or irony the inconsistencies inherent in racism, to extol the virtues of the intellect—the one sure weapon in a hostile world—and to exhort them to greater and more intense efforts in the classroom. The tactics worked. First Marvel and then Helen whipped through primary and secondary schools at or near the heads of their classes. Madison Jackson took such matters very seriously. When one of Helen's schoolmates told her that she, not Helen, was to be awarded the high-school valedictory medal though Helen's grades were better, Madison Jackson went to see the principal. His daughter then got the medal that because of her race the principal had intended to deny her.

At a time when the education of young women was not taken seriously, Madison Jackson was determined that his daughters would be well educated. "I don't want my girls to spend one day waiting on white people," he would say.

After four years at Minnesota, Marvel Jackson went east to New York and became Dr. DuBois' secretary at the NAACP—a job that DuBois, with fond memories of the beautiful Amy Wood, was glad to give her. Somehow, with Roy in Kansas City, the romance frayed, the engagement broke, and each found another mate.

Helen Jackson raced through the University in three and a half years, displaying the tenacity and determination that dominated her mother's personality. Madison Jackson did not live long enough to see her graduate. He did live long enough, however, to see her earn a Phi Beta Kappa key at the end of her junior year. And, after college, nothing, not even the bitter opposition of her mother, who wasn't quite sure about those Wilkins boys, could deter her from marrying Earl Wilkins.

Early in the spring of 1932—six months after his brother, Roy, left Kansas City to go to New York to join the national staff of the National Association for the Advancement of Colored People, and eight months before Franklin Roosevelt was elected President for the first time—Earl and Helen had the first and only child to be born of their union. I was born in a little segregated hospital in Kansas City called Phyllis Wheatley—named for a woman who, though enslaved, became a noted poet in the eighteenth century—and the first time my mother saw me, she cried. My head was too long and my color, she thought, was blue.

My father was afflicted with a profound loneliness when I was born, and so was his brother. It was a loneliness that was to persist throughout the remaining decades of Roy Wilkins' life. Though he married Aminda Badeau, a brilliant and tough social worker who had been raised in St. Louis, he would forever miss his younger brother. Except perhaps for their wives—and it is by no means sure even there—there was no one closer to either of the Wilkins boys than his brother. When Roy wrote Walter White, the Executive Director of the NAACP, in the middle of 1931 suggesting ways in which the organization could be improved, he didn't expect to be asked to come and put his effort where his mouth was. But that's what happened, and the Wilkins brothers had to separate, neither knowing that it was the last time they would live in the same city.

My memories of my father are distant now. He earned a reputation for being a tightly buttoned-up kind of person with great wit and charm, whom the ladies loved. Harrison Salisbury told me that he

and my father had been at Minnesota together and had worked on the
newspaper at the same time.

"I remember him very well," Harrison said, "because he was the
only black on the paper. He was sharp and very precise. Very precise."

My mother, though she adores his memory, will admit that he was
cocky. He had an enormous fund of miscellaneous information,
which he loved to display, in addition to his large vocabulary. He was
proud of it and he read the dictionary in his spare time just for the
fun of it.

By the time he got sick, he and my mother had gotten enough
money together to make a down payment on a small house in a lovely
middle-class neighborhood where some Negroes lived, miles away
from 18th Street and Vine, where the largest black population of the
city was confined. And it was to that house that the once fierce Amy
Jackson was attracted by the presence of her first grandchild and the
need of her daughter to go out and earn a living.

While my father was away, my mother supported the family by
going back to work for the YWCA.

The YWCA offered my mother the best way to earn something
resembling what it would take for her to support all of us who depended on her. She was something called the "Girl Reserves Secretary" at the Paseo Branch, which, in segregated Kansas City, was for
colored people. Basically, that meant that she developed and conducted programs for the uplift and betterment of young women.

During the day when my mother was at work, I would play in the
neighborhood, and there were not many friends. We lived at the top
of a hill. Down the hill from our house, there were large vacant lots
on each side of the street going all the way down to a street a block
and a half to the north that was at the bottom of a little valley. From
there, the street went uphill again for a block, where it leveled off. On
that slope of the hill, it was all Negro for a block, then all the blocks
after that were white. I observed to my grandmother, when I was
about three, that all the people living on the slope were friendly, but
that on top of the hill where it leveled off, the people had mean faces.

On our little hilltop, there were six houses, three on our side and
three facing. They were pleasant single-family houses, with good-
sized lawns that people would water and tend with care against the
brutal heat of a Missouri summer. In the house to our left were the

Marsdens. Katie was a social worker, and her husband was the principal of a Negro high school. Next to them were the Robinsons. She, too, was a social worker and her husband, "Robbie," was a railway mail clerk. Across the street were the Washingtons, and some other people whose names I now do not remember. I cared mainly about the Washingtons because they had two children, Ruby and Gwen, who were about my age.

There were large vacant fields and trees where my friends and I built houses. There were weeds and dead hollyhock stalks to use for lances. And at night, after dinner, the grownups would water their lawns and often gather to talk on our porch, the bricks still hot from the heat of the afternoon sun. While we children buzzed around catching up fireflies in pint mason jars with holes punched in the tops, the grownups would sit there in that heat and talk endlessly about their encounters with white people.

One of the favorites was about my grandmother and me in what might be called my first civil-rights activity. When I was about three, Gram had me downtown with her while she shopped in a big department store. We were on the top floor when I informed her that I had an urgent need to urinate—a word my father insisted on even from his distance in the hospital—so Gram headed for the ladies room on that floor, but we were stopped by an officious white woman who worked in the store.

She informed Gram that that rest room was for whites. We would have to go to the basement to use the bathroom for the colored. By this time, I was doing the little dance that children use to hold it in.

"Can't you see that this little boy can't wait that long?" Gram asked.

The woman continued to refuse us admittance to that ladies room, so Gram bent down and began unbuttoning my fly.

"Okay, Roger," she said. "You can do it right here."

The horrified white woman stepped aside then, and that's how Gram and I integrated a ladies room in Kansas City in 1935.

The grownups would laugh and laugh at that story and others like it. They loved stories about trivial victories over a system that was clearly crazy. In retrospect, I'm sure that those stories helped to keep them sane.

But sometimes it wasn't so gay. My mother often had to work at night, and my grandmother and I would share a lonely supper. She would remind me constantly that my milk or my water was "dangerously close to the edge" of the table, and she would belabor the virtues of such things as greens and lettuce and the balanced diet.

My father came home when I was four and died when I was almost nine. He exuded authority. He thought the women hadn't been sufficiently firm with me, so he instituted a spanking program with that same hard hairbrush that my grandmother had used so much to try to ensure that I didn't have "nigger-looking" hair.

My father put a great store in education. One of his first presents for me when he got home was a children's dictionary. I had assignments—so many words each day.

When it was time for me to go to school the board of education provided us with a big yellow bus, which carried us past four or five perfectly fine schools down to the middle of the large Negro community to a very old school called Crispus Attucks. I have no memories of those bus rides except for my resentment of the selfishness of the whites who wouldn't let us share those newer-looking schools nearer to home.

My father was not always well in those years before he died, and when he was not well enough to work, he lived and worked in the back bedroom on the first floor of the house. He would sit up in bed with a Royal portable typewriter in his lap, and sometimes he would allow me in the room if I would keep quiet and read my dictionary. If I was out in the back yard, occasionally he would take a break and make long, slim-lined paper planes and sail them out to me through the open window. They were made of yellow paper, and they would float and hang in the air, like a superb tee shot, before they would glide and sink gently to earth.

When he was well, he would sometimes take me to his office at *The Call*. When you walked in, you were hit with the roar and clang of the press and the smell of the ink. There were men in dirty clothes, with little square paper hats on their heads and ink on their bodies. They would let me watch them feed the press with paper and tend it with oil. There were other people who would sit at typewriters and squint their eyes at some place far away.

And there was the small place where my father sat, at a desk behind glass walls, where people would come in and out smiling at me.

Then three weeks after the 1940 Christmas, which was the best one I ever had, my father died at home, early in the morning, while I was still asleep. I heard a family friend tell somebody on the phone,

"No, he didn't make it," and that's the way I learned that my father was dead.

On the day of the funeral, my Uncle Roy was there from New York. I was glad to see him. He was the tallest man I knew. My grandfather too was there and we were all in my room waiting for the funeral that was being arranged in the dining room down below. I was on my knees reading the funnies spread out on my bed when I heard a strange noise. I turned around and saw it was my grandfather trying to stifle his crying and my uncle trying to give comfort. My grandfather talked about how much he had loved my father, and I remembered how much my father resented him because he had given up parental responsibility when the children were young and then claimed credit for them when they grew up.

At the funeral somebody read my father's favorite poem, "Thanatopsis," and some other people said some other words and some songs were sung. Then Momma and Uncle Roy and Grandpa and the rest of us had to take him out to a segregated cemetery—where Charlie "Yardbird" Parker was later to be buried—and put him in the ground with the rest of the colored people. According to the custom of the day, he wasn't good enough to be dead with white folks.

2 Even before my father's death, it had been decided that the family was going to move to New York. Each of my parents had a new job there. My mother was to go to the National Board of the YWCA, and the entire family moved east in February 1941.

New York did more than give life to a little boy's dream of a great metropolis. It overwhelmed it. In Kansas City, I had heard about tall buildings, famous people and subways, but I had had insufficient experience to construct a dream even approaching the reality. Even the building we were to live in astounded me. It was in that legendary uptown area called Sugar Hill, where blacks who had it made were said to live the sweet life. It rose majestically—fourteen stories of sand-colored brick—on the corner of 160th Street and Edgecombe Avenue. Our apartment was on the seventh floor. From my bedroom window, I could look down onto the tops of other buildings. And from the living room, I could see the Jumel Mansion, where George Washington was said to have stayed during the Revolution, and across the Harlem River to the Bronx, where there was another large sand-colored building, which I came to believe was the anti-matter mirror image of the building where I lived.

I lived with my mother, my grandmother and my mother's youngest sister, Zelma. Aunt Zelma was just over thirty then and was getting over a bad marriage. She was pretty and worked as a bookkeeper at the Harlem YMCA. When I first came to town as a spindly stranger, Zelma helped me cope with my loneliness on the Harlem streets, by buying herself a pair of roller skates so she could teach me how to do it. I adore Aunt Zelma.

Both of my parents' siblings and their spouses lived five blocks down the street, in Sugar Hill's other large apartment house. (The great bulk of New York's middle-class Negro population lived in these two buildings—a lot of entertainers and artists in 555, where I lived, and professionals and more sober types in 409 Edgecombe.) My Uncle Roy and his wife, Minnie, a New York social worker, lived on the seventh floor, and my Aunt Marvel, a journalist who espoused leftist causes, and her husband, Cecil, once a track star at Syracuse and now a salesman for Ruppert's beer, lived on the sixth floor.

As life in New York settled into a routine, my life came to be dominated by four women—my mother, her sisters and her mother. Nobody else had any children, not even Roy; so, everybody concentrated on me. For fifteen years, I was the only child of my extended family.

They told me that I was special. I believed it. They told me that I was smart. I believed that too. They had towering arguments, which almost always involved my grandmother, who seemed to have no capacity whatsoever to govern her temper. In later years, I would come to understand her rage, but in those years, it simply frightened me. I soon learned to deflect the rage when it was turned on me and to curry favor. Dealing with women at a deeply emotional level became a high art at an early age.

But the mores of middle-class black women and the skills for dealing with them—no matter how useful in the middle-class world of apartment 7F or in seduction scenes of all kinds decades later—were not only irrelevant with my contemporaries, they were a hindrance. Just outside our door were the Harlem streets, even if many claimed they lived "on the Hill" or in "Washington Heights." The well-behaved youngster who had just done his arithmetic homework to perfection in order to gain the privilege of going out to play was apt to be shrieking within ten minutes of hitting the street, "Motherfuck you, mothafucka!" at one of his closest comrades. It was the language of the streets and the code of entry into the one society that I needed most of all.

That society wasn't very big. There was Simmons, a mean, tough poor boy who lived down on 160th and could kick some ass and his scrawny sister, Sally, whom everybody claimed to have felt up, but nobody dared touch because of Simmons' ass-kicking tendencies. There were Lefty and Bunky and Ronnie, who lived right downstairs in 6F with whom I worked out an elaborate signal system on the steam pipes. There was Johnny Henry, who was older, nice, well thought-of by my family, my best friend and protector. Johnny Henry and I were together, listening to a New York Giants football game on the radio on December 7, 1941, when the announcement came that the Japanese had bombed Pearl Harbor. From that moment the war inflamed our imaginations.

There was Andy Kirk, whose father was a famous band leader. Andy would later become hooked on heroin, lead a wasted life and then die. It would happen to some others too—Ronnie, for instance, would die from hepatitis that he got from using a dirty needle, before he was seventeen. And Sawyer would get hooked and die after falling or jumping out of a tenth-floor window at fifteen.

And then there was Jones. He was a jolly person, with a dark handsome face, black curly hair and a great smile. His family was dirt poor, but Jones never seemed sad about it, and he was never mean. One time, when I first moved to the block, Jones came over and asked me, "How's a pussy go—triangle, square, slit or circle?" "Shit, man," I guessed, "it's a slit." There was some consternation that I had gotten it right and then congratulations all around. I had been officially accepted into the neighborhood.

Cunning, toughness and athletic ability were valued on the street, as was the necessary intellect to play the Dozens. The Dozens was a simple game. Each of two participants insulted the other's parent— usually the mother and usually in a sexual way suggesting that the speaker had personal and exquisite knowledge of her sexuality. Insults were traded before all of the assembled peers until one party was clearly bested—either because he had run out of things to say or had been so massively insulted that he burst into tears. In a matriarchal society for prepubescent boys, the Dozens was a very risky game of psychic chicken. It proceeded, usually in rhyme, often like this:

1. Saw Sally [the other's mother] last night.
2. Must've been when sweet Sue [#1's mother] was feedin' me her tasty yams.
1. Yo' momma got yams up her asshole.
2. Yo' momma's pussy got yams and cup cakes. Fucked her ass and face all over the great lakes.
   (The audience responds to each escalation—*oohooie* . . . *uuhhmph!* —indicating each time that the psychic ante has just been raised a little bit higher.)

1. Fucked yo' momma on the ice
   Baby came out shootin' dice.
(Many rhymes are in the oral literature and many contests rest simply on who has the greatest nerve and the best memory.)
2. Fucked you momma 'tween two trees
   Baby came out with black rusty knees.
1. Now yo' daddy. . . .
(There are clear rules, and a dead parent is out of bounds.)
2. . . . wait a minute motherfucka, my daddy's dead, now watch yo' fuckin' self. . . .
1. Oh, man, I'm sorry, I didn't know . . . man, I didn't mean nothin' . . .

It would break there, with both parties relieved. The showdown had been avoided and nobody had been destroyed. When no graceful way out is found, boys fight, or worse, one leaves in tears and humiliation with exquisitely crafted sounds of derision ringing in his ears.

The mother up in 7F, of course, is blissfully unaware of how courageously her little man has been defending her virtue or how humiliated he was when she walked by him and his friends on her way from work and hoisted high with a smile on her face the carefully wrapped box containing the new Joe Gordon model mitt she has just bought him. She is puzzled when he doesn't respond with pleasure. And she is also puzzled by his strange mood when he finally comes in. But, of course, there is no way to tell her that the boys swore that she was brazenly waving around a new box of Kotex.

Upstairs, except when my friends were visiting me in my room with the door closed on us and our dirty secrets, the street life of Harlem boys was not merely seven floors, but light years away. The days followed unexceptional routines. Every morning before I left the apartment, I was admonished to do well in school. It was expected that, every afternoon when I came home from school, I would do most of my homework before I went outside. Nobody ever checked it. It was expected that I would do it and do it well. It was in the genes. Though I guess we lived from one of my mother's paychecks to the next, we were of the Negro aristocracy, and brains were our capital. Though it had been years since she had lost her key down the kitchen drain while doing dishes, my mother's achievement of Phi Beta Kappa was a central fact of my young life. And I was often told stories of how first my Aunt Marvel and then my mother had astounded the white teachers in grammar school and high school by compiling perfect records and leading their otherwise all-white classes. It was quite clear that whatever the white people of that area of Minneapolis may have thought about ordinary Negroes, these Jacksons were different. And the essence of our difference was our brains—or so I was taught.

In the evenings, when my mother got home, there would be talk about my school work and talk about my room if it wasn't cleaned up. On Saturdays, to earn my weekly twenty-five-cent allowance, I had to scrub the kitchen and bathroom floors. Afterward, I'd get my quarter and join my friends. There were always at least five of us for our Saturday afternoon movie excursions. Admission was twelve cents, a box of popcorn or a bar of candy was a nickel and the double feature was Abbott and Costello or *Frankenstein* or a war movie. Going back home at dusk on Saturday, I'd have only eight cents left for the rest of the week, but I would be full of joy. Those were among the best Saturdays of my life.

On Sundays, the family would usually gather at our apartment— my mother's family that is. From the day of their broken engagement, a coolness grew between Marvel Jackson Cooke and Roy Wilkins. Although they lived in the same building one floor apart, I never saw them or their spouses in the same room or even in the same elevator at the same time.

There would be Sundays when my mother would take me down to visit my Aunt Minnie and my Uncle Roy. Their apartment was the most nicely furnished of the three in which members of our family lived. They had a dark-brown leather hassock, for example, that looked luxurious and seemed filled with luxurious soft things while other hassocks I used seemed filled with straw. Their apartment faced Edgecombe Avenue and though only on the seventh floor, it seemed much higher because just across the street, Coogan's Bluff fell away to the Harlem Valley far below. You could look out of their bedroom window and see forever: down the 155th Street Viaduct, across the 155th Street bridge to Yankee Stadium just across the Harlem River where Joe Gordon played second base and where, were I not Negro, someday I might . . .

My Aunt Minnie was a light-skinned woman with big brown eyes and brown hair. She once looked very much like my mother. As a matter of fact, when they had all lived in Kansas City, people thought the Wilkins boys had married sisters; but, though they had almost married sisters, they most emphatically had not. Aunt Minnie was an acerbic, positive woman whose forte was serving up hot rich gossip with dry flat prose.

My Uncle Roy was a distant, dignified man. He looked important, and he was regarded as important. He was Assistant to the Executive Secretary of the NAACP, after all, and everybody knew him. He smoked cigars and was cool and benign to me, speaking in a low, rich voice that I loved. But I was intimidated by him. I spent most of my time at their house looking out that bedroom window or reading the funnies in the *Herald Tribune*.

The food at Sunday dinner was delicious, cooked by my grandmother and Aunt Marvel. The talk was about current affairs, politics and inevitably about race and injustice in the country. These conversations, though, did not have the same funny bittersnap quality of those on the porch in Kansas City. Marvel believed in the perfectibility of man and in the basic goodness of American white people. And often there would be white people at the table. My mother believed in them too. We all believed there was no limit to the capacity of the society to improve itself.

The family also talked a lot about how smart I was, and how well I was doing in school. The fact was school didn't make much sense, but it was easy. Most of the kids were black, and almost all the teachers were white. The assistant principal was a wiry blond woman named Miss Arnold, who seemed primarily to be concerned with keeping order. I seemed always to do very well, but it was never quite clear to me how that happened. It was like when I was at summer camp one time and there was a sprinting race. It seemed to me that I was running in a pack with a whole bunch of other kids, but when it was over, somebody told me I'd won.

The kid who sat next to me during most of my classes in the years at P.S. 46 was a little dude named Ham, from 163rd Street. That was a dangerous block for us, but we didn't have to go past it all the time. Even so, it existed like a threat with its gang wearing green jackets with yellow letters that spelled Hornets diagonally down the backs of them. The Hornets would kick ass and steal money at the drop of a hat. They were not to be messed with.

Ham was the littlest Hornet. He was a kind of mascot, and he was not very smart. We would sit at our double desk and he would copy my work. Then he would tell me that I was "under the Hornets' protection." I never quite knew how to feel about the transaction, but I never failed to go along with it. One day, three Hornets caught me alone up on Edgecombe Avenue near 163rd Street. They gathered around me and one of them hit me in the stomach and another smacked me on the side of my head. Suddenly, I heard Ham's voice. "Cut the shit, cut the shit," he screamed. "That's my man." So, the other Hornets stopped and apologized, and it was all right. After that, each semester, I sought Ham out as my seat mate until the year I skipped a grade.

But our block was generally safe. People by and large didn't come through blocks where they didn't live. And, if they did, we knew the block. We knew the buildings, the alleys and the stairways. We had friends in every building and places to duck and hide. There was no need for Hornets' protection on 160th Street. Eighty feet from the crest of the hill down to St. Nicholas was home.

Usually, when we weren't talking about movies—" 'member when that mothafucka pulled out that sword and slashed off that cat's head . . . Yeah, but 'member when they were on the boat and that cat came up and gouged that motha's throat with his hook . . . Yea, but . . ." —or playing the Dozens, we were playing ball. Usually curb ball. If we were lucky, we had a pink ten-cent ball made by the Spalding Company called a "spalldeen." Instead of batting the ball, you threw it down at the curb as hard as you could and it would do one of three things. It would miss the curb and fly back in the direction it was thrown for a foul; it would bound out as a grounder toward the fielders as a hit or more likely an out; or it would fly up out high and far, sometimes as a fly out but more usually as a long, majestic hit.

Hour after hour we played curb ball, or occasionally stick ball. The bat was a broom or mop stick and the ball would be pitched to the batter on a bounce. We would hit toward St. Nicholas Avenue. The great hitters would hit towering flies over the corner of the apartment building at St. Nicholas, and the great outfielders would dodge the cars and catch some of those flies out in the middle of traffic on the avenue. I usually hit hard line drives, but they weren't very successful. Kids who would never get to geometry and who, if they ever got there would be destroyed by it, would figure the angles of those drives in split milliseconds and make nonchalant one-hand catches.

Sometimes when the major-league teams were out of town, there would be games between teams in the Negro leagues. Once, my Uncle Roy took me to one of those games. It was at the Stadium. When the Yankees played, the whole scene was magic. The grass was the richest green and the infield was a soft, smooth brown. There were lots of people in the stands, and the players were large white heroes.

It didn't look right when Negro teams were playing there. The players' uniforms were not as crisp, and the infield didn't look as smooth. And the players did not look as large. Although they made all the right plays it all seemed an imitation of what Rolfe, Rizzuto, Gordon and Etten might have done. But it was nice of my uncle to take me for the outing anyway.

And, of course, we would talk about baseball, and not the colored leagues either. Two major-league parks were within walking distance. The Polo Grounds, where the Giants with Mel Ott and Big Jawn Mize played, was just down the bluff. And across the river was the House where DiMaggio played with Joe Gordon and Phil Rizzuto and Bill Dickey. My friend Johnny was a Yankee fan in 1941, so I became one and have been one ever since.

Sometimes my friends and I would sit there on the benches on the bluff and instead of looking across the river we'd look south toward the Harlem Valley, Convent, Bradhurst and Eighth avenues stretching toward the park down at 110th Street. And we'd tell and retell the legends of the hard dudes from the valley. There was a gang down there called the Sabres, who, it was said, made our local Hornets seem like children. The Sabres had dudes as old as twenty, and all had knives and could stomp and even kill. They were said to be the baddest motherfuckers in the valley. And further west, toward the Hudson River, were the Rainbows, a gang of Spanish cats who wore wine-colored jackets and would slash a dude in a minute.

One day as we were sitting on the benches looking down at the path that ran through the bluff as it fell steeply away down to the Harlem River Drive and the Polo Grounds just beyond, we saw two teen-agers, one black and one Puerto Rican, approach each other. The Puerto Rican had on a wine-colored jacket and the black wore a red skullcap rimmed in black—the cap of the Sabres. Time stopped when they saw each other and circled. I did not breathe as I watched. A fist, a foot, a hand and a knife. It was fast. Suddenly, the wine jacket was fleeing to the north, while the red skullcap lurched along clutching his rib cage spurting blood. I couldn't move until somebody screamed, "Run!"

And, so I ran and cowered in the house for the night. The next day, I told my grandmother I was too sick to go to school. Since I had never lied about such a thing before, she believed me. And, just before noon, while she was out shopping, there came a tapping on the

steam pipes—*duh duhduh duh duh duhduh*. It was one of the Henry
boys from downstairs. I hadn't been the only one too scared to go to
school that day.

I never said a thing to my mother or my grandmother or my Aunt
Zelma or any other adult I knew about what I had seen on the Coogan's Bluff path that night. But, I thought about it constantly, and I
looked at their faces to see if they knew. And, sometimes, when none
of the other kids was around, I went down to the path to look for the
blood and maybe for the body that everybody had overlooked. And I
waited terrified in my mind for the Rainbows or the Sabres or the
police to come.

My mother never knew about those fears or about the Sabres or
the Rainbows either. The streets of Harlem were foreign to this
Minnesota woman, who had grown up in the Negro genteel class. The
closest she ever came to any sense whatsoever of the street was when
she would see us playing a card game that was a cross between
rummy and poker. We gambled for matchbook covers. The cover that
was filled with writing on the inside was ten dollars. The one half
filled was five and the one with no writing at all was one. It was a
game that filled the time when we were out of spalldeens and nobody
had the money to buy one.

Usually we'd play on the brownstone stoop in front of Tucker's
house just at the crest of the hill on 160th between Edgecombe and
St. Nicholas avenues. It would be early evening and my mother
would come by on her way from the subway at the corner of 161st
and Amsterdam. There, after a day of work in midtown New York
and the long ride home on the subway at rush hour, she would see me
gambling with my friends. It was a street game and we were street
boys. She was worried.

One day, soon after that, Uncle Cecil suggested I take up matchbook collecting. I told him I wasn't interested. Then my mother said
that she knew a lot of people who collected matchbooks and that she
would buy me some scrapbooks so I would have a place to keep
my collection.

And it really wasn't so bad. Everybody in the family began to bring
me matchbooks, even friends of the family. But, the best matchbooks
in the whole collection came from my mother. She had to travel a lot
trying to desegregate local YWCAs all over the country, and when
she traveled, she kept her eye out for the different kinds of matchbooks. Just the kind that would go for my collection.

I dutifully pasted matchbooks into my scrapbooks, but used the duplicates in the game.

My mother was even less successful in improving my reading habits. I was very fond of comic books. However, when she suggested that I read better things, I told her I would if she did. Since my mother was addicted to mystery stories at the time, that was the end of that.

She read those books on the long train trips that she took to the South promoting the national Y's policy of desegregation with the semiautonomous local Y's to whom, in the '40s, such a notion was an anathema. My mother was and is a gentle-appearing person with a gentle sweet smile. But she has a strong will and throughout the South she was known as "that truculent Northern Negro."

For all her sweetness, she wasn't for taking any shit from white people. One time, she was the only Negro on a dining car on a train moving from Ohio into Kentucky. The law in Ohio didn't require segregation in public eating places, but it did in Kentucky. So the white steward in charge of the car ordered one of the waiters to put up a portable screen around my mother.

My mother told the steward that she was sure the curtain would get in the way of the waiters as they brought her her food, but he ignored her. Sure enough, when the waiter brought her soup, his foot got tangled in the curtain and he spilled the soup all over the next table. The people sitting there descended in a fury on the steward and demanded that he remove the curtain. Others in the car indicated assent, so he finally relented. When he brought her another bowl of soup, the waiter winked at my mother, and the people at the next table smiled furtively. My mother just proceeded to eat her soup.

Another time, a white woman with whom she was working in the South, insisted that she couldn't quite get the hang of saying the word *Negro*. When she said it, it always came out dangerously close to *nigger*.

"Well," my mother said, putting her hand on the woman's knee, "you can say *knee* can't you?"

"Yes," the woman said, "I can say *knee*."

"And you can say *grow*, can't you," my mother said, moving her hand up toward the ceiling.

"Yes," the woman said, "I can say *grow* too."

"So," said my mother putting her hand back on the woman's knee. "*Knee, grow*," moving her hand toward the ceiling again. "*Knee, grow,*" she said again, moving her hand back and forth. "You say it with me."

"*Knee, grow,*" the woman said, along with my mother who directed the incantations with flowing movements of her hand.

So, though she wasn't exactly truculent, it wasn't hard to see how people could have found my mother a bit uppity.

At home, she would try to look after me and give me an outlook larger than 160th Street, 7F or P.S. 46, but she didn't always succeed. Once she took me to a concert at Carnegie Hall. The next time she suggested it, I declined, telling her, "I've been to the philharmonica once." But she took me to a play called *Lost in the Stars*, about race in South Africa that I'll always remember. Canada Lee, a black man with a wall eye, was the star. I would sometimes see him on the elevator in our building so it was interesting to see him on the stage.

The play was about the oppression of black people. The blacks were good, and so were the whites who tried to befriend them. But they were all thwarted in their efforts toward decency by evil people. I was enraged by the injustice, and I felt a kinship with the victims, a strong feeling that I folded up and tucked right into my soul forever.

Sometimes my mother would take me to visit some of her co-workers. One fall Sunday, she took me up to Pleasantville, New York, to the home of two white women she worked with. They were broad, tweedy types with sturdy legs. They were hearty with me and gave me the clear sense, as all of my mother's colleagues did, that I was a very special little boy.

There were a few men in her life. My mother would talk to me about her suitors, explaining that no other man could take my father's place in her heart or in mine. She might remarry, but even if that happened, my father's place in our hearts was assured. I thought that was fine, and I trusted my mother not to bring us somebody stupid.

Some time early in 1943 her work took her to Grand Rapids, Michigan, where she made a speech and met a forty-four-year-old bachelor doctor who looked like a white man. He had light skin, green eyes and "good hair"—that is, hair that was as straight and as flat as white people's hair. He looked so like a white person that he could have passed for white. There was much talk about people who had passed. They were generally deemed to be bad people, for they were not simply selfish, but also cruel to those whom they left behind.

People who could pass, but did not, on the other hand, were respected.

She saw this doctor again in the spring and they exchanged visits in the summer. By the time he came to New York, I knew that he was important to my mother and to all of us.

He and my mother were married in October 1943 when I was eleven years old. My father had been dead two and a half years.

A few months after my mother's remarriage, I finished P.S. 46 and passed on to junior high school. Because I had skipped a half grade in grammar school and had continued to do well, I was placed in the New York City Board of Education's rapid-advancement program. It meant that I would spend two and a half rather than three years in junior high school. It also meant that I entered Stitt Junior High School at considerable risk.

Stitt was located four blocks north of our apartment building on Edgecombe Avenue. Not only did that require a journey past 163rd Street with its run-down buildings, low-income people and their hard sons and daughters (Ham, my earlier protector with the 163rd Street Hornets had long since been left behind), it also meant that I was in for a severe and sustained torment called rookying. All new students were hazed at Stitt, most often and most crudely by the huge dark boys who were considered slow students. The rookies who got it worst were those in the rapid-advancement program.

All rookies were in a grade called 7A, but we were divided into groupings according to achievement, so the advanced group was marked and hated by our peers as well as upper-classmen.

When we walked through the halls, we were led by our class president. He had to walk in the front and on the outside of our double line wearing a large armband with 7AR on it. We elected the boy in the class we hated the most, and the rest of us jockeyed after each period to get a place on the inside line next to the wall, where we could walk bent over hoping not to be noticed during the day. But, we could hear the hostility from the other passing classes—"There's them cocksuckers . . . see that little yella fuck in the blue shirt, gon' kick his mothafuckin' ass after school . . . smartfuck ovathea gon' carry my books down to 125th Street an' back tonight 'fore I let him go home see his momma."

And, after a day of abject terror, they would indeed be out there on the street waiting after school. "Nigger," someone would command, "carry my books." These boys invariably seemed more substantial than I, and darker. And there would always be a group of them for each one of us. I would accept an extraordinary load of books, and before we had crossed the first street, someone other than the one who had given me the books would knock them out of my arms. Then I would get extraordinary abuse from the one who had given me the books in the first place—"What the fuck you droppin' my books for, you dumb cocksucker?" And when I bent to retrieve them, he would kick me in the head or in the ribs. And so it would go—at least once a week for every week during that semester in the spring of 1944.

But soon the semester was over, and I was once more on a train with my grandmother, heading toward Grand Rapids and my new home—and away from Stitt Junior High School forever.

We left New York on the New York Central's Wolverine, which we boarded at the 125th Street station, after it had come out of a hole in the ground at 96th Street and Park Avenue. As the train moved slowly north, across the river at 138th and then smoothly up through the Bronx, I could look back across the Harlem River, up over the Polo Grounds up there on the bluff for what was perhaps the last time and see the great high, light-sand-colored hulk that was 555 Edgecombe Avenue. And as it faded out of sight and later became fuzzier in my mind farther and farther back down the Hudson Valley, the tension in my stomach began to ease. There was anxiety about the unknown, to be sure, but the terror I had gathered in the Harlem streets over the past three years began to subside.

The train went on up the Hudson to Albany, then over to Buffalo, then across the dull Canadian plain to Windsor, then under the river to Detroit. As I sat on that train, staring out the window hour after endless hour, sitting next to my grandmother, I felt glad that Harlem was behind me. But my relief had been purchased at a real and quite substantial cost. Though I was not again to know such terror, I had also, at the age of twelve, moved beyond the last point in my life when I would feel totally at peace with my blackness.

3 When we reached Grand Rapids, my mother, who had preceded us by a month to set up housekeeping, and my stepfather—whom I, with my mother's help, had decided to call Pop, in distinction to Daddy, whose place could never be taken—met us at the station.

To me, my Pop's car was quite grand. It was a dark-green 1941 Chrysler Royal four-door sedan. The grillwork looked like two sets of matching swords laid end to end coming to a point where the tips touched. Though it was 1944 and the car was three years old, it was one of the last generation of cars produced before Detroit went to war. Though the car was a good omen, I felt the tension flowing certainly and swiftly back into my stomach as Pop swung the car out of the station lot and headed toward my new home.

I didn't know what Grand Rapids was. A tiny sliver of Manhattan had become my reality, and I could not imagine a life without dilapidated buildings and the hard, black youths who lived in them. As we drove through the three seedy blocks surrounding the Grand Rapids railroad terminal, my terror returned once more.

But then we drove past that into the city's squatty little downtown and on beyond that to my new home in the north end of Grand Rapids, a neighborhood every bit as white as the Minneapolis one in which my mother had lived as a twelve-year-old a quarter of a century before. This would be the place I would henceforth think of as home. And it would be the place where I would become more Midwesterner than Harlemite, more American than black and more complex than was comfortable or necessary for the middle-class conformity that my mother had in mind for me.

34

The driveway ran all the way down the right side of the property as you faced it from the street. The lot was about 150 feet deep and 50 feet wide. There was a backyard with grass, and near the alley there was a two-car garage and a little storage shed just behind that. It was very different from New York, but not totally alien, because there were faint echoes of Kansas City—except that all the people you could see wherever you looked were white. That was different from any place I had ever been in.

When we got out of the car, I saw a bicycle leaning up next to the house. It had a big maroon-colored frame, skinny wheels and a seat with a shaggy sheepskin cover, not the popular balloon-tired type. I looked at Pop and he smiled and nodded. He had gotten it for me, because he knew I couldn't ride in New York where the traffic made it risky. The bike was out of step, like him and me. I had a new home, a strange bike and a different father.

Robert White Claytor had been born in the hills of western Virginia, the thirteenth and last child of parents who had been born in slavery. His father had been very light and his mother a little browner as were most of his older siblings. But he had been born white with straight hair and green eyes, and his parents, mountain people from another century, had, on first glimpsing him, named him Bob-White. Later, when station and dignity required it, he changed his name.

But, by then, he had changed himself too. Three of the older brothers came out of the hills to become doctors, one became a dentist, one a school administrator, one a pharmacist and one a farmer. All the sisters became teachers. The parents had hoped that the two youngest boys would stay on in the hills and carry on the family farm and when Hunter, the one next older than Bob-White, was killed during the First World War, they insisted that their baby stay. To ensure his fidelity to the land, they took him out of school after he completed the eighth grade and kept him home working the farm.

He stayed with them dutifully until, according to the mores of the time, he became a man at twenty-one and was responsible for himself. Then, he walked down out of the hills and into a ninth-grade classroom in Petersburg and he didn't stop going to school until he had finished Meharry Medical College in the depths of the Depression. When he had finished his undergraduate studies at the University of Pennsylvania, he persuaded his brother Archer—the one who was just older than Hunter—that he had settled too low when he had taken up pharmacy and thus, he dragged Archer off to a career in medicine too.

When Robert was in college, he answered an ad seeking a house-boy for the summer. He applied and was accepted, and thus came to know the Eastmans of the Eastman-Kodak photographic company and the northern Michigan resort area around Petoskey, where they spent their summers. The experience changed his life because the East-mans were generous and encouraging people and he came to love the state where he went to serve them.

After medical school, he determined that Michigan afforded as reasonable opportunities for medical practices for himself and his brother as any other place he had seen. Archer agreed, and they decided that Grand Rapids, where there was already one established Negro doctor, was a good place for Robert to work in, and Saginaw, where there was none, would be good for Archer.

Robert was not used to having a boy around the house, and cer-tainly not a middle-class city boy whose life had mainly been spent under the direction and comfort of a number of female relatives. Nevertheless, he tried to be fatherly. One day he came home with a new baseball glove and a ball. But it wasn't a big brown Rawlings glove with the kind of pocket I could grease lovingly for hours. It was a small puffy gray thing with no discernible pocket at all. I was polite and tried unsuccessfully to be enthusiastic as we played a pitiful game of catch along the driveway in back of the house. He threw in a stiff, almost formal way and I kept dropping the ball because that mitt wasn't made for catching. We never played catch again.

From time to time on Sunday he'd take me over to Valley Field—the best baseball park in Grand Rapids—to see the local black semi-pro team, play. Ted Raspberry was the organizer and the entrepreneur of the enterprise. Mr. Raspberry was a jolly dark man who smiled a lot and had gold teeth in his mouth. Raspberry's team was pretty good and generally won. The infield chatter was sheer ecstasy.

"Come *on* baby, bump it past this motha!"

"At's okay, baby, this cat's momma didn't give him no eyes."

And after a pitcher had slipped a third strike past a batter:

"Way to go baby, you humpin' better than you did last night!"

After the games people would come up to Pop and say, "Hiya Doctor, how you doin'?" "Glad to see you out today, Doctor." "That your boy there, Doctor? Yea? Well, he's a fine-looking boy."

Pop knew I liked those games, so he took me out as often as he could.

And he was always generous and thoughtful. Because, though he didn't know just what kind of glove to buy or what sort of bike I wanted, his groping to please me all signaled a life that was very different from any I had ever known before.

Grand Rapids was pretty single-family houses and green spaces. The houses looked like those in *Look* magazine or in *Life*. You could believe, and I did, that there was happiness inside. To me back then, the people seemed to belong to the houses as the houses belonged to the land, and all of it had to do with being white. They moved and walked and talked as if the place, the country and the houses were theirs, and I envied them.

When we were settled and I could ride, I rode my bike east out along Knapp Street, past Fulton, past the cemetery and into the country, and I rode it west down Monroe and over the Ann Street Bridge over the Grand River and into the west side. The neighborhood was different there. It was a mixture of older houses and industrial buildings. The lawns were smaller over there, and the paint was peeling on some of the houses, and on some of the others it was worn away altogether. Those were the wind-beaten gray houses with the spot-sized yards that were all brown and rock hard, beaten by large feet and small into brown ugly places where broken tricycles and half-gutted Teddy bears were strewn about. The people who lived in those houses on the west side of the river were called Polacks, and they went to Union High School and played fantastic football.

One day, I rode north. By now I was gaining confidence. I knew I could find my way home and I began to think about things other than landmarks as I rode. I began, for instance, to look at the people I would pass, and they would look back at me with intense and sometimes puzzled looks on their faces as I pedaled by. Nobody waved or even smiled. They just stopped what they were doing to stand and look. As soon as I would see them looking, I would look forward and keep on riding.

I explored the north for several days. Finally, well into my second week in town, I headed south. I rode down Plainfield Avenue for a few blocks, past Creston High School where I would be enrolled in September, past Creston Heights, a few blocks on—our neighborhood shopping center, where the local branch of the Old Kent Bank was located, and then on south for miles. Grand Rapids was mainly south of where we lived, and this day I was going to find it.

I rode for miles, down and up and down again, until Plainfield changed into Division Avenue and I was again in Grand Rapids' squatty little downtown. And, I rode on past the Division movie theater and farther south until I began to see some Negro people.

I had long passed downtown and its large stores and I was now in an area where there were small commercial buildings, warehouses, small, flat factories and second-rate store fronts with people living in the rooms upstairs. Down the side streets, there were big old run-down houses and people walking around or sitting on the stoops. There were black men and women and some girls, but it was the boys I was looking for. Then I saw a group; four of them.

They were about my age, and they were dark. They were walking toward me on the sidewalk on the side of the street where I was riding. Though their clothes were not as sharp as the boys in the Harlem Valley, they were old, and I took the look of poverty and the deep darkness of their faces to mean that they were like the hard boys of Harlem.

One of them spotted me riding toward them and pointed. "Hey, lookit that bigole skinny bike," he said. Then, they all looked at my bike and at me. I couldn't see expressions on their faces; only the blackness and the coarseness of their clothes. Before any of the rest of them had a chance to say anything, I stood up on the pedals and wheeled the bike in a U-turn and headed back on up toward the north end of town.

It took miles for the terror to finally subside. Harlem had really put white fear into me.

Farther on toward home, there was a large athletic field that was ringed by a quarter-mile track and had a gridiron laid out end to end and a baseball diamond too. As I neared the field, I could see some large boys in shorts moving determinedly around a football. When I got to the top of the hill that overlooked the field, I stopped and stood, one foot on the ground and one leg hanging over the crossbar, staring down at them.

All the boys were white and big and old—sixteen to eighteen. They were wearing football cleats, and shorts and some of them wore tee shirts that said "Creston Polar Bears." They would assemble, bend over, then run very hard in the same direction. Sometimes they would throw the ball and they had the biggest thighs I had ever seen. I had never seen a football workout before, and I was fascinated. I completely forgot everything about color, theirs or mine.

Then one of them saw me. He pointed and said, "Look, there's the little coon watching us."

I wanted to be invisible. I was horrified. My heart pounded, and my arms and my legs shook, but I managed to get back on my bike and ride home.

When I came home my grandmother asked if I had had a good time and I said, "Yes." She asked me what I had done, and I said, "Rode my bike around some." She asked me if I had made any new friends and I said, "No."

"You will," she said. "It just takes time." Then she went back to her cooking and I went on upstairs and lay across my bed.

But, it wasn't very many days later that I was on my bike, standing still next to the curb sitting on the saddle and watching some boys playing on a playground not far from my house when somebody came up from behind me and said, "Hi." I looked around and saw a blond boy with blue eyes. He was sitting on a bike smiling at me. He spoke again. "My name's Jerry," he said. "Jerry Schild. What's yours?"

We shook hands, rode down to the river together, and began to talk a little.

"I know what house you live in," he said, "because I deliver your paper. Everybody in the neighborhood knows about your family moving in. There was a lot of talk. And I've seen you around, on your bike. I never saw you talking to anybody and you're new, so I thought I'd talk to you."

I didn't know what to say for a minute, so I kept throwing stones at things in the river. Then I said very carefully, "Yea. When you're new, there's nobody to talk to at first." He looked thoughtful for a little while and finally he brightened and said, "Say, why don't we take a tour of some of my favorite places around here. Places I bet you've never seen." We mounted our bikes and took off down the street. It was the happiest day I had had in years.

That night at dinner, I suppose I talked more than I had at any time since we moved to Michigan. I told my family everything I knew about Jerry and about where we had been and where we would go the next day. My mother remembered paying him for the paper a few times and remarked on what a polite, efficient person he seemed to be.

Then I told them that Jerry had said that everyone in the neighborhood knew where we lived and had talked about it. My stepfather gave my mother an imperceptible nod and then she said, "You know how we've told you about the neighbors getting upset Poppa bought the house we lived in on South Franklin. Well, it was pretty much the same here. When Pop bought the house here, the seller didn't know he was a Negro. Your Pop didn't say whether he was or he wasn't and the man didn't ask."

I glanced at my stepfather, whose green eyes were glinting amusement and then turned back to my mother. "Well, at some point they found out that he was a Negro and the neighbors started to have meetings about our moving into the neighborhood. There was even some talk about burning a cross or something, but everybody thought that was crazy except the wild man who suggested it. And so they decided that the thing to do was to try to buy the house back and they tried. But Pop told them that he had bought a house for his family and he needed it and he didn't intend to sell it. They told him they thought he would be happier with 'his own people across town,' but he told them that he hadn't found a house across town good enough for his family and that he assumed that the people around here were Americans and that those were 'his own people' so he didn't feel uncomfortable. They tried a couple more conversations, but then they gave up. They all seem pretty reconciled to it now except Mr. Stuits across the lot. But he doesn't do anything but bang his lawnmower into the fence. And since it's his fence that's fine with me."

That night I thought about Stuits and the other people on the block. Our house was just about the biggest in the neighborhood, and we had a nicer car than anybody on the block. I was pretty sure that none of the other men was a doctor and that the women probably hadn't even gone to college, much less been Phi Beta Kappa. And, though that bit of social calculus was somewhat comforting, when it was all done, the other people were still white and I was still a Negro. There was no getting around it.

Jerry was true to his word. The next day at midmorning, he rode up and we took off on our bikes on another day of exploration of all the wonders the north end of Grand Rapids held for a couple of twelve-year-olds. When it was time for lunch, Jerry led me to the sparsely stocked store in the large ramshackle building two blocks from my house. "Why're we going here?" I asked. "To get something to eat," he replied. "My folks run this store. My mom mainly. And we live upstairs."

I didn't say anything. I just laid my bike against the front of the building and followed him into the store. His mother, a large pleasant woman, greeted us warmly and gave us Spam sandwiches with mayonnaise for lunch. Afterward, Jerry took me around the back and up the outside stairway that led to the living quarters above. I met his three younger siblings, including a very little one toddling around in bare feet and a soiled diaper.

While Jerry changed the baby, I looked around the place. It was cheap, all chintz and linoleum. The two soft pieces of furniture, a couch and an overstuffed chair, had gaping holes and were hemorrhaging their fillings. And there were an awful lot of empty brown beer bottles sitting around, both in the kitchen and out on the back porch. While the place was not dirty, it made me very sad. Jerry and his family were poor in a way I had never seen people be poor before, either in Kansas City or even in Harlem. But, if Jerry minded, he didn't let on and, of course, neither did I.

Jerry's father wasn't there that day and Jerry didn't mention him. But later in the week, when I went to call for Jerry, I saw him. I yelled for Jerry from downstairs in the back and his father came to the railing of the porch on the second floor. He was a skinny man in overalls with the bib hanging down crookedly because it was fastened only on the shoulder. His face was narrow and wrinkled and his eyes were set deep in dark hollows. He had a beer bottle in his hand and he looked down at me. "Jerry ain't here," he said, and he turned away and went back in the house.

But, if I didn't find him that time, it was one of the few times during those weeks when I didn't. We filled up our time together. I even got up at dawn sometimes to help him with his weekly collections. I would get a little pocket money and a lot of company.

Then one day our front doorbell rang and I could hear my mother's troubled exclamation, "Jerry! What's wrong?" By then I was in the living room and could see for myself that something was wrong. Jerry was crying so hard, he could hardly talk. "My father says I can't play with you any more because you're not good enough for us."

My mother looked at both of us in horror, then she attempted to comfort Jerry by saying soft soothing things. When the worst of the sobbing finally eased off, she brought him a warm washcloth so he could wash off his face. "It's not fair," Jerry said. And my mother agreed that it was not fair and that it wasn't right either, but she told Jerry that she didn't see how she could tell him to disobey his father. Then she suggested that maybe if Jerry let a little time pass and then talked it over with his father again, he might come to a different conclusion. Jerry said no, he didn't think so and that she didn't know his father. My mother has a very sweet face, and sometimes an almost beatific smile, but at that moment, I saw her smile tighten into pure steel. "Oh, yes," she said gently to Jerry, "I know your father all too well."

And Jerry didn't talk about it again to his father as far as I know. He'd just sneak and see me and hope the old man wouldn't find out. But it was different. And school was about to start.

4 Creston High School was about a mile away, and served all the children from the north end of Grand Rapids from the seventh grade up. It was all-white and middle-class. Nobody talked to me that first day, but I was noticed. When I left school at the end of the day I found my bike leaning up against the fence where I had left it with a huge glob of slimy spit on my shaggy saddle cover. People passed by on their way home and looked at me and the spit. I felt a hollowness behind my eyes, but I didn't cry. I just got on the bike, stood up on the pedals and rode it home without sitting down. And, it went that way for about the first two weeks. After the third day, I got rid of the saddle cover because the plain leather was a lot easier to clean. Sometimes when I was riding home, standing up, people would yell, "Nigger, why don't you go back where you came from." And that's about all they did, except for one day when some large boys threw apple cores and stones at me.

But even then, the glacier was beginning to thaw. One day I was sitting in class and the freckle-faced kid with the crew cut sitting next to me was asking everybody for a pencil. And then he looked at me and said, "Maybe you can lend me one." Those were the best words I had heard since I first met Jerry. This kid had included me in the human race in front of everybody. His name was Jack Waltz.

And after a while when the spitters had subsided and I could ride home sitting down, I began to notice that organized football practice was being held on the athletic field and that little kids my size were playing in pickup games in the end zones. It looked interesting, but I didn't know anybody and didn't know how they would respond to

43

me. So I just rode on by for a couple of weeks, slowing down each day trying to screw up my courage to go in.

But then one day, I saw Jack Waltz there. He was playing with other boys my size in the end zone. We had now come to talk some in school, so I knew he wouldn't be rude. I stood around the edges of the group ostensibly watching the high-school team practicing, but really watching out of the corner of my eyes, the game my peers were playing. It seemed that they played forever without even noticing me, but finally somebody had to go home and the sides were unbalanced. Somebody said, "Let's ask him." And they did and I accepted.

As we lined up for our first huddle, I heard somebody on the other side say, "I hope he doesn't have a knife." One of the guys on my side asked me, "Can you run the ball?" I said yes, so they gave me the ball and I ran three quarters of the length of the field for a touchdown. And I made other touchdowns and other long runs before the game was over. When I thought about it later that night, I became certain that part of my success was due to the imaginary knife that was running interference for me. But, no matter. By the end of the game, I had a group of friends. Boys named Andy and Don and Bill and Gene and Rich. We left the field together and some of them waved and yelled, "See ya tomorra, Rog."

And Don De Young, a pleasant round-faced boy, even lived quite near me. So, after parting from everybody else, he and I went on together down to the corner of Coit and Knapp. As we parted, he suggested that we meet to go to school together the next day. I had longed for that but I hadn't suggested it for fear of a rebuff for overstepping the limits of my race. I had already learned one of the great tenets of Negro survival in America: to live the reactive life. It was like the old Negro comedian who once said, "When the man asks how the weather is, I know nuff to look keerful at his face 'fore even I look out the window." So, I waited for him to suggest it, and my patience was rewarded. I was overjoyed and grateful.

My nickname was "Wilco"—from World War II movies in which the Air Force pilots would end their radio communications, "Roger, Wilco and out." I hated the nickname, but like the feeling expressed by the fellow who said, "It's better to fail your Wasserman test than never to have loved at all," it was good to have any nickname at all.

I didn't spend all my time in the North End. Soon after I moved to Grand Rapids, Pop introduced me to some patients he had with a son

my age. The boy's name was Lloyd Brown, and his father was a
bellman downtown at the Pantlind Hotel. Lloyd and I often rode bikes
and played basketball in his backyard. His basketball wasn't like the
ones up in the North End. Up there were orange hoops hung on garage
backboards. Here the basket was made out of four pieces of wood
like a wastebasket with no bottom and it was hung on a tree in the
backyard. We didn't dribble on a smooth concrete or black-top
garage entrance, but on the uneven dirt in the backyard.

After a while, my mother asked me why I never had Lloyd come
out to visit me. It was a question I had dreaded, but she pressed on.
"After all," she said, "you've had a lot of meals at his house and
it's rude not to invite him back." I knew she was right and I also hated
the whole idea of it.

If this had been Kansas City or Harlem, it would have been all
right. Lloyd was very much like my friend Chris in Kansas City and
like my friend Jones in Harlem. But I had shared a world with Chris
and Foote from the inside out. Though my family had more than
theirs, we had suffered similar limitations and deprivations.

But I didn't share Lloyd's limitations. I looked at him and his life
from the north end of Grand Rapids as if I were seeing him through a
telescope turned backward. And though I could join him temporarily
in that small place, I had escaped those constrictions peculiar to
Negro people and I didn't want to be forced back on a permanent
basis.

And I wasn't sure my escape was permanent. With my friends in
the north, race was never mentioned. Ever. I carried my race around
me like an open basket of rotten eggs. I knew I could drop one at any
moment and it would explode with a stench over everything. This was
in the days when the movies either had no blacks at all or they
featured rank stereotypes like Stepin Fetchit, and the popular magazines like *Life, Look, The Saturday Evening Post* and *Colliers* carried no stories about Negroes, had no ads depicting Negroes and
generally gave the impression that we did not exist in this society. I
knew that my white friends, being well brought-up, were just too
polite to mention this disability that I had. And I was grateful to
them, but terrified just the same that maybe some day one of them
would have the bad taste to notice what I was.

It seemed to me that my tenuous purchase in this larger white
world depended on the maintenance between me and my friends in
the North End of our unspoken bargain to ignore my difference, my

shame and their embarrassment. If none of us had to deal with it, I thought, we could all handle it. My white friends behaved as if they perceived the bargain exactly as I did. It was a delicate equation, and I was terrified that Lloyd's presence in the North End would rip apart the balance. But my mother, either driven by manners or by a deep and subtle understanding of her son's psyche, seemed determined to press the issue.

Our fitful, but unending debate on the issue began in the late fall of my first year in Grand Rapids until just before Christmas when I got a pretty stiff case of the flu and had to stay in the house. On my third consecutive day, as I was wandering around the house bored and full of self-pity, I glanced out the window and, to my horror, discovered that the argument had become moot. Walking down the street from the bus stop, in full view of any who cared to see, were not only Lloyd, but also Bobby and her sister and brother and Lloyd's sister Joy Anne. They added up to more Negroes than I had seen altogether in my six months in the North End. And there they were. All together. Coming to my house to see me. In public view. They looked like an army.

When they got in the house, it was fine. Actually, I was glad to have them visit. They were genuinely concerned about my health, and they had brought me presents. We had a good time and my family was gracious. I asked my friends to stay to dinner, and I was glad when they accepted. I figured that after dinner it would be dark and maybe nobody would see them when they left.

I am so ashamed of that shame now that I cringe when I write it. But I understand that boy now as he could not understand himself then. I was an American boy, though I did not fully comprehend that either. I was fully shaped and formed by America, and America was both powerful and racist. White people had all the power in sight, and they owned everything in sight except our house. Their beauty was the real beauty; there wasn't any other beauty. A real human being had straight hair, a white face and thin lips. Other people who looked different were lesser beings.

No wonder, then, that most black men desired the forbidden fruit of white loins. No wonder, too, that we thought that the most beautiful and worthy Negro people were those who looked most white. We blacks used to have a saying: "If you're white, you're all right. If you're brown, stick around. If you're black, stand back." I was brown.

And there was proof in real life of all of that. By and large, the little slaves who were made on the wrong side of the sheets by the master and a slave woman were treated better. They were the ones who got some education, if any slave did, and they often got the better jobs around the house too. They were the ones who got to learn how "real" people ate and talked, and sometimes they also got freed. And since they had some white genes, they looked more like white, and when Emancipation came, they were the ones with the advantage. Negroes came to confuse color with quality and color with readiness to be accepted in white society, which so many of us craved in the pits of our souls.

America told us we were inferior, and most of us believed it. I had never had to confront much of that in segregated Kansas City or in Harlem. I was color-conscious, of course. It was in the air, and I absorbed it like oxygen. But until I lived in Grand Rapids among all those white people I had never been forced to confront the enormity of the inferiority that America had slammed into my soul, and despite the fierce pride as human beings my family had, I couldn't help but accept it. There was another saying: "Niggers ain't shit." I accepted that all right.

So, I was ashamed. I was ashamed of myself, my whole being. I was ashamed of my color, my kinky hair, my broad nose and my thick lips. I didn't look like my friends, and I didn't have their heritage. Parents didn't tell Negro children in those days of the heroism, intelligence and courage that it took for their slave ancestors to survive during that brutal time. "We didn't like to clank our chains," as my mother once said to me. And what we knew of Africa came from Tarzan movies and the story "Little Black Sambo." So, living in Grand Rapids, when I was a teen-ager, was like having been born with one eye in the middle of my forehead.

In those days, as I grew up in Grand Rapids, there were really only two figures, in the larger world, that I cared about and only one issue. The people were Harry Truman and Jackie Robinson, and the issue was race. I was to be for Truman in the 1948 election against Dewey just as, when I was twelve, I was for Roosevelt over Dewey, or when I was eight, I was for Roosevelt over Willkie, or just as at forty-four I was for Carter over Ford and at forty-eight I was for Carter over Reagan. Democrats, in formulating domestic policies, tend much more often than Republicans to take into account the problems and the pain of the little people. Blacks, by and large, are the little people. So from 1940 on, my politics were pretty much set. So, when Truman won in November 1948, I was pleased, but didn't pay much attention to what he did after that.

But if my politics had become fixed in 1940, my attitude about sports had hardened even before that; perhaps as early as 1936. When Joe Louis fought in those days, everything in the Negro community stopped. The hopes of a whole race rode on that man's skills. He would beat up the white people for us as we wanted to beat up the white people who humiliated us in our daily lives. And so it was with Jackie Robinson, the superstar who succeeded Louis in the Negro fan's imagination and whose pioneering efforts may have been made more possible by Louis' dignity in victory a decade earlier. Unlike Truman, who somehow symbolized the hope for racial decency outside our race, Jackie Robinson was us. By his skill and gallantry, he would disprove all the slanders against the whole race. We reveled in his success. It was our vindication and our way to get back for everything that had been done to us. I paid the closest attention to each twist and turn in Robinson's career. By the summer of 1949, as I was preparing to go off to Ann Arbor, he was shifting between third and second and was batting .326.

Though race and Robinson were often the same issue, race was a little different. It was not that we in my family were direct victims of racism. On the contrary, my stepfather clearly had a higher income than most of the parents of students in my high school. Unlike those of most of my contemporaries, black and white, my parents had college degrees. Within Grand Rapids' tiny Negro community, they were among the elite. The others were the lawyer, the dentist, the undertaker and the other doctor.

And that is what made race such exquisite agony. I knew that other blacks were targets of harsh job and housing discrimination; but, though being Negro did pose some inconvenience for us, those major life-numbing blockbusters were not present in our daily lives. I did have a sense that it was unfair for poor Negroes to be relegated to bad jobs—if they had jobs at all—and to bad or miserable housing, but I didn't feel any great sense of identity with them. After all, the poor blacks in New York had also been the hard ones; the ones who tried to take my money, to beat me up and to keep me perpetually intimidated. Besides, I had heard it intimated around my house that their behavior, sexual and otherwise, left a good deal to be desired.

So, I thought that maybe they just weren't ready for this society, but that I was. And it was dreadfully unfair for white people to just look at my face and lips and hair and decide that I was inferior. In high school, I thought I was doing my bit for the race when I served as student council president. By being a model student and leader, I thought I was demonstrating how well Negroes could perform if only the handicaps were removed and they were given a chance. But deep down I guess I was also trying to demonstrate that I was not like those other people; that I was different. My message was quite clear: I was *not nigger*. But the world didn't seem quite ready to make such fine distinctions, and it was precisely that fact—though at the time I could scarcely even have admitted it to myself—that was the nub of the race issue for me.

Up to then my political consciousness had been very much connected with my mother's professional life. She was smart, and before she married my stepfather, she had had the top race-relations job on the YWCA staff. By the time she resigned in 1944 after her remarriage, the Y was in her blood and, fortunately for her, it had a sufficiently extensive and structured volunteer program for the satisfaction of her fiercest and noblest drives.

Shortly after we got to Grand Rapids, she was elected to the board of directors of the Y there—the first Negro to serve in such a position in that town. A few years later she was elected president of the board—another first—and served her terms with distinction despite several resignations by white board members and a plea from one of them that Mom step down because her election had so upset the woman's husband that he had taken to his sickbed.

Other local board memberships followed, as did election to the National Board of the Y. She was active in the Urban League and one of the driving forces behind the establishment of the Grand Rapids Human Relations Commission and a charter member of it. When my sisters Judy—born when I was fifteen—and Sharon—born when I was close to nineteen—came along, I urged her to throw off some of those responsibilities and to slow down and spend more time with the children. She didn't, and I guess she really couldn't. She was fulfilling herself, and she was good at what she did. She fought for equality by spearheading efforts on substantive issues and by giving white people the eye-popping example of her excellence.

She was an idealistic and tough civic leader, and she won most of the fights she got into. I remember, though, one time when she didn't win. By then she was on the World Council of the Y and had traveled to China and to Lebanon. I think she harbored ambitions for

high office on the World Council, but one night when we were washing dishes when I was in high school, she told me about a rules
change in World Council election procedures that had slammed the
door on her hopes.

I remember her standing there with her hands in the soapy water
telling me how a powerful white American woman had made a corridor argument for the change.

"We've got to make this change," Mom remembers the woman
saying, "because otherwise any fool might get nominated."

Just as she uttered that sentence, the woman saw Mom, went
crimson and changed the subject.

"I knew then that she was talking about me," my mother said,
"and I knew that I wasn't a fool, so it had to be race."

I looked at her then, and it was the first time in a long time that I
had seen even a trace of tears in her eyes.

Another time, though, I saw her really cry. It was when my sister
Judy was about three or four and came in the house sobbing so hard,
she was incoherent. When we finally calmed her enough to understand what she was trying to say, Mom looked at me, her eyes filled
with hurt. What Judy told us was that a group of little neighborhood
kids, all white, had chased her home calling her, as best Judy could
understand it, "nickel penny." It wasn't "nickel penny" at all. It was
"*nigger* penny." I had heard the kids say it at other times myself.

Judy was still crying hard, and Mom tried to talk to her, but she
couldn't. Tears filled her eyes, and her voice broke as she said to
me, "You talk to her, Roger. I can't."

She left the room then and went upstairs, and I tried to explain
as best one could to a three- or four-year-old what had happened to
her—and why. And I tried to explain to her how irrational and
foolish prejudice was and that nothing was wrong with her, but rather
with the people who had tried to hurt her.

Finally Judy was calmed, more by the fact that her big brother was
cradling her in his arms and by the soothing tone of his words than by
any understanding I could convey to a little child about how you
defend your psyche against the madness of American racism.

When Mom came back downstairs and apologized to me for breaking down, I said I understood.

"No," Mom said, "I don't think you will until you have your own
children. You can toughen yourself up so you can take it when it

comes at you, but when it comes at your children, there are no defenses."

We never much talked about what I would do, or how I would be, my mother and I. I just watched and appreciated her through those years, and without ever forming the conscious thought, I came to the assumption that I would spend my life, as she did, blasting through doors that white people didn't want to open to us.

5 In the spring of 1945 the world began to change. One April afternoon, while I was watching the Creston High School baseball team beat South High, word came that President Roosevelt had died in Georgia. I went home before the game was over. It was my mother's thirty-eighth birthday. We observed it with long faces and silence.

In August, the United States blew Hiroshima apart with an atom bomb. I was listening to Dr. Christian on the upstairs radio when they interrupted to announce the news. I raced downstairs to tell my grandmother. "Hey, Gram, Gram. We've just blown up a whole city with one bomb. Some city in Japan is all blown up."

My grandmother looked up from her sewing with some annoyance and said, "Oh, Roger, stop your chattering. Go on back upstairs now. It's your bedtime."

A few weeks later on the battleship *Missouri*, off Japan, the Japanese surrendered unconditionally to General Douglas MacArthur. The war, which I thought would last forever, was over. I was thirteen years old, and I was about to enter the second half of the eighth grade at Creston High School.

That fall I first fully understood the central place athletics occupies in the lives of young American boys. Back in New York, most of our games had been adaptations to an environment of hard streets and high walls. There were artificial games on concrete with balls that usually didn't break windows. We played stickball and curb ball and a bastard derivative of touch football called "association." Real games were almost impossible. Larger boys pre-empted the one basketball court in our neighborhood, and the grass fields of the park down by the Hudson River were almost a half an hour's walk away.

But in Grand Rapids there was grass everywhere. And balls. And boys. High-school football was king. League games were played under the lights on Friday and Saturday nights at a centrally located field. All week long in school we would analyze the strengths and weaknesses of the next opponent. Cheerleaders, lights and several thousand people in the stands provided sufficient glamour to overcome the disappointing losses that our team suffered week after week and to fuel our fantasies of future glory.

The senior high, or first teams, were made up mainly of seniors and juniors with a few gifted underclassmen sprinkled over the roster. Then, each school had a junior varsity, or second team, made up of ninth- and tenth-graders.

And then there was us . . . the little kids who hung around the end zones during practice all week retrieving stray balls kicked or thrown in our direction or playing our own makeshift games beyond the end zones.

On Saturday mornings we would have our games. Creston High School junior-high classes were made up of groups of children fed into the school from at least three neighborhood feeder schools, and the affinity groups in the class were based loosely on the relationships from the old school and neighborhood. Each of the groups put together a ragtag football team, and on Saturday morning there would be at least one game.

And our team was pretty successful. We mainly won.

One Saturday evening after one of our sandlot games, when Creston wasn't playing at Houseman Field, I went over to Lloyd's. Lloyd's sister Bobby and all the rest were there. I had hurt my leg making a touchdown so I limped a little and talked a lot.

Somewhere around the third elaboration of the story, Lloyd said mildly that he'd like to come up and play some Saturday. I kept on talking, but all the time my mind was repeating, Lloyd wants to play. He wants to come up to the North End on Saturday. Next Saturday. Next Saturday. I was trapped.

So, after the final story about the final lunge, when I couldn't put it off any longer, I said, "Sure. Why not?" But, later in the evening, after I had had some time to think, I got Lloyd alone. "Say, look," I said. "Those teams are kinda close, ya know. I mean, we don't switch around. From team to team. Or new guys, ya know?"

Lloyd nodded, but he was getting a funny look on his face . . . part unbelieving and part hurt. So I quickly interjected before he could say anything. "Naw, man. Naw. Not like you shouldn't come and play. Just that we gotta have some good reason for you to play on our team, you dig?"

"Yeah," Lloyd said, his face still puzzled, but no longer hurt.

"Hey, I know," I said. "I got it. We'll say you're my cousin. If you're my cousin, see, then you gotta play. Nobody can say you can't be on my team, because you're family, right?"

"Oh, right. Okay," Lloyd said, his face brightening. "Sure, we'll say we're cousins. Solid."

I felt relieved as well. I could have a Negro cousin. It wasn't voluntary. It wouldn't be as if I had gone out and made a Negro friend deliberately. A person couldn't help who his cousins were.

So the next Saturday when everybody was assembling, I walked out onto the yard of Aberdeen Elementary school and introduced everybody to my cousin, Lloyd Brown. There were enough people for the sides to be parceled out evenly, so there was no trouble about Lloyd's joining the game. Lloyd was a superb athlete, and his class began to show immediately. In order not to be outdone by my cousin, I put out as I had never done before and played probably the best game of my life.

The game became our entire universe. The knees of my jeans had long since been shredded and my elbows and knees rubbed raw from rough contact with bare dirt and pebbles. But my wounds and my rags were my swaddlings of glory and I would swagger and limp with them, blood surging thick and fast inside me and muscles tense and quick, ready for the next play. And Lloyd, I could tell, was just the same. Our initial competition had given way to exquisite teamwork. We were the blazing knights of that little football field. We were one, and the game was part of us.

In the days that followed, Don or Gene or Andy would talk to me about my "cousin," and I would change the subject. Once one of them said how much he liked Lloyd and said he hoped he would come back often. I said I doubted it because he didn't feel very comfortable up in the North End. They didn't talk about Lloyd very much after that.

For my part, I felt more comfortable that fall than I was to feel for decades. I had always to be careful never to break the unstated rules that minimized my difference, the unspoken inferiority that I hoped my friends would ignore. So I was quiet for the most part, waiting for situations to develop before I reacted, always careful, always polite and considerate. By this time that state of affairs had become endurable. Sandlot football had become my first discernible athletic skill, and I reveled in it. I had friends and mastered my school work easily and well.

And the postwar fall of 1945 was a good time in America. We were no longer limited to the amount of gas my stepfather as a doctor was allowed. We could fill up the tank on Sundays and ride through the blazing autumn countryside.

But peace meant more to me than a full tank of gas. My mind had been inflamed by the war. I believed passionately in the evil of the Axis.

Hitler had obviously been a madman, Mussolini a dunce, Tojo a savage, while Uncle Joe and good Old Winnie had been warm, loving and reliable allies. I loved America, freedom, democracy and the New York Yankees.

I would sometimes lie on my back and stare up at passing clouds and wonder why God had played such a dirty trick by making me a Negro. It all seemed so random. So unfair to me. To *me*! But I never doubted the goodness of America. It was better to be American, even a Negro American, than anything else. And segregation was so stupid, its proponents so ignorant and the surge of good in the world so powerful, that things would have to change. The future belonged to America and to all of us who lived in it, including me.

But, still, I wasn't white in the pervasive whiteness of my wonderful country. The mayor and the senators and all the other important people were white. And all the big kids and important athletic heroes and all the pretty girls in my school were white.

In school I was gaining more friends, and the teachers respected me. It got so that I could go for days not thinking very much about being Negro until something made the problem unavoidable.

One day in history class, for instance, the teacher asked each of us to stand and tell in turn where our families had originated. Many of the kids in the class were Dutch with names like Vander Jagt, De Young and Ripstra. My pal, Andy, was Scots-Irish. When it came my turn, I stood up and burned with shame and when I could speak, I lied. And then I was even more ashamed because I exposed a deeper shame. "Some of my family was English," I said—Wilkins is an English name—"and the rest of it came from . . . Egypt." Egypt! Well, it was in Africa, but only barely.

And then there was the problem with girls. In the early days in Grand Rapids, my mother had a woman come in once a week to do the washing and the heavy cleaning. She was a scrawny white woman with lank brown hair, dead blue eyes and the drawn and wrinkled skin that in later years I came to associate with excessive use of both alcohol and cigarettes. Her name was MacEarlin and she came from a poorer part of the North End about seven blocks away from our house.

I didn't like Mrs. MacEarlin, because most of her teeth were gone and her gummy mouth looked horrible, but my mother said she was a good worker. The first-baseman on our high-school baseball team lived near Mrs. MacEarlin in one of those faded-out frame houses in that end of town and he had a pretty sister named Shirley. She was a grade ahead of me and had olive skin and a rich deep body.

One day I came home after school and my mother told me that Shirley had been talking to Mrs. MacEarlin about me. My breath got short and I asked her what Shirley had said.

"She told Mrs. MacEarlin that she liked you," my mother said.

"Yeah. Really, did she say that? Really?" I asked.

"Yes," my mother said. "She said she liked you because you know your place."

I didn't say anything and my mother looked at me, waiting. Then she said, "Isn't that funny. She likes you because you know your place. Can you imagine that?"

"Yeah, that's pretty funny," I said, but I didn't forget that girl's big gaunt colorless house, the deep eyewells framing the rich brown eyes or the way I first felt when I found out how she thought about me.

In fact, my sexual feelings would continue to be a problem for me for many years. At this point in my life, however, there was a steady insistence in my groin, a feeling that affected all boys my age in the school. Life alternated between constant erections and endless conversations studded with sexual fantasies, dirty jokes and sly confessions about masturbation. And we looked at the girls with their long skirts, loafers, white socks and high strapped breasts with wonder and as much imagination as we could muster. It ached terribly and the mystery could not be pierced either with endless talk or boundless imagination.

The only way to ease the pain was to run, to jump, to shoot, throw and catch. I chose track. Jesse Owens had been a national hero and Mal Whitfield and George Rhoden were coming on. I began reading sports magazines about track, and I went out for it because I needed to use my body to tell myself and the world that I was special. Very special.

Track intrigued me because I saw it as purer than life. A sport like baseball, I thought, was a lot like life. Although you stand there totally alone when you face the pitcher, the rest of the game has a team, coaches and managers. Failure is sometimes clearly pinpointed, but there are many other opportunities to spread the blame around. In track, *you* are on the line. You are on your own. Since Grand Rapids was located in one of the major American centers of Calvinism, failures at track at my school were generally attributed to an insufficient capacity to generate and to tolerate enough pain to be good. To fail at track was to prove that you lacked guts.

In my senior year, my relay team qualified for the state championship meet. We traveled to Lansing, the state capital, to compete against the powers from across the state that we had known only as distant fables: Lansing Sexton, Saginaw Arthur Hill, Detroit Northern. I was to run the lead quarter mile in our race and I was terrified that I would disgrace myself. I couldn't believe that I was good enough for that competition, and my main object was to avoid humiliation. In the blind and terrified pursuit of that goal, I lost my diffidence and forgot myself. Legs and arms flew, bodies in all other colors of uniforms could be glimpsed out of the corners of my eyes, and there were grunts and panting and the beat of calloused balls of feet on cinder. The race was a blur. I was in the pack, driving and pushing with everything I had. And finally, I saw my second man, passed him the baton and stopped.

When I had caught my breath and could look, I saw my teammate leading the race. I hadn't been humiliated, I had won.

In high school, even drained and depleted by the most arduous training and the most difficult meets, I still had plenty of throbbing unfulfilled sexual energy. They were everywhere, the girls. They all had budding bosoms, they all smelled pink, they all brushed against the boys in the hall, they were all white, and in 1947–49, they were all inaccessible.

There were some things you knew without ever knowing how you knew them. You knew that Mississippi was evil and dangerous, that New York was east and the Pacific Ocean was west. And, in the same way you knew that white women were the most desirable and dangerous objects in the world. Blacks were lynched in Mississippi and such places sometimes just for looking with the wrong expression at white women. Blacks of a very young age knew that white women of any quality went with the power and style that went with the governance of America—though, God knows, we had so much self-hate that when a white woman went with a Negro man, we promptly decided that she was trash, and we also figured that if she would go with him she would go with any Negro.

Nevertheless, as my groin throbbed at fifteen and sixteen and seventeen, *they* were the only ones there. One of them would be in the hallway opening her locker next to mine. Her blue sweater sleeve would be pushed up to just below the elbow and as she would reach high on a shelf to stash away a book, I would see the tender dark hair against the white skin of her forearm. And I would ache and want to touch that arm and follow that body hair to its source.

Some of my friends, of course, did touch some of those girls. My friends and I would talk about athletics and school and their loves. But they wouldn't say a word about the dances and the hayrides they went to.

I perceived they liked me and accepted me as long as I moved aside when life's currents took them to where I wasn't supposed to be. I fit into their ways when they talked about girls, even their personal girls. And, indeed, I fit into the girls' lives when they were talking about boys, most particularly, their own personal boys. Because I was a boy, I had insight. But I was also Negro, and therefore a neuter. So, a girl who was alive and sensuous night after night in my fantasies, would come to me earnestly in the day and talk about Rich or Gene or Andy. She would ask what he thought about her, whether he liked to dance, whether, if she invited him to her house for a party, he would come. She would tell me her fears and her yearnings, never dreaming for an instant that I had yearnings too and that she was their object.

In those days, I still knew Bobby, of course, and some other Negro girls too. But the power of American sexual imagery purveyed in the movies and in advertisements, coupled with my proximity every school day to these forbidden white beauties, overwhelmed whatever early tenderness there had been for Bobby, and what might have developed for any of the others.

But it was a Negro girl that I lost my virginity to, finally. She was known as being very fast, and in retrospect, she had to know that I had a reputation for being very slow. One night I had driven across town to go with a group of Negro kids to a student play at one of the high schools that Negro kids attended. We all rode in my mother's car and when we went home, this girl insisted on being dropped off last. It was late when we got to her house and she had had her hand on my thigh and would occasionally brush my crotch lightly as I drove, so I followed her indoors.

We were very quiet and didn't turn the lights on. As soon as I closed the door, she was against me, face up, mouth open. It was a frantic, sloppy kiss. My hand touched her breast, tentatively at first and then hard, encouraged as she ground her pelvis into my groin. By the time we got to the couch my pants were around my knees and her skirt was around her waist. I didn't know what had happened to her pants, or even if she had worn any.

In an instant, I was in her. I was amazed and more than a little frightened. It was warm and moist inside her. She panted frantically. So did I, briefly. Then it was over.

She asked, "Is that it?"

I said no. But it was over, and I was too embarrassed for any more. She stood, pulled herself together and, grinning wickedly, said, "Don't worry about it. Even you will know how to fuck one of these days. It's that easy!"

There began to be a cultural difference between me and other blacks my age too. Black street language had evolved since my Harlem days, and I had not kept pace. Customs, attitudes and the other common social currencies of everyday black life had evolved away from me. I didn't know how to talk, to banter, to move my body. If I was tentative and responsive in the North End, where I lived, I was tense, stiff and awkward when I was with my black contemporaries. One day I was standing outside the church trying, probably at my mother's urging, to make contact. Conversational sallies flew around me while I stood there stiff and mute, unable to participate. Because the language was so foreign to me, I understood little of what was being said, but I did know that the word used for a white was *paddy*. Then a boy named Nickerson, the one whom my mother particularly wanted me to be friends with, inclined his head slightly toward me and said, to whoops of laughter, "technicolor paddy." My feet felt rooted in stone, and my head was aflame. I never forgot that phrase.

I have rarely felt so alone as I did that day riding home from church. Already partly excluded by my white friends, I was now almost completely alienated from my own people as well. But I felt less uncomfortable and less vulnerable in the white part of town. It was familiar enough to enable me to ward off most unpleasantness.

The yearning for a girl, however, was not susceptible to evasive strategies. There may be few more powerful obsessions than a teen-age boy's fixation on a love object. In my case it came down to a thin brunette named Marge McDowell. She was a half grade behind me, and she lived in a small house on a hill. I found excuses to drive by it all the time. I knew her schedule in school, so I could manage to be in most of the hallways she'd have to use in going from class to class. We knew each other, and she had once confided a strong, but fleeting yearning for my friend Rich Kippen. I thought about her constantly, night, morning and afternoon.

Finally, late one afternoon after school, I came upon her alone in a hallway. "Marge," I blurted, "can I ask you something?"

She stopped and smiled and said, "Sure, Roger, what?"

"Well, I was wondering," I said. "I mean. Well, would you go to the hayride next week with me?"

Her jaw dropped and her eyes got huge. Then she uttered a little shriek and turned, hugging her books to her bosom the way girls do, and fled. I writhed with mortification in my bed that night and for many nights after.

The rest of my days in that high school were spent pretty much in that atmosphere. In my senior year, I was elected president of the Creston High School student council. It was a breakthrough of sorts.

The same year I won my election, a young Navy veteran who had just begun to practice law in Grand Rapids defeated the long-entrenched right-wing Congressman Jonkman in the Republican primary. Gerald Ford's victory was something of a breakthrough too. He was to go on to represent that district in Congress for the next quarter of a century. After the election, Howard W. Wickett, the principal of our school, called an assembly and told us that he had taught Gerald R. Ford at South High School. He said that Ford had been a fine young man, a diligent student and a splendid football player. He told us that we could all, given similar diligence, grow up to be like Gerald Ford.

II

6 There had never been any question about it—I would go to college. Even when I was a child in Kansas City, it was assumed that I would go—as my parents and their sisters and brother had gone—to the University of Minnesota. My parents talked about it because of segregation. In the thirties Negroes were barred from the University of Missouri, and Negro parents of even very young children did not then foresee a time when things would be different. But under decisions of the Supreme Court—then still contorting itself to carry out the separate-but-equal façade mandated by the late-nineteenth-century decision in *Plessy* v. *Ferguson*—states that barred Negroes from state-supported schools were required to provide them equal educational opportunities. So, Negro parents could send their children to a comparable public university where there was no segregation and pay only the expenses they would have paid if the child could have gone to the local state or university. The student's state government was required to pay the difference.

From the time I was about four, I heard my parents talk about how I would go to Minnesota under such a plan.

So, when the time to go to college actually came, I was simply fulfilling a lifelong expectation and doing just what all my white friends were doing. Only, instead of Minnesota, I decided on the University of Michigan because it had the best football team in the nation. No reason to look any further!

I didn't think of Michigan as a white school, explicitly. Of course it was white—I thought all good things in this society were—but I knew it was also integrated. Yet, in those days you knew that even the most liberal institutions would do foolish and insulting things to you

63

if you were a Negro. Michigan was no different. Though the university did not ask for racial designations on application forms—state law forbade it—in its housing application, Michigan required a photograph of each applicant. Sure enough, when I showed up at Hayden House in the East Quadrangle, both my roommates were Negroes just like me. Except they weren't just like me. They were both older than I was, and we had very little in common. The information elicited by the application form about reading habits and "other interests" had clearly been subsumed by the commonality of the color of our skins. There were, of course, no Negro floors, suites or wings of dormitories, just Negro rooms spotted at random, but with a delicate eye for balance. Throughout the dormitory, that was the pattern of integration at Michigan in 1949, and we all fell into it and held pretty much to it throughout our college years.

Beyond our room, I was beginning to perceive an even more rigid social structure. In 1949 white people and black people didn't often mix at any level of society, and the society was mirrored in the patterns of student life sanctioned and promoted by the university. There were about 20,000 students on that postwar Michigan campus and about 150 or so of us were Negroes. We lived together in the rooms assigned to us in the dormitories or we lived in rooming houses in the Negro sections of Ann Arbor that were kept by Negro couples to supplement their basic incomes. There were no integrated fraternities or sororities, and there were no apartments near the campus. There was no overt racial friction, but there was no interracial socializing either.

But I was lucky. Hayden House was one of the four houses in the new section of the East Quad. About two hundred boys lived in each one of the houses. And in that group of eight hundred boys, in addition to my roommates, there were about eight other Negroes. Six of them were sophomores and had, during their freshman year, formed a warm protective circle, which they found easy to expand to accept three new freshmen, excluding my roommates.

I wanted to be a journalist, a strange pursuit for us then, but that's what my father and uncle had been, and writing and reading were what I liked. But my choice of profession was no stranger than that of another Negro student, who was going to be a forester, and it was a lot less strange than that of the stiff loner from the West Quad who was going to be an actor. We all knew that he was crazy, partly because he never mixed with anybody and partly because everybody

knew there were no decent acting jobs for Negroes anyway. Even
after we had seen him in a few campus plays, we still thought he was
crazy. His name was James Earl Jones.

Our group was a large enough critical mass that none of us was
ever lonely. It was enough to tempt a fainthearted scholar to plunge
wholeheartedly into the wonders of idle male companionship. For
me, it was wonderful. It was the first time in five years that I had been
with Negroes and submerged in interests and values we shared. I was
square and awkward, and they recognized it, but they didn't try to
hurt me with it. They weren't cruel. "Ready to scarf, man?" Conwell
Carrington asked one day.

"What?" I replied.

"Scarf, man, you ready to scarf?" he repeated.

"What?" I asked again.

"Aw, nigger," Conwell said, "cmon. Let's go eat."

And then there was a girl. When I would head across the campus
to Spanish class in the first semester every Monday, Wednesday and
Friday at two, I would pass a tall, slim, brown-skinned girl with
dancing eyes and a lush lower lip. After a while, I found out who she
was—Ollie Mae Sanders, a freshman from Saginaw, Michigan. One
day I asked her to go to the movies with me, and after a while I
kissed her, and after that we were going steady. That was about as
good as it ever got. I had my girl and I had my Negro friends and I
usually went to class and sometimes studied.

Anytime I was between classes, or when I was cutting, I could go
over to the cafeteria of the Women's League. There would be hundreds of students in there and the jukebox would be playing all the
tunes the blacks had played by monopolizing the box. I could find the
brothers and sisters easy, because their heads would be bobbing up
and down above all the rest to the sounds of Ella Fitzgerald singing
"A Tisket A Tasket"—except when some white jerk would slip in a
nickel and play Johnny Ray whining away over some little cloud.

And we'd go to sports events to root on two levels: for Michigan
and for the Negroes—any Negroes. Though there was a fair smatter-
ing of Negroes on football teams throughout the Big Ten, there was
only *one* on any *basketball* team in the whole league—Bill Garrett of
Indiana. I can see him now, tall, graceful, pigeon-toed and fast. Garrett was good and we always rooted for him to score thirty points and
for Michigan to win by one. But it rarely happened that way. Garrett
always got his share but Indiana usually won.

Although I got along well with the white boys in college, I was too aware of our differences to ever be completely comfortable. Take the thing about nappy hair. It started when I was a little boy, two or three years old, and my grandmother would put Vaseline on it just before bedtime. Then she would have me sit on the floor with my shoulders at her knees and she would brush it a hundred times on each side. She would put a cut-off stocking, tied at the top to form a cap, on my head and twist it tight. I would go to bed then and sleep with it on and in the morning my hair would be flat on my head, parted near the center. And though my hair still wasn't straight, it had no tight little woolly balls in it. My grandmother always stressed the importance of "training" my hair.

I used stocking caps for years after that, as did millions of other Negro males around the country. Often you could see men walking in the streets with their stocking caps showing just below the brims of their hats. Nobody ever had to tell me not to wear a stocking cap in public, of course, because I was too ashamed to do it. The whole practice had less to do with neatness than denying the natural properties of my hair and showing people—white people particularly— that I wasn't a woolly head, like the raggedy blacks they seemed so to despise. Even though I would never wear the cap in public the tightness of the cap would leave an indentation—a line across my forehead and around the back of my hairline every morning. I never did manage to master that problem.

One night at college, Robinson, an unpleasant white boy from the room next door, came barging in without knocking. I had been sitting there studying, with a stocking cap on my head. My roommates looked up at him with the minimal interest they generally displayed in anything other than their books, but I was mortified. Robinson was the first white person who had ever seen me with a stocking cap on, and I didn't know what to do. Should I snatch it off or leave it on? I was paralyzed with shame, so I left it on.

Still, I probably thought less about white people those first two years of college than at any other time in my life, before or since. They had their lives and we had ours, and though I would sometimes feel wistful after football games when I knew they were going back to parties at big fraternity houses, what they did or thought was of surprisingly little interest to me in the comfortable cocoon we Negro students had constructed for ourselves.

That is not to say there wasn't civil-rights activity on the campus. There was, but it was mainly carried on by white people. The burning issue for the Student Legislature that year was a resolution it had passed that would have banned any fraternity or sorority that had not—after a seven-year grace period—gotten rid of the discrimination clause in its charter. But that wasn't something the Negroes had pushed; none of us was on S.L., as the student government was called.

Ultimately, though, I was moved enough by my sense of S.L.'s power and by my own need to add a few layers of prestige to my still slender persona, that I ran for it in the second semester of my sophomore year.

That was not long after Ollie broke off our romance to go back with some football player at Michigan State whom she had dated in high school. I had lost my girlfriend, and I lost the election, though not by much. The next semester, I ran again and won, to become the only Negro in the student government. Shortly after that, I was appointed chairman of, naturally, the Human Relations Committee.

During that year we reviewed the issue of Greek-letter discrimination and I made an embarrassed and stiff speech about how difficult it was to be a Negro in America. It was my first civil-rights speech, and I was enormously self-conscious, talking about my embarrassing difference in front of all those people. Nevertheless, I managed to bring it off, and some people told me that that had been a moving moment in S.L. history. After that I put myself up for vice-president of the organization, and though I lost I was elected to one of the lesser, but still coveted, positions in the "cabinet."

Suddenly, I was the Negro politician on campus—a job that had a good deal more weight with the white students on campus than with my Negro brothers and sisters, who simply viewed it, I think, as another one of my eccentricities—and I began slowly to develop some sense of the world outside our comfortable Negro cocoon. Around this time I read a book called *But We Were Born Free* and became a civil libertarian as Joe McCarthy's name began to hit the headlines more and more frequently.

On campus, life was more urgent. Eve Tyler came to Michigan as a freshman from Cleveland at the beginning of my junior year. I met her when five of us were cruising one night in John Edwards' Oldsmobile convertible looking over the new crop of freshmen girls. This night, during their first or second night on campus, we offered five girls a ride home from some event for freshmen women at the Women's League. I was in the back seat, and the girls piled on top of us. I couldn't see any of them. All of us talked upper-class shit to them and the girl on my lap just laughed and laughed.

Later, when we talked about them, someone said, "That girl Eve, who was sitting on your lap, goddamn, she's fine."

"I couldn't see her," I said.

"Well she's really fine and you oughta see her momma," a third guy said. "She's outta sight, pink and blow."

"Pink and blow" meant light skin and hair that would move when the wind blew like a white girl's—automatically fine. Eve's mother indeed turned out to be pink and blow, but not really as good-looking, I thought, as her browner daughter. Eve knew something of the ways of Negro life in the city, but she was "straight from the home environment," as she put it, and her ways were almost as square as mine.

Eve and her roommate, Suane Milton, the daughter of a prominent doctor in Detroit, were, by a lot of people's reckoning, the prettiest Negro girls on campus, and before the year was out, they became, by far the most popular. You had to call them weeks in advance for weekend dates, so my roommate John Loomis and I saw this as a challenge, since we elected ourselves the most desirable Negro boys on campus. We thought it would be great fun to launch a campaign to shut out every other Negro male on campus; so, we devised an ingenious strategy: coffee dates in the middle of the week for the hour before their ten-thirty curfew at the dorm and coded song requests for them on the most popular disc jockey show in town after that.

"Now the Divine Sarah Vaughn," the jock would say, "for the girls in 4 from the boys in 5."

The digits in their room number added up to 4; those in ours to 5. They thought it was sweet, and we thought it was clever—our campaign succeeded, and five years later they married us on successive weekends in June.

I rarely read newspapers in those days, except for the sports page of the *Michigan Daily*, but even the most isolated environment and my own fierce egocentricity couldn't altogether avoid the fact that Communism was an issue across the country and that Joe McCarthy was abroad in the land. I hadn't taken him all that seriously when he

first became famous—I was only annoyed that he shared the name of
the great man who had presided on the New York Yankee bench in
the years when my baseball fantasies were formed.

There had been talk of Communism in my family, of course, and
my mother was against it and thought those relatives who had flirted
with it foolish. My Uncle Roy, a staunch believer in the American
Constitution and its promise of legally accomplished equality, was
against it too.

Moreover, Joe Stalin had given Communism a bad name. Despotic
dictatorships—those of Hitler, Mussolini and Tojo—had constituted
the dark side of my earliest political sensibilities formed by war
movies, newsreels and stories about the Holocaust. So it wasn't hard
to shift the points of my political compass after the war to the despotic and crazy mass-murderer Stalin and all he stood for and led. No
analysis was necessary; Russia was an evil competitor, Stalin was a
tyrant, so Communism was bad. And right-wingers and many of
those who owned America had somehow contrived to pin that stench
on almost all efforts at change in this country. So it was best to be
careful.

One man who did not choose to be careful was an instructor
named Seymour who had taught me Spanish in freshman year. I
wasn't very good at Spanish, but there was something very loving
about Seymour as he attempted gently and politely to persuade us to
learn the material he presented so patiently every Monday, Wednesday and Friday at two. It was also charming to take Spanish from a
man who spoke with a Brooklyn accent.

So, a couple of years later, when Seymour was dismissed with two
other low-level faculty members for refusing to testify before the
House Un-American Activities Committee, I was stunned and angry.
By that time the evil in Joe McCarthy's methods had become apparent even to me. Though Seymour's problem had come at the hands of
a House Committee and not McCarthy's, the smell was the same.
And besides, through conversations with my parents and their
friends, it was clear to me that a Congressman named Richard Nixon
had given that committee a bad name too.

So the Human Relations Committee of the Student Legislature
proposed to the whole student body a condemnation of the firings,
because they abused academic freedom. Though I don't think the
resolution was my idea originally, as chairman of the committee, I

presented it to the full body with a short, but eloquent—I thought—
speech about freedom, decency and the nature of a university. There
was enthusiasm for the proposal and it passed handily.

The next day the *Daily* ran the story on the front page with a huge
headline. Shortly after that, staccato bursts of criticism were fired at
the Student Legislature from the University administration, the Board
of Regents and some prominent alumni. The overt message was that
student organizations shouldn't concern themselves with "off
campus" issues—the Un-American Activities Committee hearings
had been held in Detroit—but the clearest message was that these
kids were crazy and couldn't be trusted. And from then on there was
a gradual whittling away by the administration of the powers and
prerogatives of the Student Legislature. It was an instructive lesson in
power politics and the mood of America in the early fifties, and it
marked the dawning of my political adulthood.

Mom was a liberal Democrat, and to the extent that I had any
politics, I adopted hers. The summer vacation after the Student Legislature's venture into the realm of adult politics, I watched, enrap-
tured, the televised battles of the Taft and the Eisenhower forces at
the Republican National Convention, and I was thrilled at the eloquence of Adlai E. Stevenson's acceptance speech when the Democrats nominated him. I was working the four-to-midnight shift that
summer at the American Seating Company's west-side factory taking
metal stadium and theater seat parts out of an oven that baked the
paint on them. I hated the job, because it was hot and I was always
burning my arms on the fiery metal I had to handle. So I stayed glued
to the television at home during the conventions until the last minute
before dashing off to punch in on time. At the end of the shift I'd race
like a madman to be at the head of the punch-out line and then drive
like fury to get home, hoping that the convention would still be on.

In the Republican fight, I preferred Dwight D. Eisenhower to Robert A. Taft of Ohio, simply because I was against Taft and the rich,
selfish conservatism I thought he represented, not because I liked Ike.
I was twenty at the time, and Franklin Roosevelt had been President
thirteen of those years. Truman had occupied the rest. I had loved
Roosevelt as a black child of the Depression would, and my family
had come to a grudging approval of Truman—so, naturally, I had
too. I had never understood the general adulation of Eisenhower, and
I figured he wasn't qualified to be President. What, after all, could a

general know about running the country? He had known a segregated
life in the Army and I figured that didn't augur well for the quest for
racial justice. President Eisenhower! The phrase didn't even sit right
in my mouth.

But Stevenson! He was a different story. I didn't need any clues
from my family to admire him. He was my kind of white man. His
speech was elegant, and he was suave and urbane. I could sit and
listen to him talk all day—nothing rough, all grace, no trace of the
South in his tones. The best of the Northern liberal tradition, I
thought, a man who could be trusted to follow the best instincts of
the Constitution and lead Negroes, at least Negroes like me, to
equality.

Early in the morning on Labor Day, my old high-school friend
Rich Kippen and I went downtown to Campau Square to watch
Stevenson launch his campaign for the Presidency. He was smaller
than I had expected, and the speech was a disappointment, but there
were flashes of eloquence. That was enough for me. Though it was
a dull, overcast day, I had seen my political beacon.

A couple of nights later, on my last night at the summer factory job,
a white coworker persuaded me to do something special to celebrate
the end of our summer labors. Like me, he was a student—a small
sandy-haired junior from Michigan State. We had become friends
mainly because of the general disdain in which student summer workers were held by the regular employees of the plant—a disdain which
our four years of college enabled us to return in kind.

That night he suggested we go down to Commerce Street to buy
ourselves some pussy. Though Pop had told me that the women who
worked down there—all Negroes—didn't accept colored patronage,
I figured maybe they'd take the two of us. He didn't have a car, so I
drove and when we got to Commerce Street, I cruised slowly up and
down a couple of times while we selected the house we wanted.
Neither of us had been to such a place before, so we finally settled
on the one that looked least ominous.

We got out of the car and I locked it carefully. Then we went up
the steps and onto the porch. I felt apprehensive, but I hoped that my
light-yellow windbreaker with the University of Michigan seal on it
made me look sophisticated and a little older. An old Negro woman
opened the door and, shuffling in old slippers, led us through a dim
hallway to a room with cracked linoleum, two moth-eaten couches,

three or four straight-back wooden chairs and a big red Coca-Cola cooler.

"Wait in here," the old woman said. "If you want some beer, it's fifty cents apiece."

We both went to the cooler and pulled cans of beer from the crushed ice and gave the woman our money. She put it in a pocket of her old shapeless dress and disappeared. We sat down, worked on our beer and waited.

Finally, a younger Negro woman came out and motioned for my friend to follow her. I got up, took another beer and laid another fifty cents on the rim of the cooler.

Suddenly from the other side of walls that were very thin, I heard springs squeaking and wood knocking. The noise lasted a very short time and stopped as suddenly as it had started. Then I heard voices.

"Now you get your friend and go. We don't serve colored in here."

"He's not my friend," I heard my friend say. "I never saw him before in my life."

"Oh," the woman said. "I thought he was with you. You came up on the porch with him."

"No, he's not with me."

They came out of the door then and the woman looked at me. My friend headed toward the door without a glance in my direction.

"You have to go," she said. "We don't serve colored in here."

Embarrassed, but also relieved, I shrugged, stood up and left with as much dignity as a man can muster when he's being put out of a whorehouse. We walked down the steps and out to the car, my friend several steps ahead of me. I walked around to the driver's side, unlocked the door and got in. After I had started the engine, my friend rapped on the passenger window. I rolled it down about three inches.

"What do you want?" I asked.

"Come on," he said, "I know you're mad, but I can explain."

"Fuck you," I said.

"You can't just leave me here," he pleaded. "It's dark and probably not safe."

"Never saw you before in my life," I replied, and then I drove off.

There was nothing more to do after that summer but to go back to school, be president of my class and graduate. I had become president of the class almost by chance. One day I had suggested to my friend Crawford Young, who was to be editor of the *Michigan Daily* in our senior year, that he run for class president.

"No," he said, "I've got too much to do running the *Daily*. You run for president and I'll run for vice-president and we'll get Sid to run for treasurer. Sid Klaus was another editor on the *Daily* and a lovely guy. We sought him out, and he agreed.

Campaigning at Michigan consisted of putting up posters with your picture on them and going around to the houses where a lot of students lived and making little speeches at dinnertime. I did that and I won—to become only the second Negro ever to preside over the largest class at Michigan, literature, science and the arts. Val Johnson, a handsome, smooth-striding quarter-miler had been the first, in 1949, the year before I came to Michigan.

That resulted in my being tapped for Michigamua, the most prestigious honor society for men at Michigan. Crawford Young belonged to it, as did Howard Willens, the president of the Student Legislature, David Brown, the chairman of the Joint Judiciary Council, and Tim Green, the captain of the football team. There were about twenty of us in "The Tribe." I was close to, but not at the core of the group. I wasn't sufficiently self-confident. They accepted their positions of leadership with pride, but also with a natural ease born of belonging in a society. I had never belonged, and I was more grateful than natural. Moreover, I had learned that white America didn't like pushy Negroes, and I was always careful. I didn't want to offend white people.

After graduation, my immediate future seemed uncertain. Eisenhower had won the election and pledged that he would go to Korea to end the apparently endless stalemate there. One option was to join the Air Force and I volunteered to take the tests, reputed to be very hard, for Air Force Flight training. The recruiters looked at my credentials and I was soon given a railroad ticket to Chanute Air Force Base in Rantoul, Illinois. I got there on a Thursday with ninety-nine other hopefuls for three days of testing.

The first day was the mental exam with a minimum of language and a maximum of math. The next morning before the physical, fifty candidates were sent home. That day we had physicals, and that night forty-four more guys got their ticket home. We six survivors of that ordeal were ecstatic. Though we had been together only two days, it seemed like months; we were old comrades, survivors, in a dreary and hostile place. We knew we would make it, because the third day of testing, by all accounts, was the fun day. It tested hand and eye coordination and the ability to manipulate a simple Link Trainer. We were filled with fantasies of pounding North Korean hills in our F 104s and blowing MIGs out of the sky.

And I was the lucky one. Only five candidates could be tested at a time, and since my name came last on the alphabetical list of six, I got extra sleep. The others had to be at the testing lab at six-thirty. I was due an hour later.

On Saturday morning, the others rose, dressed and left tossing a few rude remarks over their shoulders at me as I pulled up the bed covers for one last nap. I woke up with a start at seven-twenty in the now-empty barracks room we had occupied that night. I leaped out of bed, threw on my clothes and raced out toward the testing lab. When I got inside, panting, the large clock on the wall read 7:32. I found the sergeant in charge, told him what my name was and that I was there for the physical coordination tests.

"You're too late," he said. "We're closed."

"But I'm only two minutes late," I said.

The sergeant, a big red-faced man with sandy hair, gave me a hard look and repeated, "You're too late."

"Well, when will you be open again? When's the next time I can take the tests?" I asked, expecting that he'd set a time later in the day.

"Next Wednesday, six-thirty in the morning," he said coldly.

"Wednesday!" I exclaimed. "But I've got nothing to do on this base until then."

Another pause, another cold stare—it was now 7:34, and he snapped.

"Next test is Wednesday." Then he turned, muttered "nigger" just loudly enough for one to hear, and walked rapidly to the door, opened it, passed through quickly and closed it firmly behind him.

I walked back to the barracks disconsolate. There was absolutely nothing to do on that base. I was an outsider and knew no one. My buddies would be heading north to Chicago on the eleven o'clock train. The days until Wednesday stretched ahead of me, empty. The next group of candidates wouldn't arrive until Sunday night, but I wouldn't be one of them. I was alone, and the sergeant had called me a nigger.

Despite the prospect of utter boredom, I'd have stayed but for the sergeant's last word. Instead, I took the eleven o'clock train with my friends and brooded about being drafted into the infantry and about

Eve's being at Michigan for two more years without me. I didn't know what the hell to do with my life. I chose the usual Roger Wilkins way for those days—lying and expediency. I told my parents that I had been made night blind by an accident I had had in the Bissel Carpet Sweeper factory some summers before, when a lathe strap broke and hit me in the eye. Hell, you couldn't tell your parents that you weren't going out to defend America against Communism in a jet fighter because you had overslept.

And I wanted to be a writer. Oh Jesus, did I want to be a writer! That's what Daddy had done. I once told Rich Kippen in high school, when we were both writing for the *Creston Echo*, that my main ambition in life was to write a perfect paragraph. But they weren't hiring Negroes on papers of general circulation in those days and to go back to doing what my father had done twelve years before didn't advance the ball one inch. So I did what lots of other aimless people with A.B. degrees in political science did, I opted for law school—at Michigan. That would, at least, keep the vultures away from Eve!

7 Considering my indifferent academic performance in under-graduate school, I was admitted to the University of Michigan Law School with surprising ease. I took the aptitude test in August and by the first of September I was notified that I had been admitted. So I went back to Ann Arbor in September 1953.

One day in the first semester, I was totally confused in a course that we freshmen called "The Mystery Hour," where the faculty was experimenting in teaching Contracts, Equity and Damages in one huge lump. I had understood virtually nothing of what went on in class, so I made an appointment with Professor William B. Harvey in hopes of clarifying the issues. He listened to my problem attentively. He was a small, precise man, whose Tennessee accent had been unaffected by his years of teaching in the North. He was also the law school's admissions officer.

Professor Harvey explained the essence of what he had been driving at, but although I paid close attention, his Southern accent distracted me. The South was a place I hated and feared and Southern accents from white faces made me cringe.

When I had sufficiently comprehended the course material, I expressed my nervousness over the fact that many people flunked out of law school after the first year.

"I must have had the lowest undergraduate average in this class," I said to Mr. Harvey, fully expected to be assured that that wasn't the case.

"That's right, Mr. Wilkins," the professor replied evenly.

My stomach turned.

"Well, why did you admit me?" I asked in a rage.

With no change in tone the Tennessean looked at me steadily and said, "If you had gone to some other college, you surely wouldn't have gotten in here. But we could check with your professors and we had some sense of your extracurricular activities. They all judged you to have far more academic ability than you displayed, so we took a chance.

"Now why did we take a chance?" he continued, accent unabated.

"Well, it's because we here think the Negro people in this country need leaders—well-trained leaders. And we want to do our part in helping to train them. So we took a chance on you. Now that doesn't mean you won't have to do the work. You will. If you don't, you won't stay. But that's why we took a chance."

I left his office stunned by this Tennessee man who was the instrument of the law school's social conscience—the law school's affirmative-action program for 1953. So I worked hard enough to stay and did far better than I had done in undergraduate school.

The summer before my last year of law school was to be my last vacation from any school, ever. Though I had helped pay my way through school, supporting myself entirely through law school by working in factories every summer since I had turned sixteen, I decided to try for a legal job that summer, as befitted a senior in law school, and applied for an internship at the NAACP Legal Defense and Educational Fund, Inc.

It wasn't hard to get that summer job. By then my uncle Roy had been a top executive with the NAACP for more than two decades. Though I was the only child from his generation of his family, I didn't know him well but I admired his integrity and dignity. He was, in my eyes, and in the eyes of many other people, black and white, "the highest type Negro." I was proud of him.

So I called my uncle that spring of 1955 and asked him about a summer job, and he called Thurgood Marshall, then Director-Counsel of the NAACP Legal Defense and Education Fund, Inc. For years the legal staff that Thurgood headed had been an integral part of the NAACP itself. But Thurgood had become weary of the administrative restrictions imposed in his later years by Walter White, my uncle's predecessor, so the "Inc. Fund" was formed as a separate entity which could receive tax exempt funds, as the NAACP, which engaged in lobbying, could not. The division, which over the years

was to become total and sometimes acrimonious, was amicable then
with some NAACP staff and board members serving on the Inc. Fund
board as well.

So Thurgood naturally said yes when my uncle told him what I
wanted. He had known me since I was a little boy, and now I was a
successful student at a fine law school.

So it was that I showed up at the little building just west of Sixth
Avenue on 43rd Street, across the street from White's Clam Bar, to
work for Negro equality and do battle with the evil portion of the
white population that kept our people down. I expected constant
intensity and at least controlled fury. What I found was a very re-
laxed, highly professional law office presided over by a great big bear
of a colloquial Negro—Thurgood Marshall.

Thurgood was from Baltimore, and he talked like a street nigger,
not a constitutional lawyer.

"Boy, how you been," he said, when I came in. "Glad to see you.
What do you know about the Fourteenth Amendment?"

I'd just gotten a good grade in Con Law at Michigan, so I told him
I knew a little about it, and he said, "Good. Mainly you'll be working
for Bob Carter [now Judge Robert L. Carter, who sits on the Federal
District Court for the Southern District of New York, but then was
second in command at the Inc. Fund], but first I've got a little
problem I want you to help me with." He then gave me a short
homily history of the Fourteenth Amendment—how it had been
adopted to protect the rights of the newly emancipated slaves just
after the Civil War, how smart white lawyers had twisted it into an
instrument for the enhancement of American corporations and how
slowly but purposefully the NAACP had forged it through slow decision by slow decision into a weapon designed to serve its original
purpose. Then he outlined the problem and said:

"You take the Equal Protection issue, and I'll take the rest. Need
to bone up on sump'n besides Equal Protection."

So I went out and did the research and in a day or two came back
to him with a memorandum. Thurgood read it silently and then,
instead of saying anything to me, he got up, walked out of his office
and hollered for everybody to hear:

"Hey, this boy ain't as stupid as we all thought," waving the
memorandum around. "He's got the makings of a Wilkins, after all."

That's the way it was, working for Thurgood.

After my introductory chore, Bob Carter told me and Alice Hartman, a senior at Yale Law School, what he wanted us to do with our summer. He explained that now that *Brown* was law, the Inc. Fund was afraid that the Southern school authorities would fire many of the Negro teachers and principals in the integration process.* So the Inc. Fund had made arrangements for Alice and me to go down to the New York University law school library on Washington Square in Greenwich Village and research the teacher-tenure laws in all the states that had had legally segregated school systems.

"All of them?" I asked incredulously.

"All of them," he replied pleasantly. "After all, you've got all summer."

And that was what I was afraid of. A whole summer in a law library for a student who spent his winters avoiding the law library like the plague. But Alice, a short, pleasant and utterly decent Jewish girl from the Bronx, was enthusiastic. So we went, the squarest and oddest integrated couple in the hip Village of those days and we did our work.

It was dog work. I hated it. Besides, it was defensive, not innovative and exciting. There were to be no dashing investigative forays into hostile Southern territory, just a goddamn plugging library job slogging through the codes of all the Southern and Border states. But every once in a while I'd remember some of the nice teachers I had had in my segregated elementary school in Kansas City in the thirties and I'd go back and read the next section of the next code.

I learned something about the quest for justice that summer that I was to relearn at high cost in future years: It's mainly not drama and heroics, but slog work and steadfastness, through a lifetime. It was a good lesson and there were two rewards. The first came the following year when I returned to New York with my law degree in hand and had lunch with some of the people from the Inc. Fund. They said the teacher-tenure memos Alice and I had left behind had been very

* Thurgood Marshall and the legal staff of the NAACP had embarked years before on a long crusade to desegregate the educational systems in the South, where segregation was required by law. By the early fifties, they had laid the foundations for an all-out assault on segregation in public primary and secondary schools and in May 1954 their labors were rewarded by the unanimous decision of the Warren Court in *Brown* v. *Topeka Board of Education*, overturning the fifty-eight-year-old decision in *Plessy* v. *Ferguson*, which had enshrined the doctrine of separate-but-equal in American Constitutional law. In 1955 had come the implementing decision—"with all deliberate speed"—which indicated that desegregation was to be slow, very slow, but sure.

ROGER WILKINS

good and that they had been extremely useful in fashioning strategies for litigation. I was pleased and very proud.

When law school was over, I didn't go to graduation. I went to Cleveland instead, and Eve and I got married that day. Two of my ushers were white—Tim Green, the football player, and Bob Baker, who had been an officer in S.L. and a year ahead of me in law school. The story on the social page of the local Negro paper, *The Call and Post*, announced in a headline: "Attorney Tyler's Daughter Marries in Interracial Ceremony."

In retrospect, my marriage to Eve was almost inevitable. Years before, while I was in high school, I had thought about Cleveland—a far-off sophisticated city that I didn't know, but which accepted black ballplayers—Larry Doby was the first—before any other team in the American League. *Ebony* magazine had called Cleveland one of the most sophisticated cities on race in America. I dreamed then that perhaps in that wonderful city on the lake, there would be a beautiful brown daughter of professional parents who would be like me and whom I would love. Somehow I dreamed that the girl from Cleveland would be softer—less street-wise than the girls from Detroit, who knew so much and made me feel clumsy.

And so it was with Eve—gentle, pretty, smart, good-natured, well brought-up and very pleasant. She didn't intimidate me, and she was nice to be with. Her background was right; her mother was a social worker with a master's degree, her father was a lawyer, and even her grandmother had earned a college degree—extraordinary for a woman born so close to slavery. My stepfather summed it up: "Eve is the girl of choice," he said one day when she was visiting in Grand Rapids on vacation.

Thurgood offered me a job at the Inc. Fund, but I wouldn't take it. It was too much like going into the family business. My uncle was a towering figure in civil rights and the names—Roy Wilkins, Roger Wilkins—were too similar. I wanted to be me, not a pale imitation of him, not the Wilkins kid around the Inc. Fund office. It was a thought that was to haunt me through the years as people would write letters to me addressed to "Roy Wilkins, Jr." or to "Roger Wilkins, Jr." or when I would get some new job and wasn't sure in my own mind whether I'd gotten it because I was Roy Wilkins' nephew.

At any rate, I didn't go to work for Thurgood, but rather to a private law firm that was then called Delson, Levin and Gordon.

The partner I was to work for, Robert Delson, specialized in representing developing countries. His principal client then was Indonesia, but he also did some work for Burma, India and Liberia in those days. I was going to become an international lawyer.

But Eve and I had barely settled into our Brooklyn walk-up before the inevitable happened. I had run out of draft exemptions and was called for my physical down on Whitehall Street in Manhattan. We were asked to do jumping jacks and my feet hurt. I had developed thick calluses on the balls of my feet when I ran on the track team in high school, and over the years they had become smaller, but painful, even when I walked. I anticipated problems marching during basic training, which I told the doctor supervising our jumping jacks. He laughed and soon I was classified 1A.

I took the option to be inducted from my home draft board in Grand Rapids. Eve quit her job, I took leave from the firm, we gave up our apartment and put our furniture in storage, and we headed west with Eve intending to work in Cleveland during my two years in the Army. I didn't mind any of this. On the contrary, I believed in a strong America and that the Communist world was a threat to us. I was willing to do my part.

But my feet were not. The doctor at the central induction center in Detroit took one look at my callused soles and classified me 4F. I was not entirely displeased, but the rejection left Eve and me in limbo. She had just gotten a job in Cleveland, and the prospect of going back to New York, only to have to pack it all in again if the Army decided later to take me, wasn't appealing. So, Eve's mother, then a supervisor at the Cuyahoga County (Cleveland) Welfare Department got me a job as a "Case Worker I," the entry-level job in the department. My basic responsibility was to visit each of the 114 cases in my load at least once every three months, to dictate a record of each of those visits, and to keep a sharp eye on the families and their budgets to make sure nobody was cheating—for example, by having a man in the house or having an unreported job. Nobody said much about providing social services to those fractured families, and soon it became clear why they didn't. The system made such attempts impossible. The discovery and exposure of fraud and cheating were clearly the highest priorities in the department.

I was appalled and astonished by the whole operation. Most of the other caseworkers were pretty casual about the job. They didn't seem to care much about the clients, and it became clear that some of the men were actually sleeping with some of the women in their case loads. Considering the inequality of their power positions, that was, in my estimation, pretty close to rape. Other workers, it seemed to me, were more interested in the affairs they were conducting among themselves than they were with the welfare of the people they were supposed to be serving.

As a child of the Roosevelt era, I believed deeply in the efficacy of government. Yet here, in my first sustained contact with poor Negroes, I saw that apart from the delivery of money to those who had none—a not inconsiderable service in itself—the government seemed indifferent to the possibility of helping people. I believed, in those days, that people could be helped, or at least that some of their problems could be solved. And even if you failed, I thought, you ought to make the effort.

But many of the caseworkers—all college graduates—spent a good deal of time laughing at the lower-class people to whose existence they owed their livelihoods. I remember one worker recounting at a lunch-time office bridge game how she asked a woman under thirty, who had had seven children by five different men, why she did it.

"When you come home at night," the client said, "you got a car outside your door. You can go to the movies or a ball game or just take a ride. And if you stay home, you got a TV to watch or a telephone to call up some friends.

"I don't have none of that," the woman had concluded. "I just got this," and she gestured toward her crotch. Although everyone laughed, it was unfortunately true.

Since I couldn't help all my families, I decided to concentrate on helping three of them. One was a family in a working-class home where the children were all the products of a single long-standing marriage. The husband-father was absent because he had been convicted of committing incest with his fourteen-year-old daughter and was serving two to five years in the Ohio State Penitentiary. The girl was traumatized and had gone into a shell. I tried to get psychiatric help for her. Another was an intact Jewish family with one child. They had survived Dachau, but just barely. They were virtually nonfunctional, and their ten-year-old son was frighteningly, pathologically timid and seemed to have spent his entire life in a closet. For them I sought comprehensive family service with intensive psychiatric care for the boy. The third was an intelligent young Negro woman who had had two years of college and was an epileptic. She had two children—twin boys—and no husband—the result, she claimed of a single passionate liaison with a suave gentleman about town. She wanted to work, and I tried to get her "homemaker service," and a job.

I really worked at these three cases, but I found that in Cleveland, at least in 1957, the wheels of the bureaucracy did not grind. When I left after ten months of effort, the Jewish couple was far down on the waiting list for services and no psychiatrist could be found for their son. The epileptic woman could not get homemaker service if she didn't have a job in hand, and even those employers who were willing to consider somebody with her background were unwilling to take on a mother with two young kids at home. My only "success" was with the incest victim. When I left she was seeing a psychiatrist—once every six weeks.

But I brooded continually about the inability of government to do anything really constructive about the poor people in the Hough ghetto—it became a famous place of urban rioting in the sixties— who were my clients. I was appalled at the failure of will, of ingenuity and of generosity of the richest and most powerful nation on earth in dealing with poor people, especially poor Negroes. They couldn't get jobs, and they were left to the mercy of an inadequate welfare system, while the rest of the society hummed right along, oblivious to their plight.

In the winter of 1957–58, Eve and I packed up and went back to New York—she to a social-service agency and I to the same law firm. We settled in Brooklyn again, on a nice, tree-lined street of pretty brick row houses. I had left Cleveland behind, but I could never rid my spirit of those poor people I had tried to serve.

8 Most of my energies for the next three years were directed to my work at Delson, Levin and Gordon and to building a marriage with Eve. At Delson, I began assisting the partner who was in charge of the firm's major litigation, a lovely man named Norman Moloshok, a good boss. More than anyone else he taught me how to write. He'd go through my drafts of briefs and memoranda and chop them down to concise pockets of fact and argument, regularly attacking the ambiguities contained in passages that I had liked best. But he was a kind and thoughtful teacher.

Eve went to work at the Windham Children's Service, a private Protestant child care agency that was located on lower Fifth Avenue in Greenwich Village. One of her coworkers was a neighbor, Virginia Brown, and she and her husband David became close friends. Bob and Dorothy Jackson also lived nearby and the three couples formed a tight circle. Eve and I had known Bob for what passed for forever in those years. He had been an upper classman when I got to Michigan and then he went to law school, was drafted and came back and finished just about the time I did. Dorothy was a physician, a specialist in hematology, who had gone to Meharry Medical College in Nashville (the same school where Pop went) and had done a year of postgraduate work at Michigan.

All three couples enjoyed one another's company, and all three had children in 1959. Bob and Dorothy's son, Mark, was born in April, David and Virginia's daughter, Allyson, was born in May, and Amy was born in September. When I first saw Amy, tiny and bundled in a blanket behind the glass wall of the nursery at Brooklyn's Beth El Hospital, my knees went soft. She was so little, so helpless, my daughter. I pledged to her then that I would stand between her and the world, protect and nourish her as long as I had breath.

Light-skinned Negroes often have babies who are very light at first, then over time, color comes to them. Amy was like that. She was a little white baby, indistinguishable from all the babies there whose parents were white. I thought of the extra pain she would have in life as compared to that of the "white" babies in that nursery, and I hated the unfairness of it. For a moment, my joy at being a father—of sharing with Eve the great task of raising this child and seeing her develop—was suffused with an unbearable sadness that bordered on rage. I knew then that I really could not protect her from that pain, only help her in some ways to learn how to handle it.

While I was standing there, two grandmotherly white women came to the window. They looked at me and they looked at Amy and they began buzzing to each other in low tones.

"And you should see the mother," I heard one of them say.

Later, when I was back in Eve's room and we were laughing at the story, I looked up and saw the old women at the door staring at Eve's beautiful brown face.

"Those are the ones," I told Eve in a voice loud enough for them to hear. They became flustered and began babbling to each other at the same time, trying to pretend they hadn't been doing exactly what they had come to the door to do. Then they disappeared, and I remembered what my mother had said years earlier about my sister. You could become hardened for yourself, but when the race thing came around and hit your children, you hurt, badly.

By 1960, I was no longer enjoying the practice of law. At first the work had been fun. I found it challenging to draft complaints and interrogatories, motion papers and briefs and ultimately to go to court and argue motions. Sometimes, though, my race presented problems. There were times, for example, when I would go to the offices of another lawyer for a meeting and the receptionist would take me for a messenger and simply tell me to leave my package on the desk. Minor functionaries—doormen, elevator operators and receptionists—were the worst. No matter how I was dressed—Ivy League suits and ties at almost all times in those days—at white buildings or offices I would always be taken for a messenger or made to feel that I was out of place, didn't belong.

But that wasn't really what I disliked about practicing law, or even my discovery that you had to pay court clerks occasionally to get

them to do what they were supposed to do or that a lot of the judges
in the Supreme Court, New York County, were supposed to be fixable.
All of that stank and I didn't like it, but the real problem was deeper.
Some of the senior partners in the firm had begun telling me what a
great future I had there. But I looked at them and realized that I
didn't want to be them when I was sixty or live the life that would get
me there.

I didn't enjoy spending any part of my free time with clients, for
one thing. Hustling business day and night just wasn't my thing. I
didn't like to spend time with people I didn't much care for; I had
ruled out any effort at elective politics for that reason. But even that
wasn't the main problem. The civil-rights movement was beginning
to change the face of the South, but I looked at Harlem and Bedford-
Stuyvesant and realized that the movement wasn't going to make any
great difference in those places. I wasn't sure what I was doing in a
white mid-Manhattan law office, and Eve and I considered, briefly,
my leaving the firm and setting up a neighborhood practice in
Bedford-Stuyvesant. We thought that maybe I could find real ways to
be helpful in that community if I did that.

But when I broached it to the partners in the firm, hoping that we
could form some cooperative arrangement, they urged me not to do
it, arguing that my continued development at their firm would lead
me on paths that would ultimately be more helpful to my people. I
doubted that, but after hearing some other discouraging words from
lawyers out in that community, I dropped the idea. But I still wasn't
satisfied. I was spending time and being paid to think hard about
problems that I didn't care about. My brains and my developing skills
were for hire in a marketplace that I was coming to disdain. I realized
that I was ready to take up another line of work.

9 Fortunately for me, Norman and I had been on the same side of a lawsuit with a major Wall Street firm, Clearey, Gottlieb, Steen and Hamilton. Fowler Hamilton was the Hamilton, and he became John Kennedy's appointee as Administrator of the Agency for International Development. When Norman and I sent the obligatory congratulatory notes, Hamilton wrote back and asked if I would consider coming down to Washington "to help him out." That prospect electrified me!

Mr. Hamilton asked me to come down to Washington to see him. His offices on the fifth floor of the old part of the State Department Building were once the offices of the Secretary of State. It was a massive, impressive place, wood paneling with red leather chairs and couches in the Art Deco style. There were three secretaries in the huge front office working the first multibutton console phones I had ever seen, all soft green.

Hamilton's personal office was a huge, high rectangle with a large conference table at one end. His desk was in the center of the room in front of a large window looking out over the American flag, white government buildings and a clear, blue March sky. Hamilton led me to a comfortable but opulent seating arrangement across the room from the conference table. It was the first federal office I had ever seen, and it exuded power.

So did Fowler Hamilton. He was a thick athletic man in his late fifties with thinning gray hair and a massive boyish face. He wore a well-cut blue Bond Street suit and brown, lace-up shoes that I expected also came from London.

"My boy, how good to see you," he boomed when he greeted me. "Nice of you to come down."

He led me to one end of the soft leather couch, and he sat at the other end, by the telephone. We talked. He told me how the foreign-aid program had been revamped by the Kennedy Administration, that the United States was going to pursue a more modern style of economic development, how the nation was embarking on a new and exciting experiment with the developing world and that he wanted my help in that experiment. He then talked about the job—Special Assistant to the Administrator—and how he had used these slots close to the center of power in the agency to attract exceptional young lawyers. Hamilton put a mighty store by lawyers, I would learn. He called John Kennedy "the client."

A special assistant would sit in on his meetings, meet powerful personalities at home and abroad, follow up on things for him, get the general feel of the agency and the government and then move out into other significant jobs in the agency, leaving the special-assistant slot open for yet another bright young lawyer. In the middle of all this, he excused himself to take a call from "Bill Martin." During the course of the conversation, I gathered that he was talking to William Mc-Chesney Martin, the remote and august Chairman of the Federal Reserve Board, whom I only knew through the newspapers. Later he talked to somebody he called "Sarge"—Sargent Shriver, the President's brother-in-law, head of the Peace Corps and one of the glitterati of that tight Kennedy agglomeration that was later to be called Camelot.

It was all quite a load for a thirty-year-old Negro lawyer who lived with his wife and his daughter in a garden apartment in Queens. But I still had one real worry. Washington had been a Southern city, and Eve and I were frankly afraid of the South. We had driven to Washington from time to time to visit Doris and Larry Sperling. Larry had been a classmate in law school and had taken a job in the Justice Department after that. We hated the drive. The places of accommodation on Route 40, running from the New Jersey line into Baltimore, were notorious for their racism. They had claimed the President's attention when foreign diplomats from Africa were treated like ordinary niggers by the roadside entrepreneurs. Eve and I would always gas up and eat at the last stop on the New Jersey Turnpike and pray that we had no breakdown after that.

In those days, Negro publications would often, for space in headline purposes, use "Race" in place of "Negro," as in "Race Man Appointed." The first time we drove to Washington, we talked freely about our apprehensions and what might happen to us if we were forced to stop someplace. Then, late in the night, on the Baltimore-Washington Expressway, Eve saw a sign that read, "Race traffic this way."

"My God," she exclaimed, "even the roads down here are segregated."

She laughed after I explained that the sign only directed cars to the Laurel and Bowie racetracks, but at the time her exclamation had been serious—a measure of our apprehension. So I told Hamilton that I wasn't sure I wanted to bring my family to a Southern town. The papers had reported that Ralph Bunche had turned down a job in the Administration for exactly that reason. He suggested that I speak with a Negro member of the staff, Bob Kitchen.

Bob Kitchen was a revelation. I had rarely seen such a man. He was very black, about six feet tall and almost forty years old. He had a round head, dark-tinged eyeballs and was dressed with a practiced elegance. Brown shaggy suit, off-yellow shirt, brown-and-green-patterned silk tie with matching handkerchief flopping casually from breast pocket and highly polished brown shoes all reeked of money. Kitchen moved into the room with a cool assurance I had rarely seen in any Negro, particularly in the presence of white power.

Hamilton and Kitchen greeted each other warmly and when he was seated, Kitchen began an impromptu lecture on the state of the aid agency. He told a few horror stories of programs fouled up and people failing—one so shocking about a program failure in India that Hamilton picked up the phone then and there and demanded a report from his Assistant Administrator in charge of the Near East and South Asia. Hamilton seemed to enjoy Kitchen, and we stayed on for more than an hour. All told, I was in Hamilton's office for two and a half hours that morning. As we left, Hamilton told me that he'd have to check with a couple of colleagues, "of course," but that he thought it would work out fine if I would agree to take the job. I told him I would let him know.

When we were at the elevator, Kitchen said to me, "He spent two and a half hours with you? That's a stupid waste of his time. Shouldn't have taken more than half an hour—forty-five minutes at the outside. His staff shouldn't let him do that—and they don't keep him well-enough informed. He should've known about that India thing. If he's not in trouble yet, he's going to be in big trouble soon, operating like that in this town."

In Hamilton's office I had had a hard time following Kitchen's train of thought, because he spoke a combination of bureaucratic jargon and multisyllabic words and complex sentence structures that had only the faintest resemblance to the English I understood and spoke. Hamilton had obviously been impressed, so I thought the failure to understand was mine. And he wore clothes that seemed more fitting for a highly successful show-business entrepreneur than for a federal bureaucrat. Now, here he was telling me that the highest federal official I had ever known—his job carried the rank of Under Secretary of State—wasn't doing his job right.

Later, at lunch at an Asian food place on G Street, a few blocks down from the State Department, Kitchen talked nonstop. I could still only understand about half of what he said, but I did gather this much: that he had been born in South Georgia, had grown up under segregation, had attended Morehouse College, had taught at one time at another black college, had come into the aid program in the fifties, and had served abroad in Liberia before being appointed Director of the AID mission in the Sudan at thirty-seven, the youngest man ever appointed to head a foreign mission for the aid program.

And though I couldn't easily understand his conversation, I began to understand something else. Kitchen's style, especially his verbal gymnastics, seemed consciously or unconsciously designed to send a message to the white world: "This is not a nigger, but rather, a serious educated man." I had seen other educated Negroes use pretentiously big words and complicated sentence structures, but I had never seen it done by anybody as smart as Kitchen, who had such verbal facility or such a command of impenetrable bureaucratic jargon.

I was troubled by what I perceived—a Negro bent out of shape by the power and the callousness of the white world. I figured that the way to handle oneself was the way I did it—straight on, no frills. What I didn't understand was that my particular adaptation to white power was the most grotesque of all. I dressed in Ivy League suits, shirts and ties. Simple, straight white talk had become my native tongue. I had begun to know how white people operated in the world and had begun to emulate them. I had no aspirations that would have seemed foreign to my white contemporaries. I had abdicated my birthright and had become an ersatz white man.

But, of course, what white people saw was a well-educated, well-bred, sensible Negro who, but for the unfortunate color of his skin, was very much like them. I was just the kind of person they wanted, because I was "ready"—ready to face white people without embarrassing "the race." I was just the kind of safe person white people began looking for when they tried to integrate their environment, even just a little bit.

So I felt a little sorry for Bob Kitchen as we drove after lunch in his stately white Jaguar sedan toward Blagden Avenue and the "Gold Coast," where the affluent Washington Negroes lived. I felt sorry for him because I understood too little about myself and about the nature of his life and its pressures.

He told me that life could be very good for Negroes in Washington and that I should take the job. He also repeated that he believed Hamilton was or would be in trouble. Again I thought he was crazy. Hadn't Senator Stuart Symington of Missouri, then a power in the Democratic party, supported Hamilton? Wasn't Hamilton a successful, savvy Wall Street lawyer? Hadn't President John F. Kennedy just appointed him to this high job with fanfare, hope and promises just a few months before? So what could Kitchen be talking about? What could he know?

That was late March 1962.

Eve and I talked about the expected offer after I got home and quickly decided to accept it. Though I had never been a strong Kennedy supporter, I knew he had made some good promises to Negroes during the campaign; he had hinted that he could wipe out housing segregation with a stroke of the pen, and he had called the King family when Dr. King was in jail during the campaign. JFK looked good in the Presidency, and the people around him seemed so smart. After eight-years of exile, the right people had their hands on the reins of government once more. I didn't support Attorney General Robert F. Kennedy, because he had made clear his disdain for liberals, and some said he was responsible for Chester Bowles's abbreviated tenure as Under Secretary of State. I believed in liberals; they were the wave of the future, the country's best hope, I thought. But the rest of J.F.K.'s entourage were just fine. Even Dean Rusk seemed to take on luster in the glow shed by J.F.K., and McGeorge Bundy positively glittered.

I was eager to follow these banners. I thought there were few problems in the world that couldn't be solved with appropriate amounts of American idealism, industry and intelligence. AID had been revamped, and we were ready to spread our bounty with sensitivity and brilliance throughout the emerging world. We would clash peacefully with the Soviets on those battle places of ideas, and we, of course, would win. I believed in America, the Democratic party and the efficacy of government. I still believed that I could make a contribution to racial progress by demonstrating how outstanding a Negro could be in a non-race-related job. I was ready for Washington.

When I set out, I didn't know much about government, bureaucracy, the blaze of clashing egos, power games, elemental stupidity or the limited visions and spirits of most human beings. I didn't know much about American racism either. Or about early death, alcoholism, depression, divorce, suicide or treachery.

But one thing I had discovered was sex, and not the gentle, polite sex that young people of that class and age grew to expect in marriage. Eve and I had come from puritanically constricted backgrounds. Nobody had told us much about sex, except not to do it until we got married. And, of course, we knew the difference between good girls and bad girls. Bad girls craved it, and good girls indulged in it discreetly, and in a careful set of circumstances. Good girls became good wives and, if their husbands had similar backgrounds, they didn't learn much in the marital bed, except perhaps, not to display too much pleasure for fear their husbands would decide that they were closet sluts.

But sex was in the air in those days, even before women's liberation and the sexual revolution. John F. Kennedy rumors abounded. One was that he had a favorite actress and had caused a secret tunnel to be built from the theater where she was appearing to the Carlyle Hotel where he stayed when he was in town. Even if the Kennedy stories were implausible, they made sexuality more intriguing, even for the middle class.

One night on the subway home from work, I ran into a young woman who worked nearby and who had been excessively friendly—so friendly, in fact, that I had dared fantasize that her interest might be sexual. But I wasn't prepared to pursue it, both because of my marriage and because I wasn't exactly sure *how* to in any event. But this F train to Queens was crowded, and the ride between Lexington Avenue to Long Island City under the East River is a long one. Her hip was jammed against my crotch—because of the crush of people, I thought at first. But as we talked she began to sway rhythmically and her eyes began to gleam. By Queens Plaza, the second stop into Queens, there wasn't much doubt about her intentions or mine.

"Let's get off and go back to the city," I said. My voice was hoarse.

"Okay," she replied. She was hoarse too.

We headed for a hotel I had heard about in Greenwich Village, where they asked no questions. It was a dump, but, indeed, the guy asked no questions. Upstairs, she had no inhibitions. It was let's try this, now this, now do it the other way. And her orgasms were long loud groaning things. For me, it was one explosion after another. It was dirty, it was nasty—it was wonderful.

"This woman takes sex like a man," I thought. "It's unbelievable." It was a beginning.

Eve ultimately found out about the relationship and she left me. We were separated for three months, that first time. That was a beginning too.

Just before our separation—and our scheduled departure for Washington—my old boss Robert Delson and his wife, Marjorie, gave a party for Eve and me. There were people from the firm, there were clients, there were Delson relatives—and there were very few Negroes.

"I didn't see many Negroes at this party," my Uncle Roy remarked. "That's where you come from and that's where you go back to. You can never forget your base," he concluded. "It's one of the laws of Washington."

Working with Hamilton in Washington was a strange experience. I did, indeed, attend a lot of his meetings and do research projects on whatever happened to strike his fancy. Early on, I got some encouragement. His executive secretary, Donald B. Easum, later an Assistant Secretary of State for Africa and United States Ambassador to Nigeria, told me that Hamilton had said, after I had been around for about a week, "I like the way Roger writes. It's very good." I glowed and said a little prayer of thanks to my old boss, Norman Moloshok. Then one glorious day—it was May, lovely month in Washington—Hamilton's secretary called me to ride in "the car" up to "the Hill" with "the boss," because he had an appointment with a Senator, but had an urgent need to talk to me first.

I met Mr. Hamilton at his current-model Cadillac limousine, and I waited politely, I thought, for him to get in the back seat of the car first. He deferred and motioned me in, explaining, "My boy, the one with the ranks sits on the right side. That's where the cameras are when you get out."

It was my first big lesson in Washington protocol.

On the way up to the Hill, Hamilton told me about a quick and dirty research job he wanted me to do for him in preparation for some testimony he had to give before a Congressional committee the next day. When he got out at the Capital, he sent me back down to the office in the car to begin the work. I stayed slumped in the left-hand corner of the back seat. Perkins, Mr. Hamilton's Negro driver, maneuvered the enormous Cadillac down Constitution Avenue toward "The Department," as we called State. As we waited for a light to change at the corner of 15th Street, I glanced up at a huge school bus—one of the thousands that descend each year on Washington in the late spring bringing school kids from all over America to see their government at work. The banner hung along the side of the bus identified its occupants as students from Pine Bluff, Arkansas. Only a few kids were on my side of the bus, the others were presumably looking out of the other windows across the Washington Monument grounds at the famous obelisk. Only a couple of the kids noticed me hunkered down in the back seat brooding about my work. Then the light changed and Perkins inched us forward through the late-afternoon traffic.

At the next stop, I glanced out, and there was the bus again. But this time, all the available window space was filled with young white faces, some just staring in amazement and some obviously yammering excitedly. The light changed again and we pulled away as I began to howl with laughter. These kids had probably been told at home how niggers were taking over everything in Washington, and now they had seen the proof with their own eyes—a baby-faced Negro who got ferried around town in his own massive black car. They'd have a tale to tell when they got home. I loved it.

As the summer wore on, I began to sense that Bob Kitchen hadn't been entirely wrong in his judgment that Fowler Hamilton might be in trouble. Washington is a town of boss watchers and power smellers. The people there can tell when power begins to ebb. They can smell blood in the water long before the shark has begun his bite. The murmurings began in midsummer, when I had been in Washington for only three months—and it began among Hamilton's senior staff. He was not decisive, it was said. He didn't move his paper, that avalanche of "action" memos, information papers, personnel actions, cable traffic and fiscal documents that descend on each senior foreign-affairs official each day. He was too much a lawyer, people said, and didn't understand economics well enough to master the foreign-aid program. And he wasn't "tough enough."

That last was the key. Whatever merit there might have been to the other charges—and to a greater or lesser degree, there was some—"toughness" was the key. It was partly a matter of substance, but mainly a matter of style. The fact was that as a result of the Kennedy streamlining of the agency, a vicious bureaucratic brawl was occurring under Hamilton, with old-timers trying to hang on to old forms and powers while the new people struggled—with all the arrogance that new people have toward those who have made a career of doing the government's business—to gain control of a bureaucratic monster that they surely did not fully comprehend. The fact is that Hamilton was a very nice guy who didn't like to kick ass. And Washington bureaucracies bear very little resemblance to Wall Street law firms. Hamilton was feeling his way.

You had to be "tough" in Kennedy's Washington, or at least appear to be so. It was helpful if you had some experience—"Does he have enough gray in his hair?" was one of the personnel questions I heard people ask over and over again. But one shouldn't have too much gray. In his middle fifties and looking somewhat portly, Hamilton was considered too old. It helped to be lean and laconic and appear to be self-denying. Hamilton was none of those. He was loquacious and loved the good life. Once on a trip to New York, he exclaimed to John Funari, his other special assistant, "Ah, there's wine in the air tonight, my boy." New Frontiersmen weren't supposed to pause in the pursuit of a better world to notice wine in the air.

But he did make some decisions. One was when he asked me to implement one particular National Security Action Memorandum that Robert Kennedy had personally told him to expedite with the greatest dispatch. "Nisms" were Presidential orders initialed in the National Security Council. They carried enormous weight. This one carried particular weight, because it was Bobby's baby and everybody knew it. Bobby was on the National Security Council. Bobby was everywhere in those days—he was the President's right-hand thug, as I saw it.

This Nism directed AID to accept responsibility for training police forces in developing countries—a function previously handled by the

CIA—and to set up a special office to direct the effort worldwide. The idea was a distortion of the new streamlined AID concept in which the four regional directors were to be responsible for all programs and policy in their respective areas. The regional people began pecking at this idea like geese on a just-sown cornfield and into this bloody breach Hamilton threw me. I was new, and I did not yet really understand the bureaucracy; but, to top everything off, I was a Negro.

I was not used to telling white men ten to fifteen years my senior, with distinction and experience, what to do. The only things I had on my side were the President, Bobby and Fowler Hamilton, and in that bureaucratic snake pit, that wasn't much. My bureaucratic adversaries argued, they complained, they procrastinated, they failed to return phone calls, they produced management studies "proving" that it was impossible to carry out the President's order. I wheedled, cajoled, explained, invoked the names of the great, compromised and occasionally—but only occasionally—pressed them. Meanwhile, the weeks passed, and Bobby whined, bitched and got pissed. Sometimes, to move pebbles out of the way, I had to invoke Bobby's name with Hamilton.

Finally Bobby blasted us with a hand rocket of a memorandum and suddenly, less than six months into my government career, I realized that I had to protect my ass—and in that moment, I crossed over from civilian life. It was still clear to me that these white men didn't take me seriously. It was also clear to me that I carried in my soul a powerful amount of deference for powerful white people like those I was dealing with in my agency—I was afraid of them. But I was more afraid of Bobby. So I suddenly began to be "tough enough."

"We're going to do this," I told my in-house adversaries, "sooner or later. The Attorney General wants it sooner. He wants it this afternoon. And I'm going to start giving him daily progress reports that will tell him just who's doing what and what the remaining problems are."

Within just a couple of days, most of the problems were cleared up, and we were on the road. But AID's reputation—and particularly Hamilton's—had suffered by the delay in the place where it counted most, with the tough man in the corner office on the fifth floor of Justice.

But I came out a winner. People around AID began to respect me some. I was no longer entirely a man who left no footprints. I had exercised power from an essentially powerless position. When I

walked into a room now, the automatic chain-reaction double dis-
count that flowed from the color of my face and from my youth no
longer occurred automatically. They had determined that this was a
bee that could sting—my first step in the process of accumulating
power in a bureaucracy.

But what a victory. I later was to learn that people trained by the
office that I had fought to set up did far more than to help keep the
peace that our official rationale said was a prerequisite for orderly
economic development. Some of the graduates of that program
spread across the world from Vietnam to Iran to Chile to become
some of this century's most accomplished torturers in service of the
status quo. In my innocence, I never dreamed that a New Frontier
project could have such consequences.

During the summer I made several weekend trips to Cleveland to
see Eve and Amy. I felt lousy about the separation—and guilty. Also,
I didn't like living alone, and though the myth that Washington had
far more black women than black men turned out to be true, the
game wasn't much fun. I missed Eve. I loved her. She was my wife.
But I never really took the separation too seriously. Only movie stars
and dissolute millionaires got divorced, not good solid middle-class
people like us. One day when I was in Cleveland playing with Amy in
the sandbox by the side of Eve's parents' house, Eve looked out of
the window and saw us and her heart was wrenched. She decided to
come back. And she did in September—on Amy's third birthday.

Eve and I had rented a two-bedroom apartment on the second floor
of a big old yellow house on the corner of 15th and Emerson N.W. It
wasn't exactly on the "Gold Coast," but it was close. We were within
walking distance of Kitchen's house on Blagden Avenue. We put
Amy in a wonderfully efficient and imaginative nursery school called
Tots, which was run by a black couple named Davenport. On her first
school day, Eve and I watched her skip merrily down the walk and
give a cheery wave before she disappeared on the van. Eve had tears
in her eyes.

"Our little girl," was all she managed to say.

I felt pretty teary myself.

Bob Kitchen took us in hand, just as he had taken me in hand
earlier. He was generous with his time, his friends and his contacts.
He took me to Billy Simpson's restaurant up on Georgia Avenue,
where the Negro New Frontiersmen gathered to drink and to talk. He
introduced me to Carl Rowan, then at the State Department, to

George L.P. Weaver—once introduced by Hubert Humphrey as George Long-Playing Weaver—and Ed Sylvester of Labor, to Kermit Bailer of the Housing Agency, Sam Westerfield of Treasury and Dick Fox of State. They were able men. I had not spent much of my life respecting Negro men, except the special few who had been close.

But we had a lot of sayings in the Negro community. One of them was:

> Niggers and flies I do despise
> The more I see niggers
> The more I like flies.

We laughed when we said those things, but there was no doubt that we had absorbed enough of our national culture to believe a lot of that. And I had absorbed more than my share. I had seen Negro men swagger around with diamond pinky rings and gaudy clothes, with nothing to back up their act but a few hundred bucks—all in their pocket at that moment. I had seen plenty fall by the wayside, drunken and screwing. I had never had the insight to understand the pain this society had inflicted on those men—how it bent them out of shape; how some of them had to swagger in order not to fall, and how some of them had to break. They were only human.

But these men in the Kennedy Administration were something else. Very like the old New York Yankees—and perhaps the new—they were good and they knew it. They weren't on the topmost rungs of power, but the footing in Kennedy's Washington was a little more equal. By and large, they were treated like men, and they were riding the wave of the future. Negroes were on the march in the South and Kennedy had responded, at least to the degree that he had brought Negroes into the government in great numbers and had given them unprecedented positions of authority. These men moved with a confidence and executed their offices with a competence that I had rarely encountered. They were what people had begun to call, at that dawn of our big hope, the "New Negro."

Hamilton was sliding by the fall of '62, and he knew it, and John Funari and I knew it. We were both worried, because he was our power center. I was more worried than John, because he had a White House connection, Ralph Dungan, who was the President's man on personnel in foreign affairs and also handled substantive AID stuff as well. I had nothing. Hamilton had brought me to Washington and when he left I figured I'd slide down into the bowels of AID, never to be seen or heard again even in the peripheral circles of influence in Washington.

If you didn't have power yourself, access to power was everything; and even if you did have power, people had to believe you had access to even greater power. Thus, even powerful guys like Dungan might let it slip to a nobody like me that he had briefed the President the night before as he was in his private bathroom, getting ready for a state dinner. Dungan was smart enough to know that the next day I would drop it at lunch or dinner that Ralph had told me at the White House about what he had said to the President while the President was sitting on the can. Immediacy all around. Everybody won—even the President, who was humanized in the act of taking a shit.

Watching the people in AID vie for access to Hamilton's time and attention, even in his waning days, I invented the Golden Ear Award —for that staff member who had accumulated the most minutes in the boss's presence over the year.

My access was about to go with Hamilton—no more breezing into the West Wing of the White House every week or two to shoot the breeze with Ralph. And Kennedy wasn't moving on civil rights—not worth a damn. He had proposed no new laws, he had made no ringing speeches, and he had been so cautious about fulfilling his promise about an executive order on housing that blacks had taken to sending him pens that he could use to sign with. I decided to take my shot before my access disappeared. So I called Ralph, asked for an appointment to discuss non-AID business and he said, "Sure, come on."

I was furious about the Administration's civil-rights posture. I thought it was slow, lethargic and unresponsive. Bob Kennedy was in charge of the strategy, and there wasn't a Negro within miles of his office when they sat down to decide what to do with the revolution that Martin Luther King, Jr., and the students and the NAACP and CORE were orchestrating in the South. They were demonstrating all right: They were demonstrating the unfairness and viciousness of the Southern racist system. And white people—John Nolan and Joe Dolan and Byron White and Nicholas de B. Katzenbach and Burke Marshall and John Douglas and John Doar and Ramsey Clark were the people Robert Kennedy and the President turned to when they decided on what to do about black protest—how to parcel out black rights. They were all white and the arrogance and the slowness of those people enraged me.

I began to tell Ralph exactly what I thought. He listened until I was through, and then asked me a question:

"Roger, do you really think civil rights is one of the country's three most important problems?"

It was the fall of 1962. I almost fell off my chair. This was my friend, a liberal white man, who worked in the White House, who saw the President every day—how could he ask me such a question? My explosion was instant and spontaneous. I told him it was the dumbest question I had heard in my life.

Ralph said, "Okay, Roger, look. This isn't my area, as you know. But if you write a memorandum laying out what it is you think we ought to do, I'll see that it gets to the President, okay?"

For the second time in the meeting, I almost fell off my chair.

So I went back to my office to take what I deemed my last best shot. Mr. Hamilton was dead in the water by then. Most of the time when he worked, he revised his letter of resignation. And then he went to Europe on business and came back in style—on the Queen Mary, first class. New Frontiersmen—even before the Bureau of the Budget order to travel tourist on American carriers—rode jet steerage. Hamilton, by then, an old bull fatally wounded by the lean warriors of the New Frontier, was departing with an elegant "Up yours!"

They were appalled. I loved him for it. And I had a lot of time to work on my memo—through Dungan, for the President. I talked to a lot of friends who knew more than I did—especially Bill Taylor over at the United States Commission on Civil Rights—and soaked up ideas. And then I wrote, and rewrote and rewrote. And finally sent over a "piece of paper"—the way we talked in government in those days.

The memorandum started with the premise that life in the United States was unequal and unfair and that the only power in society strong enough to force change was the federal government. It went on to argue that the moral leadership of the Kennedy Administration on this issue had been flabby despite John Kennedy's splendid campaign rhetoric on the subject. It then urged the administration to draft and send to Congress a civil rights bill that would desegregate publicly owned facilities and places of public accommodation and would also make provision for equal employment enforcement by the federal government. Finally, it laid stress on the urgent need for blacks to obtain the best educational opportunities available and said that school desegregation efforts should be pressed firmly wherever there was resistance.

The paper ended by asserting that for most practical purposes, blacks lived in a separate country and that the unkindest cut of all was to have an apparent ally in the White House whose vision or will was too limited to attempt to initiate these noble and necessary tasks.

The letter didn't change anything at first. No drums or alarms went off, and the President didn't bother to answer. After a week or so, I called Ralph Dungan and asked him what was happening. Well, he had passed it on to the President, he said, and to other appropriate people. He said he thought it was certain that I would be hearing from somebody before too long. And, sure enough, before too long, I heard from the President's special counsel, Lee White.

Lee White had degrees in both engineering and law. He also had a small cluttered office that had some pictures on the wall. In some context it would have been the office of an overworked and under-paid man—somebody to be polite to, maybe, but not someone to be taken seriously. But Lee White's office was on the second floor of the West Wing of the White House. He was a man who actually spoke to John F. Kennedy with some regularity. He was also the man in the White House whose job it was to worry about civil rights with more regularity than any others.

In Kennedy's Washington—as in any President's Washington—a good relationship with somebody in the White House was more valu-able than a gold coin, even at today's rates. Ralph Dungan, who handled a lot of the Administration's foreign-affairs personnel deci-sions, had once remarked, "The best people you know are the best people you know." If somebody like Lee White thought you were good, he just might drop your name into a conversation with the President or with Bobby when they were looking for somebody to do something important and prestigious. And, besides, it was always useful to be able to drop in a dinner-table conversation, "Well, when I was over at the White House seeing Lee White the other day . . ."

Lee is a nice man and a polite man without the arrogance that so many people who work in the White House have. He had liked the memo, he said, and he thanked me for it. But, as we talked, it turned out that he hadn't really liked it all that much.

"Do you really think that John F. Kennedy is soft on civil rights?" he demanded, his voice rising. There it was, on the table. I was young and had been in Washington less than a year. I was dazzled by the glamour of the Kennedys, if not by their politics. Like every young person in Washington, I wanted to be in close. I wanted to be invited to parties at Bobby and Ethel's house. I would gladly have given up the last five years of my life to be thrown into the swimming pool at Hickory Hill. If Lee White liked me enough, maybe that could happen.

On the other hand, I had come to that office to say some things, whether Lee White, the President or the Attorney General liked them or not.

"Yeah," I answered. "Negroes are risking their lives in the South to make this country live up to the Constitution," I replied, "and this guy is just messing around." My voice went up a couple of notches too. White came back at me with the housing order the President had just signed. We weren't exactly shouting, but the conversation was heated. I countered that the housing order was too little and too late. I argued that we needed comprehensive civil-rights legislation and asserted that the affirmative-active program within the federal government didn't impress me very much.

White cooled down at that point and explained that some thought was being given to legislation, and he asked how I could fault the affirmative-action effort since this President had issued a stronger executive order on the subject than had ever been issued before. I countered that while Andrew Hatcher, the black on the staff, was prominent—sitting up there on the stage at the State Department Auditorium during the press conferences—nobody in town had much respect for him.

"If you think you can get by with that kind of tokenism on the White House staff, what do you think other administrators are doing?" I asked.

I asserted that it was an insult to every black American that the Administration's civil-rights efforts were being directed by a Justice Department without one Negro on the senior staff.

White shrugged his shoulders and threw up his hands. "What can we do? Our staffing here at the White House is tight. We don't have hundreds of jobs lying around."

"Mac Bundy's got a big staff for the National Security Council," I replied. "I don't see any reason why you couldn't expand that by several people, or at least one."

"Give me some names," he said. So I did, right then and there. Most of them, like Sam Westerfield, who was then at Treasury, were already in the government. Others, like Clifford L. Alexander, Jr., a graduate of the Yale Law School, who had taken his undergraduate degree at Harvard, were not. White thanked me then and assured me that my memorandum had been "helpful," and ushered me out of his office.

There was no lightning in that bottle, I thought, and even if there might have been, I pissed all over it while I was in there. That view was confirmed months later when somebody told me that my name had been broached for a major job at Justice and Bobby Kennedy had dismissed it emphatically with the comment that I was "too brash." Years later, though, I got a reward of sorts when, after I had been nominated to be Director of the Community Relations Service, Lee White congratulated me and quipped, "Now people won't have to struggle with your memos anymore."

That had been a young man's memo, written out of mixed motives. There is little question, though I doubt that I would have admitted it then, that I hoped its prose and its incisiveness would cause me to be drawn closer to the glorious heart of Camelot. And there is little question that I was at least mildly disappointed when it didn't. But, there was another thing at work there. The civil-rights movement had stirred me. It was no longer enough to be an "internationalist" and to show by my example what Negroes could do if given a chance.

Partly, it was guilt. There were people in the South, both Negro and white, who had laid down their lives for this cause and thousands more who were risking theirs every day. And here I was living a comfortable life in Washington with my beautiful wife and my beautiful daughter, taking no risks at all, totally uninvolved.

And, there was access. The poor blacks in the South who followed Martin Luther King, Jr., and John Lewis of the Student Non-Violent Coordinating Committee were using their bodies in an effort to communicate with Washington. And here was I, snuggled up to the White House with all the communications skills that nineteen years of formal school and five more at the practice of law had given me. I felt that if I didn't raise my voice to speak for them, to articulate their aspirations, I was no better than a bucket of shit. It was the dawn of awareness. If Camelot lightning were to strike me, it had to be on my terms, not on the terms of the white bosses, no matter how much I wanted whatever it was in their power to give me. I would raise a voice for poor Negroes when I could.

As far as I could tell at the time, no poor Negroes benefited from that particular effort. Clifford Alexander did. Somebody told me that Bundy, who had been Dean of Harvard when Clifford was an undergraduate there, was considering offering him a job. I had known Clifford since we had been in the same swimming class at the Harlem YMCA in 1941 and I had known his wife, Adele, since she was about three and we had lived in the same Harlem apartment building and her father, our family doctor, had paid me the first dollar I had ever earned for taking care of their dog when the family was on vacation.

I called Clifford, who was then working on a housing program in Harlem, to sketch out the background of the offer that was to come and to help him assess the nature of the opportunity. He was on active reserve duty when I called, but Adele told me that Bundy had already made the offer and that Clifford had rejected it. I couldn't believe my ears. "What's the matter, is he nuts?" I asked. "No," Adele said, "he just doesn't think there's much future in it."

I called Bundy and asked whether the offer could be reopened if I could change Clifford's mind. Bundy said the offer would be open. So I called Clifford and spent about an hour on the phone explaining the functions and importance of the National Security Council staff, describing the proximity to the President and his top staff people and the advantages in all of that for a young black man—he was then about twenty-eight—coming into an administration that desperately needed attractive young black people.

Clifford changed his mind and took the job with Bundy. He subsequently moved over to the White House staff proper, was appointed by Lyndon Johnson to be Chairman of the Equal Employment Opportunity Commission, went into a lucrative Washington law practice during the Republican years, ran unsuccessfully for Mayor of Washington and then was appointed Secretary of the Army by Jimmy Carter.

But I was having career anxieties of my own.

10 Fowler Hamilton, who had brought me to Washington, resigned from AID in December 1962 and went back to New York to practice law. The President announced his intention to appoint David E. Bell, then the Director of the Bureau of the Budget, to take his place. It was standard Washington wisdom that new men brought in their own personal assistants. My colleague John Funari and I liked our jobs and entertained the faint hope that Bell would keep us on. Otherwise, we would have to sink down into the AID bureaucracy. I didn't want to do that. A person could get lost down there and never be heard of again.

Besides, Bell had a wonderful reputation in Washington. He had worked in the Truman White House, had run an institute at Harvard in the Eisenhower years, was said to enjoy the confidence of the President, and was a regular at the "mind stretching" Hickory Hill seminars that Bobby Kennedy had organized for a selected group of New Frontier intimates. He was an "in" New Frontiersman, while Hamilton was not. It couldn't hurt you if David Bell knew and liked you, and White House access might be enhanced, rather than cut off, as it was sure to be if we drifted down into the bowels of the agency.

Bell came over to meet the key people in AID. He was a tall, sandy-haired man in his early forties, with impeccable manners. He looked at John and me, and said he thought he would keep us for a while. Then he called over from Budget and said he thought it would be a good idea if he took an inspection trip of the major AID installations around the world before his confirmation hearings. He wanted to take one of us with him and said that we could sort that out among

105

ourselves and whichever one was going ought to prepare a draft
itinerary for him.

John and I decided that I should go, since he had just come back
from a trip to England with Hamilton. I prepared an itinerary that
included a stop at the headquarters of the Organization for Economic
Cooperation and Development in Paris, Pakistan, India, Thailand,
Vietnam and Korea. America had no significant aid programs in
Africa at that time.

Bell suggested that we turn it around so we would travel west
rather than east as I had proposed, because it was easier on the body
that way to throw in stops at U.S. Pacific military headquarters in
Honolulu and Tokyo, where we could get a briefing on the Far East
from Ambassador Edwin Reischauer, a great scholar before he was
an ambassador. I did this all with a sense of great wonderment, since
I had never been west of Kansas City or south of San Juan.

We left Washington on December 26, 1962. The snow was two
feet deep around the house, and the Christmas tree was still up in the
living room. Eve was pleased for me, I think. She knew how excited I
was; how I had pawed over the thick sheaf of tickets from Pan Am
and my spanking new official passport with its dull-red binding. She
and Amy kissed me goodbye in the snow at the door, and that night I
watched with awe as the 707, its powerful Pratt and Whitney engines
drooping gracefully from the wings, slid in over Diamond Head
toward the Honolulu airport. We were taken to the CINCPAC
(Commander in Chief Pacific) guest house, where I marveled to see
poinsettias growing in December in the garden. We signed the guest
book. The last guest there, the signature above ours, was Robert F.
Kennedy.

Admiral Ulysses S. Grant Sharp, CINCPAC, had a dinner for us
that night and for another visitor, Anthony Akers, the U.S. Ambassador to New Zealand. There was nobody there with fewer than three
stars on his shoulders. Except me. I was the only black person and
the only person under forty. Bell, as an Under Secretary of State,
outranked them all.

Near the end of this dinner I made a mild joke, and everybody
looked up in surprise; then they broke up in great hoots that the joke
hadn't deserved. The three-star admiral sitting on my right slammed
me hard on my back three times in a congratulatory gesture—for
speaking English, I suppose. I felt horrible.

The next morning, we were given a briefing in the CINCPAC war

room. It was like nothing I had ever seen or was to see again. There
was enough brass in that room to replace all the plumbing in Philadelphia. Two-star generals and admirals were relegated to the back
row of the little theater. Admiral Sharp and a couple of other four-
stars sat at the front-row table along with Mr. Bell, Mike Forrestal,
who was the son of the first Secretary of Defense and the Far East
Specialist on the National Security Council staff, and Seymour Janow,
the head of AID's Far East Bureau. There were name tags at the front
table, and there was one for me, right up there with the heavy brass.

A brace of bird colonels briefed us. They briefed us about Korea,
Japan, Vietnam, China—about everybody else's troop strength and
ours, about intentions, about probabilities and even about the
weather we would encounter later that day on our flight to Tokyo.
Slides came out of everywhere and projectors appeared from the
unlikeliest of places and multicolored images were produced to make
impressive points. It was quite a show.

Admiral Sharp predicted that we would have Vietnam wrapped up
by the summer of '64 or by the winter of '64–'65 at the latest.

Then we flew on to Tokyo. I couldn't have been more excited.
Japanese food, Japanese service, Japanese anticipation all the way. It
was dark by the time we got to Tokyo, and as the plane flashed down
the runway I strained to get my first sight of Japan, my first foreign
country: it was of a big red sign that said, "Coca-Cola."

That night we were entertained by the Japanese Vice-Minister of
Foreign Affairs, at a geisha house. The women were very nice to me;
they explained the food I was eating, they helped me eat it, they
purred over pictures of my daughter and they poured me endless
glasses of sake. The sake put me at ease, and the women made me
horny. But they were not to touch.

The next day, we flew on to Seoul, and on the way, the pilot
buzzed Fujiyama, as beautiful a snow-covered sight as I had ever
seen. And in Korea we saw the military. South Korea was our largest
aid recipient at the time, and the Eighth Army was stationed there.
Peril was just to the north.

When you travel with the AID administrator, it is like traveling
with Santa Claus. Nobody is naughty. Everyone is very nice. We had
lunch with President Park at Blue House and were whisked there and
back in a limousine with an American flag flying on the fender and
with a full military escort with sirens slicing through the downtown
traffic for us.

Then we went up to the thirty-eighth parallel, where the Free World ended and tyranny began. It was cold up there on the hill where they briefed us—bitter cold. We could see American troops patrolling on our side of the valley, and with binoculars we could occasionally see the North Koreans on the other slope as they went back and forth in the bunkers across on the lower slope of the opposite hill. They could have picked us off with their artillery if they had chosen to break the peace at that moment, and our guns could have done the same with them.

The American soldiers were crisp, and they moved briskly about their business as their superiors conducted their briefings for Mr. Bell. And Bell was lean, alert, intelligent, asking good questions. I was never prouder to be an American. Here was our commitment to freedom, visible and tangible on this cold Korean hill thousands of miles away from America. These soldiers had lives and people somewhere else, but they were here keeping our promises around the globe. And their purpose and their over-all goals were developed by wise and decent men like David Bell. I thought of myself as an American first, in those days, and a Negro second.

After that we went back to Tokyo and celebrated New Year's Eve before flying on to Taipei on the first day of 1963. Mr. Bell asked me to send a cable to his family for him. "Happy New Year from the Ginza," it read. It sounded awfully sophisticated to me so I sent a cable to my family. "Happy New Year from the Ginza," it read.

Our flight to Taipei stopped at Okinawa. The plane was almost empty on the first leg, but it filled with tourists at Okinawa. Bell, Janow and I had been reading our top-secret CIA briefing books on the first leg and we continued after the stop. The books had all sorts of information in them, none of it very exciting, but the contents could, I suppose, have been embarrassing for their frank portrayals of the personalities who led our allies. And, perhaps, a careful reading by an expert might have revealed something of what the intelligence community calls "sources and methods" used in intelligence collection.

I became aware of a man standing behind me and looked up at him. He looked like an ordinary Asian tourist, but he had his mini-camera aimed straight at the pages of my briefing book. I shut it and told Bell and Janow to shut theirs. The man quickly turned and began shooting pictures of the clouds passing by.

Taipei was humid and full of people. There were more briefings and more dinners. At one dinner, which was given by the President of the Republic—and which defeated even my inexhaustible appetite for Chinese food—the American ambassador, Admiral Alan Kirk, did me a favor that I shall never forget. Our host asked politely whether anybody needed a knife and fork. I choked again. Could I stand the humiliation of being inadequate in so many ways and then to top it off be the only one there unable to use chopsticks. I couldn't bring myself to the admission of this additional inadequacy, so I kept silent. Then the Ambassador boomed, "Roger and I will use a knife and a fork, won't we, Roger?" "Yes sir," I croaked. Thanks Admiral.

This trip was like a magic-carpet ride. I loved it, but, I also hated it. Except for when we were on the airplanes, or alone in our rooms, or being entertained informally, I was miserable. With the exception of one dinner in Taiwan, there were no other young people around, and no other Negroes around. There was no one with as little international experience. It brought all my old feelings of inferiority to the surface. At official times and in official places, sweat would run down my spine, I would clench my teeth and hope that nobody would say something that would require me to talk. But then, I would feel terrible because I *didn't* talk, and I imagined that everyone assumed I was as stupid as I feared I was.

Nothing much else happened during the Taipei visit except more in the endless round of briefings and tea with Generalissimo and Madame Chiang Kai-shek. The grass and the trees on their estate on the outskirts of Taipei were a bluish green, delicate, but not quite beautiful. There were men behind many of the trees—security agents. The house could not be seen for much of the long curving drive from the entrance to the grounds. It was huge, a square structure that was as gray as the dismal day we had driven through.

Our coats were taken and we were ushered down a long hall toward a huge Christmas tree, which startled me in the home of the head of this small slice of China until I remembered that Madame was a Christian. At the corner where the tree was, we turned left, and suddenly there they were, coming toward us. They looked just like the pictures I had seen of them in full color in the pages of the *New York Daily News Sunday Magazine* when I was a child. Unbidden, a fragment of an old song leaped to my mind as the old couple came down the long hall toward us. "From out of the past, where forgotten things belong," it went. I could have laughed out loud at the unconscious expression of my politics. I was for fighting for freedom, but this alliance seemed to me outdated and ridiculous.

The Generalissimo and his lady were most gracious to us. Our tea was served in a large room that, I thought at first, was simply warmly furnished. They sat in large chairs near the fireplace at the ends of two large facing couches. We would rotate places on the couches so that each of us—the Ambassador, Mr. Bell, Mr. Janow, the local director of the AID program and I—got a chance to sit and chat with each of them. One talked to the Generalissimo through an interpreter. Madame, of course, spoke impeccable English.

The Ambassador and Mr. Bell got into long conversations with them. I had little to say, so my time in the honor seats was limited. As I recall, Chiang only grunted some, while I was next to him. When the interpreter was repeating my inanities for him in Chinese, I imagine he was saying, "This dummy ain't got nothin' to say, General, so let's move him along fast." Madame Chiang said that I looked so young to hold such an important post and that Michigan was certainly a fine law school. She obviously did her homework even on the footnotes.

Since I had plenty of time to look around while the important people talked to the important people, I began to look more closely at the "large room." In the corner I noticed a large, delicately etched urn, and beautifully painted vases were set around, most decorously. There were wonderful silk screens on the walls and splendid paintings. I knew little about Western art, let alone that of the East, but the thought suddenly struck me: Shit, nigger. You're sitting in the middle of a fucking museum. Just the stuff in this room alone must be worth millions. These bastards raped the place pretty good before they got out of there. "These bastards," of course, were our allies against Communism. I was for that, but not much for them.

After that we went to Saigon, pausing only for dinner in Hong Kong, where some waterfront kid offered me his sister—"cheap." Saigon was still beautiful in January 1963, and I could understand why the French had been reluctant to leave it. What was much less clear to me was why we were there. The picture became dimmer through each day of our visit. There were briefings here too, but some of them were different. They were held out in the countryside in protected hamlets. We would go out in armored helicopters with a detachment of soldiers armed with 30mm. machine guns. We'd rise in the air with a terrible clatter and swoosh out over the beautiful countryside of Vietnam, over lush green hills, lakes, rivers and cultivated fields. Then, all of a sudden, we would drop out of the sky, down toward a cleared space near a village, and we would see the people running out and forming neat ranks to greet us.

They would clap, cheer and wave flags as we stepped from the helicopter. We would shake hands with the leaders while the people watched and smiled. We would then be taken to an insubstantial structure—the largest in town, usually—and there receive our briefings by the head man. The local American advisers, both civilian and military, would hover around as the briefing proceeded, the way teachers stand protectively near their star pupils on parents' night at school. Sometimes they would fill in gaps for him, and at others they would prompt him if he began to falter. Invariably we were told that things were now going well after a bleak period of insecurity that preceded the intervention by the Americans. Food was plentiful, health needs were being met, and security was assured. It was all very cozy—and very paternalistic.

It became clear, during these visits, that the hamlets had been selected with great care and that the briefings were rehearsed performances. I doubted that the hospitality and the enthusiasm with which we were showered, as we made our little tours of the places, were entirely spontaneous. One day, as we were walking down a dusty road under a hot sun, past a cluster of smiling and waving South Vietnamese peasants, I turned to Mike Forrestal and said, "Christ, I wish I could find out what these people really think of us and this war."

He replied, "that's the question, isn't it." Nothing more.

I thought Forrestal's reply was condescending, and I was annoyed that he had disdained to pursue the conversation. I didn't like Forrestal very much. Partly, it was envy of his self-assurance, his powerful job and his position near the center of the Kennedy solar system. But, partly I disliked him because I thought he was a snob. As in any organization, people in Washington tended to present the best nuggets of their intellect and healthy dollops of pleasing humor to their superiors. They tended to look downward humorlessly, with closed minds and impatience. It was a tribal tendency—particularly virulent in the Kennedy Administration—that I was to encounter over and over again.

The briefings in Saigon were no more assuring. The top Americans there—Frederick Nolting, the Ambassador; Paul Harkins, the military commander; the CIA Station Chief; and the AID Mission

Director—were neither crisp nor convincing. Things were going well, we were assured, though somewhat more slowly than the officials would have preferred. The South Vietnamese army was amenable to American military advice and was fast becoming an effective fighting force. The V.C., though pesky and careless and wanton in their violence, would be handled. The kill ratios were favorable, and our casualties could be borne. Nineteen sixty-five seemed a reasonable target for the wrap-up.

The one thing that was needed was *more* from home—more men, more military supplies, more AID assistance. One day we went over to see President Diem. I was very tired by that stage of the trip, but I remember him as a pleasant round-faced man who conducted our visit at a leisurely pace. The President went to great lengths to assure his visitors of the dedication of his regime to the principles of freedom and the steadfastness of his forces in the field. All they needed was *more* from America.

There wasn't anything sophisticated about the President's message. I had a firm grasp on it after the first few minutes. Chief of State or no, I wanted to get out of there, both because of boredom and because I really had to go to the bathroom. There were several points at which the meeting seemed about to wind down and Ambassador Nolting would begin to make polite exit noises, but then Diem would take off again. Agony, thy name was bladder. Finally, it was over, and Nolting was about to rise, when Diem pulled a letter out of his pocket. It was for President Kennedy. Nolting assured him the letter would be delivered with dispatch. Diem said it was important and that Nolting should read it. Nolting said he would when he got back to the Embassy. No, Diem said, Nolting should read it there, out loud. Nolting hesitated, Diem insisted. Nolting agreed. The letter was in French and very long, and Nolting had to translate it as he read. It was more of the same. Finally it was over, including endless gracious farewells and handshakes. At least four of the Americans headed for the nearest john, carrying themselves with a careful and urgent stiffness.

For once, my youth stood me in good stead. While the high-level Americans in Saigon were telling Bell, Forrestal and Janow how well we were doing, young Americans assigned to various tasks in the U.S. mission would pull me aside to whisper contradictions of their superiors. One young Army lieutenant grabbed me just after his colonel had told us that "Charlie is a coward. He won't come out and fight us in the field. He slinks and hides, but we'll get him."

"He's full of crap," the lieutenant said. "Guerrilla warfare confuses the shit out of the brass and scares the shit out of the ARVN. Charlie is kicking a lot of ass, and we've got to bribe the ARVN to fight. Even when you bribe 'em good, they don't want to fight at night or on the weekends."

I heard that message over and over again from young people in the Army, in AID, in the Embassy and even from the young CIA officer. They also said that the optimism about the future was unjustified and that the reports to CINCPAC and to Washington were exaggerated to show more enemy deaths, more pacification, more security and more ARVN improvement than was actually occurring in the country. By and large, these people appeared frustrated and sickened at being trapped in policies based on falsehoods. What they said to me had the ring of truth and supported my own intuitive reactions to what I was seeing. I asked all these people to stop by and see me when they came through Washington, and many of them did, bearing even more tales of misrepresentation in reporting South Vietnamese corruption and Communist determination.

When we left Vietnam, I was sure that the whole enterprise was a loser. I wish I could also say that a superior moral vision told me that the war was wrong, but that was not the case. My judgment was more pragmatic than that. When Mr. Bell asked me what I thought—his was not one of those minds closed to subordinates—I told him something that I was later to repeat to anyone in Washington who would listen:

"This thing isn't winnable. Charlie and the North Vietnamese have a dream, and they're going to fight for it no matter what. Our guys don't have the stomach for the fight. We'd have to keep a million soldiers in there to keep it under control, because the South Vietnamese couldn't do it, and the other guys aren't going to give up. If we pulled out, they'd just come pouring in and take the place over."

I also told him that I didn't have any faith in the American top command in Vietnam, and that I had been particularly distressed with General Harkins. Bell listened carefully, probed some, and encouraged me to pursue the contacts I had made with the younger Americans working in Saigon.

Then I thought about something else that had occurred to me

during that visit and wondered whether I should tell Bell about it. I mulled it over for a while and then decided to tell him.

"I think we underestimate the enemy," I said. "And I think we underestimate him because of racism. I don't think the Americans, particularly the high-level military people, think that little yellow soldiers are any match for American brains and material. They would take tall white guerrillas in black pajamas much more seriously."

Though Bell listened carefully to what I was saying, I still wondered whether it had been wise to say such a thing to him. He seemed utterly without prejudice as far as I could see, but I worried that that insight might make him think that I was obsessed by race and that all of my views were tainted by it. The main things a staff assistant has to sell are energy and good judgment. I didn't want my judgments discounted because my boss thought I had an obsession.

Mr. Bell didn't seem to be put off by my racial observation, but he surely wasn't convinced about my over-all thesis. I was told that he had observed to somebody else that my skepticism about the Vietnam enterprise might be a result of my never having served in the armed forces. Possible, I thought, but not likely.

The rest of the trip was more of the same, except that in India I saw Nehru and was brought to my knees in awe. He was old in 1963 and frail, like a dry, but still beautiful, rose. We went out in a party with him to dedicate a dam built by a consortium of Western companies, and with some help from AID. It was a long trip by car and some of the roads were rough. Despite his age and the heat, Nehru stood for hours in an open vehicle receiving and reciprocating the love that tens of thousands of Indians showered on him along our route. I was worried about the old man's exertions.

"He has to do it," somebody explained to me, "because they don't have television here, and this is the only way the people get to see him. He knows he is the symbol of their nationhood and feels it is part of his job to give himself to them this way."

Nehru's daughter, Indira Gandhi, was at his side constantly, with a look of concern on her face, giving strength and comfort. "That is a nice warm lady," I thought.

After those exertions and after a speech under a blazing sun, the Prime Minister had to rest before his lunch with the ambassadors of Canada, Britain and the United States, the businessmen involved in the project, and assorted other officials of government and industry. When he reappeared, the great man did not seem much recovered.

It was clear that his strength had been absolutely depleted.

There were a lot of speeches after lunch. Nehru's was a short message of gracious thanks. Everybody else was short and polite as the Prime Minister sat there, almost comatose with age and weariness, until the American ambassador, John Kenneth Galbraith, rose to his full and awesome height to add his presence to the occasion. The representative of the American nation proceeded to give a long, condescending and discursive lecture to the Indians about how wrongheaded their economic policies were. Nehru's eyes glazed. Mrs. Gandhi's face hardened. Americans squirmed. I wanted to disappear. It wasn't one of my best days as an American.

One other thing about Galbraith. Government policy in those days was that most people traveling on government business had to fly tourist class. Even officials as high as Bell were required to do so, unless the trip was so long and brutal that they wouldn't be able to conduct their business effectively if they didn't fly in comfort. So, we flew first class some and tourist some. The trip across the Pacific was first class, as was the hog-killer from Karachi to Paris. But we flew tourist across the Atlantic and on short hops such as from Bangkok to New Delhi.

Galbraith and Bell had been friends at Harvard, and Galbraith was at the Delhi airport to meet us. The 707 we had flown in from Bangkok emptied at both ends. Bell and I, in the milling and bumping that always attends airplane departures, were preparing to get off the back end of the plane with the other tourist passengers. Then there came a shout from the front: "David! David! Come off this way."

It was Galbraith. I had never seen him before, but you couldn't miss him on that plane full of short Indians and short Asians. He's around six feet seven inches. Bell himself is about six four. At six even, I was just able to watch their conversation over the heads of everybody.

"Come off this way!" Galbraith insisted.

"It'll be easier if we go off the back," Bell replied.

"No!" Galbraith shouted, "you must come off this way."

David Bell is a very nice man, and very modest. He gave me a look that said, "Ain't this the shits?"—though he would never have used those words—and we headed up the aisle, wading through the shorter brown passengers so that the American ambassador could usher the American AID administrator down the first-class ramp. Who knew what a refreshing thing it might have been for the Indian officials gathered there to have seen the administrator come out the back of that airplane. But we upheld the majesty of the United States that night by pushing against a tide of Asian humanity to do what the Ambassador thought was good for America.

Though I admired Galbraith's prose and agreed with his politics, I couldn't help thinking that night, What a *schmuck!*

11 Back home, I continued to do those things that a special assistant does for his boss: poke his nose into those places where the line operators don't want him to be, worry about potential scandals, pacify, if he can, the Inspector General of Foreign Assistance. Being a special assistant was sometimes hard on the ego. Line operatives in agencies have real jobs, like running the aid program in Africa. They want to do their jobs their way, and they want the boss's time and attention, to show him how smart they are, and they want his stroking. The competition for the boss's time was fierce, and the major administrators in the agency certainly didn't want any thirty-year-old Negro kid clogging up their routes to the boss.

Mr. Bell was too polite and too smart to relay orders through me, and he understood the needs of his top people. And, David Bell was a very self-sufficient guy. Some top people in government needed a lot of care and attention—constant briefings, petty errands run, a seeing-eye youngster hailing cabs and opening doors on trips out of town. But Bell didn't need any of that. He was enormously capable, and his ego didn't need that kind of food. I had a few general duties, like keeping an eye on operations in Africa and the Far East, the Office of Public Safety and dealing with the Inspector General. But after that, I had to search for things to do.

Finally, I figured out the perfect thing for me and for the boss. An agency head needs information. He needs it badly, because his subordinates tell him only those things they want him to know or that they can't keep from him. But he needs to know more than that—which programs are in trouble; in which country AID directors are doing badly but are being protected; where program development is ossified because of lack of bureaucratic imagination; where morale is low for one reason or another; and most of all, who the really good people are, buried down there in the bureaucracy, out of sight. AID was full of the kind of bright, ambitious talkative young people who were drawn to Washington by John F. Kennedy. Most of them had infrequent access to the Administrator, but they were full of ideas and information. And they loved to tell it all to me. The trick was to sort it out: what was malicious; what was self-serving; what was essential for the Administrator to know; and what was stuff I could handle on my own without bothering him.

I managed to turn what could easily have been a marginal existence into a useful one, and occasionally I did something that gave me great satisfaction. There was, for example, a flamboyant black man who had a long history in the agency, had achieved a high foreign-service rank, but was given nothing to do. It puzzled me. The man was a walking encyclopedia on the aid program and he seemed enormously able. It puzzled Mr. Bell too, but every time we would ask one of the agency's veterans about him, they'd mumble darkly that the man had been a security problem abroad and couldn't be trusted. So, if the security problem had been so grave, I asked, how come the man hadn't been fired instead of being kept around with nothing to do? They had no clear answers to that, only vague stuff about the difficulty of "selection out" procedures.

I called for the guy's personnel and security files. The people who had them didn't want to give them up, but they couldn't deny them to the administrator's office. I had heard rumors that the man had had an affair with a white woman when he was abroad, and I figured that was the nub of the problem. But when the files came, they were clean. Nothing about any woman, nothing about a security problem of any kind, merely reams of high recommendations and evaluations written by the man's former superiors. I reported that to Mr. Bell, and he said, "Well, if he's a good man, he ought to be doing a real job. Let's find him one." And we did, and he did fine. That felt good, a career resurrected. It turned out that I was able to help a number of sinking black careers while I was in AID.

I continued to worry about Vietnam. Slowly but surely, during the months of 1963, I collected and compiled information about our involvement there. People came to Washington and called or stopped by, and I collected what they said. I read everything I could find on the subject. I read David Halberstam's reports in *The New York Times,* and I compared everything I was learning with what our mission was reporting officially. Defense Secretary Robert McNamara had scheduled a meeting for late November in Honolulu for the high brass from all the involved agencies to confer with all the high brass from Saigon.

I put everything I had learned into two memos for Mr. Bell to take with him. One was simply a compilation of the facts that I had picked up and a comparison with the officially reported "facts" on which policy judgments were being formulated. The other was an essay on those facts with recommendations, the gist of which was that we ought to get the bastards to admit they had been lying, to get them to tell the truth, to change some of the people at the top, to scale down and to get out, if possible. When the memos were done, I had them stamped top secret—the only things I ever classified that high in an overclassifying town.

I gave them to Mr. Bell that night as he was leaving for a black-tie dinner up in the ceremonial rooms of the State Department. He always wore brown loafers in the office. That night, he had on his tux—and black loafers. A man true to himself.

Bell was taking McNamara's "shuttle" later that evening to Hawaii. It was just past the middle of November 1963 and I was leaving the next day for Puerto Rico with Byron Engle, head of the Office of Public Safety, to scout sites for a training school that AID wanted to establish. On the flight down, I read a *Life* magazine article about Bobby Baker, the former Secretary of the Senate, who had been sent to prison and who had been a protégé of Vice-President Johnson. The article said that the line on the lips of the wags around Washington was, "Whatever happened to Lyndon Johnson?"

My colleague and I were staying at the Hilton, and one afternoon we saw a lot of people clustered in the lobby. I thought it was a tourist group getting ready for an excursion.

"Kennedy es muerte," a man explained. Then he rammed his index finger into his forehead and said, *"Pow!"* Engle and I raced upstairs and turned on a television set figuring the guy must be crazy. Nobody could kill the President of the United States. But somebody had.

It was November 22, 1963. The Honolulu conference had ended that day. Bell would be heading back to Washington. I wanted to go home, and since we had finished most of our work in Puerto Rico anyway, we flew back that night. I had the cab driver take me around

the back of the White House on the way to my house. There were
lights on—a lot of them—but it was dreary and sad. I knew my
friend Ralph Dungan was in there working, because the news bul-
letins from the White House had come out in his name; Pierre Sal-
inger was out of the country, on his way to Tokyo. I thought about
going into the White House to see if there was anything I could do to
help Ralph, but I decided not to. It would have been intrusive, I
thought; and besides, there was no useful help to give. The President
was dead. Eve and I could share the grief and help each other. That
was all.

We read newspapers, we watched television and late one night
we went up to the Capitol and stood in a line in the cold to go into
the Rotunda to walk by that flag-draped coffin as tens of thousands of
other Americans were doing. It was the least we could do. It was the
only thing we could do.

On Sunday morning I was watching television. Eve was upstairs.
Suddenly I yelled, "Jesus Christ, Eve, you won't believe this! Some
son of a bitch just shot Oswald. Right on television."

The world was falling apart. It was mad. We held our child, who,
when she was three, had an imaginary playmate whom she called
"Kogy." Now she was four, and the real Kogy was dead and some
other guy too.

Next day, the government was shut down. It was clear and cold
that day. Eve and I went up to the corner of Constitution and 4th to
see the cortege go by. The sky was sparkling blue. The riderless horse
with the boots reversed in the stirrups went by. And then there was
the coffin with a flag that seemed to have redder reds and whiter
whites than I had ever seen.

"What a shame," I said to Eve.

"Oh, come off it, Roger," she said. "You didn't like him that
much."

"Well, you're right," I answered. "But he was the President, we
voted for him, and I worked for him."

"Yes," she said, "it's awful. Just awful," and she sank her beautiful long neck down into her shoulders and shuddered.

The government was back at work on Tuesday, but it was limp.
The sun had been shot out of the sky. An administration runs on
connections. They are carefully built and nurtured. For instance,
Kenny O'Donnell had real power. He was the President's appointments secretary, the keeper of the door to the Oval Office. Nobody

doubted his power, and everyone tried to curry favor with him. There were thousands of intricate webs like that in Washington emanating from Ted Sorenson, Mac Bundy, Larry O'Brien, Sargent Shriver, Bobby Kennedy, and other members of the cabinet, agency heads and bureau chiefs. It was the way the Presidential government worked informally. But all those strands carrying the current power and future dreams ultimately led back to the slender, handsome man who had occupied the Oval Office. All those carefully constructed lines were of no value that Tuesday in the Capital of America because they led nowhere.

But most people had more grief than calculation that morning. They were numb. They had shared the experience on television, in the papers and some had seen bits and snatches in person, at the White House, in the Rotunda, or on the streets. It didn't seem to matter so much to try to make sense of the garbled English of the bureaucratic memo on your desk or to probe at a meeting the endlessly troubling Bolivian sugar crop. The guys doing the talking weren't too coherent anyway. The unthinkable had happened, and they couldn't think about anything else. Only later would that little gnawing thing buried under megatons of grief and shock form itself into words: What's going to happen to me?

Sometime in those days I watched a television interview with an Assistant Secretary of Labor whom I did not know. He said, "We may laugh again, but we'll never be young again." That's it exactly, I thought. What a wise man. The man's name was Daniel Patrick Moynihan.

I saw Mr. Bell that Tuesday. His long, disciplined body was slack, the first time I had seen it so. His voice had no energy. We talked about Vietnam. He slid the folder containing my memos across the desk at me.

"That was good work," he said, "but I didn't get into it with McNamara. Harkins admitted at the meeting that his reporting had shaved the truth by about 10 percent. McNamara was so shocked and distressed by that, I didn't have the heart to tell him that somebody on my staff thought it was 25, 40, or even maybe 50 percent."

"Will you take it up with him sometime later?" I asked.

He looked at me and said, "Yes, if I get the right opportunity, I will."

I didn't press it. We were both too wiped out for any further conversation on the subject to be fruitful. I doubted that he would raise the subject with McNamara in the future. I figured that he was probably satisfied that General Harkins' admissions had jolted McNamara sufficiently to shake up the Pentagon's systems to make the thing go right in the future. I also figured that he felt that, in the current mood, McNamara wouldn't welcome sideline kibitzing from some kid special assistant in AID who hadn't even served in the armed forces. I continued to be skeptical about the Vietnam enterprise and to express doubts where I thought they would be effective, but, by and large, I turned my attention to other things.

12 Other people were killed in 1963. One of them was a man named Medgar Evers, who had been the NAACP field secretary in Mississippi. He was shot and killed in his driveway one night by a white thug for racial reasons. My uncle Roy didn't often express great warmth and admiration for young people. He didn't know much about them. He had no children. But he loved Medgar, and the murder was a shattering blow to him. "Medgar was such a fine young man," he said to me one time.

And then he thought about it some more. I was driving him to the airport in Washington, and as we looked around the Lincoln Memorial and headed over the bridge toward Arlington Cemetery, he asked, "Do you know what that Martin King did?" Then he answered his own question. "The NAACP had set up a Medgar Evers Memorial Fund to help support new youth programs and to provide some scholarships. It was an appropriate memorial for Medgar. He loved his own kids, and he was wonderful with other children too. Then King came along and tried to set up another fund using Medgar's name. Can you imagine it? Medgar was an NAACP man all the way, and King comes in and tries to take the money." The Evers family wanted all the money generated by the emotions surrounding Medgar's death to go to the NAACP. They thought Medgar would have wanted it that way, and so did my uncle.

I had never seen my uncle so incensed. He hadn't been an extraordinarily passionate man, and since he and I had never been particularly close, I was a little stunned at his opening up this way to me about King. It must mean that he's really pissed, I thought. Medgar's death had hit all Negroes hard all across the country. It was a personal, tangible outrage that put an exclamation point on the years of stupid and brutal Southern resistance to social decency.

That summer, a coalition of civil-rights, labor, and religious groups mounted the "March on Washington for Jobs and Freedom." It had been a long time abuilding. Asa Phillip Randolph, the great and honorable President of the Brotherhood of Sleeping Car Porters, had threatened President Roosevelt with such a march in the early forties. The idea had finally reached maturity. Four children had been blown up in a church in Birmingham. The civil-rights movement had spread throughout the South. James Meredith had been admitted to the University of Mississippi despite the howls of a mob of righteous white Mississippians.

And then Medgar Evers was murdered. Negroes and their allies all over the country wanted to do something. So, they came to the march. The city of Washington was fearful. There were visions of black hordes rampaging through the streets. Congressmen made dire predictions and some advised their secretaries to stay bunkered up in their apartments on the day of the march. The Administration was apprehensive but helpful. "I'll be right here sitting under my desk," one White House wag replied when asked what he was going to do. Mothers told their children not to go into town. Some blacks worried that not enough people would come. All the worries were groundless.

The night before the march, Eve and I went up to visit Uncle Roy and Aunt Minnie in their hotel room at the Sheraton Park. He slipped me the speech he had prepared and asked me to tell him what I thought of it. Uncle Roy was a fine writer and a terrific speaker, but this speech didn't move me much. Though I was polite, he could tell.

"Well, I've still got to cut and polish it," he said. "We all agreed that we would each speak only five minutes, there are so many speakers. That runs six minutes. I've got to cut a minute out of it."

I was impressed. It takes a strong constitution to cut one sixth of a tightly written piece of your own prose. I think I'd just have done the whole six minutes and the hell with it. Who'd be counting? But Roy had made a deal with his colleagues, so he was going to cut. That's the kind of integrity he had.

The day of the march was glorious. Eve and I went down to the assembly point with Clifford and Adele Alexander. There were tens of thousands of people there by the time we arrived, and more buses were coming all the time. It was like a huge family picnic. There were

people there we hadn't seen—and in some cases hadn't even thought
of—for years. Clifford went through the crowd shaking hands and
grinning. "Clifford is running for President of the March," I said.
Then all of a sudden, we were off. There had been no signal or
anything. People just started surging down Constitution Avenue, and
we went with the flow.

Uncle Roy had gotten Eve and me special tickets, so we had good
seats near the front and could see all the show-business celebrities
come in: Peter, Paul and Mary; Ben Gazzara, Lena Horne, Kirk
Douglas, Harry Belafonte, and a lot of others. The crowd by this time
was enormous under an August sun. It spilled down the steps of the
Lincoln Memorial and ran down by the sides of the Reflecting Pool
and spread out under the trees on each side. There were even people
hanging from the sturdiest branches of an awful lot of trees. The
mood was festive, yet serious. There was no ugliness at all. It was like
a huge black church social with a large sprinkling of whites.

How, I wondered, can any speaker say anything to top all of this.
The day is already a raving success, an advertisement for the civil-
rights movement in general and blacks in particular. It would be
beamed into millions of American homes that night.

But, inevitably, the speakers came. Whitney Young, Executive
Secretary of the National Urban League, told the people to take this
moment home to replicate this spirit around their dinner tables, in
their churches and in their schools and libraries. Walter Reuther and
Rabbi Joachim Prinz were good, and Uncle Roy told people that the
news had come overnight from Ghana that W.E.B. DuBois had died
in Accra at the age of ninety-three. I was proud of him for that.
DuBois' name belonged in that place, because he had been one of the
greatest of Negro Americans. Maybe nobody else had mentioned him
because he had long been a Communist. But Roy mentioned him
within the five minutes allotted him.

Then it came time for the Reverend Dr. Martin Luther King, Jr., to
say what he had to say. The first thing I noticed was that it took
considerably more than five minutes. The second thing I noticed was
that he was preaching a Baptist sermon. And the third thing I noticed
was that he was playing that throng the way a virtuoso plays a
Stradivarius. He would take the people up to the mountain top, but
sensing that they were not yet ready to explode, he would ease them
down and take them back up again. Over and over he took them up
and down, and then, at just the right moment, he repeated in a shout,

"I have a dream!" and turned suddenly away from the microphone. The place went crazy. The people made a noise as big as all outdoors. I wasn't in the mood that day for a Baptist sermon, nor was I wise enough to grasp Martin's essential greatness.

Martin King had set the tone for the day. People left that place explosively joyous. "Freedom Now!" somebody would shout. "Freedom Now!" ten others would yell out in reply. People slapped each other on the back and sometimes they hugged. "Did you hear him when he said . . .?" "Sister did you hear the man preach?" We had always known our cause was just, but it had a momentum now. There was an inevitability about it. "Freedom now," we shouted, without quite knowing what it meant, but we were sure that good things were about to happen. And the people headed back to their buses. There had been no violence, only good cheer and great joy. And now it was like the church ladies and the deacons climbing back on their buses to go home after a fine Sunday afternoon.

Eve and I carried the euphoria with us for days. We went back to New York that weekend and had a party with the Brownes and the Jacksons. We recounted the whole thing for them, and we got as high on the event as Eve and I had been on the day of the march. The group included two social workers, one educator, one doctor and two lawyers, and the talk went like this.

"Cain't say niggas can't get shit together now."

"Niggas showed the whole country that day."

"Niggas was cool. Came and listened to the preachin' and sang they song, 'We *Shall* Overcome!' "

"Freedom now, baby."

"Yea, man, we gon' get some freedom now."

In Washington, as my tread gradually became firmer in the bureaucracy, our social life expanded. We had a few good Negro friends in town and a few good white friends too. Now most of our new friends were white. They were all bright young people in the government and seemed to have limitless futures. Eve and I easily blended in—in part, I thought, because in those days white liberals were uncomfortable having all-white parties. We and the Alexanders knew one white couple who had a lot of parties. All four of us enjoyed the people and their parties, but we were never invited together. We laughed about the fact that they couldn't "waste all your niggers on one party."

I was much more comfortable in Washington now. It was clear that Mr. Bell thought I was serving some useful purpose, and I had gained a good deal of respect within the agency. I no longer had the dreadful feeling that I was in my job only because I was a Negro. I was beginning to do what I had hoped to do, show by example what Negroes could do if given the chance. And I was gaining precious entry into that white social world where useful transactions occurred and where real life was lived.

But somehow, my life wasn't sitting right in my spirit. Despite the euphoria of the summer of '63, and the sense of inevitability about our cause, the struggle was still bound to be long and hard. And there were people out there struggling. I often wondered, What the hell am I doing here in the front office of AID? And though I loved the new dimension of our social life, Eve wasn't too keen on it. She didn't dislike white people as a lot of Negroes disliked them then and some blacks do now; she just wasn't all that comfortable with them.

One night when we were going to a party at the home of a white couple who had been good friends since college days, and I was anticipating a good time, she said, "Don't drink too much, don't abandon me, and let's go home early." It was a signal. I should have paid attention to it. I just got annoyed. This was a party night, and I didn't want to put up with that kind of shit. At the time, my libido was churning about in all different directions. Though I wasn't doing anything about it, my life was beginning to fall apart. But what the hell, I didn't hear the warnings and it would take a good ten years before the whole thing went to pieces.

One of the people I met at one of those parties was a young lawyer from the Pentagon. He was General Counsel of the Army and would soon be Special Assistant to the Secretary of Defense. His name was Joseph A. Califano, Jr., and he came from Brooklyn by way of Harvard Law School and Wall Street. I heard him talking about some planes that we had in Vietnam and that our government was saying we didn't have in Vietnam. I thought this was classified stuff and here was this bastard dining out on it. If only I sat where he sits, I thought, then maybe I could really do something about slowing down this war. I didn't like Califano very much. Envy, thy name is Wilkins.

In those days, a number of us from State and AID would gather every Sunday on a vacant lot up on P Street in Georgetown for a game of touch football. I was still pretty fast and could still snare a pass the way I did when I was in high school. In one of those games was Pat Drew, a little guy who was a lawyer in AID and a great friend of Califano's. Drew was one of the white people Eve loved, and I did too. She'd always say, after we had seen him, "Gee, that Pat Drew makes you feel good." And I would agree.

One day during a game, after I had caught a pass, Drew said, "Wilkins, you're just a glory boy, and when it comes to the blocking and the hard parts of this game you're not around."

"You ass-hole," I replied. "I'm calling the next play." In the huddle I said, "Drew's carrying on a sweep around left and I'm leading the blocking." The ball was snapped. I brushed one lineman out of the way and headed downfield. Another guy came in straight up, and I bumped him on his ass and kept on going, with Drew moving right behind me. There was a third guy who had a good angle at us, so I threw my body at his legs and he went down on top of me. Drew scored. He had run three quarters of the length of the field. When he came back upfield, I was still lying on the ground catching my breath. "Just as I said," Drew said laughing, "just a glory boy."

Pat Drew married Elizabeth Brenner, a smart journalist from Cincinnati, in a Catholic church in Georgetown. Pat's brother performed the ceremony, and a lot of the women in our circle of friends helped Liz prepare for her wedding, because her family wasn't around. It was a nice day. There was a good feeling. Two nice people getting married. Marriage was "in" in those days. Eve was pregnant again, and we were very pleased.

We had moved, by that time, from Emerson Street down to the "New Southwest," primarily because the school there—Amidon— had a national reputation as one of the great public primary schools in the nation. I had never seen the old Southwest, but Eve's mother, who had grown up in Washington, told us that it had been one of the most horrid Negro slums in the country. A lot of streets were not paved, there was no running water; people had neither toilets nor urban habits. "It smelled," Mrs. Tyler once told me, "and nice people didn't go down there."

Philip Graham, the late publisher of *The Washington Post,* and a great mover and shaker in Washington, knew that was a blot on the nation's honor as well as the city's, so he began pressing first the Eisenhower and the Kennedy administrations to use the then new urban-renewal legislation to clear out the slum and to build some decent new housing. Graham made his dream come true, and a lot of upper-income and middle-income housing was built there along with some new public housing projects to take care of some of the poor people who had been displaced.

There were two public schools in the area, Bowen and Syphax. The planners decided to build a new "magnet" school, Amidon, to attract middle-class people, both black and white, to the area. The public-school administration, which was then still predominantly white, did its part with gusto. It put into place a school that featured a basic, no-frills education, but was staffed with many of the system's teaching stars. The curriculum was like the great old Woody Hayes Ohio State teams—basics, straight ahead, *boom, boom, boom.* And the kids learned. They were well above the national average. So, though Amy was not yet school age, Eve and I decided that that was where we wanted her to be.

One of the rental developments there was a place called Capitol Park. For its time, it was excellent moderate-income housing. It had a mixture of six- or seven-story high-rise buildings with many rental town houses. There were young trees and a community swimming pool. Many of the significant blacks in the Kennedy Administration had already moved there by the time a new section of the development was opened. Cliff and Adele Alexander had moved into one of the houses in the new section before the whole thing was finished. Cliff had roomed with Richard Ravitch, one of the developers, when he was at Harvard. The other partner in the project was James Scheuer, a Congressman from New York.

Eve and I opted for a smaller house than Cliff and Adele's. The house we wanted had two small bedrooms on the top floor, a modest living and dining area and a kitchen on the middle floor, a washer-dryer room, and an all-purpose room on the ground floor, where a glass wall and sliding door opened onto a small back patio. It rented for something like $212 a month in 1963. When we went to Shannon and Luchs, the rental agents, they started to give us the run-around. They couldn't rent the house until the whole new section was developed, they said. They hadn't quite figured out the rent scale, they said. They would keep our application on file, they said.

I had feared that, because to this day housing discrimination is one of the racial booby traps that can blow up in the faces of even the most affluent blacks. I went to Cliff and told him the story and asked him to pull some strings for us. He did, and we got the house. Cliff told me that when my story got to Scheuer, who had a reputation both as a liberal developer and a liberal Congressman, he said, "Oh my God. Roy Wilkins' nephew." I was thoroughly enraged by that response, not only because I didn't just want that not to happen to me, I didn't want it to happen to *any* Negro. And, I think our protest worked, because I never heard of Shannon and Luchs jerking anybody else around, despite their fears that the place would tip and go black. In fact, it never did tip.

Real estate in Washington is crazy. When we moved in, some workmen came to put the finishing touches on the house. One of the Negro workmen told Eve that he was glad that we were only renting, because the place was so jerry-built that it might go down in the first big windstorm. It was a corner house and expensive to heat in the winter and hot as hell in the summer, despite huge air-conditioning bills. You could hear the next-door stereo clearly even when it was played at moderate levels. We bought a house in 1966 and moved out of Capitol Park, which is a co-op now. Eve told me that last year, eighteen years after we first occupied that place, it sold for $120,000.

We were happy in Capitol Park. It was integrated and occupied by young people on their way up. Right behind us there was a Jewish couple from Detroit. The man, Ralph Wittenberg, was a psychiatrist, still in training, and his wife, Chris, was a brilliant psychologist. Two doors down from us on G Street were Pam and Ed Sherin. Pam was a wonderful-looking former actress who had been born in England and had been sent to America by her father to escape the blitz during World War II. Her husband, Ed, was a Jew who had been born in Hattiesburg, Mississippi, and who had come to Washington to be the artistic director of the Arena Stage, Washington's great repertory company. Ed went on to direct *The Great White Hope* both at the Arena and on Broadway. The play starred, as you may recall, an actor with three names, James Earl Jones.

Two doors down from them were the Alexanders, Bob and Jane. Bob directed the children's theater at the Arena and was later to develop it into a wondrous Washington participatory theater institution called The Living Stage. Jane, who was just starting out at the Arena then, went on to become one of America's finest actresses. Before the Alexanders lived in that house, some people named Pertchuk lived there with their daughter, Amy, who was to become a classmate of our Amy. Mike worked on Capitol Hill for Senator Warren Magnuson then. He later went on to become one of the most effective—and most hated—chairmen of the Federal Trade Commission when he tried to make American manufacturers responsible to the consumers who made them rich.

A block away lived the Schuylers, John and Kay, who had a daughter named Stacey. Kay was a tiny blonde with blue eyes, and Stacey looked like her mother had just spit her out. Stacey was our daughter's best friend. John was an assistant to Congressman James Roosevelt of California. And around the corner, there were Cliff and Adele Alexander and another black couple, Lisle and Betty Carter. Cliff was still in the White House then and Lisle had a high job in the Department of Health, Education and Welfare. Betty was beautiful and stayed home with her five children.

Sometimes when the weather was warm, I could come home early from the State Department and take Amy, who was four, for a swim in the pool. She was a happy, pretty child and a very bright one. Race was not a factor for her then. She knew we were Negro, but it didn't make much difference. She played randomly with Negro and white children, and all the parents of whatever color were nice to all the children, of whatever color. A group of us: the Wittenbergs, the Schuylers, the Sherins and Eve and I were terribly close. We had backyard cookouts together and parties in our respective homes. We were all in our middle or early thirties, and libidos were flying all over the place. But nobody much touched and everybody made jokes about the most obvious of crushes, like that one between Pam Sherin and me.

Kennedy was in the White House and then Johnson; America was well on the way to racial justice, and we were all in the vanguard of what our new and enlightened country would soon come to be.

It is different now. I am in my third marriage. Ed Sherin is married to Jane Alexander, and Pam, not remarried, lives in Princeton, and Bob, also not remarried, lives in Washington. The Schuylers, divorced, are back in their native California. The Pertchuks are divorced. As of this writing, Chris and Ralph Wittenberg are separated, and Eve lives, unmarried, in the house on M Street in Southwest that we bought in 1966, just next door to the one the Sherins had bought a couple of weeks earlier. But things were bright and shiny in 1963 and '64, even after the murder of John F. Kennedy. We laughed and laughed. A good and decent future was assured for us and for America.

13 Making the transition to a new administration in the aftermath of Kennedy's death seemed to me rude, grating and harsh. Quite simply, I resented Johnson. He was President by virtue of a constitutional contingency. He didn't sound like a President, I hadn't voted for him to be President, and he wasn't Kennedy. Besides, he was a Texan, and to me Texas was South, and he sounded South, and that's where my enemies were, more than in the Soviet Union, more than in North Korea.

That year I had been invited to make a speech at Miles College, a small Negro college in Birmingham. I had never really been to the South and hadn't even been in a Border State since I was nine. Birmingham, which blacks had taken to calling *Bomb*ingham, where Bull Conner held sway, was the last place outside Mississippi I wanted to go to. But I was told that it was a small, struggling Negro school and that the youngsters down there needed role models, so I went, but I was afraid.

I was afraid in the Atlanta airport, where I had to change planes and where I heard thick Southern accents and where Confederate flags were on sale at the newsstands. I was very subdued and quite apprehensive as I waited for my plane to Birmingham. But nothing happened. I got to the college, and the next morning I made my speech. Afterward, at a luncheon, I was befriended by a white man who taught at the college and had previously lived in Brazil. He wanted to continue our conversation about the AID program in Brazil and offered to drive me to the airport. I accepted and said I'd wait for him while he went to his office to make one phone call.

About thirty minutes later, when I was beginning to worry about missing my plane, a beautiful young blond woman appeared, identified herself as the professor's daughter, told me her father had gotten tied up and said that she would drive me to the airport instead. She was stunning—blond hair, splendid features and a slim, but full figure. I was scared shitless. I didn't want to ride through Birmingham with a white woman in 1963. I also didn't want to stop looking at her. I also didn't want to miss my plane. So, I said, "Okay."

She led me to the car—a white Mercedes—and we set off. She talked about Brazil. Her profile was glorious. I sat pressed up against the passenger door. People in other cars glowered at us, particularly when we stopped for traffic lights. She asked me about AID. I talked about the Kennedy Administration, and her skirt pulled up over her knees and fell loosely between her thighs as she worked the brake, clutch and accelerator. A young white tough gave us the finger as he zoomed by us in an old souped-up Chevy with two Confederate-flag bumper stickers. She didn't seem to notice, and I was afraid.

When we got to the airport, she insisted on coming in, though I urged her not to. There was plenty of time for the plane, so we sat in the waiting room. People stared at us, some with open hostility. I talked about my daughter. She stretched. Her breasts were larger than I had thought. Finally, my plane for Atlanta was called. I thanked her and said goodbye, but she insisted on walking to the gate with me. There was a line there, and we waited in it. There was no other Negro in the line. She was comparing racial problems in Brazil and Alabama. The hostility of the bystanders was almost tangible. She didn't notice. I wanted her to go away. I didn't want to get killed. I wanted to touch her thighs.

"It's all stupid here," she said, touching my arm innocently. "Why, in Brazil you would be considered white."

"Ain't that shit?" the man in front of us exclaimed to his companion in a thick Southern accent. He whirled to look at me with a murderous look in his eye. I looked back at him with my eyes as big as I could make them and shrugged with my hands thrust outward, palms up. He clenched his teeth and his fists and then turned away as they began to let us through the gate. I thanked her. She kissed me lightly on the cheek and left. I kept my eyes down, avoiding contact, but I heard the mutterings of Southern voices.

It was a cold, clear December night in 1963, just before Christmas, and Lyndon Baines Johnson was standing on the steps of the Lincoln

Memorial holding a candle and talking in a Southern accent, and
Eve and I were in a crowd of thousands facing him and holding
candles for John F. Kennedy. It was a memorial service for the slain
President marking the end of the thirty-day official mourning period.
Johnson's Southern cadences filled me with a feeling of dread. I
thought of Thomas Wolfe's mournful wail, "Oh lost."

But the power and the energy of the man could not be muffled. His
massive contours began to emerge against the tides of our grief and
resentment. It soon became clear that he hated Robert Kennedy. I
was told a story of something that Bobby had done to Johnson at a
meeting one day during John Kennedy's Presidency. The Vice-President was chairman of the President's Committee on Equal Opportunity, an organization of top government officials and prominent
private citizens whose purpose was to open job opportunities to
minorities.

At the meeting, to which people had come from all over the country, the Attorney General walked in unannounced, strode up to the
podium and insisted on speaking immediately, because he was busy
and had to go. He began to lash the committee for its flaccid performance. He was particularly brutal about the committee's leadership and, according to my informant, concluded by saying, "And if
this thing can't be run right, can't get some results, we'll just have to
find somebody who can run it." Then he strode out, without shaking
a hand or saying goodbye, leaving a thunderstruck and publicly
humiliated Johnson in his wake.

That was plenty of reason for Johnson to hate him. I also figured
that Johnson was deathly afraid of being the mistake that happened
between the Kennedys. There was talk, early in 1964, that Bobby
Kennedy might challenge for the Presidency, but it seemed more
likely that in his grief Bobby wanted to go on the ticket as the Vice-
Presidential nominee. One day in the spring of '64 I was going into
the basement entrance of the West Wing of the White House on West
Executive Avenue. I ran into Bobby Kennedy coming out. I knew
him a little then, so I greeted him. He knew who I was and was
pleasant, but vacant. He wasn't just detached. He wasn't there. I later
learned that the President had informed him, minutes before, that
under no circumstances would he be on the ticket in 1964. Shortly
thereafter, Johnson announced that no member of his cabinet would
be on the ticket that year.

I was going into the White House that day because I had been

summoned to see Bill Moyers and Walter Jenkins, who was Johnson's top aide. They were working on getting the Economic Opportunity Act of 1964 through the Congress. Though the program had
been fashioned under Kennedy, Johnson considered it to be the first
bill of his Presidency. He was going to lead a War Against Poverty,
but first he had to get the bill passed. Jenkins operated out of a little
partitioned portion of the office that Ralph Dungan had occupied all
by himself. The rest of the room was occupied by secretaries and
filled with boxes and files. Jenkins had the biggest pile of unanswered
phone messages on his desk that I had ever seen. The phone rang
constantly. Secretaries were in and out. The furious pressures that
Johnson put on Jenkins were a legend in Washington, but he took
time for me as if I were the most important item on his agenda. I was
impressed and thought he was the nicest man I had ever seen at work
in the White House. He wanted me to lobby for the poverty bill.
Nobody in the Kennedy White House had ever asked me to lobby for
anything, but Jenkins did.

Johnson's energy began to fill the town. He saw an unending number of members of Congress, cajoling and stroking. He was on the
phone to the cabinet. He was around the town meeting with departments and agencies. His message was always the same, "Your country needs you, I need you." His drive was infectious. He began to seem
like The President. It began to be Johnson's town, except in a few
hearts.

I had been in Washington for about two years by that time, and I
was thinking about moving on. Somehow a staff job, no matter how
useful you made it, seemed to diminish you. You were an appendage
to somebody else, not a person in your own right. My responses to
the world were still those of a young Negro. Initiative and aggressive-
ness did not come naturally to me. Those traits could get you labeled
as an "uppity nigger," and uppity niggers had a hard time in the
world. That, plus being somebody else's man, made me feel small. So
though I liked and admired David Bell enormously, I decided it was
time to leave him.

We talked about it, and he agreed with me. "I almost made the
mistake of remaining a staff man too long," he said. "It's time for you
to go out and run something. It doesn't matter how large or how
small that something is, it is the next step. You ought to do it. You'll
be amazed at how much you'll learn about yourself."

So, we began thinking about other things I might do in AID. Mr.

Bell clearly wanted me to stay in the program. He wasn't a man given to easy compliments, but he said one day, "If you stay in foreign affairs, there's no limit to how far you can go. You'll have to work, of course, but there's no doubt if you do that, you'll end up at the top." I think that was the most encouraging thing anybody ever said to me in Washington.

Before I left AID, there was one more large thing for me to do. Robert Kennedy had been appalled on a trip through the Third World to find that young people had been touched with the Communist dream while our people perfected their relationships with the people in power, largely ignoring the people who had prospects of taking over in the future. He had caused the National Security Council to send out a directive to all United States missions in the Third World instructing them to develop a youth program designed to identify and make friends with the next generation of leaders. The reports that began flowing back in the cable traffic didn't satisfy him. He thought everybody was falling down on the job, especially AID.

So, he decided to send out a team composed of three fairly young men to inspect a few United States missions abroad to determine whether they were actually doing anything. I was sent on the inspection tour, along with his personal assistant John Nolan, a lawyer in his middle-thirties as head of the team, and Jim Echols, a ten- or twelve-year veteran of the United States Information Agency, but still a fairly young man. We went to Algiers, Kinshasa—then still called Leopoldville—Dar es Salaam, Nairobi, Addis Ababa, New Delhi and Bangkok. The program really wasn't going very well anywhere, but that isn't the point.

One night in Algiers John and I decided to see the Casbah. Neither of us knew any French, so we took a young American who was working out there for the American Volunteer Service—a kind of private Peace Corps. The walkways of the Casbah were fairly broad and there were few lights to mark the way. The Casbah was built on a hill, and there were stone steps leading up on a gradual rise, bordered by stone buildings that had closed doors and shuttered windows. Occasionally, men would emerge from the dark to ask us if we were looking for women. Their voices were full of menace. We said, no, we were not looking for women, just walking. The men would disappear into the murk, but we knew they were not gone.

The passageway grew narrow as we climbed. There would be a turn here or a turn there, and we chose haphazardly as we went. The place looked like nothing we had ever seen, all shutters and cobblestones. And finally the way, which had begun wide as a small street in Greenwich Village, was almost close enough for one man's armspread to touch each wall. I was afraid of the men in the murk, and I was afraid that we would not make our way back out through all the turns we had taken. It was darker than it had been at the place where we had entered, and that had been very dim.

"John," I said, "I think we'd better go back."

I am not a brave man. Or, at least I didn't think so then. John seemed relieved to hear me say that, and he agreed. So, we slowly made our way back down to where we had begun.

Down near the bottom of the hill, where the passage was wide again, there was an open doorway and a flood of light. After all those closed and threatening doorways, the light seemed a safe haven. It was a little store—the only one there that was not shuttered for the night—that in New York would have been called a "candy store." It sold tooth paste, cigarettes, mouthwash, and other sundries. There was an old man behind the counter, and there were three hip young Algerian men in their late teens or early twenties. In America they would have been called street people—potential muggers. But, at least they were in the light.

"You want women?" one of the young men asked in a harsh voice.

"No, we're just walking," our young IVS guide said.

Then I spotted a calendar hanging on the wall. It had a picture taken on the South lawn of the White House of Ben Bella—then the Algerian president—and Kennedy, standing at attention, taking a salute. I told the interpreter to tell the young men that John was the personal assistant to Robert Kennedy. He did. The leader, who had asked us in tones full of hostility if we were scavenging for one of their women, heard what the IVS guy said and clutched his stomach. "*O-o-oh, O-o-oh,*" he said, bowing with his arms around his stomach. He bent almost double as he continued, saying, in almost a chant, "*O-o-oh, O-o-oh.*" Then he said some other words in French. The IVS guy translated.

"He says, 'Tell him we are very sorry. Tell him the President was a very great man.'"

The essence of that young man's communication to us was plain. He hurt for Robert Kennedy for the loss of his brother.

"Tell him we are very sorry."

Then they talked some more, heatedly and at length, about the death of our President. They said they didn't believe for a minute that Oswald had killed the President by himself. It had been a conspiracy. The Russians did it, the mob did it, the Cubans did it. It had to be a conspiracy.

"They get all this from the sensational French press," our young interpreter told John and me.

Then we probed the young men about their hopes for the future. The leader said he wanted to go to America to make his fortune in *"Olywoo."*

I said, "What?"

"Olywoo!" the man said to me directly.

I turned to our interpreter in confusion.

"Hollywood," he said.

"Jesus!" I said.

We began to disengage then. The young men told us again and again to tell Robert Kennedy that they were sorry. We said we would. We did some embracing as we parted from them. They insisted that we repeat their message. We did.

In the calendar picture that I had seen, Ben Bella and Kennedy had their hands over their hearts. The grass was very green as were the trees behind them. The Marine Band was in the background and a crowd of American faces. And the two national leaders, knife thin, facing the future with their hands over their hearts, were pictured there on that crumbling wall of that little place in Algiers. That calendar hung on walls all over Algeria.

A couple of weeks later, we were in Nairobi, Kenya, which is full of people of every color from darkest black to Scandinavian white, with all shades in between. People wore everything from saris to old Western clothes. Except for the whites and the dark blacks, it was impossible to tell who was what. Each evening during our stay there, we would sit out in front of the New Stanley Hotel and have cocktails. And we did a lot of woman watching. We had been away from home for a long time.

The last two evenings we were there, the most beautiful woman I had ever seen sat and drank with friends at another table. She had rich brown skin, huge and luminous dark eyes, lush, thick dark-brown hair and a fine figure. I couldn't keep my eyes off her. She was a glory, one of nature's great treasures. We speculated on what she might be—an actress, a model, an heiress, a mulatto, an Indian or a well-tanned white woman.

Later, when we boarded our Air India flight to Bombay, we found out. She was a tourist-class flight attendant. I was delighted. I stared at her as she moved about the cabin, all delicate grace. I was so awe-struck, I could barely talk to her when she served me. After a refuel-ing stop at Aden, I was thirsty and got up enough nerve to ask her for some water. She said the water taken on at Aden had been bad and would make me sick. Could I buy a soft drink, then. No, she said, they were all out.

During this exchange, something happened that I couldn't believe. At first she had just given me a warm and beautiful smile. Then—could I be seeing things?—she was flirting with me. Since there wasn't anything else to drink, I asked to buy some whiskey, neat. Then I found out that I didn't have any East African pounds left.

"Will you take dollars?" I asked.

"Dollars?" she asked. "Where did you get dollars?"

"In the United States," I answered.

"When were you there?" she asked.

"Two weeks ago," I replied.

"How long were you there?"

"Thirty-two years," I said.

Her eyes widened and she exclaimed, "Oh, you're an American, I had no idea."

I was stunned. She had taken a load off my head. This beautiful woman hadn't been talking and flirting with a Negro, a "nigger." She'd just been talking to a man, a man whom she had found attrac-tive. I was thirty-two years old, and I had never thought of myself that way. I had internalized the prevailing white American definition of me as a Negro, something less than a whole man; maybe 5/6 man. This woman's unexpected exclamation had ripped a veil off my un-conscious mind and had shown me how much America's pervasive racism had crippled me. Thanks to her, I would never be the same. I became a *man* in this world that night.

14 Back home, the Civil Rights Act of 1964 was passed in June. On the day of its passage, I went up to the Capitol and watched the leaders of the coalition that had lobbied for the bill being interviewed on the Senate steps. My Uncle Roy spotted me and called out:

"Hey, has that baby been born yet?"

"No," I said, "but soon we hope, especially Eve."

Two days later, on June 11, 1964, our second and last child, David Earl Wilkins, was born.

I was really looking hard for something to do outside the Administrator's office. Mr. Bell asked me if I would be interested in a high-level job in the mission in Vietnam or maybe Deputy Mission Director in Nepal, with the prospect of taking over there in two years. It was flattering to know that he'd think about giving me a mission of my own at thirty-four, but there was no way I wanted to take a new baby to Katmandu. I wrestled with Vietnam. I thought maybe I owed it to my country to do that, but the civil-rights movement was hot that summer. Students from all over the country descended on Mississippi to register voters. Cheney, Goodman and Schwerner were murdered in the little town of Philadelphia in July, and a month after the President signed the Civil Rights Act of 1964 into law, riots broke out in Harlem, Bedford-Stuyvesant, Paterson, Rochester and Philadelphia.

I couldn't stay out of it, so I started thinking of things I might do domestically. The likeliest thing seemed to be the new Community Relations Service just established by the Civil Rights Act. It was an old idea that Lyndon Johnson had tried to put into law in his Senate

140

days. The idea was simple. It was to establish an elite corps of race-relations specialists in Washington who would be dispatched to hot spots around the country when trouble broke out. I read the legislation and thought the concept was absurd. I couldn't figure out how Washington specialists, no matter how well trained, could dash into a community they didn't know, conduct quiet conciliation, dash out again and accomplish anything of value.

But, when I was asked to come over to see LeRoy Collins, the former governor of Florida, whom Johnson had named as the first Director of the Service, I went. It was the damnedest employment interview I ever had. The Service had been put in the Department of Commerce, on the theory that it would do a lot of its work with local businessmen who wanted racial peace, if not racial justice, and that Commerce had the closest ties to business.

We had lunch in the Commerce executive dining room. Collins never looked at me or spoke directly to me the whole time. Collins is about six feet tall, with a full head of white hair and a lined, handsome face. He has a soft Southern drawl and a gentle manner. And he had a whole pile of wonderful political stories. He told a lot of them at that lunch while he looked at his shoes, at the ceiling, at his associates, who were lunching with us, but never at me. The stories were wonderful, and we all laughed a lot, and I didn't have to say much of anything at all.

After that I was a little surprised when I was offered one of the five highest-level jobs in the agency at GS-17, two grades higher than my AID grade and four levels higher than my starting grade a little more than two years earlier.

Though the people inside the Service couldn't give me much more enlightenment about its business than I had gotten from my reading of the statute, I decided to take it.

"I can't figure out how this thing's supposed to work," I told Eve, "but when Congress is offering money and people to try to push civil rights ahead, I think I ought to try to help make it move."

My first staff meeting there was sobering. There were about ten people gathered around the conference table, and they were talking about their "Mississippi Plan." CRS was trying to devise a plan to "fix" Mississippi. I couldn't believe my ears. They were going to formulate this plan in Washington and then go down to Mississippi and sell it to the big white businessmen, and suddenly Mississippi would be better. I was aghast and appalled. I wondered what kind of

142   ROGER WILKINS

nuts I had gotten mixed up with. I didn't think any plan imaginable, especially one devised in Washington, could do that. And I knew that it would be disastrous to try to sell any plan that sought to impose a solution on the Negroes. So, I said, "I think that any plan that doesn't take into account the hopes and the aspirations of the Negroes in Mississippi is doomed to fail."

After the meeting, a Southern white staff member—there were a lot of Southern whites on that staff—came up to me and pumped my hand and told me that my contribution had been wonderful, that it was just the kind of contribution they had been hoping I would make. I didn't say anything, just scratched my head and went back to my office. But it turned out that my contributions were destined to be limited. Collins' inner circle consisted of himself and three other whites. I wasn't in it and I was the top Negro in the Service.

I screamed about that. My argument was that CRS was bound to take some lumps in the Negro community, and I was quite prepared to help take them, but only if I participated in the formulation of policy. Besides, I argued, it was a hell of a thing to run a race-relations agency in the federal government in 1964 and exclude the top Negro in the place from the big decisions. Collins and his top advisers took that to heart. They created a new division in the agency called Community Action and put me in charge of it. As a division head, I became a member of the inner circle.

The whole thing suited me fine. Community Action was supposed to develop some long-range programs for urban areas, and that is just what I wanted to do. Though little towns like McComb, Mississippi, and Bogalusa, Louisiana, provided some colorful and dreadful head-lines, I reasoned that the major racial action in America would be in the cities, and that's what I wanted to work on.

With two principal staff members, Seymour Samet, a former race-relations council director from Miami, and Jay Janis, a liberal Miami builder who decided to interrupt his career to come to Washington to work on civil rights, I began devising a plan to place CRS people permanently in a few major urban centers to work on racial prob-lems on a continuing basis rather than shoot them out helter-skelter after headlines to put out fires. This was a major departure from what the plain language of the legislation seemed to intend. But the prem-ise of the legislation was primitive. It presupposed a three-sided model with blacks on one side, white bigots on the other and per-plexed, but potentially good, white businessmen in the middle. The idea was to go into a town that had racial troubles, convince the businessmen that racial changes had to be made and then activate them to put pressure on the politicians to open the parks, desegregate the theater, or whatever it was that was causing the problem.

That model had, in fact, worked to some degree for the Justice Department a couple of years earlier in Birmingham. But it had worked primarily because Louis Oberdorfer, then an Assistant Attorney General, had roots and connections in Birmingham, roots that he could manipulate. In addition, Janis, Samet and I figured that even if you could "fix" a place like McComb, you would have affected fewer black people than live in one square block in Harlem. But the legislation clearly intended for us to operate only in places where there was a crisis. In the context of the times, it was clear that what Congress had had in mind were problems like those that had been encountered in Little Rock and New Orleans school-desegregation crises, the Southern Christian Leadership Conference's campaign in Birmingham or the bombings in McComb.

But I was convinced now that the North was the place to worry about and that the simple three-sided model constructed for Southern cities was totally inapplicable to it. Negroes in the North were watching their nightly news shows and seeing the sacrifices and the risks that Negroes and their white allies were taking in the South. They saw changes occurring in the South, they saw the President signing the Civil Rights Act with all the Negro leaders in attendance, but they saw no changes in their own lives or in the streets where they lived in Harlem, on the South Side of Chicago or in South Central Los Angeles. The furies about years of humiliation and deprivation were being fueled by the Southern Negro struggle, but they had no outlet in the North. There were laws on the books in many Northern states that guaranteed the rights that Southern Negroes were struggling for, but deprivation and inequality still existed in the grain and rough substance of the majority of Northern Negro lives. There was no outlet for the furies unleashed by the Nightly News.

One night Eve and I watched the CBS Evening News report of Stokely Carmichael's speech from Canton, Mississippi, as he and others continued the ill-conceived and lonely march of James Meredith from Memphis to Jackson, which had damned near gotten Meredith killed. Stokely had been speaking at an outdoor rally in the night. Television lights made his dark face shine and his huge and luminous oval eyes glow like those of a predatory cat. It was hot, and he was sweating, and that made his black face shine even more.

"What do we want?" he screamed.

"Black Power!" the crowd roared back.

"What do we want?" Stokely screamed again.

"Black Power," the crowd roared back.

"There's a lot of white folks in America gonna have diarrhea tonight," I said to Eve.

"Yes, baby and there gonna be a lot of pissed-off niggers in Harlem tonight," she said.

"Yes," I said. "Yes, yes," I said. I sounded just like my Uncle Roy.

And, in Harlem, in the first of the riots, *The New York Times* reported that a policeman had stood on top of a police car on the corner of 125th Street and Seventh Avenue and had bellowed, "Go home. Go home."

The answer had come back loud and clear, "But we are home, baby."

And, they *were* home. Home in the ghetto that they didn't control. Home in the ghetto where their children were not educated by the schools provided for them. Home where half the people who needed work could not find it. Home where the dope pushers and the criminals preyed on the working people who could not afford to move away from them. Home where the American dream was beamed into their homes every night and where they walked out into urine-stained halls in the morning. They were home where they were being desecrated. It is one thing to desecrate a temple or a cathedral. It is a whole different thing to desecrate a human being.

It was building in the cities, Janis, Samet and I thought, and it was a real American crisis. Not a headline crisis, but a cancerlike crisis that would eat the Negroes first and then eat the cities as some of the Negroes began to vent their hate.

The legislation did not provide for what I wanted to do. It was an idea seven years out of date. Since there had been riots in the cities the summer before, the three of us began to sell the idea around the civil-rights community in Washington that there was a continuing crisis in the cities and that CRS should be permitted to mount experimental—not permanent—programs in some of the nation's major cities. Vice-President Hubert H. Humphrey, who had been put in charge of all civil-rights activities, bought the idea.

That's an interesting thing. Congress passed a law with one thing in mind, and others interpreted it to mean something else entirely.

In the beginning, our idea was a modest one. We wanted to recruit and place one person in each of ten major American cities during the summer of 1965. That person's job would be to get to know the cities, the real Negro leaders, the white movers and shakers and the top law-enforcement people. The person would also take a good look at the pattern of federal aid being directed to the city in an effort to help us advise other federal agencies to target their aid in a way that would help ease, rather than exacerbate tensions. The Vice-President had a civil-rights task force on which all the domestic agencies were represented. We invited the mayors of our target cities to Washington to discuss, with us and with representatives of such agencies as Labor, Commerce and Health, Education and Welfare, special program needs for the summer, to try to make sure that the Administration was being as responsive as possible to minority needs in those cities. All the invited mayors came except Yorty of Los Angeles and Daley of Chicago. We picked two other cities to take their place in the program.

I wasn't able to escape Southern fire-fighting duty entirely that year. The Southern Christian Leadership Conference and the Student Nonviolent Coordinating Committee had mounted a campaign in Selma, Alabama, and we had had a field worker, Mac Seacrest, a South Carolinian, working there. Selma was a violent place. More than once I received information indicating that conspiracies were afoot to kill Dr. King. I would call Andrew J. Young, the executive of the SCLC, whom I hadn't met yet, and tell him that King shouldn't appear at night rallies for a while.

King went to register at the Albert Hotel in Selma, as he had a right to do under the Civil Rights Act. He was the first black man to do so. A white man slugged him in the face. Representative Adam Clayton Powell from Harlem registered there a few days later without incident, but the town was hot. Negroes wanted more services in Selma, garbage collection, water connections and paved streets. Mac Seacrest thought he had put together a pretty good collection of businessmen, to make some of those concessions, and it could all be put in motion if the agency dangled a few federal dollars in front of the mayor. Calvin Kytle, the Deputy Director of CRS, decided that he and I should go down and join Mac and see if we could get the thing moving. I was not overjoyed with the prospect, because I have no particular affinity for danger, and Calvin, though a sweet man, had never struck me as particularly adroit in tight situations. But, he was one of my superiors, so I went.

We got to Selma late on a February night. I was the third black man to register in that hotel. It went without incident, but Calvin got a fine large room, Mac got a smaller but still sufficient room and I was given one that was so small I had to climb over the end of the bed to get to the door. All the rooms cost the same. The next morning we went to eat in a coffee shop across the street. I was the only Negro in the place. Each table had a little card on it that read, "Please forgive the inconvenience of our having to serve colored. Right now, the federal law requires it. We are sure that our representatives will change it, but for now, please bear with us. The Management." The service, if not gracious, was efficient. And the food was excellent. I even enjoyed the grits.

It wasn't hard to understand what the Negroes in Selma were protesting about. The white side looked like an ordinary American town with nice houses, paved streets with power lines connected to the homes. The black side looked like a different town. The houses were old and run-down. Some were set on cinder blocks. The streets were not paved, and there were few sidewalks. We stopped in to see Jim Foreman, one of the young leaders of the Student Nonviolent Coordinating Committee. He was a handsome dark-brown man in coveralls, and he spoke softly and slowly. He talked about Negro poverty in the area, bad health care and sick children. He told us that the city didn't provide services to the Negroes, that their lives were bare and bleak. He was eloquent, moving and heartbreaking.

Then we went to see the businessmen, who were cautious, but didn't reject our plans to get the mayor to change things. They seemed only mildly disconcerted by my presence on the team, but as time passed, they loosened up some. One of them observed that things would be all right in Selma if it weren't for "outside agitators." I bristled.

"I have seen the underside of life all over this country," I said. "I have seen it in the North and here in the South. White people are always saying that their Negroes are happy, that Negroes are responsible for their own low condition and that the problem will just go away if nobody looks at it. Well, it won't go away and it is your problem, because it's your town and you have to fix it."

Calvin looked as if he were in pain during this encounter. He looked at his shoes, at the desk in front of him, at his hands. He wanted me to shut up, because he thought I was endangering a deal that could be brought off only by large applications of sweetness and light—all us good white folks sitting around coming to agreement together. I figured you couldn't solve a problem if you didn't even want to look at it straight.

One of the businessmen said, "Well, I think we may be able to do something, but you've got to see the mayor. He's kind of skittish, doesn't like to see outsiders very much, but I think maybe I can fix it up for you to see him. He's the key."

We thanked them, agreed to call back to find out about arrangements with the mayor and left. As we were walking back to Mac's rented car, Calvin asked him, "Do you think Roger should go with us to see the mayor?"

I was furious. I outranked Mac in the agency. It was not up to him to decide where I would and would not go. If there was some question of strategy, the three of us should work it out together.

"I'm going," I said.

Mac didn't say anything, and Calvin didn't say anything, so I went. The mayor agreed to meet us in City Hall in the middle of the afternoon. When we got there, City Hall was shuttered and shut up tight. Somebody let us in a side door and then into another side door to the mayor's office. Mayor Joe Smitherman locked the door behind us. He was a tall slender man, about my age, I judged.

He had all the shades in his office drawn. It was because he didn't ordinarily conduct mayoral business on Saturday afternoon, he explained, and if people saw the shades up they might come in. I thought it was because he didn't want people to see him receiving a group of feds, especially one that had a Negro in it.

Smitherman was nervous. He had a hard time concentrating on any one point. At one time during our conversations, he had three cigarettes lit at one time. Mac and Calvin made the basic pitch. Things had to change if tensions were to ease in Selma. And the things the blacks wanted weren't all that hard to achieve. All he had to do was to announce a program of civic improvement and a timetable to implement it. Well, Smitherman didn't know. People in his part of the country were pretty set in their ways. All these demonstrations had upset them.

I noticed a little statue in the office indicating that Smitherman had been elected one of Alabama's ten outstanding young men by the Jaycees. I said to him, "Look, Mr. Mayor. The country is changing.

All of these things are going to change at some point, so why don't
you get out in front of the change. The eyes of the entire nation are on
Selma right now. If you get out in front of it, you can be a national
hero."

Smitherman was paying attention now.

"We are young men," I continued, "and we have the chance to
change our country, to make it better, to make it the way we like it. If
you began now, showed strong leadership qualities to the whole nation, there's no telling how far your political career could go."

The mayor was definitely interested, he said. He'd think about it.
He'd be in touch. He seemed genuinely grateful for our visit and for
our advice. I actually thought he'd map out a program and go with
it.

Only a few days after that, John Lewis of SNCC led a large march
over the Edmund Pettis Bridge in Selma, hard by a billboard that
said, "Welcome to Selma, the town of 100 percent human interest."
They were attacked by a horde of Alabama State Troopers who were
on horseback and wielded clubs. It was brutal, and the whole nation
saw it on television and was horrified. People all over the nation
reacted. They demanded that the federal government take action.
They picketed federal buildings across the country and they picketed
in front of the White House night and day.

Lyndon Johnson was amazed and furious. They were picketing
him. He called the civil-rights leaders in and demanded that they tell
him why people were picketing the White House. He waved civil-
rights speeches that he had made at them. He waved the Civil Rights
Bill at them and the Economic Opportunity Act. He said his little
girl, Lucy, was being kept awake at night by the noisy picketers
outside the White House.

Lee White, who was sitting along the wall in the Cabinet Room at
this meeting, took his cigar out of his mouth and whispered to a
friend: "Do you think I ought to tell him that my daughter has been
out there with a picket every night?"

The friend snickered, and the President scowled.

The federal government was paralyzed. The President literally
didn't know what to do. He ordered the Vice-President to convene a
secret meeting of his civil-rights task force to seek advice. News of
the planned meeting leaked out, and the meeting was canceled. White
House people were furious. They thought Calvin Kytle or somebody
in CRS had leaked. The meeting was scheduled for two days later

when Governor Collins was out of town. Word came over from the Vice-President's staff that I was to represent the agency and that Kytle wasn't invited. I was secretly gleeful, because Kytle and I didn't get on all that well.

It wasn't that Calvin was a bigot. He was a native South Carolinian, who had made a career as an insurance executive in Columbus, Ohio. This was his first experience in government, and I knew more about government than he did. I was amazed at how much I had learned just watching Mr. Bell. I was gaining confidence in myself—I was doing a job I thought was important, and I thought I was doing it well. I knew I was gaining a good reputation around Washington and was so impatient with Calvin's inherent fuzziness that I often cut through it. It seemed to threaten Calvin to have a strong self-confident Negro under him. He fought me and resented me, I think. It was a syndrome I was to encounter often as the years passed.

I had been told by the Vice-President's people not even to inform Calvin about the meeting, but I couldn't do that. In Collins' absence, he was in charge of the agency, so I had to tell him; not to tell him would have been insubordinate. Calvin was distressed, and appropriately so. He was, after all, Deputy Director of the Service. My growing acquaintance and acceptance in the community of relatively important domestic-policy makers troubled him, and my growing confidence must surely have seemed arrogance to him, as perhaps it was. He called Governor Collins in Selma and reported back to me with a good deal of satisfaction that the Governor had instructed him to attend the meeting with me and to take Sam Allen, our General Counsel, along as well.

The meeting was held in the Indian Treaty Room of the ornate Executive Office Building, next door to the White House. I was always impressed with that room. It was the place where President Eisenhower had held his press conferences. The tables in the large room were arranged in a large U that Friday afternoon, with the open end near the door. A small table, obviously intended for the Vice-President, was set in the middle of the gap. Calvin and I found seats at the extreme left of the bottom of the U. I sat on his right.

After the forty-five or so people, ranging from cabinet officers down to bureau and department heads, had found seats, there was a flurry as Hubert H. Humphrey arrived with his Secret Service entourage, and the aides who worked on civil-rights problems for him.

Today Humphrey was not the ebullient, talkative, good-natured Hubert Humphrey who was the idol of the Democratic party's left. He was somber, full of business. The nation was in an uproar, and the Johnson Administration was facing its first major domestic crisis.

When we had all sat down, after rising to greet the Vice-President, Humphrey outlined the crisis in terms similar to those that had been employed privately by the President and publicly by Attorney General Katzenbach earlier in the week. The demonstrators around the country were aiming at the wrong target when they attempted to force the federal government into action. No administration in history had been more hospitable to the cause of civil rights or had done more for it. Yes, there were problems in Selma. Yes, all citizens should have the right to vote, but we were working earnestly on the problems in very tricky terrain. The pitch was all familiar to me and still unsatisfactory. We had to do something, I thought, not simply tell people what we had done and that our hearts were pure.

But then the Vice-President added something that I hadn't heard before. There might be Communist influences in the demonstrations in Selma—people who sought confrontations and provoked violence for reasons other than those stated so eloquently by the genuine civil-rights leaders. There had, of course, been murmurs coursing through Washington for years about the possibility of Communist influence in the civil-rights movement. Unknown to most of us in that room at the time, J. Edgar Hoover had been convinced of it for many years and had used that suspicion to justify to Robert F. Kennedy the recommendation that Martin Luther King, Jr., be wire tapped and bugged by the FBI. Hoover had undoubtedly pumped this bilge out through his networks, and it had been picked up and talked about quietly, but Humphrey's suggestion was the highest, most authoritative version of the rumor I had ever heard. I was disgusted. Here was one of my best and oldest heroes throwing this smelly old red herring across the road to constructive action.

Humphrey concluded his introduction by saying that it was a grave time and that the President had turned to us for guidance. He said that two men from the White House staff—Lee White and Cliff Alexander—were there to take down our words and report them in full to the President. Then, turning to his left, he asked the man sitting at the end of the U on that side for his views. It was Labor Secretary W. Willard Wirtz. Wirtz was a Chicago lawyer, who had been intimately involved with Adlai Stevenson's campaigns for the presidency. He had come into the government as Under Secretary and had risen to the top job when Arthur Goldberg, Kennedy's original Secretary of Labor, had been appointed to the Supreme Court.

Wirtz was in his middle fifties at the time and wore his gray hair in a brush cut. He was one of the smartest and clearest men in town and had no lack of self-confidence. He responded crisply. The protests in Selma were for voting rights as well as about conditions in the city. It was appropriate for the people of the nation to look to the Administration for leadership. The cause down there was just, and we ought to get a voting-rights bill up to the Congress.

Then, in an obvious dig at the Department of Justice, where voting-rights legislation was being carefully crafted and recrafted, he said, "The bill doesn't have to be perfect. There is no such thing as a perfect bill. The thing to do is to get it up there and get it up there fast."

I was delighted. There was no bullshit about this guy. Justice seemed always to be dawdling to me and Katzenbach seemed more a pettifogger than a staunch defender of the civil rights of America's Negro citizens. But, after Wirtz, the level of the contributions went down. With a few exceptions, what the rest of the people said seemed to me either soggy or silly. Then, I noticed that almost every Negro in the meeting was there with a white superior. And, when called upon, the first two or three of the Negroes said simply, "I can't add anything to what Assistant Secretary X just said," no matter how lame or uninformed that superior's contribution had been.

When he had called on everybody on that leg of the U, the Vice-President realized that if he continued in that order, HEW Secretary Anthony J. Celebreeze, sitting across from Secretary Wirtz, would speak last. So, he crossed the room diagonally and called on Secretary Celebreeze and proceeded down the leg of the U to his right. In that order, Calvin would speak just before me. I had little doubt that Calvin wouldn't say what I thought needed to be said. That hint about Communism, for example, shouldn't simply be left out there hanging. In addition, the President shouldn't just reaffirm the Administration's commitment to civil rights, he should broaden it.

But, could I say those things? I had no problem about not echoing whatever it was that Calvin had to say, but I was shy. I had never been one of those people who had put his hand up in class. I didn't like to put my thoughts out there on the line. They might be stupid. I would be exposed. People might laugh at me. And here the problem was even greater. I was one of the youngest and lowest-ranking people in a room full of Administration celebrities and personages. Nevertheless, I thought somebody had to take the Administration on. The line it had pursued all week had been dead wrong.

To do what I thought had to be done would drive me far from the role I had carved out for myself, a role where I served my white superiors with diligence and as much intelligence as I could muster without making myself an object of controversy. It was part of the self-protective covering that Negro culture had passed on from slavery through the generations. It had not been hard to do in foreign affairs with David Bell. But less had been required of me then. I found the role more and more difficult in civil rights.

As my turn to speak grew near, my anxiety level reached the panic stage. My palms grew sweaty and my feet did a little dance under the table. How could I take on Hubert Humphrey? I had loved the image of the man and the slight exposure I had had to him in Washington had done nothing to diminish that love. White liberals were my hope for my people. They were the carriers of the American morality. When we Negroes convinced them of the depth of our grievances, they would sway and move the nation to full racial justice. Wasn't that the way it had worked thus far in the sixties?

And Humphrey had power. He might be President someday. He headed the Administration's civil-rights efforts. He could be a mighty ally—or a deadly foe. I couldn't take him on, could I?

But then I thought about Jim Foreman's soft but eloquent recital of the plight of the poor Negroes in the South, his recital of white cruelty, and his description of the people's need for help.

The change had been working in me for years. I had thought that educated, middle-class Negroes were a class apart. I had heard the laughter of Negro social workers about the usages of speech and the folkways of the Negro poor. I had had a tendency to equate racial progress in the country with the good things that were happening to me.

But King's marches in Montgomery had begun to change me. I saw the glorious dignity and courage of the poor people who followed him in a simple, but extraordinarily dangerous quest for the amenities that any human being ought to enjoy without thought. And now there were the words of Jim Foreman and the knowledge that all those good things that were happening to me were based, in large measure, on the readiness to lay down their lives that those poor Negroes had displayed.

Calvin was speaking now. In my nervousness, and embroiled in my inner debate, I barely heard anything he said. I thought of my mother, who had fought for racial justice all her adult life. I thought again of Jim Foreman's words and the poor people marching along nameless roads all over the South. And then it was my turn to talk.

Are you a man or a lump of shit? I asked myself before I opened my mouth. I didn't know it then, but the gap between poor Negroes and me that had existed in my mind was obliterated for good at that moment, with enormous consequences for each of the days I had yet to live.

"Thank you, Mr. Vice-President," I said when Humphrey called on me. "I agree with Secretary Wirtz. We should send a voting-rights bill up right away.

"But there's something else that needs to be said. You said something about Communist influences down in Selma."

Humphrey's jaw tightened and his hands doubled up into fists. His knuckles were white. His hostility crackled across the forty feet of space that separated us.

"I did not . . . sir," he replied, spitting out the last word.

"Yes you did, sir," I said, "and I want to tell you that if you ever went to Selma you'd know that those people don't have to have somebody tell them to be unhappy or to demonstrate. If you lived there in those ramshackle houses with unpaved streets and no sewage and no garbage collection, you would demonstrate. I would demonstrate. Everybody in this room would demonstrate and nobody, Communist or otherwise, would have to tell us to.

"And those people ought to have the right to vote. That bill ought to go up to Congress right away, and this Administration ought not to be on the defensive talking about what we've done. We ought to say, when we send that bill up there, 'We're doing this because it's right, but this is not all we are going to do. We are for full human rights for all our citizens and this is part of what we are going to do to get them, but we're not going to stop until the full job is done.' That's what we ought to say," I concluded.

The Vice-President of the United States looked at me coldly, said a curt "Thank you" and called on the man to my right. There were only a few more speakers now, and three of them were Negroes. When it came his turn, each of them was far stronger and clearer than any of the Negroes who had spoken before me. Lisle C. Carter, who by then was serving as the number-three official in the Office of Economic Opportunity, was particularly forceful, and Sam Yette, another OEO official, was moving and eloquent. He talked about his childhood in Alabama, the deprivation of the people then and the need for the Administration to act and to act now.

When the last speaker had finished, the Vice-President thanked us all for our contributions, assured us that the President would be fully briefed and then turned to the men from the White House and asked them if there was anything they wanted to add.

No, Lee White said, he didn't think so. It seemed pretty clear to him that what we ought to do was what Roger Wilkins had said we ought to do and then get on with our business.

I was barely aware of the look of dismay on Calvin's face when Lee said that. His comment rang in my ears. What I had said had impressed this White House man more than anything else that had been said. The impact on my mind of Jim Foreman, Martin Luther King, Jr., the marchers in the South, had made an impact on Lee's mind and the result of all that was to be reported to the President as he wrestled with his decision.

I was more exhausted than pleased. What I had done wasn't a brave thing, it had simply been against my natural instincts. There was no danger that I would be killed, as there was for the people who demonstrated in the South, but I had put ass on the line for principle. I had understood that the fate of poor Negroes in our country and my own were inextricably intertwined. There was really no excuse for me to exist here near the fires of American power if I didn't understand that. Dick Gregory, the great comedian and activist, used to tell a story about an older relative who watched as one Negro family after another moved into the neighborhood where his had once been the only Negro family there.

"They moved into that house over there," the old lady would report. Or, "Now they've moved in next door." Finally, Greg said he had to tell the old lady: "Them is us."

I had understood that afternoon: "Them is me."

Calvin hadn't fully understood what had transpired in that meeting. He understood, all right, that my words had been taken seriously. He understood in some fashion that I had taken on more weight and substance inside the Administration. He didn't like those things very well and was, I think, jealous of them. One afternoon, in a fit of pique, when he was telling me that I shouldn't be so abrasive, he said that I might think it was "cute" to yell at the Vice-President in a meeting, but that it wasn't becoming at all, and not helpful.

I was taking shape now as a man. Contours were emerging: pride, devotion to a cause, confidence, arrogance. The passive, reactive, timid little boy, who would never entirely disappear, was receding, and a grown, thrusting human being was emerging. It was not a man I would always admire, like or even trust. But it was a full, non-nigger persona with which men, both white and black, would have to cope and to which women, both black and white, would begin to respond. I was thirty-three.

15 President Johnson held a press conference in the Rose Garden the day after Humphrey's meeting. He made the goddamnedest commitment to the civil-rights cause I had ever heard. Voting rights were important, civil rights were important. The nation couldn't live with segregation. It had to be eradicated. I couldn't believe it. No President had talked with such abandon about civil rights and had allied himself so completely with our cause. I was elated. I told Eve about the Friday meeting and about what I thought to be a cause-and-effect relationship between that meeting and what Johnson had said in the Rose Garden. Her response was low-keyed. I was not sure she believed me. I was not sure I believed myself.

One evening early the next week the senior officers of CRS were working late in the office. We were preparing the agency's budget presentation to our House Appropriations subcommittee for the next day. Because Collins would not be there, Calvin would have to give it, and he was in a dither. He was trying to assimilate all the material about the program that we had prepared for him. His anxieties were well founded. The chairman of the subcommittee was Representative John J. Rooney, Democrat of Brooklyn. He was a powerful man, who had a well-deserved reputation for ignorance, bad temper and worse manners. He was the only member of the subcommittee who counted; he had power over the State, Commerce and Justice budgets. He was known to shred both budgets and bureaucrats.

Despite Calvin's nervousness, we stopped our labors to turn on a television set. The President had asked to be received by a joint session of Congress for the presentation of the Administration's voting-rights bill. He could, of course, have sent it up routinely with a message telling why Congress ought to pass the bill, or he could have sent it up with a special message that the White House could orchestrate in the press for special effect. But, he was going up there himself to speak to a joint session. He was putting his ass on the line.

The speech was unbelievable. He outdid the commitments to full human rights that he had made just a few days before in the Rose Garden. Optimistic as I had been about America, I never thought I would hear a President of the United States go all the way out on a limb for Negroes. He ended up by making the anthem of the civil-rights movement the battle cry of the Republic.

"We shall overcome!" he bellowed at the Congress and the nation at the conclusion of his speech. I slumped in my chair. I had had a hand in that. It was beyond my wildest expectations. I would have followed that man to the Gulf of Tonkin.

I called Bill Taylor, a Jewish lawyer from Brooklyn and an old friend, who was Staff Director of the United States Commission on Civil Rights.

"Jesus. What do you think?" I asked.

"I don't know," Bill replied. "What do you do in this business when you get more success than you can believe—when the natural enemy becomes your leader?"

I didn't know. I just knew as I returned to work on the budget presentation, that I was euphoric. The country was on the move.

Life for me was going faster now; everything about me was on the move, especially my career and my psyche. There was a cruel line that some woman uttered about Washington parties years ago. It went that men swept into a room, exuding power, with their early mistakes hanging onto their arms. My marriage was beginning to sour as people began to notice me when I came into rooms, but Eve had been no mistake. The mistake was mine. I hadn't paid attention to or taken care of my marriage. I had married a wonderful woman who was different from me. Her childhood had been psychologically hard on her in ways that mine had not been—but that is her business, not ours. Suffice it to say that her youth had left her cautious and careful, while I was becoming a river-boat gambler.

I could serve and help save a nation. I could move a President. The details of daily life didn't interest me anymore, though my five-year-old daughter and my infant son did. I was still thirty-three and had more power in the American government than I ever could have dreamed of having—much less my father or either of my grandfathers, not to mention grandmothers. I was working for America and for justice, and Eve, who hadn't worked since Amy was born, would just have to understand that and sew the buttons, cook the dinner and wash the dishes. If I came home from my monumental labors depleted, with little left for her, well, that's just how it was. A man had to do his work, after all.

The problem is not uncommon in Washington, and it is not black or white. Nor, I suspect, does it know gender these days. The business of governing is consuming. The "other" spouse must understand that we are pursuing great purposes. Personages so full of themselves—their long hours and their weariness in just causes—often become strangers to their families.

I became a stranger to Eve and she to me. I was starting to become larger than life to myself, and unfortunately to her too. She began to think that I was magic—invulnerable and without fear. I thought any expression of my fears would absolutely crush her as I began to take ever greater risks with myself and my career. We didn't talk about serious things much after the spring of 1965, although sometimes we argued fiercely. There was, of course, no thought of divorce; we were both well brought-up.

16

Despite the euphoria after Johnson's voting-rights speech, the work had to go on. So, the next morning, Calvin led his three top aides up to Mr. Rooney's subcommittee room. The hearing was crucial. CRS was a new agency and we were justifying our first full-year budget request to the subcommittee that counted. The full House Appropriations Committee almost invariably accepted what Mr. Rooney's subcommittee recommended, and the full House, in routine matters, took the figure the Appropriations Committee recommended. If we didn't like what the House did, we could appeal to the Senate, but there we had to face a subcommittee whose senior members were John L. McClellan, Democrat of Arkansas, Allen J. Ellender, Democrat of Louisiana, and Roman Hruska, Republican of Nebraska. The liberal members of the Senate subcommittee rarely bothered to show up, so it wasn't exactly a hospitable place for a civil-rights agency's appeal. That left us to the tender mercies of Rooney.

Calvin had never faced the chairman before. None of us had. We only knew of his fierce reputation, and Calvin was scared. The hearing room was small, all smooth brown wood, and unadorned by anything other than the FBI shield. It was not an auspicious symbol. Rooney was known to have a warm relationship with J. Edgar Hoover and to use FBI agents on leave to help staff his subcommittee. Hoover's antipathy to civil rights was one of Washington's major legends. Bureau agents tried to make friends with local police forces to engender good working relations with them. You didn't make friends with Southern cops in those years by defending demonstrators. Washington was full of stories about FBI agents taking

159

pictures of whites beating marchers and then doing nothing at all about it.

Calvin pulled his chair up to the narrow curved committee table, just three feet from the hunched, bald-headed gnome of a man who was Hoover's great friend. I pitied him.

Calvin identified himself and apologized for Governor Collins' absence. He explained that the President had sent the Governor to Selma. Nobody who had eyes and ears in America was unaware of what was going on in Selma or its importance. But Rooney was not impressed. He was annoyed. He said that this hearing was an important governmental function and that he hoped Collins understood that. Then he assumed the air of a man who had been sorely put upon and forced to take testimony from an underling. Instead of calling him Kytle, Rooney called Calvin Mr. Kittle. Calvin never corrected him.

Our statute said that we were to conduct our conciliation efforts in confidence—in order to elicit the trust of those with whom we dealt in ticklish situations—so, our presentation sought to describe some representative projects without identifying the names of the communities where they occurred. Rooney wanted to know the names of the places. Calvin replied that he couldn't tell him. Rooney pressed. Calvin tried to explain the statute. Rooney bullied while the rest of the members of the subcommittee looked at Calvin in amazement and those of us who had come with him squirmed in our seats against the back wall of the little room.

Under the pressure, Calvin's answers became less and less coherent. His face became damp. His soft body seemed to wilt. He would look around at us, and his eyeballs would roll aimlessly in his head. I had never seen a man so cornered, and he was fading fast. Even Rooney noticed it and, to my astonishment, took some pity.

"Just a minute," he said to the hapless, floundering Kytle. "Take a little time, Mr. Kittle. Tell us something about yourself."

I expected Calvin to sketch out his professional career, but no, he went all the way to the womb.

"I was born in South Carolina," he replied, "but my father was a traveling man. I spent some of my childhood in Georgia. . . ."

By now, Calvin's pain had become infectious. Like him or not, his staff had become totally identified with his agony, if not his wits. It was like watching your wife sneeze with a mouthful of soup at a dinner party. Would there be no end to this?

In 1934, on my second birthday, my father, Earl Wilkins (*below right*), wrote to me from a tuberculosis sanitarium: "Great things are expected of you." His early death left my mother, Helen J. Wilkins (*above right*), a dynamic professional woman and reformer, the sole provider for our family. My maternal grandmother, Amy W. Jackson (*above left*), stayed home and raised her grandson with a firm Victorian hand.

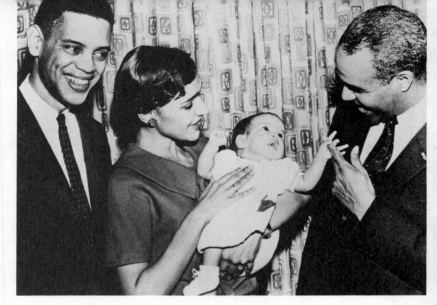

"He's got the makings of a Wilkins after all," pronounced Thurgood Marshall (*below left*) during my first week as a summer intern at the NAACP "Inc. Fund," 1955. Within two years I was married to Eve Tyler and working for a New York City law firm. In the photo above, Eve and I help tiny Amy celebrate her Junior Life Membership in the NAACP with her great-uncle Roy.

In 1962, I left New York for Washington, D.C., lured by the New Frontier of JFK and his brother, Attorney General Robert F. Kennedy (*below right*).

With AID administrator David E. Bell, a valued mentor who encouraged my initiative and agreed when it was time for me "to go out and run something." That something turned out to be Community Action, a division of the Community Relations Service established by LBJ and directed by former governor of Florida LeRoy Collins (*below right*), whom I succeeded in 1966.

WIDE WORLD

With President Lyndon Baines Johnson at the White House, 1966, just after I was sworn in as director of Community Relations Service: David Wilkins (in arms, *far left*), myself, LBJ, holding my daughter Amy's hand, and Roy Wilkins; Edna Tyler (Amy's maternal grandmother) is in the background.

I let my hair grow longer, an expression of intellectual and emotional change and a signal to my staff that their own modes of dress could reflect their attitudes.

Blacks on the move in the South—here led (*left to right*) by Martin Luther King, Jr., James Meredith, Stokely Carmichael, and Floyd McKissick—made it possible for black officials in Washington to nail down advances.

With Clifford Alexander, Jr., then Chair of the Equal Opportunity Commission, and Attorney General Ramsey Clark in Memphis the day after Martin Luther King, Jr., was killed.

Violence had barely been averted at the closing of Resurrection City in June 1968 and the Director of the CRS was drained. These years were a blur of pain and glory for me—with the pain slowly eclipsing the glory. In 1969, I left government for the Ford Foundation, to head a program specializing in experimental human service programs.

Through many years and despite acute personal travail, Representative Adam Clayton Powell, Jr., kept the faith.

In the spring of 1973, Benjamin C. Bradlee (*above left*) called his staff together and announced that the *Washington Post* had been awarded the Pulitzer Prize medal for public service for its Watergate coverage. Those who were cited: cartoonist Herblock (*left*), investigative reporters Carl Bernstein and Bob Woodward (*below*), and myself for editorial writing. Publisher Katharine M. Graham is at upper right.

The Wilkins family in 1978, on vacation in the north woods of Michigan. *Left to right:* Robert Claytor, Helen J. Claytor, Amy Wilkins, myself, and David Wilkins.

With Patricia King on our wedding day in February 1981.

By the time Calvin got to his secondary education, Rooney's eyes were glazed. Other members of the committee were staring at the ceiling or toying with their clothing. Rooney pushed Calvin back to the names of the cities and again Calvin demurred and tried to explain.

"Well there's a simple answer to all of this," Rooney said with some finality. "You don't have to tell us the names of the cities; we just won't give you any money, that's all."

Finally, it was over. Calvin had worked out some kind of compromise under which we indicated we would send up the names later on. We did, and got most of the money we were asking for.

One afternoon soon after Kytle's ordeal, I was told that the President wanted a report from me on our major-cities summer project that I was directing. He wanted it in the morning to take with him on Air Force One when he went home to Texas for the weekend. I had never met the President, who by now had firmly established his own solar system in Washington. I figured that he was only dimly aware of my existence at best and here was my chance to fix that—a report from me directly to him.

I started to work immediately. "Memorandum for the President" were the first words I dictated. Jesus! I thought. They were the most thrilling words I had ever dictated. I worked through the afternoon, went home for dinner, told Eve what I was doing and then went back to work to finish. My instructions were to prepare two memos; one was to be a two-page summary of what I had to report, and the other was to be longer, with the details. The content of what I had to report was impressive. I was determined to use the English language to make my name stick in Lyndon Johnson's mind. I labored over the drafts with no sense of time, arranging, rearranging, sharpening, polishing. Finally, I had done all I thought I could do. I got up from my desk to go home. It was five in the morning.

Eve thought I had been with a woman. It had happened occasionally in the past. I was enraged. Didn't she understand anything?— how important the nation's business was, how important I might become? After all, as I moved up, it benefited her, didn't it?

I was particularly busy that summer. My unit in CRS had recruited and deployed a person for each of our "target cities." We were directing their activities, servicing their requests and worrying like hell about riots. I was sent to Philadelphia early that summer after a

frantic call from Mayor Tate, who was afraid that his city would
blow again. Blacks were demonstrating around a segregated academy
in a black section of the city. "Rizzo must go!" they chanted about
the top uniformed officer in the Philadelphia Police Department. That
was the first time I heard the name of the man who was, in the
seventies, to make himself into the symbol of the quintessential
Northern racist mayor. Philadelphia didn't blow that weekend, but
during the course of that summer, two other cities did—Chicago and
Los Angeles. Chicago was relatively mild, but the riot in Los Angeles
made Watts a household word all over the country. That was where
people added burning to rioting and looting and where the police
began killing looters. It was also where color films of the rioting taken
from helicopters went on all the TV news shows. America was to be
different for a while.

Watts hit Washington like a thunderstorm. Everybody responded
in stereotypical fashion. Sam Yorty, the Mayor out there, began
blaming Washington. President Johnson told everybody in Washington to shut up, not to fight back. Bureaucrats sat around looking at
each other and saying that something must be done, but nobody had
the foggiest idea of what to do. Everybody wanted to go out there,
not simply because that was where the action was, but because to be
sent to the place of national crisis meant that you were important. In
Washington, it was very important to be thought important.

One afternoon, while the embers were still smoldering in the black
sections of Los Angeles, Governor Collins called Calvin, George Culberson and me into his office. Collins had been promoted to Under
Secretary of Commerce. No new director of CRS had yet been
appointed—Calvin was acting. Culberson, a quiet, dignified white-
haired man of about sixty, who had a long professional history in
local race-relations agencies, was director of conciliation in the
agency and the number-two man. I was number three. When we got
there, Collins was standing in the middle of his large office with his
longtime assistant, John Perry, a former newspaper man from the
South. Collins made his hands into fists and crossed his forearms over
his chest.

"Promise you'll never tell what I'm about to say to you," he said
solemnly. We all promised and looked solemn, although I thought the
gesture was pretty funny.

"The President is sending me to Los Angeles," he said. "I'm taking
John with me, though the President wanted me to go alone, but I

finally talked him into it. We're leaving right away. But I'm going to need more help than that. I want George and Roger to come with me. George knows about conciliation and Roger knows about federal programs. And, Calvin, you have to stay here and mind the store."

Calvin looked as if the Governor had hit him in the balls with a baseball bat, but he acquiesced. He couldn't do anything else. Collins said nobody was to know that George and I were going, that we would have to take a later plane and check into a different hotel and that he would get in touch with us. Under no circumstances was the White House or anybody else in CRS to know what was going on. When we left the meeting, Collins and Perry headed for the airport to take a nonstop flight to Los Angeles. I went back to my office and called Eve to tell her that I was going. Then I read yet another clipping where Sam Yorty was blaming the federal government for the riot.

As I collected all the clippings and information about Los Angeles I could lay my hands on, I stewed about Yorty. His charge against us—that we had caused the riot through bureaucratic lethargy—was dumb and cheap. Yet, we couldn't fight back, because Johnson didn't want to get into a pissing match with him. While I was still stewing, a wire-service reporter called to check out a tip that Yorty had refused to become involved with our special crash program. I knew that Johnson had a phobia about leaks. When he said he didn't want people talking to the press about something, he meant it. People who defied such orders often learned to regret it. But I was furious at Yorty, so I decided to take the risk. I told the guy he couldn't use my name, but could call me a "well-informed federal executive." He agreed and I told him that we had mounted a crash program for "target cities" and that the only two cities that had declined to come into it—Chicago and Los Angeles—had had riots that summer. I modestly declined to attribute a cause-and-effect relationship to the facts, I just laid them out. Then I went home to pack.

The Washington Star was on the stands by the time George Culberson and I got to National Airport that evening to take our plane to Chicago. On the front page there was a brief story about a "well-informed federal executive" telling how Yorty had refused federal aid at the beginning of the summer. I had never been a confidential source before. Though they were cloaked in anonymity, my words on the page seemed to scream, "Roger Wilkins did this." I was scared shitless.

When George and I got to Chicago to change planes, I picked up a late edition of a Chicago afternoon paper. This story was fuller. It had more of me in it, but it was still anonymous. I was really terrified by now. In Los Angeles, they played the story big. Everything I had said was in there. The phenomenon of seeing my words flung clear across this huge country and given greater and greater prominence was an eerie experience. I suspected that the story had made some television and radio news shows as well. The magnification of my voice frightened me almost as much as the possibility of Johnson's wrath. The power to reach people, to influence them was disproportionate to the source. I was to have many more occasions to worry about the disproportionate power of my printed words, but, I needn't have worried about Johnson.

Shortly after George and I went to California, Calvin, perhaps emboldened by the interview with the anonymous federal executive, gave a personal interview to David S. Broder, then a reporter for *The New York Times*. Calvin was much more explicit about the program, Yorty's refusal to come in, and the casual connection was much more strongly suggested. At first I was furious with him for—as I saw it—trying to ride to glory on my program, with which he had nothing to do. Calvin and I *really* didn't get along by this time. But in retrospect, I'm pretty sure that Calvin signed his death warrant in the Johnson Administration with that interview.

In California, our mission was fuzzy. George and I stayed holed up in a nondescript little hotel for most of the first day, occasionally taking calls from John Perry. It seemed that our mission was to induce the State of California, the Los Angeles County Board of Supervisors, Sam Yorty and the representatives of Los Angeles' poor people to enter into an agreement to establish a community-action agency so the government could begin putting money into the city through the poverty program. That may not sound hard, but in Southern California in those days, nothing was easy. Every politician had a knife out, and every politician was protecting his own back.

We seemed to have endless meetings to no particular purpose. I had no role except to keep the Governor company when he needed company. He quickly decided that he didn't need George, so he sent him home. I think he kept me simply because the problem involved Negroes. I was a Negro and might conceivably say something useful one day. Collins talked to the Mayor, to County Commissioners, to Negro ministers and to representatives of the Governor's office. We seemed just to be spinning wheels. One day early in our trip, we drove out through South Central Los Angeles and Watts. I got my first taste of ashes and urban rubble. The racial feelings were bitter. At the corner of 55th and Central a Negro mother was walking her six- or seven-year-old son across the intersection. He saw the white people in the car.

"Burn, baby, burn," he said. "Burn the white motherfuckers."

"Shush!" his mother said, glancing furtively at us as she cuffed him on the head.

On a Sunday afternoon on about our fourth day out there—I had told Eve I would be home in a day or two, because that's what Collins had told me—the Governor told us that Jesse Unruh, California's Democratic boss, was coming to see him. He wouldn't need us, he said, but we should stay in John's room right next to his and wait for his call. So we waited. We watched a baseball game on television and waited some more. Hours passed and we couldn't figure out what was taking so long, but we had been told to wait for the call, so we waited. Finally, the phone rang and John answered it.

"But Governor . . ." he said.

"But Governor . . ." he repeated.

John's face got beet-red. He held the phone away from his head and I could hear the Governor's voice going a mile a minute delivering scalding invective. Then John put the phone at his head again.

"Yes sir. Right away, sir," he said.

"What the fuck was that about?" I asked.

"The sonofabitch is crazy," John said. "He's furious at us because his meeting with Unruh was over hours ago and he couldn't find us."

"But shit," I said. "We were right here, next door, just where he told us to be," I said.

"You try telling him that," John said. "He wants us right now."

We scurried next door to find the Governor in a rage. Where the hell had we been, he wanted to know. We were irresponsible, he informed us. There were high matters to deal with, and we had gone off on a lark, he asserted. All the while he was looking at John and talking to him. His Southern-white liberalism wouldn't let him tear the hide off a Negro like that, I figured. So, like a man, I let John take the heat. After all, he was this crazy bastard's assistant, not me. But I surely couldn't figure out why he was so agitated and so irrational.

John finally got a chance to explain that we had spent the whole time waiting just where Collins had told us to wait. Though Collins heard him, I didn't think he believed him, but at least he let the matter drop. Then, suddenly, he told us that we had the deal pretty much wrapped up and since we had been working awfully hard, John and I should go out for dinner and relaxation. We couldn't believe it, but we were anxious to escape. We had spent every waking hour at the Governor's beck and call and it was good to get away from him.

We got in the car John had rented and went to a Japanese restaurant on Sunset Boulevard. Afterward, we went to a strip joint called the Pink Pussy Cat and saw some sad, scrawny women take most of their clothes off.

Later, about ten-thirty, as we were heading down Wilshire Boulevard back toward the Sheraton West, I noticed a police car dragging along beside us, just a little bit behind our car. John was driving carefully, but the police trolled along with us at light after light. I mentioned it to John, and he drove even more cautiously. Then, as he signaled for the left turn that would put him in front of the hotel, the lights atop the police car began flashing and its siren went on.

I got cold chills. One thing we had learned out there was that the Los Angeles Police Department, or "LAPD," as it was affectionately called, was not fond of Negroes. Its members had killed about thirty looters and many of them called their nightsticks "nigger sticks." Most of the Negro complaints we had heard were about police brutality.

"Come out of the car with your hands up," the officer, who had approached the driver's side with his pistol drawn, said curtly.

I came out of the passenger door with my hands up. An officer in a hard helmet stood next to the rear wheel with a shotgun at port arms.

"Put your hands on top of the car and spread your legs," he ordered.

I did as I was told and he frisked me roughly, giving me a pretty good chop to the balls as he did.

"Okay, turn around and show me some identification," he said. His voice had menace in it. He was white. His partner was white. John and I were dressed in suits and ties. I showed him a laminated card that identified me as Assistant Director of the Federal Community Relations Service. It had my picture on it and my height, weight, eye and hair colors.

"Show me something else," he said. The identification hadn't placated him. He seemed angrier now. I wondered how John was faring in his interrogation around at the back of the car. I didn't like white cops. This one, I hated, but I produced my Department of Commerce laminated identification card. It also had a picture and the physical description.

He held his gun level at me while he studied the card.

"Show me your driver's license," he growled.

This prick was really out to hassle me. I had given him plenty of identification, we hadn't been breaking the law, I was well dressed and I hadn't been driving. These bastards had just stopped us because they had seen a white man and a Negro man riding together down Wilshire Boulevard. He had no right to point that gun at me.

"I wasn't driving," I said.

"Show me your goddamn driver's license," he barked.

"I wasn't driving and you've seen plenty of identification," I snapped. "You know that person pictured and described on those cards is me. You know I work for the federal government."

"Well, I work for the government of the City of Los Angeles," he puffed, gun still level at my stomach. "Now show me your driver's license."

"I wasn't driving and I'm not going to show you another goddamn thing," I said.

He was moving the gun threateningly when his partner came from the back end of the car and said, "Well, well, we've made a hell of a mistake. Do you know who we have here?" He was being jocular and chummy.

"I don't give a fuck who they are," my cop said, glaring hatred at me, gun still in his hands.

His partner put his arm around him, turned him around and walked him off a bit, whispering in his ear. They came back in a couple of minutes. My cop had his gun down now. John's cop, still jocular, said, "It's just a mistake, fellas. We got a call about a burglary committed about an hour ago and the description of the perpetrators fit you two to a T. You can go now. Sorry about the inconvenience."

We got in the car, then, both shaking with fear and rage. Neither of us had ever been spread-eagled before and I had never had an enraged man point a gun at me before. In the car, the brush with death filled me with fear. My body was still, but everything inside me seemed to be shaking. I got John to ask the jocular cop to give us their names and badge numbers before they drove off.

When we told him, Collins was pissed, and he mused that the story would make the front page of every paper in America if we put it out. I said no, because Johnson didn't want our trip there publicized. We made a complaint to LAPD Chief Parker, and the guys were suspended for a while. Later we saw their report. They had repeated their story about the burglars and had reported that the men they had actually stopped were the Under Secretary of State and Roy Wilkins. We got a good laugh out of that and I couldn't for the life of me imagine what a conversation between my Uncle Roy and George Ball would be like.

A few days later, my one Negro friend in the LAPD told me that *my* cop had shot and killed a Chicano kid who had taken a pair of sneakers from the broken window of a store that had already been looted.

"He's a psycho," my friend said after I told her the story. "You're damn lucky you're not dead."

A couple of mornings later, Collins summoned John and me to his room early in the morning to watch TV. We couldn't figure out what that was about, until President Johnson appeared on the screen making announcements. A lot of people were in the East Room of the White House with him, among them, Associate Justice Arthur Goldberg and Representative James Roosevelt, the California Congressman, for whom my friend John Schuyler worked and who had come close enough to Yorty in the previous Los Angeles mayoral election to scare the pants off him. Goldberg was coming off the Supreme Court to become United Nations Ambassador, and Roosevelt was coming out of Congress to go to New York with him to be one of his high assistants with the rank of ambassador. How did Collins know that was going to be on TV, I wondered. What did this have to do with us? Why would Goldberg do such a foolish thing?

Later, John and I put it together, a never-confirmed speculation. Yorty's price for signing the community-action agreement was for the President to get Roosevelt out of his hair. He didn't want to run against him in the next election. The President was going to do the Goldberg deal anyway, and that classed up the event enough to sucker Roosevelt into it. The deal was struck the afternoon when Unruh came to see Collins. Collins knew it was a pretty smelly thing to do to Roosevelt, but Unruh was a tough guy. The bargaining had been hard and ugly, and that's why Collins had been so furious and irrational when it was over. And that was why he had said the deal was wrapped up and gave us the night off.

That afternoon, a press conference was held at a cavernous hall downtown to announce the deal. Representatives of all the parties were on the stage. Collins was up there too. I was horrified. So was John.

"I tried to tell him not to go up there, but he wouldn't listen," John told me.

The announcement was made, questions were asked, television cameras whirred, and still cameras clicked. When it was all over, Collins came out walking along in deep discussion with a distinguished looking white-haired man with a mustache.

"Who's that?" I asked John.

"Gladwin Hill of *The New York Times*," he answered.

"Oh, shit," I said.

Collins apparently thought that once the deal was struck, the President's admonition that he stay out of the newspapers had lapsed. Even from a distance, I knew better than that. The next morning, the story was on the front page of the *Times* with quotes from Collins sprinkled liberally throughout. That afternoon, Collins was ordered home.

I wasn't sorry. I had come out for a day or two with shirts and underwear for a short stay, and I had been there for more than a week. Eve was in a rage. I was on the phone with her almost every night. She thought I was loitering about Los Angeles fucking somebody. Besides, David, who was one, had diarrhea and she had the flu herself. I was sorry for her, but I was angry too. I hadn't seen a woman privately since I had come out there, even for lunch. And besides, Los Angeles was a national crisis. I was sorry that she and the baby were sick, but damn, wasn't that what wives of busy men had to cope with? All in all, though, I was glad I was going home.

But Joe Califano, by now President Johnson's assistant for domestic affairs, called me while I was packing. A new team headed by Deputy Attorney General Ramsey Clark was coming out to put the federal programs into place. There needed to be a link between the first team that had been out there and the second. I was it. I couldn't go home. President's orders.

Shit, I thought. How am I going to explain this to Eve?

17

Collins had been persuaded by a Negro minister to attend a Negro community meeting near Watts on his last night in town. John Perry had already gone home, so Collins and I went alone. The hall was filled with angry Negroes. The agreement on the design of the new community-action agency had shortchanged them, they thought. They waved the black-red-and-yellow booklet of guidelines issued by the Office of Economic Opportunity and screamed that there was a requirement for "maximum feasible participation" of the poor in the poverty program. They accused Collins of totally ignoring them, their needs and the program requirements. As speaker followed speaker, the fury in the room built. It wasn't just rhetoric. These people *had* been ignored, and they were enraged. It was the first furious racial confrontation of the sixties I had seen. I learned a lot that night.

I realized at once that I had made a grave mistake. I had not seen any of these people before. I had been satisfied to permit Collins to meet only with the ceremonial Negro leaders who were brought to him by powerful whites. I hadn't understood that there was a great tide of Negro humanity under the thin layer of visible leadership, and that they needed to be dealt with as serious human beings and with concern and courtesy.

These were the poor people, the voiceless people, the invisible people. They were also smart people, the world's foremost experts on their own oppression. And we had ignored them. As they flailed us, I thought of Malcolm X, and I understood him better than I ever had understood him before. Despite my commitment months earlier in the Indian Treaty Room, I had permitted a federal team to ignore these people. I had accepted a white-liberal agenda for our work. But I was not a white liberal. I was a black man, and I could forget that only at great peril to my sense of myself and to the profound disadvantage of people like those in this room.

Malcolm had sometimes talked about "blue-eyed devils" and had described whites as "enemies." Even standing there in front of people whom, in my ignorance and thoughtlessness I had betrayed, I did not think white people were all devils or all evil. But I learned that night, as Malcolm had taught, that any black who wanted to count for something decent in this world had to nurture his blackness.

He had to be *black*, not Negro. I had often thought that the gulf between middle-class blacks and poor blacks was virtually unbridgeable. That, I now knew, was a luxury that no honorable black could afford. Our community, broken and distressed as it was, had no need for the kind of stupidity I had lived with for most of my life. Even good white people, who were not devils, could guide you away from the true interests of your people because they had interests and agendas of their own or were just plain ignorant about us.

"We're going to get you for what you did to us," one furious man shouted at Collins, who was visibly shaken by the tidal wave of rage engulfing us. "And we're going to get that little darky you brought with you too."

I don't think my face changed, but inside I shuddered. Collins' face had gone dead white. But we did get out of there, and Collins and I agreed that the pounding they had given us had been amply deserved. Collins flew home then, and I went back to the hotel to wait for Ramsey Clark and his outriders.

Clark was a tall, lean man about three or four years older than I was. He was quiet and had a soft Texas accent. I went with some others to meet him at the airport and he asked me what I thought. I told him that if he did nothing else, he had to meet some poor Negroes, and the sooner the better.

"You won't know what this riot was all about unless you do," I said.

"Well," he said, dubiously, "we can't meet everybody who wants to meet with us."

I insisted. He said that maybe we ought to meet the next morning at breakfast to talk about it.

Dumb sonovabitch, I thought. Thinks he knows all the answers. Gonna come in here and meet with the politicians and all the rich people and then design some programs for the poor people.

I went to bed angry that night, but got up determined to get Clark to see some poor people. I pressed him at breakfast and then pressed him some more. "I can set up a meeting for tonight," I said. He looked at me for a long time, and then he said, "Okay. Go on and set it up."

The meeting was held in the basement of a church in South Central Los Angeles. About 150 people came and sat in folding chairs neatly arranged in rows. There were two other principal members of Clark's team—Andrew F. Brimmer, an Assistant Secretary of Commerce, who was later to become the first black member of the Federal Reserve Board, and Jack Conway, a former UAW official, who was Sarge Shriver's deputy at OEO. But this night Ramsey had them and his staff assistant and me sit in the audience. He sat in a lone chair facing the people, with a reporter's notebook in his hand.

The meeting was a virtual replay of the meeting Collins and I had had with the people near Watts. City services were terrible in their communities, the people said. The police were brutal. The bus service was so bad that old people had to take two or three buses to get to a hospital. There were no health facilities in their community. There were no state employment offices in their community. No Social Security offices. No nothing. And the community-action program had been designed without their participation.

There was rage and eloquence in that room. Ramsey asked questions politely. He wrote down what the people said. He followed up their statements with probing questions. He didn't get flustered by the rage. It went on hour after hour. He was never angry or self-righteous, never lost his manners or his interest.

I was deeply moved. I had never seen a powerful white man take poor black strangers seriously before. As the hours passed, I began to love him. It was the beginning of one of the deepest and richest friendships of my life.

Ramsey learned so much from that first meeting that he asked me to set up two more for him during the rest of the week. Between these events, the whole team worked to put together a package of programs that would help alleviate some of the problems in the poorest black areas of the city.

I returned to Washington, where my marriage continued to erode and my career to escalate. I spent a couple of weeks working in Ramsey's office helping to put together a report on what we had seen and learned in Los Angeles. At the same time, a commission had been formed in California under the chairmanship of John McCone, a former CIA Director, to study the root causes of the riot. Andy Brimmer, Ramsey and I worked hard to produce a report that would explain as fully as possible why Los Angeles had blown. The desolation in poor black communities is such an old story now, most Americans seem to have filed and forgotten it. It was a new story then. We probed and analyzed the virtual total breakdown of urban systems in black ghettos. We examined problems in health, education, credit, transportation, police protection and other service-delivery systems.

During this time, Ramsey was even more impressive than he had been in California. He was anxious to get the story out. He remembered virtually everything he had heard in Los Angeles—the names of the people at the meetings as well as what they had to say. He was more sensitive to the problems of poor blacks than I imagined any white man could be. He took their humanity every bit as seriously as he did that of his white colleagues in the Department of Justice.

When the report was finished we sent it over to the White House. After a few days, Joe Califano told us that he thought it was a wonderful piece of work and said that Abe Fortas had read it and thought it was one of the best things he had ever read. I was elated.

A couple of days later word came that McCone had thrown a fit when he heard about our report. It would pre-empt the work of his commission. He would quit if we were published. That was the end of our report.

During the fall, CRS just limped along. The President left the directorship unfilled, and Calvin was in the uncomfortable position of acting as director without any visible sign of support from the White House. Morale in the agency went to hell. People reasoned that if there had ever been a situation where the agency should have been involved, Los Angeles had been it. Yet, it had been virtually ignored as an institution. One assistant director working first for the Under Secretary of Commerce and then for the Deputy Attorney General did not constitute a ringing White House endorsement of the Service or its competence. The President's failure to appoint a director didn't help matters any.

Then word came that the President intended to shift the Service from the Department of Commerce into the Justice Department. That was the last blow. Justice wasn't trusted in the civil-rights community. It had too often seemed an impartial arbiter between two equally

valid competing views in the South when the basic civil-rights assumption was that we were right and the Southern bigots were wrong.
The disdain of the Civil Rights Division of Justice for our field men,
who were ardent, if sometimes amateurish civil-rights advocates, was
well known. Attorney General Nicholas DeB. Katzenbach, a former
University of Chicago law professor, seemed bloodless and academic
when he approached civil-rights issues. People in the Service suspected that Nick wanted to get CRS into Justice and then bury it.

I was disconsolate until I heard that Ramsey had been put in
charge of the shift. And I had always had my doubts about Commerce as an appropriate home for the agency. One day Governor
Collins had arranged for Dr. King, Andy Young and some other top
SCLC officials to come to Commerce to lunch with top people there
to try to persuade them to get top businessmen around the country to
push hard in their communities for civil rights.

King talked, Andy talked and some other SCLC people talked. The
Commerce people said very little, but when they did they talked a
different language. They were unmoved by the black men's plea. King
and his people were puzzled. I was dispirited. There was to be no
help from the top of Commerce.

There was one other good reason for the move. However tepid his
views were on civil rights, the Attorney General at the cabinet table
had a voice of authority on civil rights. The Secretary of Commerce
was out of his field there.

So, we stumbled along in limbo in the fall of 1965, doing little,
waiting and unhappy. Then Calvin decided to oppose the President
on his priorities in the housing program. Some of his views got into
the papers and he was consequently invited to lunch by Rowland
Evans and Robert Novak, the syndicated columnists, who were not
deemed friends by the White House. I urged him to turn the invitation down. He said no, that he would go and that he wanted me to go
with him. I said I didn't want to go and wouldn't unless he made it an
order. He did and I went. Calvin talked a great deal at that lunch
about how misguided he thought President Johnson's urban priorities
were. I sat there silent, glum and depressed—just one block from the
White House.

Several days later, after the column had appeared, quoting Calvin,
I came back from lunch to find several urgent messages from Calvin's
assistant, Harry Wilkinson.

"The White House called this morning. Calvin's finished. He's to be out of the building by close of business today. You are in charge of the agency for the time being," he told me.

I called Joe Califano at the White House, and he confirmed Harry's information. Calvin's demise had been swift, sure and brutal, and I was to muddle the place along until the President decided what to do with it. Then Joe asked me if I knew Nick Katzenbach. I did, but not well. He suggested I get to know him. Eventually Collins took me over for a ceremonial meeting with the Attorney General. Nothing of great consequence was discussed. I was being looked over.

A couple of weeks later, I went with Ramsey to a White House meeting to review the CRS budget for the following year. Halfway through the meeting, Nick Katzenbach, Cliff Alexander and Harry McPherson, a special assistant to the President, joined us. They had a secret. They looked at me with their mouths closed, but they all looked like they had just been chewing canary feathers. I was sure the decision had been made. I was to be the new director. The first director had been a mature Southern politician. Now Johnson was going to a thirty-three-year-old Northern urban black. The notion was breathtaking.

That night Eve and I went to a private preview of the newest James Bond movie, *Goldfinger*, at the Motion Picture Association screening room on I Street. I had carefully left the phone number with Joyce Davis, our baby sitter. Sure enough, during cocktails, Jean Firstenberg, our hostess, announced excitedly to me that the Attorney General was calling me. At Washington parties, that kind of phone call did wonders for your stock.

Nick told me that the President had decided to appoint me Director of CRS on his recommendation. I thanked him and said I'd do the best I could. He then asked me how my commission should read—what state should it say I was from. In my new exalted status, I immediately made a major blunder.

"New York," I said, "because that's where I came from before I came down here and that's where I'll go back to when I finish up here.

"And," I added, "I want Bobby Kennedy to introduce me at my Senate confirmation hearing." Kennedy, by now, was the junior Senator from New York.

Now, what did I say that for? That was *tsuris* I didn't need. I had heard that Johnson hated Kennedy. I was soon to learn just how deep that hatred ran.

Before I was through talking to Nick, Cliff Alexander came up to me and said that Joe Califano was on the line. Joe asked me some personal details about my background and then said, "Stay on the line—right on this line."

Since I had only one line in my hand, I knew what that meant and sure enough, in a second, the voice of the President of the United States boomed at me:

"Roger, this is Lyndon Johnson."

"How are you, Mr. President?" I managed.

Then he talked to me—read, probably—about all these wonderful things he had heard about me and that my uncle was a great American and the country was in trouble and this was the most difficult job he had ever given to a Negro. It was all heady stuff, and all I could blurt out was, "I'm with you, Mr. President."

Not much cool there. The next morning it was confirmed on the front page of *The New York Times* in a story under Tom Wicker's byline. The President had chosen me as the new director and when the Service was shifted to Justice, I would be an Assistant Attorney General of the United States, the first black to achieve that rank. It was the best and the worst that ever happened to me.

A few days later, Nick Katzenbach told me that there were too many Presidential appointees from New York and that I should be from the District of Columbia. I knew what that meant. The President didn't want Bobby Kennedy introducing me to the Senate committee. I said, "Okay," but with a mule's ignorance, I decided to have Kennedy introduce me anyway. D.C. had no Senators, so I had a hundred to choose from. I chose Kennedy.

At about that time, Dr. Robert C. Weaver was sworn in as the Secretary of Housing and Urban Development, the first black to achieve cabinet rank. While he was being sworn in in the East Room of the White House, Johnson told my Aunt Minnie, Uncle Roy's wife, that he was going to have that kind of ceremony for me too.

I was embarrassed. Cabinet officers get sworn in at the White House. Assistant Secretaries or Assistant Attorneys General get sworn in at their boss's offices in the departments. Johnson was obviously going to make me an exception for Roy's sake and for the political mileage he could get out of appointing a black. During my Washington years, Roy and I had kept our distance. I didn't want to be subsumed by him—I still wanted to make my own way and find my own identity. He understood and wanted it that way too, for his own reasons. He had enough problems in the movement without people draping his nephew's blunders around his neck.

But, I needn't have worried. During the days before my confirmation hearings, I got several gentle reminders from the White House personnel people that I was from the District of Columbia. I ignored the warnings. The last one came as I was sitting down in the witness chair for my hearing. Kennedy was already settled in the chair to my right. Senator Magnuson, the chairman of the committee was ready to pound the gavel when I was told that I had an urgent call from the White House and had to excuse myself. In that call, I was reminded for the last time that I was from the District of Columbia. I said I understood that and went back to take my seat just in time for Kennedy to begin his introduction. Astonishingly enough, his hand was shaking under the table as he introduced me to the committee.

I was confirmed in due course and then there was a deafening silence from the White House about the swearing-in. I was in limbo. I was confirmed, but still the Director-designate because I hadn't been sworn in. Finally the Secretary of Commerce and I agreed to end the impasse by scheduling the ceremony for his office and notifying the White House. Word came back quickly from Jack Valenti that it would be held in the White House. I was asked for a list of my guests. I put Kennedy's name on it. Word bounced right back that my list was too long, that the ceremony was going to be in the White House theater—a little thimble of a place—and that I had to cut some guests.

I cut some guests but left Kennedy's name on the list. The list was still too long, I was informed. My stubbornness, foolishness and loyalty to the memories of Camelot had limits. I cut Kennedy's name and the names of some people Johnson wanted for political purposes. Word came after that that the list was just fine.

On the day of the ceremony Johnson made a wonderful speech about what a terrific fellow I was. It had been written by Jack Rosenthal, Nick Katzenbach's public-affairs assistant. The President was warm and gracious to my mother and stepfather, to Eve, who held the Bible, to Aunt Minnie and to Uncle Roy. He was captivated by Amy, who was six and beautiful, and he even tried to be nice to David, who cried the whole time. But he would not speak to me in my brand-new blue suit. Not a word—just a stony stare. It was scary as hell.

A few nights later, Thurgood Marshall, who was Solicitor General

of the United States, a neighbor, and an old friend, called me while
we were having dinner.

"Come over here right now," he said.

"But Thurgood," I said, "I'm eating my dinner."

"Right now," he commanded.

So I walked over to his house, and he looked at me hard and
asked, "What the hell did you do to the President?"

"Aw, I didn't do nothin' to that sonovabitch," I said.

Thurgood, who had known me since I was a child and had known
my uncle for even longer, and who had once said to my mother about
me that "he has the Wilkins arrogance," looked levelly at me for a
long time.

Then he told me a story. He had been sitting in his office that
afternoon when the President had called and told him to get over to
the Oval Office right away. Thurgood said he thought from the
urgency of it that some major case before the Supreme Court had gone
sour. He expected a major meeting, but when he got there, the President was in his office alone. The conversation went like this:

PRESIDENT. You know Roger Wilkins?
MARSHALL. Yes.
PRESIDENT. Well goose him in the ass, then. [*Making an upward circular
motion with his right hand, middle finger extended as he said it.*]

That was the meeting and that was the message the Solicitor General of the United States was to convey to his young friend.

Lucky for me, I appeared on an obscure local television talk show
a few Sundays later. A foreign journalist was expressing skepticism
about the President's commitment to civil rights. I lashed back at him
with some heat in defending a commitment that I was sure was there.
I didn't think I had done so well on the show, and Ben Holman, an
Assistant Director of CRS, who had gone with me to the studio,
agreed. I shrugged, figuring that nobody would see a local talk show
that ran at eleven-thirty in the morning.

But Johnson saw it. He called me and told me that I was the
TV star of the Administration—a regular movie star. He told me
again at a meeting at the White House. Then he invited Eve and me
to a state dinner for Indira Gandhi.

Eve looked ravishing that night. Many women spend $500 or
$1,000 for dresses when they are invited to a state dinner at the

White House. Eve had bought a $13 piece of material and fashioned it into an evening gown. She was the best-looking woman there. When we went through the receiving line, Johnson grabbed my hand and pumped it like he was drawing the last bucket of water from the well.

"This is the movie star of my Administration," he told the Indian Prime Minister. "A regular movie star. And so is his daughter and so is his beautiful wife here."

All my sins were forgiven, at least for a time.

18 The next three years were a blur of pain and glory. I grew as a bureaucrat, a figure in the Department of Justice, a factor in the civil-rights movement and a quasi-public person. But the unraveling of the private person, which had already begun, gained momentum in ways that I neither understood nor saw. Some things in the next few years were easy. It was easy to decide to promote the ablest man on the staff, George Culberson, to deputy. It was easy to decide to hire the brightest and most committed people we could find and to make ours one of the most integrated staffs in town. It was even easy to deal with the black men who wanted to coerce me into giving them big raises, figuring that I would be embarrassed if black people left the staff just when I took over.

"You are a grown man," I would say. "You have responsibilities to your family and yourself. There's no way I can stand in your way if you see a way to improve your career."

Most guys stayed after hearing that little speech. The one who left cried as he went out the door and asked if I would leave his spot open for him in case he didn't like it where he was going. I told him, "No."

It was even easy dealing with Chairman Rooney. I had learned from watching Calvin. It was pretty awesome sitting in that chair right opposite the Chairman. The Chairman was bad enough, but the chief of staff who sat next to him with a lap full of potentially embarrassing clippings, which he would slip along under the table to Rooney, was pretty frightening. But I remembered the year before.

"What was the most important thing your agency did last year, Mr. Wilkins?" the Chairman asked.

"The summer program with ten target cities, Mr. Chairman," I replied.

"Name the cities," he demanded, quick as hell.

And I gave him each and every one of them. He had convinced me the previous year that there was no holding back from the man who had the money. Mr. Rooney just smiled as I reeled off the names. He and I never had a bit of trouble after that. But, I had learned from David Bell too. He had never said anything. I had just watched him testify. The committee might be dumb, uninformed, rude and abusive but the Administration witness had to be polite, well informed and cooperative, no matter what the personal cost. It wasn't fair, but that was what you had to do to get the money, so I did it.

Finally, Ramsey made it easy. He, as Deputy Attorney General, stood as a buffer between me and those whom I could not abide. I heard Nick talking one day about John Lewis, a young black minister who served as one of the early leaders of the Student Nonviolent Co-ordinating Committee. Nick acknowledged that John was a brave man, but indicated in a joking way that he thought John was stupid. I had always seen John as a quiet and powerful moral force for good. There was no question about his courage, proved time after time in Southern campaign after Southern campaign. And his intelligence wasn't the point—and wasn't insufficient in any event. He was risking his life day after day to make America a better place and I despised the high and mighty Attorney General of the United States for sitting in his office and making fun of somebody who I thought was a truly great man.

Ramsey kept us apart, and after CRS had been in Justice for a few months, the President sent Nick over to State to be Under Secretary there. I was ecstatic. Ramsey became Acting Attorney General, and after Johnson had tortured him for several months, he appointed him Attorney General. Ramsey agreed with what I was trying to do with the Service and told me, "Just go ahead and do it. If you have problems, come and see me."

That was the hard part, turning the CRS into the kind of agency I wanted it to be, an advocate for poor blacks, Chicanos and Puerto Ricans in the big cities. That was not exactly what Congress had told us to do. But, then, what the President was telling us to do wasn't exactly what Congress had told us to do either. Congress had wanted us to hit a hot spot, work intensively on the crisis and then go on to the next one. That was essentially a Southern model, but the action had turned North and the Congressional notion was too simplistic for big urban centers. The President, on the other hand, wanted us to quell riots. That didn't make too much sense either. With no coercive or financial powers, it was not possible to make people do what you wanted them to do.

What we could do was to speed up the process of change wherever we could get a handle on it. We could find the kinds of community leaders that had finally come to my attention in Los Angeles, help them define their goals realistically and then get them the kind of hearing from the powerful people in their cities that they would never have gotten without our help. We could go into cities in the wake of a riot, when the city fathers in business and politics were deeply scared, and persuade them to put together local efforts to help the minority poor that they would never have considered without a riot. Finally, we could act as the advocates within the government for the pleas of poor people for help.

There were some in the government, including John Doar, the legendary head of the Civil Rights Division in those days, who wanted us to be the eyes and ears of the Justice Department in the black ghettos. I resisted his suggestion and others like it, and I was successful because Ramsey always backed me up.

As those three years passed and black radicalism increased in the cities, it was hard enough for CRS operatives to overcome the suspicion that they were "agents" of the Justice Department. Some of our guys were in enough danger as it was. To accede to John's notion would have put them in greater danger and would have been a betrayal of the people we were trying to help. Moreover, most of the staff, militant and dedicated as they were—or *became*, as a result of the deprivation that their work made them see—would have rebelled if such an order had come down from me or even from Ramsey.

There was no precedent for an operation such as that which George, Ramsey and I decided to mount. There was no book to follow. We had to grope our way, improvising from a solid base of conviction and a growing base of experience as we went along. It was intangible work, virtually unquantifiable and therefore sometimes unsatisfying. To our wives, Congress and dinner companions, it was like describing smoke. Yet we were involved with some of the most decent, most earnest and noblest people in America. And, our cause was surely just.

The agency was set up to deal with crises. It was clear that the major racial crises were in our big cities. Riots were a symptom of the crisis. But the real crisis was the shameful deprivation of poor non-white people who lived in those cities. Nobody liked riots, especially the blacks who got killed in them. The only way to stop them was to end the deprivation and the desperation of the poor.

But the hardest part of those three years was me. I started on that job when I was thirty-three, and I left it when I was thirty-six. I had grown up slowly and carefully in white America. I had studied how it operated, learned what it would tolerate from a black man and what it expected and I controlled myself to fit the mold that I thought was expected. I was a black man with a law degree, excellent credentials, a beautiful wife and two children, and I spoke standard English fluently, sometimes eloquently. My commitment to poor black people was clear. But my commitment to white America was still strong, and my personal sense of deprivation was powerful.

I had spent thirty-two years with my head firmly in white America. Though I had lived among black people and had spent some of my life in black communities, the symbols of power, beauty and goodness that I had grown up with were all white. Human fullness was white. The symbols of foolishness, degradation and shame were black. I had a full nose, thick lips, kinky hair and brown skin. I could be like white, but I could not be white.

Black shame was all around me. My parents never talked about slavery or my ancestors, for example. Images of Africa were images of backwardness and savagery. Nigger was bad, sometimes despicable, while white was good. Our bodies betrayed us, and the darker and more African our bodies were, the greater the betrayal. Once, when I was a little boy, I said to my mother after a friend of my parents left the house:

"Mr. Bledsoe is black, isn't he mama."

"Oh," she exclaimed. "Never say anybody is black. That's a *terrible* thing to say."

Next time Mr. Bledsoe came to the house, I commented, "Mama, Mr. Bledsoe is navy blue."

Even if our parents tried to counteract it, we internalized a substantial portion of what white America told us about ourselves. When I was a young man, I would try to avoid going to the toilet on airplanes because of the shame I felt because I was not white. I didn't want white people looking at me, the intruder, on the airplane. Neat, tidy and clean though I was, they wouldn't sit next to me unless every other seat was filled.

And then, there were the personal encounters. The minute you walked into a place, you knew a chain reaction went on in the white person's head. You might hate the unfairness of the judgment, think it was irrational and stupid, but you knew it was being made. Although I would cringe at it, a little piece of me accepted the judgment and craved approval. And in some practical sense, that approval was necessary—to get into schools for example or to get jobs.

So, for us there was a rejection of our intrinsic values as human beings, a rejection of the strengths and glories of our African and American past. We threw out most of what was good inside us and put on the whitest face we could.

It was psychological destruction of an indescribable magnitude. Psychological genocide. White America did this to us, but most of us were its unwilling accomplices.

People who didn't understand that, which means most white people, didn't understand what was happening when Stokely Carmichael started talking about black power, when people began saying that black was beautiful, when black kids in the movement began telling whites to go work on the racism in their own communities, when Negroes began calling themselves black and when blacks began wearing their hair long. But Stokely and the other young intellectuals in the movement knew what they were doing. They were purging themselves of all of that self-hate, asserting a human validity that did not derive from whites and pointing out that the black experience on this continent and in Africa was profound, honorable and a source of pride.

Simple as it now seems, in those days it was hard to tell people that. Some older blacks didn't want to hear it, and a lot of whites didn't either. In the summer of 1966, when the words black power were on the lips of most of the black youth in the nation, I became directly involved in my uncle's business for the first and only time. I was scheduled to speak at the NAACP convention, but I flew out to Los Angeles early in an attempt to persuade Roy to moderate his keynote speech in a way that would not alienate him from most of the black activist youth in the country.

The text of his speech contained a pretty full attack on those who espoused black power. My uncle and I had a long talk about it, and I persuaded him to tone down a lot of his rhetoric. But he still wasn't comfortable with the notion of black power. He thought it sounded a call to violence, so before he gave his speech, he restored a line I thought was gone. When I heard him utter the words, "Black Power means black death," I knew he had lost the youth. Roy knew how to grab a headline and he got it across the nation. I was sorry about it, but his vision was different from mine. I think that line more than any other made him the target of the black youth and radical communities.

Another time, in the fall of 1967, after the Newark and Detroit riots, there was consternation at the White House about the pervasive mood of blackness sweeping black communities around the nation. There was a suspicion in some minds that the riots resulted from a conspiracy of black-power advocates. In order to prevent misgivings growing into panic, I wrote a long memorandum attempting to explain the new wave of black thinking. I showed it to Ramsey, who told me it had made things clearer for him, but that he didn't think they would understand it at the White House, and it might work against me. I went around Ramsey then—the only time I ever did so in my years at Justice—and sent it to Vice-President Humphrey, who was still nominally in charge of the government's civil-rights effort.

About a week later, I got it back with a note from one of his assistants saying that the Vice-President had found it "enlightening" but that he did not think it a propitious time "to send it across the street"—that is, across East Executive Avenue, from the Executive Office Building to the White House. So much for that effort to explain to the President and his top aides something about an important intellectual and psychological transformation that was going on in the country.

Much of the new black thought settled inside me, but rested there alongside some lessons from white America that couldn't be purged. The sense of deprivation, the sense of exclusion would not go away, but lingered, like a ghost, from my adolescence. In the late sixties, I had money, power and prestige. I certainly didn't want to be white anymore—the movement had touched me deeply enough to get rid of that—but I had a keen sense that something was missing. Perhaps it was the ease and assurance that, in so many white people, seemed to flow from the absolute knowledge that America was their country.

One tangible aspect of that deprivation was white women. My sexuality had been formed amidst the images of unobtainable white

women. Like most American boys of my age, I had fallen in love with
Elizabeth Taylor when she appeared in *National Velvet*. The sex
goddesses of my adolescent fantasies were white women like Janet
Leigh, on the silver screen, and closer to home, the nubile young
beauties who ran up and down the halls of Creston High School.
"This is perfect beauty," white America seemed to tell me, "and you
can't touch one bit of it."

By the time I was thirty-four, I had been with one or two white
women, and I knew they weren't magical, but the taboo against interracial sex made it more tempting. Gnawing memories of adolescent
deprivation and the powerful images of the white goddesses remained.

And so it was in the summer of 1966 during the riot in Chicago
that I invited a tall slender young white woman with long dark hair to
my bed. She was a member of my staff and had long pretty legs that
looked wonderful in a mini skirt. We were in Chicago at the same
time in the same hotel by chance, not by design. Her name was Mary
and she was a graduate of Smith College and we mainly talked that
first night, but it was a beginning.

Mary meant a lot of things to me. There was wonderful sex, youthful, exuberant and free. There was her whiteness and the fact that at
twenty-two she wasn't all that much older than the inaccessible girls
from high school. And she came as close to being a hippie as a
government employee could come, so she reminded me of those wonderful images I had seen in Greenwich Village so many years before
—white girls with long flowing hair walking with black men—couples
who I imagined had the ripest and most abandoned sex. Her youth
was especially important. Something was happening in the generation
behind me and I didn't understand it. There were the Beatles, the
marijuana and Bob Dylan. There was an expanding consciousness
that seemed better than the constrictions I had grown up with. Mary
put me in touch with all of that.

Finally, Mary did that thing for me that young women often do for
older men who leave their marital beds for them. She told me I was
brilliant, wise, courageous and strong. My ego was reflected off her
slim white thighs. The relationship started as a sexual lark, but it
deepened and would not end. It was not exactly a shot in the arm for
my already troubled marriage.

Sexual and romantic conflicts were not the only ones I had in those
days. As young black intellectuals clarified their thinking, I found
their views of America increasingly persuasive. For the first time

white America had turned a hard eye on the poor black ghettos of the nation. I walked through those ghettos and saw the degradation and the despair there. Mothers would tell me of their yearnings for the education of their children. And I saw the children wasted by drugs in their early teens. I saw families of six or eight living in one dirty room. I heard police officers speak of these people with contempt. I listened to the young blacks asserting that America was ripping off their lives. One thirty-two-year-old woman with four children said to me, "Yeah, mister, my children run the streets. My husband can't get a job—only part-time work sometimes. He can't read so good. So I do day work. It's hard cleaning up dirty houses, and when I get home I don't have no energy. I can't control those children, only feed them the best I can."

I would pack the hurt from such encounters—and there were thousands of them in those three years—'way inside me. There was nothing else I could do with it. And when I heard young blacks argue that American democracy and liberalism did not reach this human pain in the middle of their cities, I agreed with them. When they said blacks had to band together to take over some control over their own lives, I agreed with them. When they said that white America had been vile and evil to blacks over the centuries and that the evil still continued, I agreed with them.

When they called for revolution, I understood the emotional release it gave them, yearned for that kind of release myself, but ultimately disagreed with them. Black power might not mean black death, but black revolution in America would surely mean black suicide.

I yearned for the release and the comfort of living and working in an all-black environment. Yet I knew I could best help such people right where I was, close to the top of the American government, even though I was painfully aware of the inadequacies of my own programs and their meager resources against the monumental need and aware too of the sluggishness of even the Great Society in responding to those needs. Some of the strongest and clearest black people in ghettos across the nation often distrusted my staff and me because we were middle-class, and they suspected us of being spies for the Justice Department. We were outside the mainstream of the intellectual ferment going on in the black community in those days. And we were always in conflict, because our instinct and our honor demanded that we serve the interests of the poorest black communities, while our roles as government employees put increasing pressures upon us to maintain order and calm in the cities.

The conflict was real and excruciating. I let my hair grow longer after the fashion of the times, as an expression of intellectual and emotional change and as a signal to members of my staff that their modes of dress could reflect their attitudes, especially since they needed to work with some pretty tough, ideological community groups. Soon we had people with long Afros, dashikis, beards, even necklaces with animal teeth dangling from their necks. White staff members were at a disadvantage in the fashion switch, but they did the best they could.

The change didn't bother Ramsey, but the rest of the government was dismayed. Over at the FBI, Hoover and his people seemed convinced that we were dangerous radicals and tried to undermine us at every turn. A report submitted by a member of Doar's Civil Rights Division on a meeting he attended at CRS started, "It looked like a black power meeting," the report began. I guess it did. But serious business was transacted at both.

I tried to reconcile the intensity of the feelings we got from the streets and the government's insistence on order by arguing that the riots were a contagious phenomenon born out of oppression and desperation. Order could be achieved either by massive repression or a powerful and sustained effort to achieve justice for the people of the ghettos.

The madness of the conflicting demands practically split my skull apart on successive days in May 1967. We were trying to help a black community group in Washington sponsor a new nonprofit housing development a few blocks from our offices. One day, after lunch, I walked through the blocks where the group was proposing to clear and to build. The neighborhood had originally been full of small brick townhouses, but it was crumbling now. Partly inhabited houses stood among houses that had completely crumbled and others that were disintegrating. Preschool children were playing in rubble-strewn lots littered with cans and bottles. A drunk in ragged Army clothes was urinating in a doorway, and apparently able-bodied men who had no work were standing on a corner talking and passing a bottle around.

The next day I attended a meeting in the White House that the President had ordered to plan for the summer in Washington. He didn't want a riot in the town where he presided. The Secretaries of

HEW, Labor and HUD were there, as were the Attorney General and two of the commissioners who then ran the District of Columbia. When we began talking about plans and problems, one of the commissioners held up the latest edition of *The Washington Post*'s Sunday magazine, *Potomac*. It had a picture of the hottest disc jockey in town on the cover wearing a sleeveless sweatshirt, dark glasses and a goatee. He worked for a soul station, called himself Moon Dog and broadcast hot soul music and citizen complaints. He was big and very black.

"This is the kind of problem we have," the commissioner said. "This man inflames the people with the things he says on the air."

The commissioner apparently had never heard of the First Amendment.

Lisle C. Carter, Jr., by now Assistant Secretary of HEW, answered him.

"Wait a minute," Lisle said. "The people don't have to be told what their problems are. They know what the problems are. And their problems are the real problems we've got to deal with in this city."

There was no way I could bring the human devastation I had seen the previous afternoon into this room in the White House. I tried, and got blank stares from most of the people there. From Ramsey I got a look of understanding.

Working for the government created other problems as well. One late spring night in 1967, the executives at the Department of Justice and their wives were invited by the Supreme Court to a reception at their splendid courthouse. Eve and I found it difficult to deal with the glitter of that place that night. The intractability of inner-city problems and the refusal of most of white America to understand the human pain weighed heavily on us.

That night, even the glamour of the Supreme Court held little enchantment for us. The large room where the reception was held was elegant. The hors d'oeuvres were splendid and the Justices and their wives were gracious. Ramsey was laconic and wry, and his wife, Georgia, witty and charming. But apart from Eve and me there were only two other people in the room who were not white, Cissie and Thurgood Marshall.

Somebody suggested that a group of us go out to dinner, but Eve and I didn't feel like it. Instead, we drove across the bridge to the forgotten part of town called Anacostia, where a lot of poor blacks live. Even the river that separates them from the rest of town is mostly forgotten. Everybody knows the Capital is nestled by the Potomac, but few people outside Washington ever heard of the Anacostia. We drove up a street, now called Martin Luther King Jr. Boulevard, toward St. Elizabeth's Hospital, where Ezra Pound was kept after World War II, then angled down off to the right to look at a deteriorating public housing project I wanted to see.

The place was grim, the houses little better than lots of barracks-like structures one sees in the black townships in South Africa. We ended up on an unpaved dead-end street, where ragged, barefoot children were playing among the rocks by the roadside. As I twisted in my seat to turn the car around, I was struck by what I saw.

"Jesus, Eve, look at that."

She looked and gasped. What we saw was a panoramic view of official Washington, the grand monuments, the floodlit Capitol and RFK Stadium, lit up for some official event. It was the most breathtaking view of the city I had ever seen. It was where we had just been drinking with the Justices of the Supreme Court and the administrators of the Department of Justice and their wives. It was where I worked and moved easily with the men and women of power. It was the view these ragtag children saw every night—a world utterly foreign to them; a world that seemed a thousand miles away.

Not everything seemed bleak to me in those days. Some things were good, like going to meetings with Lisle Carter. He was a tall, dark lawyer from New York, whip-smart, who didn't suffer fools gladly. His way of dealing with unpleasant meetings was to destroy his adversaries with incisive comments, walk out or go to sleep. My standard for judging black people in government was whether I trusted them alone in a room full of powerful whites. Lisle passed that test. So did M. Carl Holman, a poet and former college professor, who was then serving as Deputy Staff Director of the United States Commission on Civil Rights. And, so did Ed Sylvester, a former Detroit businessman, who headed the Labor Department's Office of Federal Contracts Compliance. Lisle, Carl and Ed were all several years older than I and personal friends.

After I became Director of CRS, the four of us started meeting informally at lunch to discuss what each of us was doing and to determine whether there was any way in which we could help each other. Once this paid off handsomely, when Carl got word in the late spring of 1967 from his friend Richard G. Hatcher, a black City

Councilman from Gary, Indiana, that the Democratic machine against which Dick was running for mayor, was stealing him blind.

Carl called me on a Saturday afternoon and asked if Justice could help. I called Ramsey, who got Hoover to send a squad of FBI agents into Gary to investigate the election fraud and sent Jim Turner of the Civil Rights Division to oversee the investigation. The machine was stealing all right, and the feds stopped them dead in their tracks. As a result, Dick was elected mayor of Gary at about the same time that Carl Stokes was elected mayor of Cleveland.

Dick ultimately became the first black president of the United States Conference of Mayors.

The first time Hatcher came to Washington after his election, he came over to see me, and we talked about his plans for Gary. Then, I took him over to meet Ramsey. On the way, I asked him, "How do you get on with the black militants in Gary?"

Hatcher gave me a long look and said, "We *are* the black militants."

I knew I would like the man.

There were other collaborations among the four of us over those years, and my professional relationships with them deepened into family relationships. Our wives all liked one another, and mainly they liked all of us as well. We spent many evenings together, and we always spent New Year's Eve together. I had the best social time of my life among those quick, intelligent, effective black people. There was warmth, laughter and shared values.

I was more comfortable in that group than with black professionals, who spent a lot of time thinking about making money. And though I had a lot of white friends, I was more comfortable with these people because I didn't have to screen anything out. It was a time of self-conscious blackness and with them my blackness lay on me in soft, warm folds.

The summer of '67 was grim. The big riots that year were Newark and Detroit. The looting was fierce. The killing of blacks was fiercer. There was a lot of indiscriminate shooting. Innocent people were shot in their apartments. Richard Hughes, a liberal Democrat, was Governor of New Jersey. Though moderate Republicans like William M. McCulloch of Ohio and even conservative Republicans like Everett Dirksen of Illinois had been enormously effective in getting the civil-rights bills passed in 1964 and 1965, I believed that it was the liberal Northern Democrats who would lead the country to racial justice.

Yet, despite clear proof of indiscriminate killings of some blacks during the rioting, Hughes issued a statement that seemed to condone the police methods. Law and order must be preserved, he said, lawlessness had to be stamped out.

On the heels of my immersion in the black-consciousness movement, Hughes's statement showed me the face of white America naked and ugly. The problem wasn't regional discrimination or prejudice. It was racism all over the country—deep, thick and pervasive. Order was more important than social justice. The psychological distress, economic well-being and inanimate property of white people had a higher premium than the lives of poor blacks. When racial problems came North, the liberals there could be every bit as racist as Southern bigots. But Northerners were more oblique about it, more defensive, cleverer and, thus, far harder to deal with. And there was no North to push the North as the North had pushed the South. Our moral leverage was evaporating as quickly as Northern racism was exposed. I was sick and disgusted with the America that I now saw more clearly than ever before.

Sometime after the Newark riot and before Detroit, Georgia Clark, Ramsey's wife, went home for a visit to Texas. Eve and I had Ramsey over for dinner alone one night, because he was tired and we thought it would be good for him to have a quiet dinner at home with friends.

Something happened that night that Eve and I could not control. We started talking about Newark, about the deaths of the black people there and the wanton use of force against them. We talked about our sense of betrayal, our sense of outrage at America. The more we talked, the more intense Eve and I became about our judgment that the late fifties and the early sixties hadn't changed America after all. This generation of white Americans just couldn't take the humanity of poor black Americans seriously. Our words came tumbling out of us.

We were not attacking Ramsey as he sat on our couch sipping a brandy. He agreed with much of what we were saying. He was just the catalyst for the expression of our despair. It took about two hours before it all ran out of us. Then we had a little more brandy and sat there quietly, suffering in the gloom of our vision of America. About eleven, Ramsey rose to go home. We watched him walk across the quiet street. The tall slender frame of the Attorney General of the United States was stooped. His head was down and his jacket thrown over his shoulder. He walked that way until he reached his old Oldsmobile convertible, got in and drove away.

Eve and I felt terrible. We had invited our friend over for a peaceful evening. Instead, he had received a load of our pain. We felt sorry for him. We felt sorry for our country.

19 A few weeks later, on a Sunday night, Jim Madison, the head of the conciliation division of CRS, called me to say that his field man in Detroit had reported that trouble had erupted earlier that night when a cop had shot a black at an unlicensed drinking place, or "blind pig," in the middle of the black section of town.

"How bad is the trouble?" I asked. "How widespread?"

"We don't know that yet," he replied.

"Well, report it to the situation room at the Department," I said, "and let me know what else you hear."

I heard nothing more from him before I went to bed that night, but at about five the phone rang. It was Ramsey.

"We've had a pretty bad night in Detroit. Governor Romney has been on the phone with the President several times asking for federal troops. The President wants us at eight. We'd better meet in my office at six-thirty."

Warren Christopher, the brand-new Deputy Attorney General from California, was in Ramsey's office that morning, as were John Doar and George Culberson, my deputy. As in so many other crises, we sat there in that small corner office where Ramsey worked, just behind the grand one he used for ceremony, with insufficient information to make the judgments we knew had to be made. George and I reported the fragmentary information we had collected from the field. Widespread burning and looting and shooting, a few deaths. We didn't know how many or which side they were on.

Ramsey had similar information. In addition, he had the President's accounts of his conversations with Governor Romney. Though

194

Romney wanted federal troops, he was unwilling to make the necessary declaration that the situation was beyond the state's control. What he hadn't said, of course, was that he was planning to run for President on the Republican ticket in 1968 and he didn't want such an admission on the record. The President, on the other hand, didn't want to use extreme measures unless emergency conditions really warranted them.

I stood up and rubbed the head of Lincoln that Ramsey kept on a window sill as I often did when we were squeezed into an awful corner. There's got to be some better way to run a country than this, I thought as I stared down at the gathering morning traffic at the corner of Tenth and Constitution.

When it was time to go over to the White House, Clark, Doar, Christopher and I went. Culberson went back to the office to try to collect more information on what was going on in Michigan. We were directed to the Cabinet Room and a couple of minutes after we settled in our chairs, the President came in with Robert McNamara, Secretary of Defense. The President went over the information he had and described his dealings with Romney. He wasn't very charitable about the Governor's behavior so far, which he characterized as a bit hysterical and substantially uninformed. During the middle of the meeting, Cyrus Vance, who had just resigned as Deputy Secretary of Defense because of a serious back problem, walked into the room.

Then Johnson went around the room and asked everyone for an opinion. I thought we shouldn't send any troops in until we could get some high-level civilians on the ground to see what was really going on. Others thought the President couldn't wait that long for fear of inviting the charge that he had fiddled while Detroit burned. After a little more discussion, the President announced that he was going to send a civilian team in to head the operation. Vance would lead the team, which was to include Christopher, Doar and me, from Justice, and Dan Henkin, a press spokesman, from Defense. He would send the 82nd up to Detroit, but they would be stationed outside the city, at the Michigan State Fair Grounds, until we civilians decided that they were needed.

Then Johnson delivered a fierce monologue about what he didn't want to happen. If the troops were ordered into Detroit, he didn't want them walking around with loaded guns unless their commanders thought there was a sufficient emergency for them to carry them. No bayonets. No bullets.

"I don't want my troops shooting some ni—" he glanced sharply at me and stopped. Then he started again, "—some pregnant woman."

Then he pulled a phone from its cradle by his chair under the cabinet table, handed it to Ramsey and had him call Governor Romney to inform him of the plan.

As we were being dismissed, the President touched my arm, looked at me for a long moment and then said, "Have a safe trip, Roger."

It was his way of saying that he was sorry that he had almost said "nigger" in front of me. I was amused, because I was sure it was one of the mainstays of his uninhibited vocabulary.

At the door of the Cabinet Room, John Doar and I paused to use the phone there to start the arrangements for our trip.

"Who are you taking with you?" John asked me.

"Nobody," I answered. "I already have a man there. If I get there and find I need other people, I'll send for them. Who're you taking?"

John mentioned three names. I knew the first two, but I asked about the third.

"Who's Jesse Queen?"

"Don't you know Jesse Queen?" John said. "He's a Negro, *but* he's soft-spoken and he takes orders well."

I just looked at him and then turned to the phone to tell my office that I wouldn't be in that day.

Smoke was rising from Detroit when our plane flew over it. There were plenty of flames licking high as we came down the freeway on our way to police headquarters at 300 Beaubien.

"It's a great town if you're a fire buff," Christopher told Ramsey later on the phone.

We then met with Governor Romney, Mayor Jerome Cavanaugh, the head of the Michigan National Guard, and the police superintendent. They didn't know what to do. They had no moves planned. We were astonished to learn that the Guard Commander had thousands of troops in reserve, despite Romney's assertion that federal troops were needed. What was the level of violence, we wanted to know. Well, they didn't exactly know. The fire department was reporting a high incidence of sniper fire. So was the National Guard. It was dangerous out there. A blanket curfew had been imposed. Liquor stores were closed for the duration. They didn't know what else to do. I had never seen as impotent a group of men in my life. It was clear that the whole thing was in our hands.

When the troops got on the ground, Cy decided to bring them
into town to patrol the east side of the city, freeing the Guard and
the local and state police to handle the west side, where most of
the action had occurred. What we needed most at that point was
information more reliable than the hysterical reporting of the fire
department about the level of violence in the city. I was the community-relations guy. I was the guy with a field man on the ground. I
was it. My job was to go out and get the smell and the feel of the city,
find the significant blacks, take their temperature and forge the links
between our group and the black community.

The pattern of our days was set. We would get to our headquarters
in the police department by seven-thirty, eat lunch at our desks and
go back to the hotel at about five-thirty. We'd clean up and reassem-
ble in the Vances' suite—Gay Vance was there with Cy—for cocktails. Since bars and liquor stores were closed, Mayor Cavanaugh had
provided Cy with a good supply of booze. Then we'd have dinner
together in the hotel dining room. At about seven-thirty, we'd leave
Gay Vance—a gracious, charming and attractive lady—and go back
to work at headquarters. Everybody but the duty man—we took
turns at that—would break at twelve-thirty or one to go back to the
hotel to sleep. The man on duty had to stay at the office all night to
handle any emergencies and to wake the rest of us if all hell broke
loose.

The cocktail-dinner break became a ritual. It was the one oasis in a
long and grubby day. We always did it together. We all looked forward to it.

When I made my rounds of the city at night, it was eerie. There
was no traffic on the streets, and the city was very dark, because the
National Guard and the police had shot out many of the street lights
for cover. There were armed checkpoints all over the city. There is no
experience quite like being stopped at gunpoint by armed and uniformed men in the middle of an American city. I would ride with my
field man, who was also black, in his civilian car. As we approached
checkpoints I would pull out my leather-encased Justice Department
identification, hold it out the window and call out "Department of
Justice." I was not going to risk being shot by a scared kid with a rifle
in his hands.

I saw no evidence of the sniping that the fire department talked so
much about. Occasionally, there were gunshots, but invariably, when
we checked them out, we found they came from some trigger-happy

Guardsman who had just shot out a street light. There was danger in
the streets, though, and it came from the forces of law and order. I
quickly learned that I was safest on the east side of town where the
disciplined Army units were on patrol. The west side was downright
frightening. The Michigan Guard was made up of white country kids
who didn't know the city and were scared of blacks. If they hadn't
been so dangerous with loaded rifles in their hands, they would have
been ludicrous with those baby faces under their battle helmets.
Moreover, Michigan State Police were pretty rough customers, and
the Detroit Police had a long-standing reputation for brutality against
blacks.

One night I was riding out on one of Detroit's main west side
arteries, with two black staff members, when a convoy of seven state
and local police cars went screaming by in the opposite direction.
They screamed at us to get off the streets because there was sniping in
the direction from which they had come. We headed for the sniping,
but didn't see any. Finally, we decided to cruise down a side street to
see what was happening when the convoy caught up with us, lights
flashing and sirens screaming. They flagged us down at the corner of
a large avenue, just as an old white Buick with a black man and
woman in the front seat and two black children in the back turned
into it.

"Come out of the car with your hands up," somebody shouted at
us with a bullhorn.

The three of us came out of the car, credentials out, hands up
shouting, "Department of Justice, Department of Justice."

We found ourselves surrounded by more than twenty armed white
men aiming loaded rifles, shotguns and pistols at us.

"You're curfew breakers. What the hell are you doing on the
streets?" a rough voice demanded.

"Department of Justice, Department of Justice," we kept yelling.

The blacks in the other car hadn't come out immediately, and I
saw and heard cursing men go in after them and the ripping of
clothing. The cops hadn't responded to our identifying shouts and
shouted obscenities at us behind raised rifles.

Thirty-five years old and dead at the corner of Grand River and
Joy Road, I thought. My father had died when he was thirty-five.

After the longest, stillest moment of my life, the cop who was in
charge understood what we had been yelling. He motioned for his
men to lower their firearms and stopped the others from snatching the

people out of the Buick. It turned out that the man in the Buick had a special pass to be out at night because he did essential work at a G.M. plant, and his wife and two children had picked him up there to take him home. The officers apologized to us and told us they had to be careful, but advised us to get off the streets because they were so dangerous.

We got back in our cars, and the old Buick, which had a broken spring in the rear, went on off down Grand River, spewing exhaust fumes in its wake.

"Motherfuckers," I heard the man yell as his car limped on down the street. When I got back to headquarters, and made my report, including that incident, the three-star general who was in charge of the troops looked at me for a long time and then said, "Jesus, Roger, you're lucky to be alive."

Echoes of Los Angeles. The Detroit police killed a lot of black people during the Algiers Motel incident that night.

Detroit was full of black consciousness and intellectual ferment in the summer of 1967. A number of the major black thinkers lived there. One of them was the Reverend Albert Cleague, who started as a Congregational minister, but who by that time had renamed his church the Church of the Black Madonna. He was one of the black people I thought it important for Vance to meet if he were to have a full understanding of what was going on in the city. It was ironic that Cleague, one of the major apostles of black consciousness, was a very light-skinned man with light eyes.

Vance masked his surprise when Cleague met him at the church door. The two men were cordial to each other and got on easily. After they had talked for a while about the problems of blacks in Detroit, the minister offered to show Vance through his church.

"What denomination are you?" Cleague asked.

"Episcopalian," Vance replied.

"Oh, it's about the same," Cleague said.

Some black-consciousness thinkers felt that whites had done a terrible psychological thing to blacks by giving us a white god. During the riot, somebody had gone onto the grounds of a white monastery located in the heart of the black west-side area and had painted the face and hands of a statue of Jesus a deep, rich brown. Cleague chatted about such things with Vance as he headed him down the aisle toward the back of the church. When we got there, Cleague turned us around. Since I knew what we would see, I watched

Vance's face. It blanched and his mouth dropped open.

Above the altar in this church, where a stained glass window might have been, was a huge oil painting of a Madonna against a background of deep blue. She was holding a baby. Both she and the baby had Africanoid features and were shiny black.

"Very impressive," Vance managed to say.

"Yes, I think so," Cleague said.

In addition to restoring order, we tried to put a group of prominent and powerful whites together with a representative group of black leaders so they could begin a process of improving the lives of the poor blacks in the city. Everybody told us that the key to such an effort was Walker Cisler, then head of the Detroit Edison Company. Cisler was said to be the mover who made things happen in Detroit.

One afternoon, after John Doar and I had spent the day at the federal prison in Milan, Michigan, interviewing people who had been arrested during the rioting, we learned that a meeting with Walker Cisler had been arranged. He had invited Mr. Vance to the Detroit Yacht Club for dinner.

"The Detroit Yacht Club?" I asked John, who had taken the call.

"Yes," John said. "I thought you ought to know that."

The Detroit Yacht Club was notorious among Detroit blacks. It didn't allow them to eat there.

"We're going to dinner there tonight. I thought you ought to know that," John repeated. "And I think Mr. Vance wants you to call him at the hotel."

So, I called Cy at the hotel. He asked how it had gone at the penitentiary, and I told him. He then said he'd see me back at the headquarters later in the evening. Everybody else in the group went to Cisler's dinner at the Detroit Yacht Club—as part of a mission that had black people, their lives and their aspirations, at the center of it all.

But many good things came out of Detroit. Cisler and some others helped form the New Detroit Committee, which still exists as part of the National Urban Coalition; it has done many constructive things in the city over the years. The auto companies opened up a number of jobs and instituted innovative training programs. Henry Ford became deeply involved over a long period of time in the affairs of the inner city. After a while, the embers cooled, the troops went back South, and we returned to Washington.

On one of our last nights in the city, John Doar and Warren

Christopher decided that they wanted to join me on my nightly
rounds to make sure that the city was now as calm as I had been
reporting it to be. We got a driver and a car from the federal motor
pool and set out. The driver, who was black, was clearly reluctant to
be out on those eerie streets at night, but he had no choice. Christopher
sat up in front next to him, and Doar sat behind him. I sat in the back
behind the driver.

At the first checkpoint we reached, the Guardsman approached the
car from the passenger side and he could see Christopher and Doar.
He asked politely for their credentials and passed us through quickly.
At the next checkpoint, the Guardsman approached from the driver's
side, and he could see only two blacks. Perhaps because the car had
federal motor pool markings on the door, perhaps because there were
white men in the car, and perhaps because I was tired, I was sloppy. I
didn't have my credentials in my hand as he came up to the car and I
reached inside my suit pocket for them as he was standing there.
Suddenly I felt cold steel on my neck.

"Don't move another muscle," the Guardsman said.

I froze with my hand in my pocket. Doar and Christopher quickly
identified us, and the man removed the muzzle of the gun from my
neck. Months later Christopher remarked at a meeting how different
it was when the car had been approached on the black side from how
it had been when approached from the white side. I was glad he remembered.

On one of our last nights in the city, when things had calmed
down, I arranged to have dinner with my college roommate Dr. John
Loomis and his wife, Suane. I met them at the home of one of her
affluent relatives, who was also a doctor. The major north-south arteries on the west side were typical slum-commercial and had been hit
very hard in the arson and the looting. Yet a number of the east-west
streets between these major arteries contained some of the finest
housing then available to black people. Suane's relatives lived on such
a street only a few blocks each way from some of the major devastation areas. Before we went out to dinner, the relatives, John, Suane
and I discussed the riot. It was going along quietly when the lady of
the house, who had many diamonds on her fingers, turned to me and
demanded:

"What is it that *they* want?"

I looked at her for a long time. This was the kind of middle-class
Negro that I'd been running from all my life. Diamonds on her fin-

gers, Cadillacs in her garage, and brown skin stretched across her strong boned face. What do *they* want?

"Jobs and dignity, I guess," I replied.

"Well, there's not much dignity in burning and looting," she replied haughtily. I closed my eyes. I had to go through this with white people all the time.

"No, I suppose not," I said without opening my eyes, "but I guess there's also not much dignity in sitting there quietly while the society chokes the life out of you and your children."

20 Shortly after I got back from Detroit, I was at a meeting at the White House when somebody came in and said the President wanted to see me. The President was alone in his office. He motioned me to a chair and asked me how it had been in Detroit. I outlined what we had seen, what we had done and what I thought. I didn't tell him about the Detroit Yacht Club. He asked me what the government should do. I said I thought it was mainly education and jobs. He asked whether it had been as dangerous as the newspapers had said. I said not for everybody, but yes, for blacks. Then I told him about Joy Road and about the gun muzzle on my neck.

He looked at me for a minute and then got up and led me over to the French doors leading to the Rose Garden. We stood there for a minute looking out toward the golf green that President Eisenhower had put in. The President put his hand on my shoulder and still didn't say anything. Then he looked down at the floor. It was pock-marked by Eisenhower's golf spikes.

"Look what that sonovabitch did to my floor," he said.

I laughed and he smiled, and he said quietly, "Thank you, Roger." And I said, "Thank you, Mr. President," and then I left and went back to my meeting.

I wasn't much of a Johnson fan then, but I liked him a lot that day. I didn't like him because of the war. I had wavered on it for a while during the period when he was the President "who would finish what Lincoln had begun." He had been my President then, driving toward the kind of America I had dreamed of and he had put me in a position to help him do that. In that frame of mind, I accepted his

judgment that the security interests of the United States required that
we stay the route in Vietnam. Wiser friends of mine, including Eve,
didn't buy that for a minute. By the fall of 1967, neither did I.

The first major Washington peace march was held that fall, and the
government's nerves were frayed. Ramsey summoned those of us who
would be involved in managing the demonstration in one way or
another to a meeting late one Saturday afternoon in September. We
weren't going to approach this march the way we had approached the
March on Washington in 1963, he said. Yes, we'd provide them with
a line of march, but no portable johns, no amenities, nothing to make
them comfortable.

"We won't be brutal, but we may elbow them in the ribs a little
bit," he said.

I couldn't believe my ears. This was my pal, Ramsey, the decent
guy in the government, the guy Johnson was furious at because he
wouldn't put Rap Brown and Stokely Carmichael in jail. I thought his
attitude was all wrong. These people were citizens. They had a right
to express themselves. The government ought to be self-confident and
open about it. I stewed about it all weekend, and on Sunday night I
called him at home and asked if I could see him in his office first
thing Monday morning.

I told him that I had been appalled by what he had said on Saturday. I didn't think the government's approach was right; in fact, I
thought it was dreadful. He explained that most of the cabinet members wanted to stop the demonstration completely. In fact, Mc-
Namara had even proposed that there be legislation preventing
demonstrations against the government in Washington during times
of war.

I stood up and began to stroke the head of Lincoln again. "What
the hell does that sonovabitch think he's running: the Ford Motor
Company or the United States government?" I said. "Hasn't he ever
heard of the First Amendment? You're the Attorney General. You're
the guy who has to tell those guys what the law is. They're not
allowed to push people around who have something to say."

"You're right," Ramsey said. "Okay, you've made your point."

Under Ramsey's leadership, the government's attitude toward the
march became more cooperative.

Late on the night of the march, Ramsey asked me to go over to the
Pentagon to see what it looked like. The demonstrators were wonderful. They were orderly, courteous and enormously helpful to one

another. The grassy bank leading from the parking lot up to the lawn where the mass had assembled was slick as glass, having already been trampled by thousands of pairs of feet. I slipped as I tried to climb up, and suddenly five pairs of hands were grasping at mine and up I went. On the lawn, I entered a crowd of gentle, smiling white kids who were, for the moment, imbued with an intense sense of camaraderie. Even the few crazies I saw in the group were spaced out, but gentle.

I reported to Ramsey that night and then went home. On Monday morning, I got a call. He wanted me in his office right away.

"Look at this," he said with disgust in his voice as he tossed a thick memorandum across his desk at me.

It was the memorandum to the Attorney General from the Director of the FBI. The memorandum was a report about the same people, the same place and the same time I had reported on in the early hours of Sunday. "Scum," the demonstrators were called in the first sentence. "Slime," they were called in the second. The memorandum went downhill from that.

"Sick," Ramsey said when I had finished reading it.

"Sick as hell," I agreed.

I didn't know it then, but that march signaled the absolute end of the civil-rights movement as we had known it in the sixties. Many idealistic young whites, having been invited out by black militants, had already left it. Now there was a new and powerful channel for their idealism, the antiwar movement. Black militants wanted little part of that movement. It was a white thing. Johnson had marched off to war, leaving domestic affairs to others. He was furious at Martin Luther King for condemning the war, and he didn't like the black-militant rhetoric either. The civil-rights landscape of 1968 was to be different and bad.

Johnson's disenchantment with the civil-rights effort had been signaled a few months earlier when he decided to unveil his equal-housing proposals to the civil-rights community in the Cabinet Room. In earlier years, Johnson style might have dictated that such an event take place in a grander setting before a larger audience. This time, he simply invited the leaders: A. Philip Randolph, Martin Luther King, my uncle, Floyd McKissick of CORE, and Whitney Young, civil-rights lobbyists such as Joe Rauh of the Leadership Conference on Civil Rights, Dave Brodie of the American Jewish Committee, Clarence Mitchell of the NAACP, and Andy Biemiller of the AFL-

CIO. A few of us civil-rights technicians from the government sat around the back walls of the Cabinet Room.

The President was late. While we were waiting for him, Bill Moyers arranged where people were to sit, so the pictures would come out right. Vice-President Humphrey was there, providing good cheer during the waiting time. Finally, the President arrived and his greetings were courteous, but perfunctory. He chided my uncle for being on an airplane when the White House was trying to summon him.

"Leave numbers," he said to Uncle Roy. "Always leave numbers."

When everybody was seated, he asked the Vice-President, who had taken his place across the table from the President, "Are you in good voice today, Hubert?"

"Yes, Mr. President," the Vice-President of the United States replied.

"Then read this," the President said, as he skidded the proposed legislation over the table top to him. "My voice is hoarse. I've got a cold. But read it fast. I'm in a hurry."

"Yes, sir," the Vice-President said. He began to read. Fast.

I was sitting right behind Johnson and I wondered idly where the coffee that was often served at such gatherings was. Nobody had been served anything except the President, who had an oversized metal container in front of him that he kept drinking from. Since I knew what was in the bill already, my mind wandered during the reading, but kept coming back to Johnson drinking out of that big container. I got thirstier and thirstier. Johnson kept shifting impatiently in his chair.

"Faster, Hubert," he demanded. "Faster."

Humphrey picked up his reading pace and ripped through the text.

Johnson pushed a button under the table. Ah, I thought, at last he's going to serve us some of that Tab, or whatever else it is he's been drinking. Then one of the Navy Filipino mess men who serve at the White House came into the room in his white coat with a big tray bearing one container, just like the one Johnson had in front of him. He took away Johnson's empty and placed the new one in front of the President. Johnson picked it up and took a big swig.

When the Vice-President had finished his reading, nobody in the room expressed much enthusiasm for what they had heard. There was a lot of desultory talk. It was all downbeat. This was a meeting that was clearly going nowhere. Finally Johnson told his guests that they had to be patient. All the things that had to be done couldn't be done at once. There was a silence in the room as the cold-water message sank in.

Then there was a voice. "Now wait a minute, Mr. President," it demanded. I couldn't see who it was at first. Then I realized, it was none of the leaders—not Roy nor Martin nor Whitney. It was Clarence Mitchell, the Washington representative of the NAACP. Clarence was a big burly man who had been around Washington for a long time. He was sometimes called the 101st Senator. He operated out of a small, unprepossessing office on a run-down strip of New Jersey Avenue and was known for having the courage of his convictions.

"You don't have any right to tell these people to be patient. They've been patient for more than three hundred years. And many of them still live in the worst housing in the country, can't get jobs and have the worst education available for their children."

Here was the President in a foul and stingy mood, kicking the Vice-President around, and Clarence was telling him off in public. He was passionate and eloquent. He hit the table. He had tears in his eyes. He went on for about four minutes as the President heard him out. When he stopped, the President, in a soft voice, said, "Okay, Clarence. I've heard you. I was just talking about political realities, not my personal feelings."

The fact was, though, that Johnson's personal feelings had soured. The government turned nastier toward militants. Though Ramsey shielded most of it and never spoke ill of the President, to me it seemed clear that there was a good deal of pressure on the Department of Justice to find some way to put Rap Brown and Stokely Carmichael in jail.

It came in other ways too. Stokely called me one day and said he was having trouble getting his passport and asked if I could help. I called a couple of people in the State Department and said it was stupid to jerk him around, if that's what they were doing. Then I forgot about it, but a month or so later, I ran into Stokely at National Airport. He was beaming. His passport had come through, and he thanked me profusely. I didn't know whether my calls had had any effect, but I accepted the thanks anyway.

The President's rage at Martin Luther King for turning against the war was monumental. Martin was a flat-out ingrate. In the late winter of 1968, when word came that Martin was planning to lead a poor-people's crusade to Washington in the early summer, bitter words started circulating around the town. I had a different view. I hoped the thing would work.

My doubts about King had been resolved in Chicago in the summer of 1966, when John Doar and I saw him at about midnight of the day when the Illinois National Guard had rumbled into town. He was attempting to mount a campaign in the city, but was not getting very far. Word was out that he had taken an apartment on the city's black South Side. Washington cynics had suggested that it was probably the only gold-plated ghetto apartment there. It wasn't gold-plated at all. It was a typical ratty third-floor walk-up. When John and I got there, Martin had the living room filled with poor black ghetto kids. The heat in the room from the Chicago summer mixed with all those bodies was oppressive. Kids were on every available piece of furniture, standing around the walls and sitting on the floor. Andy Young, dressed in a short-sleeved shirt, chino pants and white tennis socks was sitting on the floor too.

Martin was talking to these tough street kids about the futility of throwing rocks and Molotov cocktails at tanks and armored cars. While the kids talked, Martin listened patiently. Some of them seemed barely aware of who he was. Others were so inarticulate, it was difficult to understand what they were saying. He answered each one with care, sometimes repeating what he had said just minutes before because one of the kids had repeated a question. Martin listened and talked until every kid had had a chance to say what he had on his mind and had received an answer. There were no cameras there, no news people. Just two Assistant Attorney Generals of the United States who were required to hold their business while the Nobel laureate conducted his seminar on nonviolence for youngsters whose lives mattered not one whit to most of America.

When it was over at about five in the morning, Martin took John and me through the railroad flat, through the rooms where some of his children were sleeping, to the kitchen. He woke up his wife, Coretta, who made coffee for us and then we did our business as the sun was rising over the ghetto. I was impressed.

But his Southern campaigns had run out of steam, and Northern blacks did not welcome him. He had been laughed at and booed in a meeting in Los Angeles. His efforts to mount a campaign in Cleveland had fizzled, and he seemed lost in the massiveness of Chicago. I wasn't sure that he wasn't a man whose time had passed. A conversation that we had had in early March of 1968 in Miami about his vague plans for the poor-people's crusade didn't reassure me. I hoped that he would find a format that would give him the traction to reassert the kind of moral force that had been his forte.

On the night of April 4, 1968, I was sitting in a Washington apartment, seeking advice about my conflicts over Eve, my children and Mary from Marian Wright, a close friend, who was a genuine civil-rights hero. Marian was a wiry black woman, who had been born and raised in South Carolina and had attended Spelman College in Atlanta and Yale Law School. When I first knew her, she was the only black civil-rights lawyer in Mississippi. She was tough, smart and highly principled, and she never seemed to have my problem of reconciling her commitment to poor blacks with her private tastes that ran to Porsche automobiles and skiing in Aspen. If her engagement to a white man ever gave her conflicts, I never knew it. She was not yet thirty.

I was there to draw strength from this wise and concerned friend. I was strung out, strength depleted and vision destroyed. The Kerner Commission had produced an excellent report on the causes of the riots, and Johnson had buried it. I had fought him on it—gone public in opposition on the front page of *The New York Times*. I was told that he despised me. The feeling was mutual. Poor blacks in the cities and in the rural countryside in the South were no better off for all our huffing and puffing in the administration, and the nation seemed to be tiring of them. And my personal life was tearing me apart. My relationship with Mary was deeper and thicker, yet I was not prepared to get a divorce—Eve was a fine woman and I adored my children.

But there was little talk going on between Eve and me by then. Whatever revelations I made about my inner life, I made to Mary. Whatever comfort I sought, I sought in Mary's bed. But Mary was white, and black was beautiful in those days. One of the most searing charges that black women could hurl at black men was that they talked black during the day and slept white at night. The charge hurt me because, in my case, it was true. It was also true that Eve and I had been trapped by the John Wayne myth of the strong, silent man. If there were fears in our house, she was the only one who could express them. If I had shown my own, she would have become even more troubled, I thought, and so I bundled them up and carried them over to Mary.

But, there were the children. I remember the day when David, who was then about one, first learned to crawl down the steps. We called Amy, who was still four, to watch. She stood for a minute comprehending this marvel and then said in the most loving tones I have ever heard one human being utter about another, "My brother." Later, when he was a little older, David came to love the Beatles. We gave him a number of their records and when I came home from work, he loved for the whole family to sit in the living room and to listen to *Sergeant Pepper's Lonely Hearts Club Band.*

When it was just the family, we would eat together in an alcove in the kitchen. Just behind my seat at the table, there was a wall phone, which I could use without getting up from the table. One night, the phone rang and it was Ramsey, who was still in his office. We talked business and when I hung up, David, who was then about three, asked, "Who was that?"

"The Attorney General," I replied.

"The Dirty General!" David exclaimed.

We all laughed, and the next day, I told Ramsey that we had a new name for him in our house. He laughed and said, "That's redundant. All generals are dirty." And that's the way some of us in the Justice Department felt about the Vietnam war in those days.

Ramsey and Georgia Clark adored our children, just as we adored theirs, but there was something special about the relationship between Ramsey and David right from the beginning, and there still is. One night when we were entertaining—we normally had three other couples over, and this night was no exception—Carl and Mariella Holman were the first to arrive. They are black. Mariella is a beautiful woman whose mother was black and whose father was Japanese. I once asked Mariella: "What the hell are you?" "Jigger," she replied with a wink. "Half Jap, half nigger."

The next to arrive were a famous columnist and his then wife. They are white, and she clearly couldn't figure out why she had to come out of Cleveland Park all the way down to the unfashionable Southwest to have dinner with all these black people. Although Amy was being most gracious serving the hors d'oeuvres, the woman was quite uncomfortable and didn't want to be there. David was still very small then, and he was the only one the woman would talk to.

"Why are you still up?" the woman asked him.

"I want to see my fwiend," David replied.

"What's your friend's name?" the woman asked.

"Wamsey," David said.

"How old is your friend?"

"Oh he's about this big," David said, spreading his arms.

Pretty soon the doorbell rang and the Attorney General of the United States walked into the room and David flew into his arms shouting "Wamsey!"

The woman's face almost fell off. She changed her attitude completely and after the children went to bed, we had one of the best nights of talk at our table that we ever had.

That was my home and those were my children, and I didn't want to leave it or them, but there was unhappiness in that house, and it wasn't getting better. So, this particular night, I skipped the Attorney General's executive meeting at Justice and took my troubles to Marian, who was patiently sorting out the issues with me when the phone rang.

She lifted the receiver, made some short exclamations and then turned and looked at me, horror in her face.

"It's Peter"—her fiancé, who worked for Robert Kennedy—"Martin has been shot in Memphis. It's bad."

I called Ramsey's office and got Warren Christopher. Yes, Martin Luther King had been shot, late in the afternoon, he was in the hospital, it looked bad and I had better come in. It was another night in Ramsey's office like so many others. What to do? We now knew that Martin was dead. The word was out to all CRS people over the country. Report reaction if there is any. What should the President do? We talked. Then Ramsey talked to the White House. Then we talked some more.

Phones rang. Somebody would pick them up. Finally, during the night it was settled. The President would call in the civil-rights leaders and have a meeting with them. He would not go to Memphis to see Mrs. King as some of us had hoped he would. Ramsey would lead a delegation instead. Cliff Alexander, chairman of the Equal Employment Opportunity Commission, and I would go with him. His press man, Cliff Sessions, would also go and Cartha "Deke" De Loach, Mr. Hoover's liaison man with the Attorney General's office would be along, because we needed to know quickly everything they knew. They had a lot of physical evidence, including a blanket and a rifle. It was a lone man, they informed us. They would get him soon. It was after one when we left to go home to sleep if we could.

It was just before six the same morning when we gathered in the courtyard at Justice for the trip out to Andrews. Faint light was coming into the sky as De Loach drove his blue Mustang into the courtyard to be met by an FBI operative, who whispered some words in his ear and then drove the Mustang away. The physical evidence was in the lab, De Loach said. There was a whole table full of it. The lone gunman was being tracked. He would soon be apprehended.

On the flight down on the Air Force Jet Star, De Loach was full of optimism. The Bureau was at work. At one point, he opened his briefcase. I thought he was going to show us some evidence or a report. All he had in there was a pistol and a sandwich. He ate the sandwich.

In Memphis, we went onto the Electra that the Rockefeller family had provided for Mrs. King to take her husband's body home. She was courageous and calm and gracious as she accepted the President's condolences and our words. We spoke to A. D. King, Martin's brother, who looked like a bloated and faded version of Martin. It was said that A.D. drank too much.

Inside the terminal building, we spoke to Ralph Abernathy, Martin's successor, who thanked us for our concern in the rumbling and eloquent cadences of the Baptist preacher he was and we spoke to Andy, who acknowledged our presence, but wasn't really there. We spoke to the mayor and to the blacks who were leading the sanitation men's strike, which had brought Martin to the city in the first place. We saw the picketers, all black men, walking with such large gaps between them that each seemed alone. The signs on their backs and chests read, "I am a man."

All through the day, we listened to Deke De Loach. The Bureau was getting closer. It was a lone man on the run. He was driving a white Mustang with Mississippi tags. He had been going west. Now he was going east. Everything pointed to him. The Bureau would soon have him.

The press was all around. They wanted a statement from Ramsey. We had reports that rioting was beginning around the country. Washington was on fire. Cliff Sessions drafted a statement with some calming words in it. There was a lone gunman on the run. We would probably have him soon.

I read the statement before Ramsey delivered it and said it was okay. That was a terrible mistake. I didn't believe much else the FBI said. Why the hell should I have believed De Loach? Because, I believe, a single madman was much easier to deal with emotionally than the notion of a conspiracy. Conspiracy was more evil than my emotions were prepared to accept. And, I did not know then that the FBI had sent Martin a tape designed to induce him to commit suicide. So I didn't demur when I had a chance to stop Ramsey from making a statement based on FBI information and which would thereafter convince black radicals that he had had some part in a cover-up, if not in the conspiracy itself.

We flew home that night and as the Jet Star came up the Potomac toward Washington, I could see in the distance what looked like a needle framed by an orange blur. Soon I realized it was the Washington Monument backed by the glow of flames devouring the riot-wracked city. We had the pilot circle slowly and could see the long, thin strips of flame along the streets where the rioting had been. It looked like the tracks of runs made by planes loaded with incendiary bombs. Reports we had gotten indicated that scenes like this were occurring all across the country.

That was Friday. Saturday, I took a night flight to Atlanta. The King family had requested that a senior Administration official whom they trusted be sent down to help with the arrangements for the funeral. On Sunday, Vernon E. Jordan, Jr., then the head of the Voter Education Project, picked me up at Paschal's, a black hotel on West Hunter Street, and took me over to Sister's Chapel on the Spelman campus, where Martin's body was laid in state. There was a long line of people, and they were very quiet and very sad. Many were crying, and some were white. The casket had a glass top and Martin's body seemed small.

We walked back to the West Hunter Street Baptist Church through the clear air of a perfect Palm Sunday. Vernon showed me the public housing project where he had grown up and told me about his mother, who ran a catering business and had insisted that he be a man. Ralph Abernathy preached a sermon that day to Martin in heaven. Some of the sisters in the congregation fell out. Others talked in tongues. Tears fell from my eyes.

After church, I took a white staff member of mine to lunch to discuss what had to be done. We were eating fried chicken in the dining room in Paschal's when Willie Ricks, an SNCC field worker, who had a reputation as a wild man, came in wearing a black leather jacket and sun glasses. Willie started hollering about revenge against white people. Atlanta was tense that day, and people tried to shush Willie, but he would not be quiet.

"Shit, ain't no white folks in here," he said.

Somebody pointed at our table. For the first time, I realized that my colleague was the only white person in Paschal's.

"Shit, they ain't nothin' but agents," Willie said.

People stared. For the first time in my life, I understood how a white man must feel when he took a black guest to his segregated club. The hostility was almost tangible. After that, I did not meet with my staff at Paschal's.

During the afternoon, a committee was formed to carry out the funeral. Reverend Wyatt Tee Walker, who had been Martin's executive secretary before Andy, was the chairman. Walter Fauntroy, a minister and a member of SCLC, was on it, and so was Yvonne Braithwaite of Los Angeles, who would join Walter in Congress when he was the nonvoting delegate from the District of Columbia. And I was on it. My job was to get logistical help from an Administration headed by a President who had sent down the word that there was to be absolutely no federal involvement in the funeral except for my presence. But there were too many people there. We needed blankets and we needed cots and we needed some food. Joe Califano knew the President's orders, but he responded to my requests anyway, and we got a good deal of help.

While I was at meetings or on the phone, my people were taking the town's temperature. It was hot, about to snap. People were in a rage. Only their grief kept them in check, but no one knew for how long. Late that night when I got back to Paschal's, Willie Ricks and a lot of other hostile-looking people were milling around in the lobby. As I walked toward the elevator, somebody hissed, "Agent." Everybody turned and looked at me. There was a narrow path through the people to the elevator. "Let's get him," somebody else whispered. The path began to close. I had two choices. I could turn and run and forever after be known as the agent that people had run out of Paschal's during Martin's funeral, or I could keep on going and get the shit kicked out of me.

I kept on toward the elevator. As the people came toward me, I saw a man facing the doors in a denim jacket and jeans. He seemed the only one in the place who hadn't noticed what was going on. As the crowd closed, the man turned and took everything in immediately. It was Stokely Carmichael.

"Roger!" he exclaimed. Then, throwing his arms wide to embrace me, he said, "My man!" The crowd disappeared.

Tuesday, the day of the funeral was bright, warm and clear. My staff and I had done as much as we could to arrange with security people a smooth and orderly day. But though I knew that spaces in the church were limited, I had failed to foresee the unbelievable crush at the door. I was worried that someone would be squeezed to death. Then, suddenly, oddly, I saw a giant making his way slowly and inexorably through that terrible press of humanity. It was like a determined man battling through a gale. Slowly he pressed on, and finally the door was opened and he ducked through. Wilt Chamberlain was not a man to be denied on a basketball court or at the door of the Ebenezer Baptist Church.

Celebrities were there, some to grieve and some to be seen. They followed the mule-drawn cart to the cemetery, and Robert Kennedy, who was running for President, smiled and waved at the people who greeted him along the way.

I hated those smiles. A man was dead. And I was furious at Johnson too. Martin's life had been full of important people and they all wanted to be inside the church. I had relayed the family's request that only the President come and if he couldn't then only Vice-President Humphrey. Johnson wouldn't come, but rather than honor the family's wishes he sent a whole planeload of Washington dignitaries, who took seats that could have gone to the people who risked their lives on lonely roads with Martin.

I got up before dawn the next morning to go back home, and I stopped at the place where the open-air service had been held. Light was beginning to show above a drizzle as I walked through the place where the people had been. It looked like the leftovers of any American crowd with the lines of chairs in disarray, overflowing refuse containers and trash on the ground. I made my way up to the spot where Martin's body had lain. There were some wreaths and other leftover flowers there. I stood for a minute in the damp, because I had been too busy the day before to do my grieving.

"Thank you, Doctor," I said, through my tears. Then I left to go to the airport.

Late that afternoon, Ramsey had his regular Wednesday staff meeting with the Deputy Attorney General, the Solicitor General, all the Assistant Attorneys General and the heads of the Bureau of Prisoners, Immigration and Naturalization Service. Hoover never came. I don't know whether Ramsey ever asked him or not, but in my three years at Justice, I saw him exactly twice. Once was at a White House reception and the other when I ran into him accidentally on the elevator. A man from John Mitchell's Justice Department told me that he came to Mitchell's staff meetings.

"What does he say?" I asked.

"Garbage," the man replied. "Just garbage. It's embarrassing. Everybody looks at his shoes when he talks."

Even without Hoover, I didn't like these staff meetings and I almost never went to the twice-a-week staff lunches. The fact is that I was still rarely comfortable in large groups of men where I was the only black. At Justice, I sensed an arrogance that I found unwarranted and unsettling. Their demeanor always suggested to me that they knew more about sophisticated life than I did, and their conversations about the law and what they were doing rarely included me. It was as if I were a mascot, nice to have around so the class picture would be integrated, but not really an equal. The aura surrounding some of the people who ran the Department under Ramsey was not unlike that of the all-white staff under Robert Kennedy; they assumed that blacks were irrelevant at the top level, even in civil-rights matters.

It was a ludicrous assumption, and difficult for me to bear. They knew about being white in America. I knew about both being black and being white. I had been to most of the places they had been to—a first-rate law school, a law firm and around the government. I had been around whites most of my life. And I had studied them since I was twelve, because I had to, to survive. But, I also knew about being black and I was studying what it was like to be black and poor. I had a far broader grasp of the sociology and the politics of America than they did, yet I was the outside token. It stank and it hurt.

This night was particularly hard. It had been a week since Martin had been shot. Most of the men in the room had had time to absorb it as a major, but remote, news event. Then they went back to doing tax or antitrust work. Some of them had dealt with the shooting's after-effects; they had been sent to Baltimore or Chicago or Memphis to deal with the riots there. But I had been immersed in the tragedy for the entire week. And a man I had known and respected, a leader of my people, had been murdered. I had seen him in his casket.

Ramsey called for reports from the people who had dealt with the riots. Warren Christopher reported on Chicago. Fred Vinson, who was in charge of the Criminal Division, reported on Baltimore. Steve Pollack, who was in charge of the Civil Rights Division, reported on Memphis. Some of the reports were bloodless. There were a couple of

comments that were light and flippant. But there was no sense in any
of those reports of the gaping psychic wound that the murder had
inflicted on black Americans and that had driven so many of them
onto the streets in a rampage of destruction.

Finally, Ramsey called on me to report on Atlanta.

"Black people all over America hurt right now," I said. "They've
suffered an enormous loss, incalculable. There's a terrible chasm between black people and white people in this country, and for more
than three hundred years, black people have been trying to reach
across that chasm to heal the division in this nation. But white people, by and large, don't reach back. Some blacks, because of what
happened last week, are going to give up trying. Some of us won't
give up. I'm going to get up tomorrow morning and keep on trying,
but I don't know how long I can do that. Or how long I'll want to do
that. Now, Ramsey, I'm tired and I'm going home."

I got up and walked out and went home. I hadn't really been home
in a week. I was exhausted, and I wanted to sit with a martini and
look at my children and talk with them and Eve. Amy and David
would make up games to amuse Eve and me while we listened to
"Sergeant Pepper." Those times at the end of the day were the best
times we had. I wanted that night. I needed it. But the phone rang
five minutes after I got in the house. It was Ramsey.

I don't know what happened in the meeting today, he told me, but
Fred Vinson is very upset. He thinks it was something he said that
offended you. He wants to come over and see you. I said no, that I
didn't have time or energy for white people that night. Ramsey was
persistent. Fred was a good guy, he said. He hadn't meant any harm.
I told him to tell Fred that it hadn't been anything in particular that
he had said, that it had been what everybody had said and the whole
scene and that he should go home. Ramsey pressed on and implored
me to call Fred and ask him over. So, I finally gave in.

We put "Sergeant Pepper" away and when Fred came, he said he
hadn't meant to offend me. He understood about blacks. He was from
Appalachia. His family had been poor. It was all the same, he said.

It was a conversation I had had many times with white people who
had grown up poor. They had known deprivation. They had been
outsiders. They knew. It was all the same. Even Katharine Graham
once told me it was all the same, and she had never been poor.

It is not the same. Being poor and white in my generation was not
the same as being black and middle class. And, it was surely not the

same as being black and poor. And, being rich and white is not remotely the same as being a black of any kind.

But Fred really did feel bad. There was no question about that. He wept great gobby tears on the carpet, this son of a former Chief Justice of the United States. I continued to resist his notion that it was the same, but I told him gently that he hadn't wounded me, that tomorrow would be fine and that we'd get on. He left then, and we did get on okay after that. The children wanted to know why the man had cried in the living room.

"Because I made him feel bad at work," I told them. I felt heavy in my soul, but I didn't tell them that.

21 In the wee hours of a June morning, the duty officer at the Department called to tell me that Robert Kennedy had been shot in Los Angeles. Eve woke up and I told her. There were no words to say. On Saturday, a number of us in the Department were in Ramsey's office watching the services at St. Patrick's in New York—Andy Williams singing "The Battle Hymn of the Republic" and Teddy Kennedy making his brave and eloquent eulogy—when the word came over from the Bureau that James Earle Ray had been arrested in London.

We couldn't prove it, but Ramsey and I figured that Hoover had arranged the timing of the arrest to upstage the news of Kennedy's funeral. Hoover had hated the Kennedys.

That night, the slow train from New York finally got to Union Station with Bobby Kennedy's body and all the principal officers of the Department of Justice were on the curb in front of the building on Constitution Avenue when the cortege came by and paused for a moment on its way to Arlington Cemetery. We stepped from the curb, bowed our heads and retreated into ourselves. The best hope for poor people and for what passes for the left in American politics has just been blown away, I thought.

But the Poor People's Campaign came to Washington anyway, without Martin, without Robert Kennedy and without much political support. The campaign was doomed from the start. The Administration granted the demonstrators a permit to erect their camp on the mall to Lincoln's right in front of the Memorial. But SCLC couldn't get the logistics together. The leaders didn't come to town to set it up, and it was a mess from the beginning. To make matters worse, it rained for days, turning the camp site into a sea of mud, and I worried so much about a possible epidemic that I arranged for the Public Health Service to send a team in there.

Marian Wright by now had moved her operations to Washington and was able to spend full time pumping intellectual and programmatic substance into the poor people's demands. Carl Holman and I worked all day for the government. Most nights he joined Marian's efforts, and on many nights I did. It was a two-shift job because SCLC seemed only to function late at night. Each day the leaders of the campaign would take their followers out of the camp and demonstrate at one of the domestic departments of government. Then they would be invited in to make a presentation to the leaders of that department. Occasionally, Ralph would testify before a Congressional committee. We would work on the statements and the testimony, and then we would present them to Ralph in his room at the Pitts Motor Hotel. The followers, of course, were living in makeshift accommodations down in the muddy, nasty camp ground. When we finished at about three or four in the morning, we'd go home and sleep and then get up and start all over again.

Neither Carl nor I felt like double agents. Of course, by day we'd push inside the government for the things we'd helped SCLC shape the night before, but I had no sense then, nor do I now, that it was an adversarial position. Our Administration was saying that it wanted to be the most humane in history. The poor people were trying to tell them how to do that. And we were trying outside to make that voice more articulate, and inside to make the government hear it.

But, it was a weary and battered government by now, licking its wounds and feeling sorry for itself. Its emotions were depleted and its compassion was thin. We were worn down finally to a modest goal: to get the government to agree to provide free food stamps to people whose incomes were a dollar a day, or less. Ramsey was with us.

But, the Agriculture Department wasn't buying it, and a lot of others weren't either. I heard one man argue that some of the poor people might barter free food stamps for liquor. But—hosanna!—we beat Agriculture. The President went for the idea, a tiny victory in a year of disasters. But when the President called Wilbur Mills of Arkansas, chairman of the Ways and Means Committee through which enabling legislation would have to go, Mills told the President that if he wanted a tax increase to finance his war in Southeast Asia he better forget free food stamps. The President forgot them. We lost—or at least the poor people did.

The mood in the camp turned sour. My staff people began reporting increasing instances of violence there. The violence became so widespread, the newspapers picked it up. It was beginning to be unsafe for outsiders of any color to be in there.

The camp ground was under the jurisdiction of the United States Park Police, a force which charitably could be described as lacking in any community-relations sensitivity whatsoever. They just didn't like niggers. On several occasions, there were exchanges between the Park Police and the campaigners—stones and bottles from one side, tear gas from the other. The mood got uglier. The permit expired on June 24, 1968. Congress was furious at us for having granted the permit in the first place and contemplated passing a law making it a crime for anybody to be on that land without a permit.

That would have been a disaster. There were people in the camp who had become so attached to it, they were claiming it as their land. They would never leave, they said. Some people in there had guns, others had knives and lots of them had clubs. The Park Police hated them by now, viewed them as scum, and were aching for a confrontation. That confrontation would surely have left a lot of dead poor people at the foot of Lincoln's Memorial; it would have been a national disaster. The leaders of SCLC knew that and we at Justice knew that. We were all in the same vise, but we couldn't let it seem that we were in collusion. Overt SCLC cooperation with the Justice Department would have disgraced the organization.

But we all knew that our mutual problem had to be solved. We agreed to a meeting out of sight—at my house on Sunday, June 23, Eve's birthday. Her parents were in town to celebrate the occasion. I asked Eve, my children and her parents to leave that afternoon, and good soldiers, they did as I asked. Ramsey came and a lawyer named Christene Clark, whose husband Leroy was actually the lawyer for the campaign, but he was out of town. And Andy Young came representing SCLC. Abernathy was out raising money somewhere.

Our problem was to induce the poor people to leave that plot of land without bloodshed. The obstacle between life and death was the rage and instinct toward violence on both sides. We finally developed a simple plan that would enable those who were furious inside the camp to protest by getting arrested one place or another and, on the other side, to give the major policing responsibility to the District of Columbia Police Department rather than to the Park Police. Ralph would lead the great majority of the people on a protest march to the Supreme Court steps the next morning. Protests were not permitted on the steps, so anybody who wanted to get arrested there could do so.

Meanwhile, a small group of people who felt most strongly about the plot of land would stay there and be arrested by the District Police, but, they would have to be unarmed. It was agreed that Andy would put the plan to Ralph and the other leaders for approval and that I would go in with the first wave of police because I had a better sense of where the camp's danger spots were and would probably have a better rapport with whoever was left than any of the police. Finally, somebody had to go into the camp that night to firm up the details after Andy had gotten Ralph's approval.

After the meeting, Ramsey said, "I'm sorry, Roger. I would go in there tonight if I could, but you know I can't." He said what we both knew to be true. It had to be me. What we both thought and didn't say was that if somebody other than the leadership recognized an Assistant Attorney General in that place at that time, he'd likely come out dead. It was arranged then. Andy would supply me with a pass to the camp, and a false identity, and I would go in for the night meeting. When the time came, I put on a pair of dirty chinos and a dashiki that my sister, Sharon, had made for me, stuck my false pass in my pocket, checked one last time with Ramsey and went off.

The people on my staff, who had had the run of the camp in its early days, and who had been viewed as allies, were barred from it by now. They had no interest in risking their necks inside in any event. But we kept people near the gate to keep an eye on things, and the man assigned there that night was Ronald T. Gault, a young black from Chicago. I tried not to play favorites on my staff, but Ron was my favorite, and I think he knew it. I had alerted him that I was going in. When I got there, he walked silently with me to within fifty feet of the gate. Then he stopped, there in the dark and gave me a soul shake.

"Take care, my brother," he said.

"Yeah, right," I replied.

Then I walked alone the rest of the way to the gate. I was scared shitless. I gave the guards at the gate the pass that had been used and worn, and I gave them the answers about where I was from and where I was sleeping that Andy had given to me. They looked at my face for a minute and then they let me on through. It was dark in that camp and eerily silent. Occasionally, a figure would come close out of the dark with a board or a club in his hand and then pass on by. I finally got to the headquarters tent and told the guard that I had business with Andy Young. That he had sent for me. I prayed that Andy was inside.

I was told to wait because an important meeting was going on. I told him that I was supposed to be part of the meeting. He wanted to know who I was. I told him the name on my pass. He had never heard of it. He decided I wasn't important. I had to wait in the darkness and the silence until he felt like moving. He was a very big man. Finally, he let me in.

All the top leaders of SCLC except Ralph were inside the headquarters tent. Sterling Tucker, head of the Washington Urban League, was there too. They had agreed to the plan. We smoothed out details, who would do what in the morning. I assured them that the D.C. cops would be in charge and that to the extent possible, I would control the behavior of the cops. It was agreed that the Reverend Hosea Williams would stay inside the camp after Ralph had led the marchers out and would try to persuade those who remained to give up their guns.

"There's a lot of crazy motherfuckers in here, Roger," somebody said. "If they weren't crazy when they got here, they got crazy from the mud and the tear gas and the cops."

Andy was sitting on the floor by the door of the tent hugging his knees as I was leaving. He is a Congregational minister.

"I don't know what religion you are, Roger," he said, "but you'd better pray to some god tonight."

I got out without incident.

The next morning, I put on a suit and tie and went to the Department to go over the final plans with Ramsey and the rest who would be manning the command post there. I learned that the Park police couldn't be entirely excluded, but was assured that they would be under the firm control of the D.C. police. Then I went to the mall to wait for Ralph to lead the main body out before going in with the police. Ralph came out late, but when he came, he brought them out singing in good spirits under a clear June sky.

After Ralph and his people were gone, Tulley Kossack, from the Criminal Division, and I went in with the police. I had never seen so many cops in my life. They were ready and armed for a massive infantrylike assault. Any resistance to that kind of force would have been an invitation to a massacre. We moved from east to west. Most of the people were gone. Some who were left fell to the ground to be arrested.

Then I saw the commander of the Park police. He was shouting, almost out of control. He was whipping his men up, not calming them down. I took a walkie-talkie from Tulley and called Ramsey on the open frequency asking to have him relieved of his command. He was, instantly. It probably ruined his career.

When we got near the assembly tent, I could see Hosea Williams preaching. Now a lot of bad things have been written and said about Hosea through the years, but he was magnificent that day. He was preaching the way I've seen no man before or since. He was preaching guns, knives and clubs out of people's hands and persuading them to be arrested nonviolently.

After I saw that, I figured it was over, so I left the camp. I was frightened, but a part of me wanted to be in there with those people who proclaimed to the richest nation on earth that there was poverty and despair in its midst that it could ignore only to its everlasting shame.

When I got through to Ramsey's office, Warren Christopher told me they had reports that there were still some people with guns in the southwest corner of the camp who were determined to shoot it out with the cops after they had made their arrests. He asked me to go back in to check it out.

I was afraid, but I went back in. There were some people, and a few of them had guns, but their leader was talking them out of there onto buses just outside the fence. I joined him in his plea and the people saw the awesome police forces moving slowly but inexorably toward them and they left. And then it was over. Nobody was dead.

When I returned to Ramsey's office, the staff was having sandwiches for lunch. I ordered a sandwich and a beer. Ramsey ordered a beer too. Ramsey raised his to me, and I raised mine to him. He smiled and said I had saved America that day. That made everything better.

Later in the afternoon, we heard that some of the people who hadn't been arrested at the Court were gathering in the black community at the corner of 14th and U streets in an ugly mood. I went up there and listened to Jesse Jackson preaching to them from a flatbed truck. "I may be poor," Jesse chanted, "but I am somebody." The people responded. Jesse looked huge, handsome and commanding. After a while, the crowd dispersed.

Martin would have been pleased, I thought. Andy, Ralph, Hosea and Jesse—all his brothers had been valiant.

But the turbulent year 1968 wasn't over. In June, Sam Dennis and Phil Mason, two of the men assigned to our Chicago regional office, told me that Rennie Davis, one of the leaders of the antiwar demonstrations planned for the Democratic National Convention in July, was anxious to see me. The New Mobilization Against the War, the "New Mobe," was having a hard time coordinating its planning efforts with the government of the City of Chicago, and they wanted to see if CRS could help. I knew nothing more about the antiwar movement than I read in the papers, but if there was a problem and I thought our staff could help, I figured I ought to go.

Dennis, Mason and I met with Rennie Davis in a booth at a dimly lit restaurant in Chicago's Loop. Davis was earnest, clean-cut, bespectacled. It was hard not to like him. He said that the New Mobe was an umbrella organization for a range of antiwar groups, and that they hoped to attract 100,000 people to Chicago during the convention to demonstrate against the war. There would be a carefully planned program, he said, with plenty of events—concerts, teach-ins, rallies—all culminating in a counter convention to be staged the night the Democrats nominated their candidate. The intention of the organizers was for the entire protest to be nonviolent.

But they were being thwarted in their planning, Davis said, because Chicago officials wouldn't cooperate in the planning for the demonstration in any meaningful way. The mayor's office had shunted them off to a young, low-ranking official, who had no power and did not follow up on their meetings. Could the Community Relations Service possibly build them a better bridge to the city's officials? I was on unfamiliar terrain and couldn't judge antiwar people's intentions the way I could those of the civil-rights people. But, Davis was hard not to believe. I told him I would talk to some people in Washington and would be back in touch.

Back home, I took a chance and put my chips on Davis. I wrote Ramsey a memorandum reporting on the conversation with Rennie and included my opinion that the demonstrators did indeed intend to be nonviolent. But, I added, without the kind of closely coordinated planning that we did in Washington, violence was not only possible, but probable. "Violence at the convention will be a national disgrace, and a national disaster," I concluded. I urged Ramsey to have the President send a high-level emissary to encourage Mayor Daley to engage in serious joint planning with the demonstrators.

I was worried, because an antiwar demonstration in Chicago had turned nasty a couple of months earlier, and the Mayor had made a "shoot to kill" comment. The Chicago police had been unrestrained and I didn't want a replay of that during the convention. Ramsey decided that the President was by now so sour on the Department of Justice that he wouldn't act on my recommendation, but he thought somebody ought to try to convince Mayor Daley, and he chose me. I was doubtful that Daley would see me as sufficiently important to have a real influence on his decisions.

Nevertheless, I gave it a try. Together with Wes Pomeroy, a police expert in the Department, and Tom Foran, Boss Daley's hand-picked United States Attorney for the Northern District of Illinois, I met with Davis again. Then we went over to see Daley. The theory of my pitch was simple. If the officials who would be in charge of policing the demonstration could meet and work along with the leaders of the New Mobe, there would be a better chance of staving off crises should things begin to heat up during the week of the convention.

The Mayor was gracious, all packed into his dark-blue suit. His eyes were twinkling at the beginning of the meeting, because he remembered that I had been helpful during the riot of 1966. The thing that always overwhelmed me about Daley was the massiveness of his jowls. I couldn't keep my eyes off them, even as I talked. When I said the New Mobe planned to have predesignated marshals to control their demonstrators, those jowls started shaking and turning red. Tom Foran looked at the floor. Wes Pomeroy looked at the ceiling. I looked at those jowls and tried to continue, but Daley interrupted me.

What was this stupid stuff about marshals, he wanted to know. The Chicago Police Department could handle anything that might come up. Chicago knew how to deal with its own people. If there was any violence, it would come from outside agitators. He had just talked to Carl Stokes, the Mayor of Cleveland, who told him the riot there had been conducted by outside agitators. Why didn't the Justice Department spend its time tracking down those people instead of sticking its nose into Chicago's business?

This tirade lasted for about twenty-five minutes after which he

ushered us out, saying that, if we had any other business, his administration would be happy to cooperate. The liaison person would be the
same ineffectual official who had been of absolutely no help to the
New Mobe. And then we were out. It had occurred to me during his
monologue that Daley thought, probably because I was black, that I
had been talking about black demonstrators. He had never given me a
chance to say a word to correct his misapprehension.

"It's too bad one of you wasn't speaking Urdu," Wes said outside
Daley's office.

"Why?" I asked.

"Because then, you'd have *known* you had a communication
problem."

Later Ramsey told me that after my visit, Daley had called President Johnson, Senator Dirksen and the President of the United States
Conference of Mayors, asserting that I was the most dangerous man
in America and he didn't want me in his town again.

Ramsey decided the problem was significant enough to give it another try. This time, he sent Warren Christopher to see Daley and
again Wes went along with him and again Daley turned our ideas
down. Afterward, Wes told Mike Royko, the columnist, "The only
difference was that Daley seemed to dislike Warren Christopher less
than he disliked Roger Wilkins."

Violence did break out at the convention, of course, and it was a
disaster and a disgrace. Among other things, it didn't help Hubert
Humphrey's chances against Richard M. Nixon. I watched the violence on television and was disgusted. The police were beating the
hell out of—not blacks—but white America's children. Bad as it was,
I thought there was a silver lining. I told Ramsey that since the whole
nation had seen the Chicago police go berserk, there would be pressure for stronger police community-relations programs and civilian
review boards.

I was wrong. The polls showed that the people were, by and large,
on the side of the cops. No cops were put on trial. Tom Foran's office
brought charges against seven of the demonstrators. Tom handled the
case, although it seemed to me that he had a clear conflict of interest,
since he had been in on one meeting with Rennie and one with the
Mayor and had even acted as a go-between for me. I testified for the
defense at both Chicago Seven trials and was delighted that none of
the demonstrators had to go to jail.

22 The rest of the year was downhill. I was exhausted in both mind and body. The plight of poor blacks was constantly on my mind. Every time I saw a little black kid, I would wonder whether his parents had jobs, what kind of house he lived in, whether he had an older sibling in jail, what his education was like. I wondered whether he, like my friend Chet Carter, now one of Washington's leading black businessmen, would be told by a white teacher that he should go to vocational school because he wasn't college material.

Sometimes my concern with inequality was more immediate. In the summer of 1968, I decided to take up jogging. On my first night out, I put on a pair of old chino pants and a sweatshirt and struck out. About four blocks from my house, I heard somebody shout, "Hey, boy!" I figured he couldn't be calling me, so I kept on running and the shout was repeated, more insistently this time, but I still ignored it until a car came abreast of me and a searchlight was flashed in my face. It was a D.C. police car; a cop had been calling me. The car stopped and two cops came out, guns drawn. They spread-eagled me against the car and frisked me. I told them to reach in my rear pocket, that I had some identification there. In those days I didn't go anywhere without my Justice Department identification and that night I was glad of it.

The cops checked the identification, put their guns away and began apologizing profusely. It was another case of a "mistaken identity"— just like Los Angeles three years before—another criminal call where the person sought looked just like me. I believed that as much as I believed the world was flat. They had seen a black man running, and

228

that was enough for them. An equally innocent poor black man who didn't have my credentials in his pocket might have been dead or at least gone to jail in any one of the encounters I had with the police in Los Angeles, Detroit and Washington, D.C.

It was clear during the summer of 1968 that the country hadn't changed much for poor blacks.

By now, a lot of people were talking about blacks having control of their own communities. I had a lot of sympathy for that. White-run institutions that were supposed to serve them, whether they were schools or hospitals or welfare departments, just couldn't take the humanity of poor black people seriously. There were enough new-model service-delivery systems supported by the Office of Economic Opportunity to convince me that highly motivated black people could do it better. There was a lot of idealism abroad in poor black communities then, a lot of caring, a lot of love. If white America was going to be cruel and heartless to these people, then maybe we could create a layer of caring black professionals and aides between the white bureaucracies and the people they were mangling.

But whites weren't going for that either. They called people who propounded such theories "separatists." It was a very bad word in their lexicon. Very few people in the government outside CRS bought the idea either. And, in New York, the teachers made Albert Shanker into a powerful labor leader, by supporting his resistance to community control of some black schools.

And in Washington I was torn between my enormous distress at the plight and pain of poor blacks and a government that was less and less willing and able to do anything about their lives.

I had had it. Seven years in Washington, four and a half of them spent trying to push the government into doing the right thing, had left me depleted.

A good part of my rage was directed at Lyndon Baines Johnson. To this day, if you ask Washington old-timers who the most memorable character of their time in the Capital was, most of them will answer, Lyndon Johnson. That is my answer too. And if you ask most knowledgeable blacks who was the best President for blacks, most of them will answer, Lyndon Johnson. Again, that is my answer.

But, when I left the government, I hated him. We were all so tired in that government then that we all needed to go home. I always thought that a Humphrey Presidency would have been a sad old thing because so many of the people helping him would be the tired, frazzled, beat-up leftovers from the Kennedy-Johnson years. But, I voted for him because I thought even that would be better than Nixon. And, besides, for all of the manhood that he gave up to be Johnson's Vice-President, I liked Humphrey very much and knew him to be a good man. But, in that late fall of '68, passions were high and divisions were deep.

Johnson despised us at Justice, because we wouldn't put Stokely Carmichael in jail. White people all over the country wanted scapegoats for the riots and Stokely and Rap Brown were the likeliest targets. Rap did something profoundly dumb. While he was under indictment somewhere, he took a rifle on an interstate flight. That was a federal crime, no getting around it. So, we arrested him. But the only thing you could get Stokely on was speech.

People thought he inflamed blacks to riot. In those days, blacks with suits and ties were a fairly rare sight on airplanes. Invariably some white person sitting next to me on a plane would see how I was dressed, watch me open my briefcase and go to work on some papers and ask me what I did for a living. When I answered that I worked in the Department of Justice, they would ask, "Why don't you people put Stokely Carmichael in jail?" It never satisfied them when I said that he had committed no crime that we knew of. He was a black-power person and that was bad.

During those years, I did an experiment to find out what it was like to be a black-power person. I had business in Cleveland and I went on a plane from Washington wearing dark glasses, a dashiki, beads around my neck and jeans. I never got ruder treatment in my life, except maybe when all those white people went off to the segregated Detroit Yacht Club for dinner and left me behind. Ticket agents and flight attendants almost snarled at me, and I was shunned by the other passengers. Nobody sat near me. When my business was done, I came home in a suit and tie. People smiled at me, and though I was still young, some even called me "sir."

Sitting in the Oval Office, Johnson was not different from the other white people. He had started his time there saying that he would "finish what Lincoln had done." He got the Civil Rights Act, the poverty program and the Voting Rights Act through Congress. He went up to Howard University in June of '65 and made the most sensitive speech about the plight of poor black Americans that any white man could make. My heart was in his pocket.

But the war engulfed the poor man, and then Martin came out

against the war. Johnson was distracted and angry, and his cities were burning. His soul hardened against us then, I think, and he liked very few of us. Uncle Roy opposed Martin on the war issue and the President liked him. By then, my wavering on the war was over and I opposed the President. I once went to Ramsey and said, "I've got to quit this fucking government, because I hate this war. Johnson is sending poor people, blacks and whites, over there to get shot up for nothing. And one of these days my children are going to grow up and ask me: 'Daddy how could you have worked for that man at that time?' " Ramsey told me that he and I had done all we could to stop that war and that we had a job to do in Justice. He also said that he could assure me that if I left, "they"—Ramsey was always punctilious about not speaking ill of the President—would put some hambone in my job and that would be bad for black people. I loved Ramsey, so I stayed, though I'm not sure even now that I should have.

I'm sure Johnson knew how we felt, so he hated us, and besides, we wouldn't put Stokely in jail. We would have periodic meetings in Ramsey's office about some speech of Stokely's or other. There were some people in Justice who were anxious to prosecute, but Ramsey never wavered. Once I did, and Ramsey looked at me in horror. I'm pretty sure now that I was wrong that night and I'm also pretty sure that Ramsey was constitutionally incapable of prosecuting somebody just for speech, although the prosecution of Dr. Spock and his confreres came pretty close. I wasn't in on that decision, and Ramsey and I have never talked about it much, but I guess that that is one call that he would like to have back.

When it came to the end, the atmosphere in Washington was poisonous, and I had contributed my bit. After John Gardner had quit as Secretary of HEW—over disgust at the Vietnam War, I assume, though he never said so—Wilbur Cohen was put in the Secretary's chair. After that, to my astonishment, there was a ground swell of opinion around town that I should be appointed Under Secretary. It got so far that a Johnson insider, Les Carpenter, wrote in his column that I was a shoo-in for the job. I hadn't taken the shit seriously until then, but at that point I became alarmed on two counts.

The first was that by that time, I honestly didn't want to take another appointment from Johnson, because it would have indicated that I approved of him in 1968, and I didn't.

The second was a horrid and huge personal secret. One night in 1967, I went to the White House Correspondents' Ball as a guest of a

black guy, Wally Terry, on *Time* magazine's staff. I left home early
that morning without breakfast and put my tux in the car. Then there
was a lousy, furious day and I didn't get a chance to eat lunch. That
night, I changed into my tux in the office and drove up to the Sheraton Park Hotel. By this time in my life, I had begun to lap up the
booze pretty well, and that night was no exception. I threw at least
three very dry martinis down on an empty stomach, and then I drank
a good deal of wine at dinner. After dinner, I went up to *The New
York Times* party and soaked up some more booze—scotch, I guess.

The last thing I remember is a conversation with Robert Semple,
who is now Foreign Editor of the *Times*, but who was then in the
paper's Washington Bureau. Semple asked me about possible riots for
the summer.

"Riots," I screamed. "The only thing any white fucker wants to
talk to me about is fucking riots."

Then, I went with a woman. To this day, I do not know who she
was, only that she was white. We went to her apartment somewhere
in Northwest Washington and we must have tried to do sex. I only
know that because the next day I found lipstick on my underpants.
Booze unleashed my rage in those days and I must have been such a
mess that the woman put me out. But I didn't want to go, because I
wanted the comfort. And I ended up in a back courtyard screaming
her name, whatever it was, at the top of my lungs. Sorry lady. And
pretty soon, there were headlights on me, and the police put me in the
back of a van and took me away. I slept peacefully in the back of that
van and on a hard board in the cell of a police station after that.

That's the only time in my life that I have ever been put in jail, and
I woke up with a triple horror. The first was the potential headline:
"Black Assistant Attorney General Jailed as Drunk." The second was
that goddamn Hoover. Even if this shit didn't make the papers,
Hoover would know about it and use it against me—such was the
power of J. Edgar Hoover over the minds of officials in Washington,
both appointed and elected.

But the third was by far the worst. During all these years, Momma
had been working her way up through the hierarchy of the YWCA.
She had first been a regional vice-president on the National Board
and then the executive vice-president—first black all the way. Now
she had been elected President of the National Board, the capstone of
her professional life and the day she was to be installed at the Y
convention in Boston, her fucking son wakes up in a jail cell.

Well, fortunately for me, Washington cops know a lot about covering up for important personages. I must have been a ludicrous sight,
because I was outraged about being in jail, as if it was the cops' fault.
I insisted that they drive me home. They convinced me that that was
not their job and that maybe it would be smart of me just to pay the
$10 fine for being drunk and disorderly and to get the hell out of
there. So, I paid and called Eve, who was justifiably outraged, and
then made my way out of the police station with as much dignity as I
could muster in my soiled tux.

But, that wasn't the half of it. I had made plane and hotel reserva-
tions for Amy and me in Boston. We were going up there to surprise
Momma on her installation. Eve said on the telephone she guessed
that that trip was off. I said hell no, Amy and I were still going. And,
I got a cab, went home and cleaned myself up. While I was undress-
ing, Eve and I discovered the lipstick on my underpants at the same
time. Then Amy and I went off on the plane and Eve had to go
looking for our maroon Valiant because I had no idea where in the
hell I had left it.

Momma wasn't to be installed until the afternoon, so I had
planned an elegant day for my beautiful seven-year-old daughter. I
had made a lunch reservation at a fine Boston restaurant called Locke-
Ober's, and Amy and I went there to eat in an upstairs room. She
looked so pretty and so innocent that day, I couldn't stand it. Eve had
put her in her prettiest dress, and she had high white socks and black
patent-leather shoes. She was gorgeous, and it was 1967, and liberal
white people were delighted to see neat and clean black people in
public places. And so they smiled when the slim, indulgent father and
the beautiful child came in. And when I pulled Amy's chair out for
her, she piped up in a little girl's voice, "Why are you doing this for
me here, Daddy? You never do it at home." And everybody laughed,
even I.

Momma was amazed and delighted when her granddaughter and
her son surprised her at her installation as the first black president of
the National Board of the Y. I thought then of her will and her
greatness and of Arthur Miller's fine line: "Attention must be paid." I
paid attention to that wonderful woman that day and I was so proud
of her. And I remembered what I could of the night before among all
those nice ladies, who were smiling at us, and I was so ashamed of
myself.

I don't for one minute condone that night. I was an ass-hole. But, I think of it a lot when I think of nuclear weapons and the pressures of Washington and Moscow and of New Delhi and of Pretoria and the other places. And I think of James Forrestal, the first Secretary of Defense, who committed suicide. And, I think of Walter Jenkins, that nice man whom I met in Johnson's White House, who was caught with another man in the G Street YMCA. And I think of myself and the other people who crack a little bit, out of everybody's sight. And when I think of those pressures and of good people cracking and of nuclear weapons, I become afraid for all the people on this earth.

At that time, though, I was only afraid for myself because of my secret, and so I never told anybody. But when it became clear that the idea of promoting me to Under Secretary of HEW was going to be presented to the President, I had to get serious. I had told Ramsey over the preceding weeks that I wouldn't take another appointment because of my Vietnam objections, but he had brushed all that aside. So, then I had to go to tell him the nasty secret, and it was the hardest thing I ever did in my life. I stood there in his small working office stroking his bust of Lincoln, as I always did in times of stress—like the night that Martin died—and I told him. And I told him that Hoover would splatter me if I went up for another confirmation because he didn't like niggers, especially uppity ones like me.

When I had finished, Ramsey got up and came around from his desk and he hugged me. Then he said:

"I'm sorry that happened, Roger. I love you like a brother. You're right about the nomination. We'll have to kill it. But, if the FBI wants to get you, they'll have to come through me!"

It was surely time for me to leave. I was offered the Vice-Chancellorship for student affairs at the University of California at Berkeley. Despite the fact that my favorite professor from Michigan, Roger Heyns, was now Chancellor, I thought it would be another stressful job that was guaranteed to tear me three different ways. I turned it down.

I went around to some of the wise elders I knew, seeking advice about what to do next. A clock had been ticking in my head from the time I left AID. It kept reminding me that there was a real world out there that was very unlike government. After 1966, the ticking became louder. The king had tapped me on the head with his sword, and people met me with cars at airports. Sometimes there would be reporters and camera crews. I slipped into all of that easily and sometimes gracefully, but I knew it had to end.

Ernest Dunbar, a senior editor of *Look*, wrote a masterly piece for the magazine about life for black people out in the world. They had to get up in the morning and go downtown to meet the *man*, the white man. He talked about the real American economy where the good manners in United States government were replaced by the profit motive; where a black person's competitors in the company were there permanently, not for a limited time in the sun like a political appointment; where profit, jealousy and personal success defined the contours of life. I knew that one day, I would have to go back out there, and I knew that I didn't want to be a lawyer.

John Gardner, the former President of the Carnegie Foundation and one of Lyndon Johnson's secretaries of Health, Education and Welfare, thought that the Ford Foundation would be a good place for me to explore. He put me in touch with McGeorge Bundy, who by now was president at the Foundation, and we talked. The conversations went easily and two jobs were offered. One was in international affairs and the other was to run, under the supervision of the Foundation's Vice-President for National Affairs, Mitchell Sviridoff, the Foundation's largest domestic program. The program gave money for programs in job training, inner-city education, drug rehabilitation, black economic development and projects for other American minorities. It sounded just right, and the money sounded fine, so I agreed to take it after I left government in January.

The decision to go to Ford was typical of the pattern of my life; it was a mistake and probably an inevitable one. The Ford Foundation was another way station in the white establishment. At a time when the divisions between black and white and between black and black had never been greater, I chose to work once more with a white institution, a decision that was to do little for my peace of mind, but much—for better or for worse—to teach me about the nature of white racism.

There were by now a variety of strong and well-developed strains of black ideology, each in its own way suggesting that blacks could survive in America only if they banded together outside of, and largely in opposition to, mainstream white American life. The ideologies were based on searing and emotionally appealing analyses of historical and systematic white destruction of black people and their aspirations in America. Instead of turning away from Africa and slavery in shame as most of the older generations of blacks had done,

the younger generation was pulling it out in plain view and almost
reveling in it. The attempted destruction of tribal and kinship ties, the
imposition of a foreign religion and a white god and the insinuation
into black minds of white America's racist fantasies were marshaled
and rehearsed endlessly.

The crippling imposition of the white fantasy upon the black
psyche most enraged and infuriated me. I hadn't understood until
the late sixties. I had bought the fantasy of white superiority, the
notions that my thick lips and kinky hair were somehow inferior to
the genetic legacies of Europe. I had been ashamed of my skin, my
genes and myself. White America was not simply fraudulent, it was
full of a systematic and deliberate cruelty that had deprived my fellow
black Americans and me of our essence as human beings—self-
respect and internalized dignity.

Those realizations and the rage that flowed from them impelled me
toward a stronger feeling of kinship with other blacks than I had ever
experienced before. And yet, that closeness was more difficult to
realize than ever before, because the new ideology carried with it a
new hierarchy of color and social class. A true ghetto childhood,
laced with poverty and deprivation, provided the strongest credential
of blackness. The Black Panthers, with their recruitment of street
youngsters from what they called the "lumpen proletariat," provided
one model for true blackness. Although the press, most whites and
some blacks were appalled by the Panthers' flamboyant use of weapons as an organizing tool, other blacks were drawn by their programs
of service to the black poor. Around the country hundreds of thousands of blacks who had overcome impoverished backgrounds and
had achieved some training were now finding ways to serve the black
poor through funded community agencies or neighborhood groups
that had grown up in response to the newly dramatized needs of poor
urban blacks.

But, by training, adolescent experience and work history, I was
distanced from this group. My earliest twelve years in middle-class
black communities in Kansas City and in New York didn't provide
the requisite black credential. Once a white member of my staff asked
me where I had lived as a youngster in New York and I replied, "In
Harlem." A black staff member interjected, "Shit, he lived above
145th Street, that's Sugar Hill, not Harlem."

I was struck at that moment by one of history's little ironies. When
I was young, I had heard the older people in my neighborhood insist

that they lived in Washington Heights, to distance themselves from the poorer people who had lived in the Harlem Valley. Now it was the style to claim that you had lived in Harlem to distance yourself from the richer people uptown.

My acculturation as an adolescent in a white middle-class neighborhood had deprived me of easy access to black street language or the sinuous body movements that would have made me comfortable day by day in a storefront in San Francisco or Cleveland. My parents had armed me for life in an integrated America, and now the enraged and romantic part of me didn't want to go there, but I was not equipped culturally or psychically to spend my life in the deepest pools of black America. I could tell myself over and over again that my blackness was as valid as anybody else's; that my experience, though it had been fairly unique, was totally that of a black in America. And I could tell myself that I had kept the faith with the black movement in the sixties as best I could. But I couldn't escape the nagging taunt hurled at me by a black kid in Grand Rapids when I was sixteen, that I was a "technicolor paddy." And I couldn't escape the feeling that I had sat out the sixties wars behind a desk in Washington while the real soldiers like Martin and Andy and Hosea and Stokely and Rap had put their lives on the line.

So I was going to the Ford Foundation instead of a ghetto storefront and that, of course, was the right thing to do, not just because of how I was formed, but because I could do things there that people in the storefronts could not do nearly as well. But, I couldn't find a spiritual peace that I desperately needed, to prevent the constant conflict between black and white America that seemed almost to threaten my sanity.

The conflict was laid out plain one night, when Eldridge Cleaver came to Washington in the fall of 1968 campaigning for President. I had no intention of throwing my vote away in a year when Richard Nixon was making a serious run for the Presidency, but I wanted to hear Cleaver. He was speaking at Howard University, at Crampton Auditorium. I wanted to go, and Mary wanted to go, and a white couple who were friends of ours also wanted to go. I had a late meeting, so I told them I would meet them there. I didn't think about it too much, but as soon as I walked in the auditorium it was clear that I should have.

Crampton Auditorium has about 1,500 seats, and it was jammed when I got there. There were about ten white people in the place and

I was going to be with three of them. The black audience had decorated itself with the stylistic and sartorial symbols of black rage. There were long, blown out Afros; dashikis, of course; beads of bullets and bones; African dresses; red-green-and-black headbands; and stylized black fists hanging on chains from black necks under dark faces with hard and angry looks. As with so many black-power meetings of the time, this "political rally" was to be a celebration of black rage.

As I walked in wearing a gray suit, blue oxford-cloth button-down shirt and dark-blue tie, I ran into Skag, one of my street contacts in Washington. There was no question about Skag's black credentials. Though his skin was as light as mine, he had on dirty purple pants, a black-and-silver dashiki with no undershirt, and a single outsized bullet hanging from his neck. Skag had grown up poor in the middle of black Washington, had been a street hustler, and had been sent to the Lorton Reformatory, just outside Washington, on a drug charge when he was sixteen.

One of my field men had found Skag trying to put together a Head Start program with a group of welfare mothers over on Georgia Avenue and an after-school study and athletic program for grammar-school boys. The place that Skag had talked some guilty Jewish landlords into giving him was a beat-up old ground-level floor-through that once had been a paint store. The floors were not level, the paint on the walls was peeling, and there was no light except what filtered through the big front window. In these makeshift surroundings, seven serious black ladies had divided fifty little black preschool children into five groups, each with a different activity. One woman was reading a simple life of Frederick Douglass to a group of attentive three- and four-year-olds; another woman was teaching freedom songs to a group of children who held hands as they sang after her, "We shall not be moved." One group was reading; still another painting. The women obviously cared about the children, and the children were responding. I was moved.

Skag was pleased that I had come. He knew that if I was impressed, I would try to get them some money.

"This man can call Sargent Shriver on the telephone," he said to a number of the women working there, referring to me as "My brother Wilkins."

A few days after the visit, I met with him in my office to go over his proposals for funding with Mary, who would work with him on the fine points if we decided to try to help him. Skag started a deep-black rap as he sat in a blue leather club chair in my office.

"We develop the skills, you see," he said, "but with the pride that black people need to survive. We screen these ladies. They are strong black ladies from the neighborhood. They know what it takes to survive out there, and they are ladies who have got black love. The children respond to that, don't you agree, brother Wilkins?" I agreed and asked Skag about his recruitment plans for more staff and for children, how he was accepted in his neighborhood, and how he would mesh with the D.C. school system. Skag had answers. He knew this person and that; he was always making connections with the "strong mothers" in the neighborhood; he had great contacts with the teen-agers to whom he expected to expand the program.

Mary and I were both impressed. I told Skag we would help him and that he should provide Mary with the information needed to put together a full proposal. Skag was so high at the end of our meeting that he took off his dark shades and there were tears in his eyes when he said, "This lovely lady has heart. We gon' move with her help. And you, my brother, are beautiful."

Mary looked at me and her eyes were misted. She was a true white radical in those days. She adored the black struggle and distrusted most things white. She thought—and she was right—that her radical-ism affected me and my judgments. She was far less impressed with my performance in White House meetings than she was with my forays into poor black areas and my response to them.

Weeks later, when I walked into the Cleaver rally, Skag's funding proposals were working their way through the federal bureaucracy under Mary's careful eye. As I began to sense the rage that filled that auditorium, Skag separated himself from the crowd and came toward me.

"My man," he said. "My man." Our hands met and flipped in the prolonged handshake that led one black friend of mine to say, "When you niggers get through with all that shit, the revolution will be over."

"The lady's up there," Skag said, when we'd finished shaking hands. He pointed and I saw Mary and our two friends, three white faces in a sea of black with one empty seat beside them. In that sea of dashikis, black fists and rage, it was the last seat in the auditorium I

wanted, but the only place I could go. So I thanked Skag and left him
to climb the steps to where they were with people looking at me in my
white people's downtown clothes.

Cleaver came on and he made a disjointed speech, full of fury and
hatred for invading and oppressive police forces. Then he asked:
"What's the name of the police chief here?"

"John Layton!" the crowd roared back.

"Then chant after me, 'Fuck John Layton!' "

The crowd did—"Fuck John Layton!"

Then Cleaver would say it. Then the crowd would say it. Then
Cleaver would shout it. Then the crowd would shout it. My need for
black fellowship didn't go that far, so I kept my mouth shut, as did
Mary and our two friends. People noticed. A few heads turned; then
more, as the chants went on. I saw Skag see the heads turning and
follow the eyes toward us. I saw him notice that our mouths were
closed and then he looked once again at the angry faces staring up.
Suddenly, he thrust out an arm and pointed a skinny yellow finger.
"Agents," he hissed. Then, standing, "Agents!" he shouted. All eyes
turned toward us as the chanting about John Layton continued.

"We'd better get out of here now," I said to the others, whose faces
mirrored my own fear. I got up from my seat and moved down the
aisle, Mary and the other couple behind me. Nobody followed us,
except with their eyes.

We didn't withdraw our support from Skag's program, and eventually Skag got his money. From what I heard, the programs worked
very well for a couple of years. More women became involved, and a
larger and larger segment of neighborhood children were enrolled.
Then, under President Nixon, the money began to dry up. Skag
drifted away, people said, but some of the women kept it going for a
while until there was no more money and then the programs disappeared. Nobody could say just what became of Skag. And there was
surely no one who could say what became of the children.

What I had learned had more to do with me than anything else.
However much distance there was between me and poor black people, I had learned a lot about being black in America. I knew that by
now I was too burned-out in Washington to do much for those children I cared about. Others might come to it with new energy, new
insight. Maybe seeing things from a new angle, from the Ford Foundation, would give me some invigorated approaches. But in late 1968
I was just marking out the days, working with the staff in an effort to

put down on paper in a programmatic way, the things we had learned over the three tumultuous years in which I had headed the agency.

Despite my weariness with government, the Nixon people told me they wanted me to stay on. Richard G. Kleindienst, the Deputy Attorney General-designate, came over to our building for a briefing and a tour. Kleindienst was a stocky man with a big broad face and the manner of a man who might have been a successful insurance salesman in his native Arizona. Instead, he came with a reputation as one of the meanest and shrewdest conservative political strategists in the country. But he was determined to make me like him. He began by telling me how poor he had been when he was growing up in the little town of Winslow, Arizona, and about a really good black friend he had grown up with. He asked me to stay on the job, told me that John Mitchell wanted me and that the President-elect wanted me. I said, "No."

Then one day I got an urgent call through the White House switchboard telling me that Daniel Patrick Moynihan wanted to get in touch with me. I didn't know Moynihan, and didn't think much of him since his report on the black family, which seemed to blame black poverty on the weakness of the black family structure rather than on white oppression.

Moynihan had signed on for the Nixon Administration and was helping out with the transition. He said he wanted to see me, so I suggested a couple of places in downtown Washington where we might meet for drinks or for coffee. He turned down each of my suggestions and insisted that we meet at the "Harriman House." I wondered what the "Harriman House" was—I thought it was some official building I knew nothing about, but finally at his insistence, I agreed and asked him where the "Harriman House" was.

"Oh, you know," Moynihan said airily, "on N Street."

"Oh yeah," I said, keeping the astonishment out of my voice. Of course I knew *that* Harriman house, but I had hardly expected Pat Moynihan to invite me for drinks at Averell Harriman's home, but that's where he insisted I meet him.

Almost everybody in Washington knew where that grand brick mansion in Georgetown was, but few had been inside it. I was let in by a butler, who was expecting me, and I walked through rooms that made me keep my jaw clamped tight shut. There were paintings everywhere, French Impressionists and Post-Impressionists mainly— Degas, Renoir, Matisse—all originals. The notion that one man actually owned such things astounded me. Before I could master my stunned feelings, I was led into a sitting room where Moynihan, behaving as if he were totally at home, received me grandly.

I wasn't sure what I was there for, but walking up to the house, I speculated that Moynihan had followed the Administration closely enough to conclude that I had spent more time in the streets than any other black high in the government and that I might have some insights that would prove useful to him. In the spirit that Ramsey had urged upon us at Justice, I decided to be as helpful as possible and to make three points.

The first was that community-action programs, fragile and uneven as they were, had succeeded not simply in providing services to the poor, sometimes in ways that were unique and innovative, but had the added benefit of developing a whole new level of community activists and leaders who were capable of revitalizing urban life. The second was that American cities, especially the black segments of them, differ enormously and that in developing its urban policies it was imperative for the new Administration to keep in close touch with local leaders through the Community Relations Service and the Office of Economic Opportunity. Finally, I wanted to tell him that it was important for the Nixon people to pick their top blacks carefully and to make sure that these people were permitted to keep their credibility in the black community while at the same time given regular access to the White House. For many of us in the Johnson Administration, the last year and a half had been like the sound of one hand clapping. We had broken our necks figuring out where the pressures and the pain in the black community lay, who the most helpful people out there were, and what the most useful contact points of black people and government were. Then, armed with this information, we would be handed decisions made behind our backs or asked to meetings where information from white experts received the most attention. I wanted to help the new Administration avoid that mistake and to spare the blacks who would replace us the pain and humiliation that we had experienced after Lyndon B. Johnson had marched off to war.

We chatted about the art while the butler brought us our drinks, and Moynihan told me that I had a fine reputation. I thanked him, said that I had learned a lot and began to tell him about the value of the community-action program when he interrupted me and took off on his own theory of community action, which was not nearly as

optimistic as mine. He gave a splendid monologue full of broad ges-
tures and hyperbole spouting from mobile pink cheeks.

When he ran down, I tried to make the point about the individual-
ity of the cities and again I was interrupted in midsentence by a
torrent of florid prose. This time it was Moynihan's theory of urban
development, every bit as devoid of self-doubt as his theory of community action. It was the same when I tried to give my view of how
the top blacks in the new Administration should be treated. By the
time we had spent an hour together, I had managed to utter about 3.8
sentences. Moynihan had said everything else. At that point, he
looked at his watch, stretched, and with the ease of a practiced Washington name dropper and press sycophant, the Presidential assistant-
to-be said, "I've got to be going. Having dinner with Joe and Polly
Kraft."

Neat. The new boy in town establishes that he's really an old boy
in town, off to have dinner with the distinguished Washington columnist and his distinguished Washington hostess-wife. As we walked
out the door together, Moynihan repeated that my reputation was
good, and that the new people would want to keep me on.

The light dawned at that point. I had been puzzled by his lack of
interest in the knowledge the black Assistant Attorney General had
picked up in three years of visiting the nation's black ghettos. But it
hadn't been a debriefing session. It had been a job interview, which,
of course, had been just as upside down as a debriefing session. All
Moynihan had observed was that I could drink a martini and listen
politely as he declaimed in the manner that later led John Oakes of
The New York Times to write of him as a Shakespearean actor. I
chuckled as I watched Moynihan cross N Street, headed up toward
the Krafts' and thought of Ramsey's dictum: "If you're talkin', you're
not learnin'."

A few days later, I got a call from a young man who was helping
Secretary of Health, Education and Welfare-designate Robert Finch
put his new team together. Mr. Finch would like to see you, the man
said, and if it would be convenient, could you come at two next
Thursday. I knew this had to be a job offer that I wouldn't take, but I
agreed to the appointment. Finch was reputed to be a very shrewd
fellow, and I was curious about anybody who was close to Nixon and
slated to be one of the powers of the new Administration.

When I got to the reception area that Finch was using on the fifth
floor of the HEW building, I realized that this was Finch's black-

appointments afternoon. My buddy Ed Sylvester, who by this time was an outgoing Assistant Secretary of HEW, was there, and so was Ruby Martin, a lawyer, and acting head of HEW's Office for Civil Rights for the previous three months.

While we were waiting we shared our amusement at Finch's schedule and told other tales of powerful white folks' insensitivities during our years in Washington. I told about my riding in the front seat with William Stallworth, CRS driver-messenger, when I was going anywhere. Every time I went for a meeting at the White House, the guards at the South West gate would see the two black men in the car and tell us we could leave our packages with them. I would patiently identify myself each time, and they'd let me in. But one day when one of the guards said, "You boys can leave your package with me," Stallworth had had it out with them.

"Dis here man Assistant Attorney General of the whole country," Stallworth announced before I could say anything. "He Attorney General Clark's right-hand man. You don't let him in right now, he'll 'boy' you!"

Ruby told of going in the basement entrance of the White House on West Executive Avenue and being asked by the guard on duty there for the package he was sure she had to deliver. Without answering, she read upside down, the list of attendees for the meeting to which she had been summoned and put her finger by her name and said, "There I am. I'm here for a meeting with Mr. Watson."

The guard reddened and stammered, "Uh, uh. You're the only—"

"Woman," Ruby finished for him.

But Ed's story was the best. He's a light-skinned black man, and when he was director of the office that made sure large government contractors complied with affirmative-action requirements, his program had become embroiled with Crown Zellerbach because of its employment policies at its plant at Bogalusa, Louisiana. Crown Zellerbach went to the state's most powerful Senator, Russell B. Long, and told him that he had to straighten out a problem with a black bureaucrat. In due course, Ed was summoned to a meeting in Long's office with the Crown Zellerbach people.

Prior to the meeting, there was the usual milling around and when Long came in, he didn't realize who Ed was and decided to tell a story to pass the time until the black bureaucrat arrived.

"Did you see what Stokely Carmichael said in the paper?" Long asked his fellow Louisianans. "He said, 'For every one of our

churches the white folks burn down, we'll burn down one of theirs.'
No wonder people follow that fellow," Long said. "He's got a program."

They were the kinds of easy, comforting stories about white stupidity and black perseverance that the grownups used to tell back in the
heat of the bricks on the front porch in the evenings in Kansas City,
and that the black people in Soweto, outside Johannesburg, still tell
today. Those stories are an assertion, in the face of white power, of
the strength, intelligence and dignity of black people.

Finally, I was summoned for my job interview with Mr. Nixon's
friend, the man who would soon head the largest domestic department in the government. When I walked in the room, we shook hands
and Finch directed me to a chair. It was a mean little room, sparsely
furnished. Wilbur Cohen, Lyndon Johnson's outgoing Secretary of
HEW, had surely been niggardly in providing space and facilities for
his successor to go about the chore of putting his top team together.
When we sat down, Finch looked at me and said, "Mr. Wilkins, everyone says you have done a fine job in the government. I would like
you to be my General Counsel."

Just like that. The man had heard me say, "How do you do, Mr.
Finch," and he was offering me a Presidential appointment in his
department. This guy was obviously crazier than Moynihan. Either
this guy is stupid, I thought, or the General Counsel will have no
power or he just wants a nigger for window dressing.

"No thank you," I said.

Finch's jaw dropped. "I don't want you to answer right away," he
said. "I want you to think it over."

"I don't need to," I said politely. "I had decided to leave the government no matter who won, and I have a new job at the Ford
Foundation." I paused, then I added, "And, anyway, I wouldn't work
for Richard Nixon."

"Why not?" Finch asked.

"Because Nixon has displayed no understanding of black people
and no interest in learning about them," I said. "In addition I thought
his law-and-order campaign was divisive and raised resentments
against blacks and war dissenters."

Finch took my views about his boss and friend with equanimity,
thanked me for my frankness and asked me to reconsider my response to his offer. I told him that I would call him in a couple of
days if he liked, and we shook hands and parted. Finch also offered

jobs to Ruby and Ed that day. They too turned him down.

A couple of days later, I made the call to Finch's office to confirm that I hadn't changed my mind. Kleindienst continued to try to persuade me to stay on at CRS. Every time I saw him, he would throw his arm around my shoulder and joke with me about my anger at white America.

"You're from the upper class," he would tell me, grinning. "I'm just a poor white boy from the sticks. I need somebody like you to show me the ropes in this big town."

Though I knew he was basically full of shit, I liked Kleindienst. He wasn't a tight-assed guy full of Puritanical pieties. He was clumsy about race, but easy to be with if you could make allowances. Kleindienst taught me something. Bad guys don't necessarily come in rough packages. They are often among the most pleasant people.

Kleindienst, Moynihan and Finch taught me something else—especially Moynihan and Finch. The transition between the Johnson and Nixon administrations occurred before the women's movement had taken hold of the popular mind, so I hadn't yet grasped the concept of women's liberation or considered how women had been forced by male society into compliant, powerless roles. But by January 1969, even without the analogy of the women's movement, which was to sharpen black perceptions of the nature of the society in which they lived, blacks had a sharp sense of being ravaged. Finch didn't know me, and he didn't care about me either. He just wanted things to look right. And he had the power to offer me a good title—General Counsel of the Department of Health, Education and Welfare—the status of a Presidential appointee and whatever salary that paid in those days—about $37,000, just what I was making in Justice—with all the glory that comes to a parade-ground pony. I realized that that was the way women were often treated too. Black or female, it really didn't matter—it stank. And, that's what I had learned so far in Richard Nixon's America.

Fuck you, Finch, I thought. Fuck you, Moynihan; fuck you, Kleindienst. I am black, but I am a strong, free American black man and I am going to be myself.

That assertion did not come easy. There was a black fellow whom I knew at the time, who would say, when a black person got a very good job, "They're buying black high and that guy made a good sale." This man had once been a candidate for an important job in the United States government and he had wanted it very much. The man went around Washington lobbying with his friends and making the proper connections. People responded to him in those days, because he was a dark man with very black skin and from the South, an authentic black. Finally, he got an interview in Lyndon Johnson's White House and another black man was present and described it to me.

"The nigger came in," the witness said, "and he had on a brown tweed suit and a soft oxford-cloth shirt with a red-and-blue silk tie with a handkerchief to match flowing out of his jacket pocket. The white man sat him down and was sweet when he talked to him about the work. The nigger was cool until the white guy asked him about his background, then the nigger went off," my witness told me.

"I was a little boy," the job candidate said, "when the Klan came at night to our house. My daddy got me out of bed when they were in the front field and he snuck me out the back door and hid me in a hollow and said, 'Lay there now, don't move and be quiet.' Then he ran off, but the Klan was coming and they passed me by while I was laying in the hollow. After they passed by me, I raised up my head—I was only eight—and I saw a flash from a shotgun and I saw my daddy fall. I lay there in that hollow until morning and then I went to my daddy and took him in my arms. He was dead."

"The white guy was crying," my informant told me, "and the nigger was crying and I know and you know that none of that ever happened," my informant said, "but the nigger damn near got the job on the strength of that story."

That black man had been selling black for all it was worth in those days. And who can say he was wrong? There were buyers then for that.

Kleindienst and Moynihan and Finch didn't ask for that much. They didn't need my mind or my knowledge. All they needed was my brown skin. I decided that there'd be no sale.

There was nothing left to do then but resign, pack up and vacate the premises on the arrival of the new President. I resigned to President Johnson, as you do when you are serious about getting out. If you have a Presidential appointment and hope to be kept on, you send your letter of resignation to the new President and hope that he'll implore you to stay. Mine was a long letter, full of the sweet earnestness that was designed to enrage a President who by now cared as little for me as I did for him. I lauded, as one of the major accomplishments of his Administration, the community-action program, which I knew he had come to hate as a major cause of contention and unrest in urban America. And I thanked him for having given me the opportunity to work for Ramsey Clark, whom I described as "the best man I ever knew," knowing full well that Johnson disliked Ramsey even more than he disliked me.

I was packed up and out of my office on the day before the inauguration and had to get a pass to get into the Department of Justice building in order to take my children to see the inaugural parade. Amy and David and I stood on a balcony and watched the bubble-top limousine come up Pennsylvania Avenue. Richard Nixon's face looked small and pink, and Mrs. Nixon seemed an even smaller, still figure in the back seat next to him. They passed by. An era was over, and it was time to leave that place where I had become more vulnerable, less pliable and too enraged for my own good.

23 Eve and I flew to Jamaica on the first day of Richard Nixon's Presidency. I guess we both hoped that sun and water and sleep in an independent black nation might restore our depleted reserves of energy and hope and the gentleness, concern and love that we needed for our marriage. It didn't work out that way.

It had been bitter cold in Washington, and we had worn heavy clothes against that weather, though we knew that we would land in tropical heat. Eastern Airlines had misplaced our bags and we rode out east from the Donald Sangster Airport in Montego Bay toward the Colony Hotel, itching and sweating. We knew that this was the playground of the affluent whites from the northern part of the Western Hemisphere. We had no idea how black tourists would be accepted, but our experiences in the world made us expect that we might be treated rudely.

The man at the reception desk was a small, precise, light-skinned Jamaican. Apart from him and the rest of the hotel staff we could see around there, Eve and I were the only blacks at the hotel. I felt awkward in my heavy clothes with no baggage while people strolled by in tennis clothes, slacks and beachwear. Old anxieties die hard, and I worried that the man behind the desk would pretend that he could not find our reservation. But, he found it without difficulty. He also served us without warmth; he was aloof, cold.

We were led to our bungalow by another Jamaican, this one quite dark. He too was cold and seemed unconvinced by our story of lost baggage. The maids we encountered walking along the palm-lined path were broad, squat and dark, wearing gay brown-and-yellow dresses with *gailees* on their heads. They glanced quizzically at us as we passed, offering no greetings.

The hotel was a collection of small bungalows arranged around a large building that overlooked the ocean and served as the dining room, bar and stage for the shows in the evenings. The bungalows were connected by curving walks that passed through flaming bougainvilleas, palm trees and cultivated tropical flower beds. It was our first tropical hotel and it was lovely, and even the man who led us to our rooms brightened some when I tipped him though we had had no bags for him to carry.

But though our bags caught up with us the next day, we felt out of place there in that tropical beauty. We were the only black guests, and we were being served by black people who were obviously poor. Most of them moved slowly in the heat, their heads down, and would give us a reluctant "sir" or "ma'am" if we spoke to them. We were served by black waiters on the terrace overlooking the ocean at breakfast and dinner. They cleaned our rooms and brought us towels when we were at the pool or raked the beach and arranged our chairs when we lounged by the ocean. Men and women dressed in old clothes—sometimes little better than rags—would come along the beach selling fish or trinkets. They would plead deferentially and then go on.

The problem for us there was very simple. We had come to enjoy the sun and the water and the rum, just as the white people did. But, we were not white, and we brought with us a different sensibility than most of the white people did. We cared about black poverty and cringed at black pain at home, and we couldn't turn that off just because we were someplace else under the sun. It was not the natural order of things for us to have black people serve us nor was it easy for us to absorb the enmity of black people, who seemed to think that by purchasing a little bit of leisure, these two brown Americans were somehow trying to deny their African heritage and their kinship to the black workers as well.

Black Jamaicans didn't swim in the ocean there, or in the pool; they didn't eat on the terrace or drink at the bar. They just came to serve or to entertain. They could be seen after work, hitchhiking along the road or just trudging toward one of the wooden shacks we could see tucked away in the hills. For the first few days of our stay, the staff kept us at arm's length, and the white guests regarded us with curiosity. The staff was wary, viewing us as intruders, we suspected, whose brown skin made us no better than they, but who had pretensions of being white.

We hacked at that reserve with resolute pleasantness and good manners until some of the people who worked there began to speak frankly to us about themselves.

"Jamaicans can't use this beach or come to these hotels," a bar man told me. "And Jamaicans don't own these hotels. A few of us get jobs here, but for everyone who has a job, there are probably ten out there who need them. This is all arranged for rich white people from Canada and the States to come and play. Then the profit goes back to the States or Canada or Britain."

It was anomalous for us to lie in the sun being served by black people while becoming increasingly aware of how little their political independence meant in the absence of any significant transfer of economic power to black hands.

Though a few of the workers there warmed to us, a number of others seemed to view us as handmaidens of their oppressors, especially Malcolm, the haughty wine steward, who seemed to revel in my ignorance about wines. Malcolm's nose would go up in the air when he served me, and he would look into the distance with barely contained impatience when I tasted a newly uncorked bottle, as if nothing could be more ridiculous than the notion that I could taste anything at all. Malcolm intimidated me thoroughly until one day I borrowed a corkscrew from him for a picnic we were planning at the beach at Negril, about fifty miles from the hotel.

Negril was beautiful and largely untouched in 1969. It was a seven-mile crescent of clean white beach that sloped gently down to a blue sea. An old woman tended frail bamboo structures back in the palm trees, and there, for a dollar, we changed and stored our clothes. She also sold us some Red Stripe beer. There were no hotels on the stretch of beach that we had chosen, and so Jamaicans could swim there. We spent the afternoon among a number of Jamaican families and a few other tourists, drinking wine, eating cheese and salami, walking along the uncluttered white sand and occasionally swimming.

And the drive to Negril was marvelous too, along a winding road that twisted and dipped through lush tropical growth along the ocean and occasionally came upon small settlements of little wooden buildings that looked very much like West Africa. When we got back to the Colony we were tired, but ecstatic. It had been the best of our days in Jamaica.

"How did you like Negril?" Malcolm asked me carefully as I returned his corkscrew.

"I loved it," I gushed. "We've never seen a beach as beautiful as that or ocean water so clear. And I was glad finally to see Jamaicans enjoying the ocean. It was wonderful."

To my amazement, a wide smile broke on Malcolm's face. "I am from Negril," he said. "It is the best place in Jamaica."

Malcolm became our friend after that, and he talked to me about the poverty and the crushing unemployment that Jamaicans suffered and the indignities that they bore from the tourists. They were depressing talks, but it was good to have Malcolm as a friend. He had finally decided that Eve and I were co-conspirators and not fellow travelers of the white tourists, whom he viewed as oppressors, even though they were necessary to his livelihood.

At night after the shows where Jamaicans would come and swallow fire, or walk on glass or contort their bodies for the pleasures of the hotel guests, the hardiest clusters of tourists would merge into one group at the bar for the last few drinks of the evening. Malcolm was in charge of the bar at those times and toward the end of our stay, when I went to pay my bill, he would shake his head imperceptibly and roll his eyes toward the drunkest of the white guests there. I didn't understand at first, but then it became clear that he was laying my bill off on a white man.

It was his way of saying, I supposed, that black was black and you had to strike tiny little blows against heedless use of human life however you could. It was touching, in a way, and also pathetic. The whole vacation had been touched with pathos. Black was black everywhere, it seemed, and white people could enjoy themselves immensely in the midst of black poverty without even noticing it. I left that beautiful island tanner, more rested and substantially sadder than when I had arrived. It was not a good augury for my reentry into the real world.

The Ford Foundation has been described as a pile of money surrounded by a sea of people who want some. In 1969, it was among other things a place where an out-of-office public-service person could do good works while marking time until another, more congenial administration could come to power. It was also an enormously productive bureaucratic paper factory, a large group of people working in an architectural marvel, and an institution grappling with its conscience over race while firmly in the grip of affluent, middle-aged white men. The fifteen-member board of trustees was all white, all middle-aged to elderly, and all male.

The two highest blacks in the organization were directors of two of the programs in the national affairs division, headed by Mitchell Sviridoff, a man who had made a tremendous reputation in putting municipal human-service programs together and running them, first in New Haven, Connecticut, and then in New York under John Lindsay. Chris Edeley, the other black, headed an office that gave grants for innovative legal programs. I was hired to head a program that specialized in experimental human-service programs. And that was one of the problems.

Mike Sviridoff was a short, stocky energetic man in his early fifties. He had started out as a sheet-metal worker and had been a highly effective labor-movement politician before Mayor Richard Lee tapped him to be one of the key members of his highly effective administration in New Haven in the late fifties and early sixties. Though Mike often commented on the fact that he had never earned a college degree, he was a highly intelligent, tough, shrewd man. Human-service programs, particularly manpower experiments, were his babies. They were also my responsibilities at Ford.

I should have read the handwriting on the wall early. I hadn't been at the Foundation very long when Mike grabbed my arm in one of the elegant, brass-trimmed elevators in the building and told me, "We just spent a million and a half of your money at lunch."

I blinked at him and gulped. My annual budget in those high rolling days was $27 million, but about $15 million of that was channeled to old commitments and another $5 million or so to semi-promises that program officers had been whipping into shape for some time. So, Mike's announcement that he had just committed a million and a half of my free money stunned me.

"Bundy and Lou Winnick and I just had lunch with John Gardner and Pete Libassi of the National Urban Coalition," he continued amiably, "and we made a commitment to them of $1.5 million that will come from your budget."

I felt anything but amiable. I was having a hard time comprehending the words I had just heard. The National Urban Coalition had been established in the late sixties, under John Gardner's leadership, in an effort to mold a coalition of business, labor and black leaders to begin to address the problems of the inner-city black poor. Yet, here were Bundy, Sviridoff and Winnick, all white from the Ford Foundation, meeting with Gardner and Libassi, both white of the Coalition, deciding on the nature and level of the Foundation's support for that organization.

Gardner was a decent, liberal man as was Bundy. I had known Pete Libassi for years—since he had served as the General Counsel for the United States Commission on Civil Rights. Sviridoff had the reputation as one of the most enlightened municipal administrators of the decade, and I assumed that Winnick shared his views. And certainly the Ford Foundation under Mac Bundy was bidding to become the most racially enlightened institution in the American establishment. Yet none of these men had thought to ask Carl Holman, by now the Executive Vice-President of the Coalition, or me to the meeting. And the money was to come out of my budget.

I do not think that Mac Bundy or John Gardner acted out of malice or racism. It was simply thoughtlessness. But, Mike's cavalier announcement of the decision told me how he did business, and how he viewed my role in the Foundation. I balked.

"I'll quit before that money comes out of my budget," I said. "If you and Mac want to make a handshake deal with John Gardner, that's fine. But don't take it out of my budget. Take it out of Bundy's discretionary funds or your own. I don't know anything about that grant, none of my program officers worked on it, so I'm not prepared to fund it. I'll send Bundy a note this afternoon telling him how I feel."

Now it was Mike's turn to have trouble comprehending. "Oh, there's no need to make something big out of this," he said in a jocular tone. Then he chuckled, but it was a nervous chuckle.

I smiled and said, "I'll send you a copy of my note to Bundy," and got on the elevator and went on down to my office.

That was the beginning of the end for Mike and me. Mike is an amiable and charming man who spent much of his social time in those days with associates and subordinates. He could be a very generous friend to those who went along with him. But it was necessary to go along in order to bask in the warmth of the circle that he created and dominated. Mike was an acknowledged expert on manpower programs, and he was learning fast about putting together local economic-development programs. He also thought he was an expert on blacks, the kind of white man who thought he knew more about blacks than we did ourselves.

One morning I went up to Harlem to meet a young friend of mine who had called me in a good deal of distress. We had coffee in a grim little place on 125th Street in the shadow of the overhead railroad station through which thousands of suburban white commuters rode twice each day without much thought of the lives below.

"You know, I been a Panther for a long time now," my friend said over the grits and eggs that I had bought him because he was hungry.

"Yes," I said, "I figured that."

"There's a lot of killing among them brothers now, man," he said disconsolately. "I'm scared."

My friend was eighteen years old, a high-school dropout and very smart.

"Why're you scared?" I asked. "Somebody after you?" I blew on my coffee, looking straight ahead at the cracked mirror of the little luncheonette. I was acting cool, but the conversation about the possible death of this bright young black man chilled me. He could contribute something to himself and society; he could get killed; or he could destroy himself. Those were his three choices, and the first seemed least likely.

"Look man, it's a power struggle," my friend said. "With Huey in prison, those West Coast cats are coming down with some heavy ideological shit. The brothers back here don't buy the new shit that's comin' down. At least most of us don't, but a brother who didn't, got blown away down the street selling the Panther paper the other day. I don't buy it. People know I don't buy it. I could get blown away too."

"People are enforcing ideology with bullets?" I asked.

"Yeah."

The Black Panther party, founded in Oakland by Huey Newton and Bobby Seale, had come apart at the top. Newton was facing charges that he had murdered a policeman in California, and Seale had been charged by federal officials in Illinois with conspiracy to foment the riot at the Democratic convention in Chicago. While the Panthers were still trying to operate their service programs in some of the big cities around the country, their revolutionary ideology had grabbed the guts of thousands of ghetto kids across the nation. With the founding leadership and many of their legitimate lieutenants in trouble with the law, a violent struggle for the heart of the movement was taking place on the streets.

"You care enough about all that ideological shit to take a bullet in your head?" I asked.

"Shit, man," my friend said. "I don't want to get shot, but I care about the people."

"How much good you goin' to be able to do for the people if you're dead?" I asked. "Why don't you just get the fuck out and go back to school?"

My friend had finished his food by now and I had finished my second cup of coffee. He looked at me for a long time before he answered my questions.

"Let's take a walk," he said finally. "I want to show you something."

I paid the check and we left.

"Now just look at what you see as we walk," he said, as he steered me west along 125th Street, toward the Hudson River. He acted as if I had never been on 125th Street before. I remembered 125th Street when the trolleys ran along it, when Blumstein's seemed a glorious department store, the Apollo Theater a magic place and the Theresa Hotel a haven where middle-class people went in their best clothes to Sunday dinners. Now there was a large hole at 125th and 7th Avenue where a disputed state office building was to be built. Blumstein's wasn't glorious anymore, and many of the businesses and clubs were closed and gone, mere store-front shells.

People were out this weekday morning, many of them just standing and looking, a day stretching before them with nothing to fill it up. My friend walked me all the way over to Eighth Avenue and then we turned downtown. Soon I began to see large crowds of sidewalk people at the corner of 116th and Eighth Avenue. Even at that early hour, it was not yet ten-thirty, there were a lot of people standing and milling around between 116th and 115th on the east side of Eighth Avenue. Before I could ask what was going on, my friend said:

"Drugs, man; that's what you're seeing. That's what this corner is all about. You wanna get fucked up? Just come down here and they'll sell you something."

As we got closer, I could see that most of the people there were men, some young, some not so young. There were women too, and cars came along, slowed, were met by somebody from the sidewalk, then moved along again.

"Most of those cars got customers in them," my friend said. "And some of them got cops looking for their payoffs. Look at that dude over there," my friend said, pointing to a young man in red slacks and a black shirt, who was bent over almost double, his head slowly bobbing up and down. "That's what you can buy at this market—somethin' that can make you forget you're alive."

My friend and I watched for a short while from the opposite side of the street and then walked a couple of blocks in silence. Then he said, "That's what I mean when I say I care about the people. The Panthers ought to be about cleanin' up shit like that," he said. "The cops ain't gonna do nothin' about it. They don't give a shit for poor niggers. That's what the Panthers ought to be all about and not this fightin' among ourselves to be the leader."

I told my friend that I didn't think he could do much about all of that if he didn't even have a high-school diploma. "I know there's some good shit in the Panthers," I said. "And I also know that there's some very bad shit in the Panthers. The way it is now, the bad shit's more likely to get to you than you are likely to do anything about that corner. If you want to get back in school, I'll try to help you."

"Okay, man," he said, shaking my hand at the subway station at 110th, "I'll think it over. Thanks for breakfast."

I got to the office that day just in time for a meeting with Mike and some people from outside the Foundation. The Panthers were very much in the news in those days and one of the white visitors asked me what I thought was going on inside the organization.

"Well," I said, "I think—"

I didn't get any farther. Mike cut in then to give a long version of his theory about the Panthers. It was rough, speculative and, considering what I had just learned, largely wrong. But Mike had his theories about black people. When he finished, he looked at me and asked whether I had anything to add. I said no.

It was not a good time for me all around. I was living in a hotel during the week and commuting to Washington to see Eve and the children on weekends. The absences weren't doing our marriage any good. Our conversations became rarer and leaner. Mary was still in Washington and still in my life, and though our relationship was no longer pure, unalloyed bliss, there was still life in it.

The marriage got worse and worse. Neither my job nor the circumstances of my personal life were doing much to ease a deepening depression. Finally, I told Eve that I thought we ought to separate, that I needed to leave. She thought I was mad. Perhaps I was. She was hurt and enraged. I left.

Work at Ford went on, and it was not all terrible. Mac Bundy was a bright spot. There are people who will never forgive him for having been Lyndon Johnson's National Security Adviser while the war was being escalated, but that was not a thing between us. It had happened when we had barely known each other, and it was something we never talked about.

Mac mediated disputes between Mike and me in a calm, judicious way. His role in this respect probably kept me at Ford a year longer than I otherwise would have stayed. One night when I was staying alone at the hotel, Mac and his wife, Mary, invited me to dinner at their Fifth Avenue apartment. It was during a time when the Foundation, especially Mac, was taking a lot of heat for travel and study grants that had been made to a number of Robert Kennedy's assistants just after Kennedy had been killed in 1968.

Marian Wright and Peter Edelman had gotten married just after the grants had been made, and one of the news stories reporting on the wedding said that they were going to take a round-the-world honeymoon on a Ford Foundation grant. The legend in the foundation world was that Wright Patman, the old Democratic populist curmudgeon from Texas—scourge of the banking industry, and private foundations, and not known for civilized views on race—exploded at the thought of Ford paying money to send a white man around the world with his black bride. His response to that story began a Congressional review of foundations, which led to the imposition of a tax on foundations for the first time.

That night the subject came up at the Bundys' table, where Mac, Mary and I were dining alone. Though the "Kennedy grants," as they were called, had been made before I got to the Foundation, I was responsible for administering them.

"I know why you made those grants," I told Bundy. "You were at the White House when John Kennedy was killed and you saw how devastated and distraught all those people were left. You figured that these guys could pull themselves together if they were given some projects to do and some time to do them in."

I hadn't been looking at Mac when I talked. My eyes were fixed on the opposite wall, remembering those days in November 1963. But when I turned and looked at Mac, he had his face in his hands. When he looked up, tears were brimming behind his clear-rimmed glasses. He nodded his head jerkily.

"Yes," he managed. "Yes."

At that moment I wished that my friends who thought of this man as a cold-blooded war criminal could have been there.

When the reports on the projects came in, Peter Edelman's was by far the best. It was a book-length study of youth programs around the world, sensitive and perceptive. I should have had the wit to send a copy to Wright Patman, but I didn't.

24   My relations with Mary did not thrive in the freedom
      we got from my separation from Eve. The age differ-
      ence, a difference in temperament, and the claustro-
      phobia that a person who grew up near the desert
around Tucson felt in the East took its toll. None of the problems
that Mary and I developed over our time together ever seemed to me
to be based on race. We had been involved in the civil-rights struggle
together for so long and had discussed the issues so much that Mary
usually seemed to me lacking in racial identity. It was clear that on
many issues—the relative lack of distinction in the white population,
the extent to which blacks ought to separate from the white community, and the length that I should wear my hair—Mary was more
radical than I, perhaps to compensate for not being black in a decade
when one's color seemed to take on moral value.

But in December 1969, months after the flames that Mary and I
had enjoyed had died, the conflicts that might have lurked in that
relationship became concrete in a different form. A delicate dark-
haired woman with fine features and a striking figure came to interview me for a book that she was doing on Robert F. Kennedy. When
she called me to make the appointment, she identified herself as
the former wife of William Vanden Heuvel, a familiar New York
political aspirant and a fairly close associate of Robert Kennedy's. I
had never heard of Mrs. Vanden Heuvel, but the breathy rush and
jumble of her words on the telephone was appealing.

Mrs. Vanden Heuvel turned out to be even more appealing in
person than she had been on the telephone. She kept on getting
tangled up in the wires of her tape recorder as she tried to find the

260

outlet behind the couch in my office. The tentativeness of her approach produced an impression of the woman's vulnerability that I was later to learn was something less than the whole story.

But, it was partly true and enormously effective for an interviewer. To help this woman out, I found myself remembering things that I thought I had long forgotten. Each time I would come up with a new nugget of information to her half-formulated question, she would give me a smile suffused with shy gratitude. When the interview was over and she was stumbling over her mike and her cords, she thanked me profusely, and several days later, I received a warm and effusive note of thanks for giving so much of my time to her project and expressing the hope that I would review the transcript in order to make sure that it was correct. I was anxious to see that woman again, and so, in January 1970, when the transcript had come back, I went over to her Central Park West apartment early one evening to go over the material and have a drink.

Jean and I had one drink and then another. And then I took her out to dinner that night, and later another. Her smile was bewitching. It would begin and her head would tuck down and sideways, then the smile would begin to fade as if a cloud of doubt were passing, and then the teeth would show again and the smile would rush to fulfillment, powered by a shy giggle. Jean's bones were as thin as her features were fine. Her hair was very dark and her skin very pale. Her touch on hand or cheek was light, sometimes tentative, always affecting. She had a way of making a man feel strong, capable, protective, supported and, ultimately, loved and loving.

It was clear from her apartment that Jean was not poor. It was a large place overlooking Central Park; it featured a large sitting room, draped largely in blue, highlighted by a red velvet rail at the fireplace and a deep easy chair covered in the same material. The art ranged from a fanciful Man Ray disk on one wall, to a Jules Feiffer strip autographed "to Jean," to a line self-portrait in profile by William Faulkner. I figured the money had come from her husband since Bill's name had been prominent in New York politics for as long as I could remember. I thought that Jean's maiden name was Styne and that her father was Jule Styne, the songwriter. But was I wrong!

Her father was Dr. Julius Caesar Stein, usually called Jules, who had started a talent-agency business in Chicago, then moved it to Hollywood, where, as President of the Music Corporation of America, he had been a dominant—some would say *the* dominant—force in the movie industry. Jean had grown up as a princess in the Canyons above Los Angeles and though she rarely talked much about it, had such memories as being brought with her younger sister in their best clothing out on the lawn to curtsey to such people as Charlie Chaplin and J. Edgar Hoover.

Sometimes Jean's tentativeness would dissolve almost into incoherence, which was often incongruously linked with a sincere and effective proffer of strength for and belief in me. She was generous to her friends, emotionally and materially.

Jean started to introduce me to her impressive circle of friends. There was Gillian, large, galloping, loving and warm, who lived in the building next door to Jean and who was a sometimes awkward, large-boned beauty, cerebral and brooding. Gillian was Jean's best friend and though her father had been curator of the National Gallery, Gillian was just Gillian from next door, easy to be with. And then there were Jason and Barbara Epstein, stars of the literary world, he at Random House and she at *The New York Review of Books*. My relationship with Jean often landed me at evenings at the Epsteins' with Stephen Spender or Lillian Hellman or, at the least, Bob Bernstein, the lovely man who heads Random House.

Then one night, Jean said we'd been asked to drop by the home of another editor, Aaron Asher, of Holt, Rinehart and Winston. So we went and, in addition to the Ashers, there were the photographer, Inge Morath, and her husband, Arthur Miller, and there was also, sitting across from the Millers, Philip Roth.

The Senate was scheduled to vote the next day on President Nixon's nomination of G. Harrold Carswell to be an Associate Justice of the Supreme Court. Roth was expounding; he had no doubt that the Senate would confirm Carswell. I thought I knew better. I knew that he had been hip-deep in a land deal that was designed to transform a public recreational facility, which by law was required to be desegregated, into a private country club, which maintained its segregated character. And I knew that Marian Wright Edelman had been launching a successful campaign to bring Carswell's history of racist rulings to light.

So, that night in the Ashers' living room, with the Millers looking on, I told Roth that I thought the nomination would be defeated. So we made a bet. The one who lost would have to take the winner and his lady to the restaurant of his choice for dinner.

The Carswell nomination was defeated the next day. Though I

called him a time or two, I saw nothing of Roth until a chance encounter years later at the airport in Barbados. He and a woman were just landing on the island and I was in the embarkation area. He slapped his head when he saw me and said, "God, I still owe you that dinner. Well, come on, at least let me buy you a drink."

This was said as the gate for my plane back to New York was opened and the crowd was surging around me.

"Sure, Philip," I laughed. "Great way to pay off a debt."

The fact is almost everybody lost on the deal. Roth lost the bet. I lost, because Roth never paid. The liberals lost, because the President came back with William H. Rehnquist. Rehnquist's youth at the time of his appointment seems virtually to assure a very long tenure. He has proved to be a more effective opponent of the liberal interests than the rejected nominees could ever have been. The only winner was Richard M. Nixon, who managed to appoint an effective conservative to the Court.

There were few political victories for people like me in the days of 1970. After Edward M. Kennedy went off the bridge at Chappaquiddick Island, there was no credible threat on Nixon's left, so he veered right. Local police forces, energized by the FBI, cracked down on the Black Panthers around the country—in Philadelphia blacks were rounded up, stripped and made to stand naked in the cold; in New Orleans, sweep arrests were made; in Chicago, special police attached to the State Attorney's office fired scores of bullets into a Panther residence and killed Fred Hampton, leader of the Illinois Panthers, in his bed. In the spring, it was revealed to the American people that the United States armed forces had made an incursion into Cambodia.

All of this had an impact on the artistic and literary circles in New York in which Jean moved and to which I was gaining access not only through her, but through my own activism as well. Late in 1969, I had been asked to attend a meeting at the home of the playwright Lillian Hellman. Miss Hellman then lived on East 82nd Street, just down from the Metropolitan Museum. When I got to the meeting, I recognized Burke Marshall, the head of the Civil Rights Division under Robert F. Kennedy, the writer William Styron and his wife, Rose, Norman Dorsen, a distinguished NYU law professor and civil libertarian, Blair Clark, a writer and former radio journalist, the cartoonist Jules Feiffer and Robert Silvers, editor of *The New York Review of Books*. The drawing room where Miss Hellman settled us had a gentle and softly faded ambiance that was touched by elegance; the books and the pictures of Dashiel Hammett suggested the richness of Hellman's past.

The times were bad, Hellman said, by way of explaining her reason for calling us together. They reminded her of the McCarthy time and she thought there was need for a group of concerned people with influence to band together in an effort to alert the American people to what was going on and to try to reverse the course on which the government seemed bent on taking us. There was no disagreement in the room about the characterization of the situation or the need to do something. After an initial round of agreement and amplification on the basic theme, the discussion turned to the practical questions of whom to recruit, possible sources of money, potential projects, and time and place for the next meeting.

That night, Jean and I had dinner with Felicia and Leonard Bernstein at their penthouse apartment on Park Avenue.

There was a strain in all of this. I had known when I left the government, that I had to forge a new identity, or at least to consolidate the old one, which in large measure had been based on a charter from a President who was no longer in office and at a time that no longer existed. Now I was getting a new identity from associations with some of the most glittering people in America. But, there were problems about that—profound ones.

An identity built on association is almost as valuable, I suppose, as fool's gold. It would be absolutely destructive of the ego of one who doubted the value of what he had already accomplished and was on the way to hating what he was presently working on.

Occasionally, my name would slip into a gossip column. "Roger Wilkins of the Ford Foundation," it would say. That was perfectly respectable in print, but the reality was becoming more and more difficult to live with. One day, for example, a black man and a white woman—both professional educators—who had founded a private minischool for poor black kids in the West Philadelphia ghetto, came to have lunch with me at Ford. Theirs was exactly the kind of effort that I loved; innovative, concerned, respectful and loving without condescension. It was for me the purified essence of the black consciousness movement of the late '60s.

We had lunch in the dining room on the eleventh floor of the elegant Foundation headquarters. While the orders were being taken by starched employees of Restaurant Associates, a company that owned some of the most expensive restaurants in the city, I showed

my visitors the view of the East River, the United Nations and Tudor
City visible out of the glass wall on the east side of the dining room.
Over paté, they began to tell me how they had conceived the school
program and why. While we ate our steak and lamb chops, they told
me how they had built their curriculum, and over chocolate mousse
they told me how they had scrabbled for the funding that had kept
them alive so far.

After lunch, I led them along a walkway, eleven stories up in the
glass-roofed core of the building that served as a greenhouse for the
tropical foliage planted around the pond in the garden. The woman
looked down at the trees, bushes and pond hundreds of feet below
and pulled her head back.

"The height makes me dizzy," she said.

"The expense makes me dizzy," her male companion replied, looking at me. I just nodded. I knew how he felt.

The elevator we took down to the third floor, like all the others had
leather walls, large brass-trimmed hand rails and recessed lights. I
asked them why they had come to me since they understood education was not my primary responsibility.

"We came to you because you're black and because, on the basis
of your reputation, we thought you'd understand what we're trying to
do," the man said.

I just grunted in reply. When we reached the third floor, we walked
down a corridor defined by gray, cloth-covered walls and parquet
floors. My office had a glass wall that looked out onto the garden and
past it to the natural park in Tudor City outside. The room was filled
with modern furniture—a couch, a square coffee table of polished
walnut, two square-backed chairs with material that matched the
couch and wood that matched the coffee table, my rectangular desk
and the large, elegant credenza behind it.

"We need $25,000 to get us through this year," the man said. "If
we can make it through this year, I'm sure we can get state and local
grants in Pennsylvania that will put us on a permanent footing."

I sighed. I had seen these people because a good friend of mine
had told me they were doing a first-rate job in their attempt to develop an alternative to the failing Philadelphia public-school system.
My friend had asked me to see them as a favor to him. I had known
what they would ask, and I had checked before they arrived to see if
there were anything we could do.

"I'm afraid there's nothing I can do for you," I said.

Their faces sagged. I tried to explain. "My program only does education in conjunction with the people here at Ford who specialize in education," I began, attempting the impossible task of making institutional constraints plausible to working idealists. "We have a little bit of money that we can put up together with theirs if they are interested in the project, and if it fits within their guidelines," I continued, hating each bureaucratic word as it came out.

"I've talked to Ed Meade, my counterpart in education, and he's not interested. He has a number of pilot projects like this, and he doesn't need another one. That leaves me powerless to help you," I concluded, "because I don't have authority in this program to fund education projects by myself."

They looked at me, their faces blank. I looked back at them, trying to keep my face blank.

"But we're talking about fifteen little black kids whose minds are being opened up like never before, man," the black man said. "What does all that stuff you were just talking about have to do with that?"

"Won't you even come to Philadelphia to look at the school before you turn us down?" the white woman asked.

"There's no reason for me to come to Philadelphia except to make myself feel worse than I do now," I said. "I don't have the money or the power to make the grant you're asking for."

"But, brother, you understand the needs," the black man said plaintively.

"Yes, I understand the needs and if I had the money in my pocket, I'd give it to you. But I don't have it, and weird as it sounds, there's no place in this Foundation that I can get it for you. I'm sorry. I really am."

I stood up then and started moving them toward the elevator. There was no use prolonging this agony. We walked down the corridor on the polished floor and then waited for the elevator in silence.

"I'm really sorry," I finally said.

They just shrugged and looked downcast. When the elevator came, they thanked me and stepped in. As the door was closing, I heard the man say, "We could run our school for three years with just what it cost to build this elevator."

I walked back to my office, hands in my pockets, head down.

The other problem with my daily life as it was evolving then was that the Ford Foundation was the only place where I had any daily connection with blackness—thinly strained and awkward as the connection often was. The places where I had drifted and where I was building an identity outside working hours were all white. And there was not much occasion for the exercise of robust blackness inside the Ford Foundation. Minor victories had to provide sustenance over long arid spells.

One of my program officers asked me one day how to make out the check for the community-development corporation in Bedford-Stuyvesant. The organization was really two corporations. One was called Development and Services. Its president was John Doar. His group was white, and it was designed to give technical assistance and guidance to the operating corporation and to deal on its behalf with the white corporate world. The operating corporation, called Bedford Stuyvesant-Restoration, was headed by Franklin Thomas, a black man who had been a Columbia University basketball star, and an assistant district attorney. His staff was largely black, and it was his corporation that actually mounted the projects in the community.

I had always thought that the two-corporation construct was paternalistic and that whatever services were provided by the white corporation could, somehow, have been fitted into the structure of the corporation the black man headed. It was as if the business community couldn't entrust money to a black hand unless there was a white hand holding it.

"What's the problem about the grant check?" I asked.

"It's always been made out to John Doar," the program officer replied, "but now Frank Thomas wants it made out to him. I also hear that Doar has called the treasurer of the Foundation and insisted that the check be made out to him."

"Is there any program reason for the check to be made out to one as opposed to the other?" I asked.

"No," the program officer replied, "none at all."

"Good," I said. "Then notify the treasurer's office that I won't sign a payment authorization unless it's made out to Thomas as president of Restoration." So much for that bit of paternalism and condescension.

Some things did make coming to work worthwhile. Putting money and technical assistance into the Watts Labor Community Action Committee was one of them. The program was the brainchild of a number of United Auto Workers' officials, particularly Jack Conway, who had been one of the members of Ramsey Clark's team in Watts in 1965. The union had picked Ted Watkins, a black auto worker, to head a program designed to bring jobs, businesses, houses and services into Watts. The combination of Watts, strong union backing, and Watkins' brilliant entrepreneurial instincts made WLCAC one of the brightest spots in America's ghetto landscape.

Ted Watkins is a powerful, dark-skinned man with a shaved head and limitless enthusiasm for his work. On my visits to Los Angeles, he would take me on tours of WLCAC projects in his gray Lincoln sedan carrying the vanity license tag, "WLCAC." Watkins was a factory man, a nonideological blue-collar bulldog. While some of Los Angeles leading black-power theorists would spend days decrying the racism of Mayor Yorty, Watkins would be down in City Hall obtaining new grants or donations of surplus property.

"He's the only mayor we got," Watkins would say, when asked about his thick, rich relationship with City Hall. "I don't have time for denouncing. I'm too busy building."

A ride through Watts with Watkins was like a walk through the Cloisters with a Rockefeller. He would point at a run-down gas station and talk enthusiastically about WLCAC's plan to buy it, revitalize it and put youngsters to work running it. A moderate-size grocery store would be turned into a "supermarket" as soon as WLCAC bought it, and Ted would charge through the aisles checking on inventory, through the office checking on sales volume and through the back storerooms checking on the newest trainees hired from the neighborhood. Neither Watkins' vision nor his energy appeared to have limits. Only occasionally did he betray weariness. One day after he had shown me a new housing-rehabilitation project that WLCAC had just initiated and Watkins hoped would employ about 75 community youths and ultimately provide good housing for 200 families, I asked Ted what he estimated the true unemployment rate of Watts to be.

He looked at me for a minute and then said, "You mean everybody who is looking for a job and everybody who isn't looking, because they know there's nothing out there for them?"

"Yes," I said. "That's what I mean."

"Fifty or sixty percent," he said grimly. He looked at me for a few seconds and then, not taking the time to reflect on the enormity of what he had just said, he motioned impatiently. "Come on. There's a lot more for you to see to justify all the money I want you to give us."

Giving Ted Watkins as much money as we figured he could use effectively was not a problem. The problem was that energetic, able, charismatic and effective as Watkins was, his program was only a small part of the answer for Watts, and the rest of the answer wasn't even in sight. I saw millions of black Americans trapped in conditions that could be guaranteed to make them suffer throughout their lives, and I saw no promising answers in the framework of American politics. I had a strong romantic impulse, which had recurred since my years as a lawyer, to turn my back on the white world and live in a black community, not only to declare my emotional loyalties in a racially divided America, but also to see whether I could help to devise better answers from a physical vantage point dead inside black America.

But other romantic and deep American impulses were taking me away from America's black ghettos. Instead, I was spending many of my evenings on Central Park West or joining Jean's friends in the newest cultural trend or artistic fad. My night world was virtually lily-white and far more distant than the actual three thousand miles that separated Central Park West from Watts. Jean's sensitivity, warmth and perceptive intelligence were enough to keep me involved in our relationship, but she had also given me the keys to the candy store. Instead of standing with my nose pressed to the window, I often found myself inside rooms with people whose names were Mailer, Vidal, Javits, Kennedy or Bernstein.

Those who were Jean's friends seemed as devoid of racism as any group of whites I had ever encountered. Whatever problems people had about Jean and me, they kept to themselves. Once, in Roxbury, Connecticut, at Arthur and Inge Miller's home, at a party celebrating Arthur's birthday, a grand dame of a Russian *émigrée* took me to be the bartender. Everybody thought it was pretty funny and I didn't mind.

Normally, there was simply easy acceptance of me, as if I had earned my way into those drawing rooms just as everyone else had. Yet, because my work was not individualistic, creative or as celebrated as that of most of the people I saw around me, I didn't believe I belonged.

Felicia Bernstein, Leonard's delicate, intelligent and beautiful wife, was one of my favorites in Jean's circle. She was Chilean and had been an actress before she married Leonard. I always thought she should have been a queen.

One evening when Jean was having a small dinner party, Felicia told me a story about her father-in-law.

"Lennie's father always discouraged Lennie's musical aspirations," Felicia said. "He wanted him to be a mathematician. After we had been married for a while, I asked my father-in-law why he had been so mean to Lennie about that.

" 'How was I to know he was going to be Lennie Bernstein?' " the old man answered.

Felicia knew about my insecurities and once, when she heard me say I had been the first black to do this or that, she stopped me.

"You know, Roger," she said, "you sound like you're keeping score. This isn't a game. It's life, so stop keeping score and go and live it."

The company of Miller, Bernstein *et alii* was all heady stuff; I loved it, but it tore me apart. I was enjoying a kind of life that was far beyond the actual or even the imaginative grasp of the poor blacks to whom the serious efforts of my life were supposed to be committed. This was the life where people escaped even the mundane problems that ordinary white people had. It was as if, by entering that world at night, I was betraying everything I told myself I stood for during the day.

One March day in 1970, I went up to meet a young man in the basement of an Episcopal church on Edgecombe Avenue in Harlem. The young man's name was Sam. He had light skin, a left eye that had a tendency to wander off on its own and a sweet, soft manner that suggested a patience with the problems that his organization was encountering. Sam and his group were working on housing when I met him, and he didn't want Ford money; just my sense of how he was doing and a connection that would make him feel comfortable when he thought it would be useful to him.

Sam had the people in the church basement divided into several work groups. Some of them were simply taking telephone complaints from local residents about their landlords. Others were interviewing people who walked in off the streets with complaints. There was a third group of complaint processors, who knew just where and whom to call in the city bureaucracy in order to get action for the helpless old people of Harlem who were filing into that church basement, sitting on rickety folding chairs and waiting to be interviewed at tables made of large warped boards and saw horses. These were not hipsters or drug pushers, but people who had worked out their lives and were now being used badly by circumstance and society. They sat quietly waiting for their turn at the service desks, in old clothing, looking stoically at the world through rheumy eyes.

Sam walked me out of the church and told me about his dream of mounting a major housing-rehabilitation program in Harlem.

"We've got some great housing up here," Sam said, "and if we can get it together, people will live better up here than they ever did."

He seemed oblivious to the cracked sidewalk where we stood, the litter on the street, the loose dirt on the space between sidewalk and curb, and the worn and crumbling look of the houses on the block.

"How are you going to get it together, Sam?" I asked.

"We've got some beautiful brothers and sisters up here," Sam said. "They're into helping each other and helping the community. It is beautiful energy we're building up here," Sam said, "and we'll get a lot done, you'll see."

I shook Sam's hand and turned away to go. My eyes were full of tears that I didn't want him to see. Sam, the man of beautiful energy, was nineteen years old.

It was one of those unusually warm March days, and it was late in the afternoon when Sam and I parted, too late to go back to the office. I was due at Jean's for drinks with friends early in the evening, so I decided to walk the sixty blocks or so from Sam's Harlem church to Jean's Central Park West apartment.

Abandonment of real estate had already begun to afflict Harlem by the spring of 1970, and as I walked over toward Eighth Avenue, I saw a number of buildings that were gutted shells with paneless windows staring like hollow eyes at a street filled with day people, who in an hour or so, would become night people doing the same thing in the dark that they had done in the sunlight—nothing, because there was nothing for them to do. The buildings that had not been burned-out or abandoned for some other reason were old and often crumbling. At many of the corners there were stores, with faded signs and tired-looking vegetables. There was litter and garbage everywhere. The Sanitation Department didn't seem to visit often, and the people didn't seem to care much.

Some men sat on stoops, others on folding chairs that they had brought from small, musty apartments upstairs. Many of them were engaged in the long, seemingly aimless conversations that so often occupy the hours of old men. But not all of these men were old. Some of them, in their scuffed shoes and patched jackets, were no older than I. Many of them drank from containers in brown paper bags. And all the talk was emphatic—everyone was certain of his own points. The vehemence of each speaker suggested he had a stronger identity than that presented on the street; he was merely passing through on his way to some place else where he counted for more than he did here.

Farther down, on Eighth Avenue, I came upon the drug center that my young Panther friend had shown me months before. Now, in late afternoon, there were twice as many people on the stretch of sidewalk on the east side of Eighth between 116th and 115th streets as there had been when I walked by before. The people wore brightly colored clothes, for the most part. Many of the men wore gaudy, light-colored hats. Some of the movement through the thickness of people was flamboyant, a swinging of hips and a dipping of head that communicated the mover was cool and unapproachable. More of the movement was like quiet gliding, making minimal use of arms and legs, moving lips and jaws imperceptibly, passing things from one to another with quick fingers. Some people went in and out of the dark and shoddy bars on the street. Some people just stayed in one place, bending rhythmically from the waist, apparently hearing and seeing nothing. They were, according to the argot of the street, on the nod.

I went on. Farther down Eighth, I saw some small children playing. They were very dark, and some of the boys had on short pants even though it was only March. The boys were throwing around a soiled toy rabbit that had once been yellow, trying to keep it from the two girls who had been playing with them. The girls were not happy, it had apparently been their toy before the boys had come. Just as I approached them, the boy who had the rabbit gave the toy a wild heave. It went high in the air, over my head and into the doorway of one of the buildings from which I had seen some of the children emerge just a few moments earlier. The children were puzzled. They didn't know where the rabbit had gone. I ducked into the doorway to get it and was struck, almost repulsed, by the powerful and acrid smell of dried urine that filled the place. I picked up the rabbit, tossed the dirty thing to one of the girls and kept on walking.

Amy was ten then, and David was almost six. My daughter was a little older than the children playing there, but my son was just the right age. They did not live with me, but I saw them often. I missed them. They were not poor like these children and didn't have to find thin pleasures on dirty streets. But they were black children in America, and these children on Eighth Avenue in Harlem reminded me of them, and I was filled with almost unbearable sadness and terrible senses of loss and guilt.

A couple of blocks farther down at 110th Street, Central Park began and Eighth Avenue became Central Park West. It was not the Central Park West with the large and well preserved buildings in Jean's neighborhood. The buildings up on the black end of the famous street were old and not well kept. But it was not central Harlem anymore. There were no more run-down and exorbitant convenience stores. There were no people sitting on the stoops, on folding chairs or milk crates. And later, in the low 90s, it was better preserved, more like the Central Park West that people knew from movies and literature.

Soon I was passing buildings where I had chatted with Saul Steinberg in a room on one evening or with Arthur Schlesinger, Jr., on another, or with Lucas Foss on another. All of the rooms where I remembered seeing those people were lovely places, and the evenings were usually charged with intelligence and wit. I was only fifty blocks away from Sam and that church basement on Edgecombe Avenue.

Finally, as the shadows of the large apartment buildings facing east were lying long across the park, I came to Jean's building. The door-man who knew me well by now, smiled and nodded me in, and I went up. A lawyer I knew and liked and his lovely blond wife were already there. Jean was in the back of the apartment, still getting ready. I greeted my friends, poured a lot of Beefeater gin over ice in a wide, short glass, added two drops of dry vermouth and an olive and then joined my friends looking out of the window at the play of shadows on the still barren trees in the park and at the white people walking home from midtown. They would not walk nearly as far north as the place from which I had just come, and that place and those people would not cross many of their minds during the evening to come. I took a deep slug of my martini. And then I took another one as I thought about Sam and the people uptown, and then I fixed another one so that the alcohol could numb what I could not reconcile.

Jean's parents had heard of our relationship and thunder began rolling east from the hills above Hollywood. I never met Jean's father, a circumstance that neither of us regretted. Dr. Stein was a great philanthropist, having given millions to the Jules Stein eye institute at UCLA but, according to his daughter, was given to the vicious and casual use of the word "nigger," as in, "What are you doing with that nigger?" Jean filtered out many of her father's strongest opinions, but she did tell me once that, when he heard that I had an estranged wife, he commented, "I hope she has a knife and kills him."

I wasn't terribly troubled by what the Steins had to say, except for the fact that their attitude bothered Jean more than she was willing to admit. I was amused and endlessly fascinated at how much discomfort our relationship was causing the grand couple out on the coast. After each of Jean's encounters with her parents, I would do my best to draw details of their latest assault on us out of her. Finally, though her father would not meet me, her mother could not contain her curiosity and announced one day when they were visiting New York that she was coming over for drinks. Jean could have prevented the meeting, but the imp in her was as strong as the curiosity in me.

"You don't have to come if you don't want to," Jean said, grinning.

"I'll be there at five-thirty," I said, laughing.

Mrs. Stein was already there sitting on a couch in the blue library when I got there. She must have been nearing seventy by then, and she was a striking woman with thin beautiful features, exquisitely kept white hair, a strong body in an expensive blue suit. It was clear, looking at her, how Jean had come by such delicate beauty. We were introduced, and Mrs. Stein was polite and so was I. Conversation was sporadic, disjointed, aimless and difficult until Mrs. Stein hit upon a topic that she thought suitable. She began talking about her work for the Hollywood Canteen during World War II.

The Hollywood Canteen was probably the most famous U.S.O. center in the country and powerful Hollywood figures like Mrs. Stein did their part for the war effort by making sure that the soldiers, sailors and marines who came there for relaxation and entertainment got only the best before they went off to offer their lives for their country. But there was a problem at the Canteen, according to Mrs. Stein. It was the Communists. The Canteen it seemed was democratic. Its doors were open to servicemen of the United States, regardless of color. But the Communists were always pressing for the white girls to dance with the colored servicemen. Now, the white girls were some of the nicest girls who could be found, according to Mrs. Stein, and what the Communists proposed was out of the question. But she and the other powers behind the Canteen fought off the Communists and kept that rest and rehabilitation center safe for all our servicemen and for the American way, Mrs. Stein informed me triumphantly.

During this recital, Jean could hardly contain her amusement. Her eyes danced with mirth.

"You know, Mrs. Stein, that reminds me of a story," I replied. "It is said that before World War II, there was an annual cotillion down in Charleston, South Carolina, where the loveliest and the finest young women of the state would be presented. Well, during the war, there was a shortage of men, because so many had gone off to fight. So, one year, the woman who was arbiter of Charleston society and who ran the cotillion called a nearby Army base for help.

" 'Captain,' she said, 'I want you to send over fifteen of your finest young men to the cotillion tonight to be with some of our finest young ladies.' The captain agreed and then the woman said, 'And, there's just one more thing. Don't send any Jews.' Again the captain agreed.

"The night of the dance, when everyone was assembled, there was a knock at the door, and the arbiter answered and saw before her fifteen of the biggest, blackest buck niggers she had ever seen.

" 'There must be some mistake,' she exclaimed in horror.

" 'No, ma'am,' the leader of the blacks said, 'Cap'n Goldstein, he don't never make no mistakes.' "

Jean doubled up in silent glee when I finished the story. I just looked at Mrs. Stein, my face blank. She stared back, almost as expressionless, but scarlet started at her collar and spread quickly to the roots of her supremely coiffed white hair. She finished her drink quickly after that and got up to leave. She told me it had been nice to meet me. I told her that it had been nice to meet her. Then she left, and Jean howled with laughter until she cried.

But every once in a while, the pervasive whiteness of the world I was looking at in those days got to me in ways I couldn't handle with either humor or liquor. The 1970 dinner of the Gridiron Club in Washington was one of those occasions. In his book on *The New York Times, Without Fear or Favor,* Harrison E. Salisbury describes the Gridiron Club and its dinner:

> There is no institution in Washington so hallowed as the annual Gridiron dinner. The Gridiron club is an assembly of troglodytes, the wise and stuffy Old Men of Washington journalism. Their names might or might not be known beyond the confines of that Chinese Wall which

Raymond Clapper insisted encircled the nation's capital but within the walls their names were golden . . .

In reality the occasion was a turnout for every lobbyist and power broker in the capital.

From his vantage point, Harrison can afford to be offhanded about the dinner and its meaning. But in 1970, when I was still thirty-seven and still had my nose pressed up against the window of the candy store, I was delighted to receive an invitation from Tom Wicker—decidedly not a troglodyte member of the Gridiron Club—to that year's dinner. I accepted with alacrity and delight. The notion of hobnobbing with the nation's elite turned me on.

A few days after I accepted, I got a call in my Ford Foundation office from a woman in the social secretary's office at the White House. President and Mrs. Nixon would very much like me to come to a prayer breakfast at the White House on the Sunday morning after the dinner. Nixon's first year in office had been rough on blacks. He had tried to dismantle some civil-rights enforcement programs and weaken the Voting Rights Act of 1965. He had made no noticeable progress on his stated intention of winding up the war and had clearly abdicated the role of moral leadership on civil rights that Kennedy and Johnson had undertaken. In addition, I thought prayer breakfasts in the White House on taxpayers' money were probably unconstitutional as well as tacky.

But when the invitation first came to me, I wanted to go. It was like being invited to an Andy Warhol happening. I wanted to see the latest tacky trend myself. But Eve, with whom I was then joined in one of our periodic reconciliations, said she'd have nothing to do with those creeps and their cheap uses of the White House. That sobered me up pretty well, and when I thought of it, I agreed with her. But what about protocol? Could you decline an invitation from the President on mere matters of principle? I checked with some of my wisest elders: Uncle Roy, Dr. Kenneth B. Clark and Mac Bundy. They all said I had to go; that you couldn't turn the President down because you thought he was tacky. But I couldn't see why not, so I called the woman in the White House back.

"Mrs. Wilkins and I won't be coming," I said, "because I don't think it is proper to have prayer breakfasts in the White House and besides, I think Mr. Nixon's policies are damaging to blacks," I told her.

"Oh, that's a shame," the woman said. "You know, we have lots of coloreds at these occasions. Sometimes they're even the preachers."

It turned out that the Nixons had invited all of the out-of-town guests of the Gridiron Club to the prayer breakfast, and on the night of the dinner, I caught the President—all dressed up in white tie and tails, sitting about twenty feet away—staring at me intently. Our eyes locked only briefly before the President turned away, his eyes blinking in a rapid, nervous way. Though we had never met, he had to know that I was the black who had turned down his invitation with those rude comments, because I was one of only two blacks in the group of more than five hundred men in the room. The other black was Mayor Walter Washington, of Washington, D.C., so the uppity one had to be me.

It was a white-folks' night. There were no black members of the Gridiron Club or women members either. Despite the distinguished company, the humor made me think I had stumbled into the locker room of a segregated country club. The parties after dinner weren't much better, but I did meet one fellow there whom I liked. His name was Nick Kotz, a Pulitzer prize winner, who at that time was writing for the *Des Moines Register and Tribune*. Nick looked as disgusted as I, and he sensed my feelings. He offered me a ride home, and on the way we agreed that someone ought to write about the dinner—expose it.

"You ought to write it, Nick," I said, "you're in the writing business."

"That's exactly why I shouldn't write it," Nick said as he maneuvered his old blue Mustang carefully through the deserted streets of Washington. "You're not in the business, so you ought to write the piece."

We never settled on who should do it that night, but a week or so later, I got a call from a woman who identified herself as Meg Greenfield, the deputy editor of *The Washington Post*'s editorial page.

"I've heard from Nick Kotz that you have some pretty strong feelings about the Gridiron Club dinner," she said, "and that you've thought about writing about it. We'll give you as much space as you need on the editorial page."

I was stunned. I didn't have that much faith in my writing ability, and I wasn't sure whether it was good manners to do what she had asked me. I told her that I would think about it. The first thing I did was to call Tom Wicker and ask him whether he'd mind if I wrote

about the evening. Tom, a fiery red-headed liberal from North Carolina, whose columns in the late sixties and early seventies blazed with
indignation at the outrages and the injustices in American society,
laughed at my question and said, "Hell no. Help yourself. We sure
deserve whatever you dish out."

So I began to write in the way I did in those days. I dictated to my
secretary. My secretary, Gloria, was an appreciative audience.
"Wheeeeew!" Gloria said, when I got to the end. "It's awfully emotional."

I polished the draft a couple of times, and a few days later, when I
was in Washington, I took it up to the *Post*'s office on L Street. I had
never met Miss Greenfield before and had met the Editorial Page
Editor, Philip Geyelin, just briefly at the Gridiron dinner. It was a
polite, but hesitant meeting. They seemed a bit uncomfortable, and
I was actually quite shy about handing over a piece of writing for
somebody else to judge. It was like handing in a paper in high school.
I didn't like the feeling one bit.

A few days later, though, Miss Greenfield called me in New York
to tell me that they loved the piece and would run it in a few days. I
asked her to let me know the exact date, because I wanted to give
Mac Bundy at least one day's warning before the thing became a *fait
accompli*. She called me back in a few days to say that it would be
published on March 26, 1970, which happened to be one day after
my thirty-eighth birthday. On March 25 I told Bundy that the piece
was coming, and I gave him a copy to read.

There are a lot of little truisms about racism that pass along
through black culture. Some of them are so frivolous that they are
funnier than they are painful, while others hurt both on the surface
and much more deeply. An example of the first is the saying, "They
all look alike." I remember once, for instance, ringing the doorbell of
a lady's apartment at an hour when it was indiscreet for me to be
there. As I was waiting for the door to open, somebody came out of
the opposite apartment. I recognized him. It was Merv Griffin. He
gave me a puzzled look and then said, "Andy?" in a quizzical voice. I
knew it would be equally indiscreet for my buddy Andy Young to be
at that place at that time, so just as the door opened, I said, "No, I'm
Julian Bond," and then stepped inside.

Much more painful and destructive than that is the knowledge that
many, perhaps most, white people believe that they see and think
more clearly than black people, and that when there is a clash of

opinion, surely the white person must be correct. The sense that the black mind doesn't work very well has severely damaged black lives and careers since blacks were first introduced onto this continent more than three hundred years ago.

On the evening of the twenty-fifth, I was packing up to leave my office to go out and celebrate my birthday with Ron Gault and the woman with whom he was spending his time, Charlayne Hunter, a beautiful Georgian who was a reporter at *The New York Times*. My office phone rang. It was Mac Bundy, who had been talking informally with some of his trustees.

"Irwin Miller says that Julian Bond was at that dinner. Your piece says that he wasn't. You'd better check that," Mac said.

"Julian wasn't there, Mac," I said. "I didn't see him and I checked the guest list. He wasn't there."

"Irwin says he was," Mac said.

"No, Mac, he wasn't there," I said.

"Well, here's Irwin," Mac said. "You'd better talk to him."

Miller came on the line. "Hello, Mr. Wilkins," he said, "how are you?"

"Fine, Mr. Miller," I said.

"Julian Bond was at the dinner," Miller said.

"I don't think so," I said.

"I saw him," Miller said.

"Where was he sitting?" I asked.

"Well he was sitting near me," Miller said, "next to somebody—I can't quite remember who it was."

"Was he sitting next to George McGovern?" I asked.

"Yes, that's who it was," Miller said. "He was sitting next to George McGovern."

"Mr. Miller," I said, "that was me. Julian wasn't there."

The piece ran the next day in the *Post*. It took up all the space under the Herblock cartoon on the editorial page. This, in slightly abridged form, is what it said.

A Black at the Gridiron Dinner

When it was all over, a number of men had tears in their eyes, even more had lifted hearts and spirits, but a few were so dispirited that they went upstairs to get drunk. We had just heard the President and Vice-President of the United States in a unique piano duet—and to many old Gridiron Dinner veterans, it was a moving showstopper. To a few others, it was a depressing display of gross insensitivity and both conscious and unconscious racism—further proof that they and their hopes for their country are becoming more and more isolated from those places where America's heart and power seem to be moving.

The annual dinner of the Gridiron Club is the time when men can put on white ties and tails and forget the anxiety and loneliness that are central to the human condition and look at other men in white ties and tails and know that they have arrived or are still there.

The guests are generally grateful and gracious. But the event's importance is beyond the structures of graciousness because it shows the most powerful elements of the nation's daily press and all elements of the nation's government locked in a symbiotic embrace. The rich and the powerful tell many truths in jest about themselves and about their country. I don't feel very gracious about what they told me.

Some weeks ago, to my surprise and delight, a friend—a sensitive man of honor—with a little half-apology about the required costume, invited me to attend the dinner.

The first impression was stunning: almost every passing face was a familiar one. Some had names that were household words. Some merely made up a montage of the familiar faces and bearings of our times. There were Richard Helms and Walter Mondale and Henry Kissinger and George McGovern and Joel Broyhill and Tom Wicker and William Westmoreland and John Mitchell and Tom Clark (ironically placed, by some pixie no doubt, next to each other on the dais) and Robert Finch and Ralph Nader and, of course, the President of the United States.

One thing quickly became clear about those faces. Apart from Walter Washington—who, I suppose, as Mayor had to be invited—mine was the only face in a crowd of some five hundred that was not white. There were no Indians, there were no Asians, there were no Puerto Ricans, there were no Mexican-Americans. There were just the Mayor and me. Incredibly, I sensed that there were few in that room who thought that anything was missing.

There is something about an atmosphere like that that is hard to define but excruciatingly easy for a black man to feel. It is the heavy, almost tangible, clearly visible broad assumption that in places where it counts, America is a white country. I was an American citizen sitting in a banquet room in a hotel that I had visited many times. . . . This night in that room, less than three miles from my home in the nation's capital, a 60 percent black city, I felt out of place in America.

That is not to say that there were not kind men, good men, warm men, in and around and about the party, nor is it to say that anyone was personally rude to me. There were some old friends and some new acquaintances whom I was genuinely glad to see. Ed Muskie, who had given a very funny and exquisitely partisan speech (the Republicans have three problems: the war, inflation, and what to say on Lincoln's Birthday), was one of those. I was even warmly embraced by the Deputy Attorney General, Mr. Kleindienst, and had a long conversation with the associate director of the FBI, Mr. DeLoach.

But it was not the people so much who shaped the evening. It was the humor amidst that pervasive whiteness about what was going on in this country these days that gave the evening its form and substance. There were many jokes about the "Southern strategy." White people have funny senses of humor. Some of them found something to laugh about in the Southern strategy. Black people don't think it's funny at all. That strategy hits men where they live—in their hopes for themselves and their dreams for their children. We find it sinister and frightening. And let it not be said that the Gridiron Club and its guests are not discriminating about their humor. There was a real sensitivity about the inappropriateness of poking fun that night about an ailing former President but none about laughing about policies that crush the aspirations of millions of citizens of this nation. An instructive distinction, I thought. . . .

As the jokes about the Southern strategy continued, I thought about the one-room segregated schoolhouse where I began my education in Kansas City. That was my neighborhood school. When they closed it, I was bused—without an apparent second thought—as a five-year-old kindergartener, across town to the black elementary school. It was called Crispus Attucks.

And I thought of the day I took my daughter, when she was seven, along the Freedom Trail, in Boston, and of telling her about the black man named Crispus Attucks who was the first American to die in our revolution. And I remember telling her that white America would try very hard in thousands of conscious and unconscious ways both to make her feel that her people had had no part in building America's greatness and to make her feel inferior. And I remember the profoundly moving and grateful look in her eyes and the wordless hug she gave me when I told her, "Don't you believe them because they are lies." And I felt white America in that room in the Statler Hilton telling me all those things that night, and I told myself, "Don't you believe them because they are lies."

And when it came to the end, the President and the Vice-President of the United States, in an act which they had consciously worked up, put on a Mr. Bones routine about the Southern strategy with the biggest boffo coming as the Vice-President affected a deep Southern accent. And then they played their duets—the President playing his songs, the Vice-President playing "Dixie," the whole thing climaxed by "God Bless

America" and "Auld Lang Syne." The crowd ate it up. They roared. As they roared I thought that after our black decade of imploring, suing, marching, lobbying, singing, rebelling, praying and dying we had come to this: a Vice-Presidential Dixie with the President as his straight man. In the serious and frivolous places of power—at the end of that decade—America was still virtually lily-white. And most of the people in that room were reveling in it. What, I wondered, would it take for them to understand that men also come in colors other than white. Seeing and feeling their blindness, I shuddered at the answers that came most readily to mind.

As we stood voluntarily, some more slowly than others, when the two men began to play "God Bless America," I couldn't help remembering Judy Collins (who could not sing in Chicago) singing "Where Have All the Flowers Gone?"

So later, I joined Nick Kotz, author of "Let Them Eat Promises," and we drank down our dreams.

I don't believe that I have been blanketed in and suffocated by such racism and insensitivity since I was a sophomore in college, when I was the only black invited to a minstrel spoof put on at a white fraternity house.

But then, they were only fraternity brothers, weren't they?

Even though I wasn't in Washington to get its full force, the reaction to that piece stunned me. I received at least twenty phone calls from Washington in my New York office that day, and at least a hundred letters in the following days. The *Post* apparently was flooded with letters responding to what I had written. A week after the piece appeared, the *Post* devoted its entire letters column to responses to the piece. Most of them were highly emotional, but only a very few were critical. The most striking of the responses was a private note from Benjamin C. Bradlee, Managing Editor of the *Post*. I didn't know Bradlee, but he was already a Washington celebrity, if, for nothing else, for his friendship with John F. Kennedy. Bradlee's letter was short and to the point.

"I'd be damn proud to work on the same newspaper with you," it read.

Though I wasn't applying for a newspaper job and wasn't contemplating one at that time, I was thrilled with the letter. A few days later, Phil Geyelin asked me to see him the next time I was in town. I agreed. We had a long, roundabout talk in which he suggested that I might think about coming onto the *Post*'s editorial page staff. I told him that I didn't think I had been at the Ford Foundation long enough. He told me to think about it, and I said I would. Then he suggested I meet the publisher, Mrs. Graham, before I decided, and one Sunday he drove me over to Mrs. Graham's mansion in George-town for an introductory conversation.

Mrs. Graham was at once more attractive and less self-possessed than I had expected. There was a nervousness about her movements, an uneasiness in her eyes and what friends of mine later would iden-tify as "Locust Valley Lockjaw" in her voice. Yet, dressed casually on a Sunday afternoon during which she was supervising preparations for a dinner that evening in honor of former President Johnson, she looked younger than her age and more vulnerable than I thought such a powerful person would ever appear. I have no recollection of our conversation, but from it she learned that I spoke and wrote standard English and that my fingernails were clean. Afterward, Phil made the offer firm, but I rejected it because I thought I owed Mac Bundy more time than I had given him.

But the time I was giving Mac was becoming more and more difficult to give. Men get ugly when they are locked in a battle inside an institution, and that happened to Mike and me. He had games that I wouldn't play. One of those involved the Foundation's practice of paying for a membership in a club for officers over a certain rank. I didn't want to join a club. It was not my style, and I thought that that particular perquisite was especially stupid. But somehow it was sug-gested to me that the Harmony Club of New York—a club which I understand to be composed of upper-class German Jews—might be interested in an application from me, because a number of the mem-bers thought it was time to desegregate it.

I was indecisive about the idea, more out of politeness than any-thing else. Desegregating high-income social clubs was not high on my agenda. I was still not easy with large clusters of white men in social situations, and I had no interest in spending time at the club. Notions of the contacts I might make for politics or my career didn't entice me. Nevertheless, I didn't say no right away, simply because I knew that the people who were interested in desegregating the club were sincere about it, and it was a decent purpose, whether or not it was a priority of mine.

But, soon it became clear that Mike Sviridoff and I were to be a joint entry. We were to be sponsored by the same members and put up for membership at the same time. That put a whole different cast on the enterprise. Mike was a Jew with roots in Russia or Poland, and with no college degree in his background. A woman I knew whose husband and father-in-law were members of the Harmony Club told me that there was no way that a person with such a background could hope to get membership. I was the black Brahmin, the trail blazer. I'd probably get in. And, Mike would get in on my back.

Bull shit, I thought; I won't do it.

Nevertheless, an application for membership appeared on my desk one day, and I looked it over indecisively, thinking that maybe I was being pigheaded in denying Mike something that meant a great deal to him. But as I looked over the application and saw how much personal information it sought—even the maiden name of the applicant's mother—I balked. From time to time in the weeks that followed, Mike's secretary pushed me to complete the application, and I expressed a disinclination to do it.

Finally, I exploded. "If Mike wants to get into that club, let him apply by himself. It's a waste of the Foundation's money and my time, and I'm not going to carry Mike into that club on my back, and you can tell him that."

She seemed dismayed, said, "Okay," and left my office. I didn't hear anything more about the club, and I never did learn whether Mike had ever gotten in.

That was just one of many episodes in the disintegration of our personal and professional relations. I was finding the work at the Foundation less and less satisfying, and my own situation there less and less comfortable. Though Mike, with a little help from me, had been successful in getting Vivian Henderson, a black economist who was President of Clark College in Atlanta, elected to the Board of Trustees, the Foundation was still pretty much a white, male, elitist institution. But when news of the Cambodian "incursion" hit America with the force of a national sonic boom, young Americans on campuses and in institutions all over the country began questioning the legitimacy of the major mechanisms of the country. The Ford Foundation was no different.

Staff members in their twenties began looking at the way the place operated as they never had looked before. They had always previously accepted their minimal involvement in basic decisions.

Cambodia came at a fairly advanced stage of the Ford budget cycle. The preliminary budget that was to go to the trustees for tentative approval at their June meeting had almost been completed. I was distressed because Mike was proposing to cut my budget substantially. Since the Foundation expected to put five million dollars into a police training program that he felt would be of benefit to blacks, there was less need to spend money on manpower training, economic development, innovative urban education and drug-abuse programs.

That was pure sophistry, and the intention to cut my budget seemed to be just one more indication of the waning interest in liberal circles in the plight of the black poor. Thus, though I wasn't involved with their protest, I was sympathetic to the skepticism that the younger members of the staff were expressing about the Foundation. I had proposed to the chairman of the board of trustees months earlier that Marian Wright Edelman be considered for membership. I thought there ought to be a second black on the board, at least one woman and somebody under forty. Marian would have brought all three attributes to the board. But, I had not even received a reply to my note.

So, when Mac convened the vice-presidents and the program directors of the Foundation to consider responses to the criticisms leveled by the young staff members, I was not inclined to defend the interests of the institution. The discussion finally focused on the demands that young people had made about gaining a larger role in the development of the budget.

"But we're pretty far down the line with the budget," Mac said. "There's not much opportunity for more participation. I suppose we could let them read what's going to the trustees, even though there's no longer any real chance to change it."

"Let them read cake," I said from the back of the room. Everybody laughed, including Mac and me.

"Wilkins, you sonovabitch," Mac said, "if I hear that outside this room, I'll have your head." He was laughing, and I was laughing, but I think he knew he had heard my real attitude toward the Foundation.

At about the same time a National Guard officer at Kent State panicked and ordered his men to fire into a crowd of demonstrating students. Four were killed and others were injured. A group of armed black students at Cornell occupied a building and were pictured, as they left, armed to the teeth. The Weathermen were at large and the Internal Security Division of the Department of Justice—a bastard outgrowth of the McCarthy period that Ramsey had wanted to abolish—was sending a lawyer named Guy Goodwin around the country to convene grand juries at the whisper of a suggestion that a

Weather person had passed through. From the outside the impression was that the Nixon Administration was completely out of touch with thought in the country other than that of older, successful Americans. The black movement was at a virtual standstill. Martin Luther King was dead. Whitney Young had only a few months to live. CORE had shriveled to a small band of people who posed as ideological purists, but who would come to be accused by New York authorities as extortionists and confidence people. My uncle was aging, and so was the NAACP under him. Nixon was dismantling the Great Society, and his slogan that one shouldn't "throw money at problems" had become popular with politicians and editorial writers all over the country.

Even from my pessimism of 1967 I could not have anticipated a country as desolate as the America of 1970 seemed to me to be. My personal life seemed to mirror that larger gloom. Jean and my job were in New York. Eve and my children were in Washington. I could not choose. Paralyzed by guilt, a sense of duty, hunger and growing hopelessness, I sank further and further into despair.

Then I received a phone call from my old friend Liz Drew, Pat's wife.

We exchanged pleasantries and then she asked, "Are you sitting down?"

"No," I said. "Should I be?"

"Yes," she said.

"Okay," I said, "go ahead."

"Pat Drew jumped off a bridge this morning and killed himself," she said.

"What did you say?"

"Pat Drew jumped off the Calvert Street bridge this morning and killed himself," she reported.

I slumped in my chair. Pat Drew, one of the sweetest men I had ever known; Pat Drew, my friend in AID; Pat Drew the New York lawyer, Pat Drew my absolute contemporary, not yet forty, had jumped off a bridge and killed himself.

"Jesus!" I said. "What can I do?"

Liz told me when the funeral would be and asked me to be a pall bearer. She said Joe Califano had interrupted his vacation at the Jersey shore and was with her now.

The next morning, I ran into Paul Firstenberg and Rod Wagner, two other AID contemporaries of Pat's who were also on their way to the funeral. We were standing morosely at the American Airlines gate waiting for our flight, when I heard a gruff and hearty voice call my name. It was Richard G. Kleindienst, now high in the saddle as Deputy Attorney General of the United States. He threw an arm around my shoulder and asked how I had been. You'd have thought he was an old Army buddy from a common foxhole, the way he carried on. He insisted on upgrading my ticket from tourist to first class on his credit card so that we could sit together. I was too wrung out with grief and the intimations of my own mortality to resist.

"You look terrible," Dick said when we had settled on the plane. "What's the matter with you?"

I looked at him for a long time before answering. Early in the Administration, Dick had given Liz Drew an interview for a piece she was doing for the *Atlantic Monthly*. In it she quoted his use of brutal and threatening language about dissenters, the kind of language that gave civil libertarians chills in the night. In a telephone conversation that we had after the piece had been published, Dick denied the quote and called Liz a bitch.

"A friend of mine died. I'm going to his funeral," I said. "His name was Pat Drew. You know his wife, Liz."

Dick screwed up his face in pain and sympathy. "What happened?" he asked.

I gave the details of his suicide as Dick shook his head in disbelief. Then he asked, "Are they Christians?"

After a while our conversation drifted away from the Drews, and I began to twit Dick about various policies the Administration was pursuing. Finally I got to the war.

"Just what is it that makes this war worth the lives, limbs, and money that we're investing in it?" I asked.

"It's worth anything to defeat Godless communism," Dick replied, and his jaws snapped shut.

We parted at Washington National, and some time later, Liz received a very gracious note of condolence from him.

25 I left Eve for the second time soon after that. The guilt about my decision and the fear about the damage I was doing to my children flashed through me like a river at flood tide. At Justice and at Ford, I had been somebody to whom a lot of other people turned for guidance, leadership or favors. I had once told Eve that I felt like the big black whale lying in the water that everybody wanted a bite of. Once late in the evening I was on a plane on my way home, very tired after having made a speech in Detroit. A black man sat down next to me, recognized me and asked for help on his economic-development project in San Francisco. I gave it to him. Another person found me hung over and weary at a New Year's Day brunch. I gave him some help, too. But now, the big black machine was running down with no strength left for friends or family.

A few days after I left Eve, there was a pounding at my door in the wee hours of the morning. It was Charlayne Hunter. Ron Gault was in the hospital. Could I come and help. As we headed for the hospital, Charlayne put the story together for me. Ron had been having a drink in an elegant and fashionable eating and drinking place on the upper east side, Maxwell's Plum, with a black woman who was light enough so that she looked white. They were standing at the bar between one and two in the morning and Ron was the only easily identifiable black in the place. I had long since decided that the most dangerous place in America for a black man was where white men had been drinking for a long time without women and the black was with a white woman who looked good.

A white man at the bar mumbled something to Ron. He had leaned

forward and asked the man to repeat what he had said. The next
thing he knew, he was on the floor with a fractured skull, a bottle
broken over his head. The white man was gone.

Ron's broken skull stood for me as a metaphor for the continuing
idiosyncratic, dangerous and pervasive racism in this country. Pat's
death was a reminder of my own that I had never taken seriously
before. And Eve's sadness and anger stood not as a metaphor, but as
living proof of my wickedness, my foolish weaknesses, the certainty
that my children would sustain severe emotional damage and ringing
demonstration that my life had neither core nor purpose. Jean was
my only salvation.

The world began to seem mad to me. Who in his right mind would
choose the rigors of the city with its asphalt and exhaust fumes when
he could as easily walk in a meadow and, at worst, smell a compost
heap. I began losing patience with even the most minor chores of
urban life—waiting for elevators became difficult, and riding a subway from the east to the west side of New York virtually impossible.
I soon lost energy for almost all tasks. I even gave up fighting Mike,
for it seemed to me that even when I won something, nothing really
changed on the streets for the people I yearned to help. Working at
Ford made me feel like a capon. I had come to hate it. I wanted to
get out of there.

Then, one night that fall, a good friend of mine asked me to talk to
his manic wife, who was having trouble. I took her to a place on
Columbus Avenue in the low 90s with a bar, some tables and a
piano. The woman talked about herself. She talked a lot and she
talked fast, about her talents, about the unfairness of life. The words
came out in torrents, so thick and fast that after a time, I could no
longer hear the piano. Pretty soon the sentences no longer had meaning for me. All I heard was one long loud wail of anguish that became
louder and more insistent with each passing drink. After almost four
hours I walked her home. Then, I walked home and went to bed. But
the woman's madness had shaken up the shards of my own unsettled
consciousness. I had destroyed my life, I thought, and had exposed
myself to danger in a world full of peril. The blow on Ron's head, the
stone on Pat's grave, the unhinged state of that woman's mind proved
all of that. The only safe place, it seemed to me, was back home with
Eve and linked to my safe job at the Ford Foundation.

Things were happening to me there. I was taken into the Council
on Foreign Relations. I was appointed to two mayoral commissions

and received invitations to more and more official receptions and parties in both Washington and New York. It was clear to me that America would have a need over the years for wave after wave of distinguished black people in political and civic life in order to demonstrate that racism in America was over. I was destined to be one of those. All I had to do was to play the game, make all the appropriate moves, and I would be a big black Poo-Bah when I got old, honored and taken care of by a grateful country.

But I didn't want it. That world made no sense to me anymore. I wanted out of all that safety, predictability and bureaucracy. I didn't want to be that person I had become and surely didn't want to be the person I was becoming. I wasn't quite sure what or who I wanted to be, but I knew what I didn't want, even though it terrified me to take a different, uncharted path. But, I got up out of bed the next morning with no sleep and got dressed and went to the Ford Foundation and quit.

The word spread rapidly to granters around the country, partly propelled by Mike, who called as many as he could to tell them that I was leaving, but not to worry because he would look out for their interests. I began to get calls from black people across the nation telling me that I couldn't quit, that I was the black beachhead at the Ford Foundation and that I owed it to the "community" to stay there. My Uncle Roy took that line and was vehement about it. It was the only time in our relationship that he ever screamed at me.

The accusation that I was acting selfishly and deserting the black cause weighed heavily on me. But I knew I had worked long and hard for blacks. I had become a projectile that slammed almost willy-nilly into predominantly white institutions, encountered racism there, and tried to make things better. By the time I left Ford, I had been the top black in AID, the Community Relations Service, Justice and Ford. I hadn't sought fights and confrontations, but I was incapable of leaving a serious racial problem alone.

I was worn now by almost a decade of that kind of effort, fighting belly to belly with powerful whites, and I was coming apart. Maybe, in appropriate circumstances, I might owe the community, at a moment of crisis, the act of putting my life at risk, but I did not owe it a course of conduct that was sure to result in the unraveling of my mind.

My closest friends understood that and saw the unraveling. They told me that it was my obligation to take care of myself and they undertook to help take care of me. Mac Bundy had long talks with me and asked me to stay on for a year with him as his assistant working on special projects. I agreed.

He was also concerned about my personal life. "If I were my mother," he said, "I would tell you not to get divorced."

"But since you're not your mother, you won't. Right?" I replied.

Mac laughed and said, "Well, I can only tell you I think divorce is the most painful of all human experiences. Death is final. Divorce hurts more."

I was to learn that he was right.

Then, Mac said, "You know, I hate for you to leave the Foundation, but it's the right choice. I shouldn't have had you in that box down there. The caponlike existence of a philanthropoid is not for you."

I was amazed. Capon. It was the word I had used, but never to him. Philanthropoids, to me, were people who hovered around people who were actually doing things of value. The most useful thing a philanthropoid could do, I thought, was to separate the thinkers and doers among grant applicants from the frauds, help the doers think their projects through and then get out of the way and let them do their business. But, the capons flutter around long after their function has been performed, beating wings, stirring up dust and getting in the way.

The mantle of impotence that I had assumed on joining the Foundation became a garrote as I attempted to confront, from the Ford Foundation, the profoundly racist tendencies in American society. Mac understood that I had to leave, and he also understood that I was in terrible shape. Much later, I learned that he called the psychologist Dr. Kenneth B. Clark and asked him for advice on how to help me.

"Roger is too valuable to lose," Kenneth told me Mac had said to him.

So, Kenneth and Ramsey formed a pact, which they presented to me as the Clark and Wilkins team for *ad hoc* work on *pro bono* projects. The most notable of these was a serious study of the raid on Black Panther headquarters in Chicago by the special police attached to the Chicago State's Attorney's office. There were some other projects as well, and, apart from whatever substantive good the projects may have done, they gave Kenneth and Ramsey the opportunity to schedule periodic breakfast meetings with me to determine whether I was continuing to disintegrate or beginning to heal.

Other friends rallied around. Carl and Mariella Holman made special trips from Washington as did Ed Sylvester, Lisle Carter and Marian and Peter Edelman. Richard Harris, the fine writer at *The New Yorker*, was always there for me. It was as if they had all noticed a tree beginning to fall and had come around to support it at the point where it was cracked until it could support itself once more.

One of the things my friends urged me to do when I quit was to go away to an island where there was some sun. So, I decided to do that, and Jean and I planned a trip to Martinique. Vernon Jordan, who was by then directing the United Negro College Fund in New York, called solicitously to see how I was doing. When I told him that I was going to take off for a week or so with Jean, he asked, "Why are you taking her?" I suspected that many of my friends thought that Jean was a large part of my problem.

"Because I love her," I replied firmly.

Vernon was to say later to others, "He said it in a way that meant, 'Nigger, mind your own business.' "

So, my friends stood back and watched what Lisle Carter called my high-wire act with some misgivings. They all liked Eve, but nobody thought it wise or appropriate to suggest what I ought to do.

Jean and I went off to Martinique, Jean with gentle kindness and I with bloated expectations about the restorative powers of a week under the Caribbean sun. Our hotel there was across the bay from Fort de France, the main town of the island. It could be reached by a winding hour-long auto ride or by a twenty-minute trip on a ferry across the water. The hotel's beach was disappointing, a narrow, crowded and undistinguished strip of sand that had little grace or charm. The island, though, was full of lush green rubber trees and much of it had that robust overpowering green look of a rain forest. Though the days were pleasant enough, the food at the hotel was quite ordinary, so one night we decided to take the ferry over to Fort du France to get a good meal.

Though on paper Martinique was an integral part of France, in 1970 it had the look and smell of a colony. The white people lived well and ran the place. The blacks had menial roles or no jobs at all. Fort du France was a quaint little town set around a town square near the water at its center and ascending into the hills on the perimeters. The place was charming at sundown, and we chose a small, lovely French restaurant on the second floor of a small building that faced the town square. The food was not exceptional, though better than that served at the hotel. The patrons were interesting. There were no other blacks in the place, and most of the whites looked like service-station owners out for an evening with their wives.

There was a feeling of hostility in the place. I was particularly struck by the hostile stares of a couple of rough-looking fellows at another table who couldn't seem to take their eyes off us, particularly me. They would stare at us with what I thought was unveiled anger then mutter to each other with great intensity. I asked Jean if she had noticed those two. She had, and they seemed menacing to her too. We hurried to finish and paid and left, hoping to be out before the two angry men were through. There was a definite coldness in the trans-action when we paid, and we were glad to descend the stairs and enter the square again.

It was night now, and the square was almost deserted. I thought the hostility had to do with her being white and my being black.

"Do you really think so?" she asked. Jean was aware of my acute racial sensibilities, and by now, she had come to trust my instincts about such things.

"Yeah," I said, "I really think so. What else could account for that hostility? These people never saw us before."

"I guess you're right," she replied. "This isn't Paris. The people here are the Colons, the pits."

Just then, a group of young blacks came near to us, stared in our faces, laughed nervously and then skittered away. We paused to look in the window of a place that looked like a recreation center that featured a pool table. A man inside stared at us for a moment, made an ugly face and dropped the shade.

The ambience of the town square was beginning to be almost as menacing as that of the restaurant. I looked back to see a flood of light spill into the square as the restaurant door was opened and I saw four shapes emerge. Two were women and the two others—quite large—appeared to be the two men who had been so angrily preoc-cupied with us while we were eating. I led Jean in a circuitous route toward the ferry dock. It was time to get out of there, I thought, but the man at the slip said that the ferries ran infrequently at night and the next one to our hotel wouldn't leave for an hour.

I began to feel real fear. We had encountered nothing but hostility from whites or frightened curiosity from blacks since we had come to this town. We had obviously tripped over some invisible line between the permissible and the forbidden. We weren't sure what the exact nature of our transgression had been, although its general contour was pretty clear. We couldn't tell how serious it was, but the lack of any civility whatsoever from whites and the apparent fear that our behavior caused blacks led us to believe that we had done something pretty serious and might be courting real danger. The thought of wandering around that creepy town unprotected at night absolutely chilled me.

I looked at Jean, who didn't look any happier about the situation than I felt.

"I know," I said. "Let's go to the Hilton and have a drink. We'll be safe there, and then we'll come down to the dock just in time to get the ferry. Okay?"

"That's a great idea," Jean said.

We found a taxi and went to the Hilton, which was the most welcome Hilton I have ever seen, before or since. The service was polite and people didn't appear to take any notice of us. We began to relax, and I even began to entertain the notion that we had been the victims of my paranoid fantasies, so powerful that Jean was swept up in them. When forty-five minutes had passed, we paid up and went outside to find our cab driver waiting for us. He was pleasant enough, drove us back down to the dock and left. It wasn't until the lights of the cab had disappeared around a distant corner that we learned we were still fifteen or twenty minutes early for the ferry. There was nothing for us to do but wait, with our apprehension rising in the darkness, and the lights of our hotel twinkling dimly, a long way off, across the water.

After a few minutes, another prospective passenger arrived at the pier. He was black, and from his shambling, unsteady gait, we surmised that he was drunk. He made his way toward us, mumbling under his breath, apparently, a self-absorbed, pleasant drunk. Then he saw us. He did a slow-motion double take, his features slowly struggling to comprehend just what it was that he was seeing. When it finally came together for him, his eyes widened and he did a little jump backward. Then he hurried on by, head down, talking audibly to himself, apparently agitated. He walked up and down the dock, talking, moving his hands wildly and aimlessly. He would look at us, say something to himself in a wild kind of way and then move on away.

"What's he saying?" I asked Jean, who speaks French.

"I can't make it out very well," she said. "All I can get is something about God and trouble."

While we were once more contemplating on the depth of the racial taboo we were violating, another black man came to the dock. The newcomer was younger, about twenty, in clean, well-fitting work clothes with his pants tucked into high combat boots. The man was very dark, almost six feet tall and had the build of a National Football League halfback. As soon as he saw us, his face clouded with anger. He looked at us briefly, turned on his heel, walked about ten feet away and pulled out a cigarette. With another surly look at us, he sat down on a bench to wait.

Jean and I looked at each other. This was no paranoid fantasy. We had seen sharp changes in the demeanor of the two men as soon as they got a good look at us. We had caused fear in one and had elicited great anger from the other. It was as if white and black strangers had arrived in a little town in Mississippi in the early fifties, knowing nothing of the social mores of the place and not being fluent in the language.

I could see the ferry now as it moved almost imperceptibly through the water toward us. All I wanted was for it to get to us before anybody else came. However we had affected them, these men were surely no threat. I just didn't want any whites to get to the dock before the boat came. And I thought we were going to make it as the boat swung wide to come up to the dock, when Jean nudged my arm and nodded in the direction of the street from which we had come. There were five white men, all in their late teens or early twenties, weaving toward the dock as if they had picked up substantial loads of alcohol during the evening.

Shit, I thought. Shit, shit. This was the last kind of group I wanted to see in this place at this time. I remembered Ron at Maxwell's Plum, and my fear of horny, loaded and lonely white men late at night. Just about the time I saw them, some of them began nudging each other and nodding toward Jean and me. Some of their faces hardened as they saw us while others appeared surprised and curious.

"This could be real trouble," I said to Jean. "Stick close to me."

She looked at me, her brown eyes wide, and just nodded, saying nothing. Now the strong young black man was looking at us with a look that was more quizzical than angry. I spoke to Jean again, about something inconsequential, but I was sure the man heard me.

His look changed from anger to comprehension. He was certain now that I was speaking English, not French. He smiled at me and nodded, and I smiled and nodded back. I was not a native intentionally flaunting local taboos and carelessly endangering whatever black bystanders there might be when appropriate wrath was visited on my head. Rather, I was a stranger who didn't know what fates he was tempting by standing here in the night with this good-looking white woman. As the white men approached, the younger black man's smile faded, but his posture softened. It was clear that the rage he had been feeling had diminished.

As the ferry docked, the five young white men stood nearby and stared openly or leered at Jean and me. The drunk black man saw them and went away, apparently deciding to avoid whatever it was that might happen on that small boat during the twenty-minute crossing. The young men got on the boat and then we did. They did not take their eyes off us and I didn't take mine off them. The black men went alone to the back of the boat and sat down and watched. The five white men gathered at the middle, near the wheelhouse, and Jean and I moved a little forward toward the bow. When we were all on board, a man came out of the wheelhouse and pulled the ropes into the boat and the small ferry chugged out into the bay.

The young men maintained a steady low conversation in French, watching us all the time. The light from the wheelhouse illuminated the faces of two of them. They were puffed with alcohol, eyes red. They looked like very unpleasant people. They moved a bit forward out of the light and toward us. I moved a bit toward the bow. They moved again. Each move was small and each was separated by perceptible intervals. But, it was clear. Our space was shrinking and we were being chased, ever so slowly. There would be an inevitable confrontation—five young men against a man, a woman and, perhaps, if he were bold—the strong black in the stern. Any way we sliced it, it would be ugly, humiliating and probably painful. I could practically taste the fear in my mouth.

"Stand right here," I said to Jean, squeezing her hand before I released it.

I went over to the white men and approached one who had just lit a cigarette.

"Pardon me," I said. "May I have a cigarette." I had quit smoking a couple of years earlier, and I hated the notion of taking smoke into my lungs. But at that moment, the alternative for that evening was worse.

The man looked at me in confusion and made a gesture that he hadn't understood. His companions stood frozen, watching.

"Cigarette," I repeated and then placing two fingers at my mouth and inhaling.

"Oh," he said. "Oh," he repeated as he extracted a blue packet of Gauloises from his pocket and offered me a cigarette from it.

"Thank you," I said, taking it. "Do you have a match," and again I gestured, this time as if lighting the cigarette.

"*Oui,*" he said quickly, and he lit my cigarette with a lighter he had pulled from his pocket. His friends were no longer frozen. They were watching, the attitudes of their bodies substantially less stiff than when they had been cutting down the deck space available to Jean and me.

"Thank you very much," I said, smiling and withdrawing.

"You're welcome," my benefactor said in heavily accented English and he smiled.

The tension was gone. It was as if someone had let the air out of a balloon. In the act of requesting a cigarette and a light, I had transformed myself from an object, a symbol of something that stirred primitive fears and hatreds in these men into a person, with human qualities that they could recognize. I had become an American who smoked cigarettes and said thank you. It was enough. The human connection had been accomplished, and we would not be attacked.

Late that night, Jean awakened me and said, "Roger, you are the bravest man by far that I have ever known."

The next day, we were on the beach and I was reading a segment of Charles Reich's *The Greening of America* in *The New Yorker*. An American woman asked me what I thought about the piece. We talked about America, about politics and about the future. I was gentle with her, but I suggested differences of view on most of the things we touched upon. Later, as we were having a drink on the small terrace of our room, Jean brought up that conversation.

"When you're black, you have to know everything that everybody else knows to get along in this life," she said. "You have thought about all the things that an intelligent white person has thought about —your identity, politics, your children, the future of the country. In addition to that, you know all about being black, how America deals with black people, what you have to do as a black person to survive, how to raise black children so they can survive. All of that."

"All of that," I agreed.

"It's a whole extra thing that black people have," Jean marveled. "I'd never quite seen it that way until I put what we went through last night together with the conversation I listened to today. A whole extra dimension," she repeated. "And white people don't even know it, and they don't give black people credit for it."

"Yep, Jeanie," I said. "I think you've got it just about right. Except for the extra stress. You left that out." I smiled at her and took her hand and we sat silently sipping the end of our drinks as the sunset faded.

26 After the week in Martinique nothing was changed, except that I was a little more rested, and even more deeply convinced that racism was all-pervasive. Martinique had fueled the paranoia that resulted from my disintegrated state and raised its level above what virtually all blacks need in order to survive. I had once observed that "any nigger who ain't paranoid is crazy," but this was ridiculous. I came back to New York no less guilt-ridden about my wife and my children, no less fearful about my children's future, no less rootless and no less frightened and lonely.

Somewhere in the distant sky, I could hear my grandmother rumbling, "You are a bad boy, Roger."

I believed her and I couldn't even contemplate what my father would have thought about his mess of a son. I was almost thirty-nine years old.

I lived with terrible guilt that was mainly about the children, but not entirely; it was about Eve too. No one who knows Eve Tyler Wilkins could ever, by any stretch of the imagination, call her a bad woman. On the contrary, she is a very good woman and a fine mother. We almost never had screaming fights. She did not waste my money, drink or go with other men. We were just constitutionally different in profound ways. Eve was cautious and wanted security, and sometimes it seemed to me that I fled from security when it beckoned. Eve wanted a quiet life, and I kept on going out looking for high adventure—I thrived on it and got bored in between adventures. Eve once observed that I only seemed to come alive and function at my peak when there was a crisis. My boredom with the life that most suited Eve was almost tangible. I would become grumpy, irascible and yearn as deeply as I could for something else.

But, when I was away from her, I would gradually forget those moods and times and remember how comfortable we sometimes could make each other. After all, by that time we had been friends for twenty years and had been married for fourteen. I would almost forget why I had left. The world's view was simple—Roger left Eve to be with a rich and glamorous white woman. I knew that that wasn't entirely true, but in my despair and extraordinary need for self-laceration, I would begin to believe what the world had to say.

And, of course, there were the children. We had moved from Washington to New York during the reconciliation and they all lived in a nice house in Cobble Hill, a neighborhood undergoing rapid revitalization just south of Brooklyn Heights. In 1970, Amy was eleven and David was six, and they went to an integrated private school—St. Ann's—in Brooklyn Heights. I adored them, and when I would visit them, as I did regularly, it was like putting a lance through my own heart.

It wasn't that the children were obviously troubled; they didn't seem to be. I knew, of course, that the separations had to have a huge impact on them, but it didn't seem to show, then. They had had both black and white friends in Washington, and that was also the case at St. Ann's. Amy was making a good adjustment to the school, and David had become an avid collector of junk. Discarded hub caps and broken-down pieces of machinery just appeared in the house. One day when I was walking him from school, he saw a giant discarded motor that looked like it came from a commercial air-conditioner.

"Can I take that home, Dad?" he asked.

"If you can carry it, you can have it," I replied and that was that.

But, to take them out to meals, which is what I most often did, was usually excruciating. People of eleven and six are not the most interesting table companions, and guilty fathers are worse. I had deprived myself of the easy day-to-day contact with them, and the yearning and the loving and the missing on both sides of the table made it extraordinarily difficult to have easy visits. I see men with young children at restaurant tables on weekends, and my heart goes out to the children and to the fathers too. I am glad those days are over for us.

But there were some good times too, like the wonderful fall Sunday when I drove the children up to Inge Morath and Arthur Miller's home in Connecticut. It is a wonderful place to spend days because they live in a big old comfortable white farmhouse, and Inge has turned the silo into her photographic studio and Arthur uses the barn as a wood-working shop. There is a meadow, a pond and woods, and through it runs a spring that feeds the pond. The children had never met Inge and Arthur, who weren't there when we arrived, so I showed Amy and David some of the chairs and other furniture that Arthur had made and then we took a walk. It was a fine, clear, sunlit October day, and we walked far into the woods. When we came to the spring, Amy and I stood holding hands as David flopped on his belly to drink. When he finished, David looked up from his prone position and said, "Oh Daddy! Isn't it clean and good?"

Things like that often came out of his mouth in those days. He once told me that spring was his favorite season "because it is a leaf's birthday."

By the time we finished our walk, the Millers were home and the adults talked, while my children played with their daughter, Becky. After we had dinner, the children and I headed on back to Brooklyn. It had been a wonderful day.

Some weeks later, David was trying to make me remember some person, but the clues weren't clear enough. Then, the light struck his mind. "You remember. That carpenter we went to visit up in the country. Mr. Miller."

Arthur loved that when I told it to him, but many of my visits with my children were very sad, and when I would stand on that desolate subway platform at Bergen Street late in the evening after having dropped them off, I would wonder from time to time whether a leap in front of the train would give me peace. But, I knew that whatever scars I had inflicted on the children were as nothing, compared to that which would be left by a father who had taken his own life. It was, in large measure, the children who kept me going. Nevertheless, most of the time, I still felt like a horrible person.

Bad boy or not, there was one last thing for me to do in my capacity as a foundation executive. It was to make explicit my professional reasons for leaving the Ford Foundation. My battles with Mike were simply metaphors for what was wrong with the place. Granted, Mac had opened the windows to a lot of fresh air since the days when his predecessor summarily threw representatives of the NAACP Legal Defense Fund out of his office because he didn't think that kind of activity was appropriate for Ford Foundation funding.

But the place was still run by successful, middle-aged white males. The assumption about their omniscience was overpowering, and there were not enough kinds of people in the Foundation—young, non-white, female—with any power to challenge the status quo. It was terribly lonely there.

I dictated a short memorandum setting forth my views about the Foundation and showed it to Mac and asked him if I could read it to the trustees at their December meeting. The memorandum, particularly its charge of racism, distressed Mac profoundly, but he agreed to arrange for me to read it to the trustees. I learned much later that he had done so over quite strong objections of some of the trustees, who thought that employee views of the Foundation, even those views that led an employee who had been highly valued to leave, were not of sufficient weight to take up their time. Mac prevailed, and I entered the board room and read to the men assembled there—Henry Ford II, Edwin Land, Judge Charles Wyzanski, Bethuel Webster, Robert S. MacNamara and Kermit Gordon among them. This is what I read.

I deeply appreciate this opportunity to speak to you for the last time as one of your program directors.

There is one thing which I consider to be of overriding importance that I feel absolutely compelled to tell you. By not doing so, I would betray my own conscience, the black, brown, red and yellow citizens of this country whom I have tried faithfully to represent in this institution, and also the trust which you have reposed in me.

Except for one (a very new arrival) all of the men in this room are white, older than I am, and very successful males. No matter how much you may disagree among yourselves, this group represents a very tight and homogenous vision of American society and the world.

Please do not misunderstand what I am saying. There are men in this room whom I respect and some whom I revere.

The fact is, nevertheless, that there is no one in this room whose vision was formed by growing up on a red reservation. And that is a valid American vision.

There is no one in this room whose vision was formed by growing up in a brown barrio. And that is a valid American vision.

There is no one in this room whose vision was formed by growing up after Hiroshima. And that is a valid American vision.

There is no one in this room whose vision was formed by growing up wearing pigtails and skirts. And *that* is a most valid American vision.

There is no one in this room whose vision was formed by growing up on one of the teeming continents of Asia or Africa, or of Latin America.

For a Foundation that takes pride in being an international organization, these are valid institutional visions.

From excruciatingly painful personal experience, it is clear to me that the burden that you have placed on Viv Henderson of being the sole voice for all those voices that are excluded from this room is very heavy indeed.

You might also close your eyes and think about the weekly officers meeting where the basic day-to-day operating decisions of the Ford Foundation are made and think of the voices from other places and other rooms that are not there. The burden placed upon your two black program directors who do not go into that room has been very heavy indeed. Soon there will be only one, and I do not envy my friend and colleague, Chris Edley.

Finally, there is that stark image of the thirty or forty leaders of the International Division sitting around the conference table in Mexico City where mine was the only skin that was not white.

There are people in the Ford Foundation whom I love and there are things that it has done which make me proud to have been a part of it. But the exclusion of these voices of pain, rage, feminine joy and youthful anguish set up for me a screeching sound of silence that makes my spirit weary and my soul cry. America has through all her days been governed generally by successful, rich, thrusting, white men over forty-five. American is in deep trouble today and it is because America cannot hear or will not hear those sounds of silence.

It may be true that homogeneity promotes a comfortable and civilized discourse, but it does not, I believe, promote those rasping and some-times painful encounters that can lead us closer to the truth about our country and about the world. There is pain in America and around the globe, but except for Viv, the carriers and the criers of the most ex-cruciating human pain do not sit in these chairs when it really counts for the Ford Foundation. Finally, I would say that people do not talk to men like you this way because they want your smiles, your approba-tion, a part of your power or your money.

This is a most important and certainly unique American institution. America needs the best that this institution can offer, and that cannot happen in my judgment the way things are.

I love America and I guess in a funny way I love the Ford Founda-tion. I hope that I have done my duty to both by saying to you what I have just now said.

Thank you very much for listening to me today.

And, then after the dawning of 1971, I left the glass and gilded office on the third floor of the Foundation and was given a smaller space below ground, which I could use when the work that Mac wanted me to do required me to be in the building. But, mainly, I was not there. I began thinking seriously about becoming a writer then, but my friend Richard Harris, who had just published a splendid book on the Department of Justice, warned me not to do it. "It's a mug's game," he said. Nevertheless, Jean lent me a writing table, which Ramsey and Georgia Clark let me put in their then sparsely furnished apartment in Greenwich Village and I went there to try to work or write.

It was terrifying. My umbilical cord to the world had been cut. No longer did each day bring a flood of bureaucratic papers or grant proposals across my desk for signature or review. No longer did each day bring that torrent of telephone calls and messages that reminded me that I was a significant man. No longer did each day bring a clamor of people struggling to get a fragment of my time, a shard of my attention. Each day brought nothing. I was alone.

I had shed all that had puffed up my importance in order to go back to something more basic. And I did get to something more basic—myself confronting myself, alone, without props. I was a man of no value, I thought, who had ruined his life, abandoned his children, shredded his career and made himself a laughingstock for those who didn't take him seriously enough to despise him. One day I met somebody for lunch on the east side, in the forties. After lunch, at about quarter to three, I was in the Grand Central subway station when a delivery boy carrying a large, thin rectangular package wrapped in black brushed by me in a hurry, knocking me off stride. I watched him. He had someplace to go. Somebody would miss him if he didn't arrive somewhere at a certain time. He had a place and a function that I didn't have.

I thought about suicide. I could walk in parks and not hear children. I would read as much of the newspaper as I could, and all I could see were calamities. I could see old friends and know from their looks—a kind of veiled, wary watching—that they were worried and sad, some of them, because their friend had gone off the active list. It was easier to see strangers.

Jean was quiet, watchful, steady and supportive.

"Don't worry," she would say. "This is just a short phase. You'll come through it all right." It is possible that I might have gone under, that year, without her. It is clear that I held on to her for dear life. And there was just enough to do so that I couldn't feel that I had entirely disappeared. There was a flow of tasks from Mac. There was Lillian Hellman's Committee for Public Justice, of which I had become chairman and which was trying to push prison reform and to mount a conference on the governance of the FBI. There was also the project to review the Panther deaths in Chicago; it was cochaired by Ramsey and my Uncle Roy. And I was trying to do a little writing. But my energy level was low, my work output was down, my capacity to concentrate was limited, my attention span was short and my confidence was gone.

Toward the middle of that year, a search committee of the National Urban League board chose Vernon Jordan over Cliff Alexander as the successor to Whitney Young. It was a change of guard and a change of generation. Vernon decided that he wanted a consultation with some of his contemporaries and friends as he contemplated his new responsibilities. He asked Kenneth Clark to convene an informal meeting at his house in Westchester on an early summer weekend.

The whole crew was there; the core of the sixties that I had known and cared about: Carl Holman, by now a vice-president at the National Urban Coalition; Marian Wright Edelman, now director of her own Washington-based research program; Ed Sylvester, now director of a foundation designed to stimulate minority business enterprises; Lisle Carter, now a vice-president at Cornell University; and Andy Young, gathering his strength after one defeat, for his second run at a seat in the House of Representatives.

Kenneth had us there for two days of talks about race in general, about the future of the country, about the National Urban League and about what we could do to help Vernon. These were my kinds of issues. The people were among my dearest friends on the earth. But I couldn't function. I couldn't assert anything with certainty, and I had no faith in my ability to analyze a problem. At a meeting I would normally have enjoyed hugely, I felt thoroughly uncomfortable.

At the end of our meeting, Vernon drove Andy and me in to the city. It was a lovely day as we came down the Major Deegan, past the Yankee Stadium and over the bridge and into Harlem. We reminisced the way good friends do on an easy balmy Sunday. Somehow our talk about things past, the kinds of things we had done and the sense that these two were now moving toward new approaches to the old set of problems made me begin to think about new departures that I might take.

The writing I was doing was going nowhere, and I couldn't make a living on hit-or-miss projects. The better thing to do was to recognize that this was the seventies and to begin finding my own new approaches to the problems we had all cared about. My thoughts began to run back to the offer I had received from *The Washington Post*. I wondered whether that might still be good or whether I might not find some other newspaper to write for. I was in better spirits when Vernon dropped me off. I wasn't so sure that the weekend had helped him, but it may have done something for me.

Jean had been agitating for us to take a vacation that summer, but I didn't think I had done enough work to warrant a vacation. Jean insisted, however, and slogged around in the Hamptons until she found a place where she thought we would enjoy ourselves for a month. The Hamptons—far out on the South shore of Long Island, distinguished by miles and miles of wonderful beaches—are where most of literary Manhattan goes for the summer months. The Hamptons are snooty and full of social calibrations about who had invited whom to what parties and why. They have more to do with status than with sun and sand. Needless to say, there are not any black people around there to speak of—or to see, or talk to.

But, when the late afternoon light slants on the green potato fields and some congenial people gather to put flame to food on a deep white beach, the glory of the place could block out, for a bit, a fundamental understanding of what the place was and the dogged memories of the barefoot children running through hydrant water in dirty gutters.

It was on such a night that news spread across the Hamptons that George Jackson, the Soledad Brother, the man who had become the national symbol of the oppression of blacks in the American prison systems, had been killed in an "escape attempt" at San Quentin prison in California, just north of San Francisco Bay. I shuddered at the peril in which black people found themselves, and I wondered for the fiftieth time what in the world I was doing in the Hamptons. I had to write about George Jackson's death, so I called Harrison Salisbury, who was the editor of the Op-ed page of the *Times* and I asked him if he would like a piece on Jackson's death. He said he would be delighted. It went this way:

EAST HAMPTON, L.I.—August in East Hampton is a lovely time. Gusts from the ocean hint fall, and the late summer sun casts a soft light over brown meadows, green potato fields and deep blue ponds. People fret over communal picnics, speculate over names included or left off weekend guest lists, and compare notes on the household help available in the local talent pool. In serious moments, a disgruntled intellectual may talk of emigrating to Ireland or of the alienation of modern man and his ceaseless search for identity.

Then comes the news from California. George Jackson couldn't get to Ireland. He couldn't even reach the San Quentin wall. The paper said that in the yard at his prison Jackson received a rifle bullet "on top of the head . . . that went through the base of his skull, down his back alongside the spine, fracturing a rib and leaving from his lower back."

Talk on the beaches and at backyard cocktail parties turned to the inconsistencies in the official reports and to speculation about prison authorities having set him up to die. Jackson, the general judgment goes, though for perhaps good reason—imprisoned for up to life for a seventy-dollar robbery—was a desperate man and alienated from our society.

Jackson was certainly alienated from East Hampton's late summer ennui and that strain of American life that encourages people to fritter their lives away heedless of casual and calculated cruelties inflicted on people who do not belong, but he was not alienated from himself. He was the ultimate nigger and he knew it. A man of intelligence and dignity, George Jackson was one of those against whom American law contorts, degrades and mocks itself. For a crime for which a white youth might have received probation for two years, Jackson served eleven years—most of them in stench-filled solitary cells—at the mercy of officials who had some need to break his will. He told Angela Davis in a letter, "They created the situation. All that flows from it is their responsibility. They've created in me one irate, resentful nigger—and it's building—to what climax?"

George Jackson never really had a chance to live the life of the empty spirit, worrying about status, his next promotion or the right place to live. He suffered the final American degradation—he was poor and black and smart and a prisoner.

Jackson knew the value of seventy dollars and a black life in the California prisons. He wrote often that he never expected to be given back his freedom—to leave prison alive. But he also made clear that his soul was his own. He refused to cede his spirit to coarse prison authority in return for the mean favors of a system that could pen men for years in cramped "adjustment-center" cells smaller than a family bathroom, behind solid metal doors with two-inch by five-inch slits to see the "free" corridor area outside. To preserve his mind, Jackson read everything from Stendhal to Engels. To preserve his body, he did exercises in his

cell for six hours a day. To preserve his soul, he resisted prison brutality and evolved a philosophy of rebellion which he preached to all
who would listen. He saved his soul and lost his life following the pre-
cepts of the prisoner Sologdin in Solzhenitsyn's *The First Circle*: "The
most rewarding past . . . is the greatest external resistance in the
presence of the least internal resistance. Failures must be considered the
cue for further applications of efforts and concentration of willpower.
And if substantial efforts have already been made, the failures are all
the more joyous. It means our crowbar has struck the iron box containing the treasure. Overcoming the increased difficulties is all the more
valuable because in failure the growth of the person performing the
task takes place in proportion to the difficulty encountered."

No matter how hard they pressed George Jackson's face in the slime,
he always thrust his hand toward the sun.

The state says George Jackson was a murderer, and perhaps he killed
a man or more, but if he did, he did it inside an iron circle of hell where
the agents of a careless people have almost unlimited sovereignty over
the bones and spirits of the men they keep. Death of prisoner and
keeper alike are the natural consequences of state-sponsored savagery.
If some men kill to prevent the theft of the goods of their store or their
family jewels, might others not also kill to prevent the theft of their
lives and their spirits?

In East Hampton and other places—where iron boxes are rarely
struck—people will speculate briefly on the nature of Jackson's life and
the reasons for his death and go on to the next headline. Whatever the
details of his last day—whether or not he had a gun in his hair—the
brothers, not Soledad, but mainly black—George Jackson helped define
for all time our iron boxes and some of the ways to approach them.

In his time and in his place, he built a powerful life and suffused our
spirits with the nigger suffering and the steel force of the Black Every-
man he had come to be. In California they could snatch his life for
seventy dollars, but the bullet that split his skull and creased his spine
could not kill what he had become.

And now, as August wanes, waves lap quietly on the sandy Hampton
shores.

That may not have been the best piece I ever wrote, but it certainly
was the least popular. Whites didn't like it because it plucked at one
of the last twinges of guilt before the *Gestalt* of the sixties disappeared altogether. One good white acquaintance took me to task for
several hours at a dinner party a couple of months later.

Some blacks also thought I had a hell of a nerve writing such a
piece from the Hamptons. They wanted to know what I thought I was

doing attempting to have it both ways, living the high white life while rambling on like a badly wounded nigger.

Though the attacks on the conflict between my life and views were sometimes phrased in almost the same way, the black complaint was much more painful for me. The white complaint really had as its base an outrage that I would voice a black complaint when they had included me in a rarefied segment of their world. The black complaint, on the other hand, said, look, you've escaped the daily pain of black life, so don't come around here with some eloquent cries trying to convince us you didn't.

The piece was not in any measure an attempt to assert black authenticity for myself, or plead that it be bestowed on me by others. It simply expressed how I felt about George Jackson's death at the place where and time when I learned about it. The black complaint hurt, because it signaled a thinning of my connections with the black community, connections that were vital to me if I were to preserve any semblance of mental health. Much later, Angela Davis told me that she had loved the piece when she read it in the Marin County jail where she was awaiting her trial for murder. I wish I had known that then; it would have helped a lot. The bulk of the black response was, in a sense, an outward manifestation of a truth I had been wrestling with privately—that the conflict I had set up for myself in adopting the life that Jean lived was probably more than I could bear and had to be resolved, one way or another.

The Washington Post began to look better and better as an alternative. Soon after getting back from the Hamptons, I reopened conversations with the *Post*. To my delight, Phil Geyelin seemed as pleased to hear from me as I was eager to talk to him. The job negotiation with Geyelin was extraordinarily pleasant, but mystifying. Geyelin is a ruddy man with thinning red hair. When I was negotiating with him, he had been editor of the editorial page for four years and had won a Pulitzer Prize for editorial writing just the year before. Geyelin had grown up on the Main Line in Philadelphia and was in his element, moving in the top rungs of the Washington political-journalistic establishment. Mrs. Graham called him "Philsy" just as she called Bradlee "Benjee," and she talked about what a marvelous job Philsy was doing, especially commending his wonderful touch with the people who worked for him. Geyelin was at the top of his game when I talked to him in the fall of '71.

Our lunches were pleasant, and Phil would laugh a lot, throwing his head back and letting out a small roar or screwing up his nose and just snickering a little. He made it plain that he wanted very much for me to work for him and that I would not be assigned to writing about the District of Columbia, as people from the *Post* had suggested during our first round of conversations. The *Post* couldn't pay nearly as well as the Ford Foundation, but promised me early adjustments. My only reservation was that, never having worked at a newspaper, I couldn't quite envision how my days would be spent.

Finally, one day after one of our lunches during which I had virtually agreed to his terms, I went back to the office and had a talk with Jim Clayton, one of his senior staff members. Jim was a gray man. His face had little color, his hair was gray, and it is difficult to remember any color in his clothes. He had been a distinguished Supreme Court reporter and was one of those journalists who, by dint of hard work, had learned more about the kind of law that is practiced and handed down at the Supreme Court than most lawyers in the country.

Clayton made the editorial process simple and comprehensible.

"Just imagine an extraordinary dinner party conversation," he said, "but imagine that all of the people there are intelligent and extremely well-informed. That's what you have here in the editorial conference every morning after everybody has read all the papers. During the course of the conversations, it is decided what everybody will write and then you go off and do it. You call sources, you get out clips and read them and you figure out what you're going to write and then you write it."

I thanked Clayton for that information. It sounded like a kind of thin day to me, but I wasn't ready to assume that it would be an easy job. I told Phil before I left the *Post* building that day that I would take the job.

I was excited. I was going into the kind of work my father had done. I would sit at a machine and work there. At the end of a day something would exist that I had made. It wouldn't have existed but for me. There would be a tangible product that I could take in my hand in the late afternoon and judge.

I was also afraid.

But, the issue was decided, and I went back to New York to get ready for my move back to Washington for a new challenge and an entirely new career. I would turn forty just after going to the *Post*. It was a massive departure at a relatively advanced age. People in

New York began saying goodbye in the loveliest ways. Many of them really seemed distressed at the idea that I was leaving the city. Although the notion of a new and different job bolstered my self-esteem some, I still had a good grip on strong feelings of uselessness. It was hard to believe that in a city as massive as New York, anybody would be missed.

By this time, I was having major problems with my relationship with Jean. I kept telling her that I couldn't handle the conflicts that our being together stirred in me; that it seemed to me that it diminished my ability to reconstruct a coherent sense of myself. Jean generally dealt with my misgivings lightly and with good humor, as she did with the rest of my expressions of doubts in those days. Her attitude seemed to be that it was simply a phase I was going through, and that it should be treated with patience, good humor and large dollops of encouragement. And that was how she was dealing with the doubts I was expressing about interracial relationships as we went to a dinner at the home of Sheila and Joe Okpaku, who, in the course of it, were going to say goodbye to me.

Sheila is beautiful and one of the first black female graduates of Harvard Law School. She was at the time a civil-rights lawyer. Joe is a Nigerian businessman who, in those days, owned a publishing company that I had helped him start in my days at Ford. They seemed to me to be a couple whose love and personal interplay was nourished and enhanced by their blackness. I envied them that, and I was somewhat embarrassed to be going into their black home with my white woman. They were about to have a baby, enlarging the black community by one black human being who would be the product of the genes and the nurturing of two exceptionally able black people. Into that black strength, I was taking my weakness and I was ashamed, not of Jean, but of me.

When we got to Sheila and Joe's, Douglas Turner Ward, the driving force and guiding light of the Negro Ensemble Company, was there. Doug Ward had provided more showcases for more black actors than almost anyone else walking around. His artistry, whether on the stage—he is a fine actor—or behind it—he is also a fine director—was an assertion of black strength and sensitivity. Nobody could deny the glory of Doug's blackness or the blackness of his contribution. We were introduced to Mrs. Ward. She was white. Jean looked at me and grinned.

It was an easy and pleasant evening at Sheila and Joe's and I was

sorry that we had to leave early, but we were expected by Marion
Javits, who was having an evening for the Russian poet Yevtushenko
and the American foreign-policy expert Henry Kissinger. It was late
by the time we got to the Javitses' Park Avenue apartment, and
some people had already left. We ran into Warren Beatty in the
lobby. He was leaving. When he saw us coming in, Beatty grinned
and said, "God, what a swell-looking couple."

Jean grinned at me again.

Upstairs, Yevtushenko was just leaving, and the Javits party had
dwindled to a small group sitting around the living room focused on
Henry Kissinger. Kissinger was sitting on the far edge of the couch,
and Nancy Maginnes, who would eventually become Mrs. Kissinger,
was sitting next to him. Sherry Henry, the radio personality, Harrison
Salisbury, Senator Javits, Charlotte Salisbury, Barbara Walters, Jasper
Johns, the English publisher George Weidenfeld, and Marion Javits
were all there.

India and Pakistan had been engaged in a brief but bloody scuffle.
America was bombing North Vietnam, and Jack Anderson had got-
ten hold of a batch of National Security Council documents and had
published some of them, including one that indicated that President
Nixon wanted the United States government to "tilt toward Pakistan"
in the battle on the Subcontinent. Richard M. Nixon was encouraging
Middle America to believe that school integration could be resisted
because busing was undesirable. It was the winter of 1971–72.
Nixon had been in office for three years, and Vietnam had become
Nixon's war. Somebody at the party had apparently asked Kissinger
about the Anderson revelations, and he was explaining them with a
heavy voice, polysyllabic words and complex sentences. I had never
seen Kissinger before, nor he me. I was the only black in the room.

As I walked in, Charlotte Salisbury reached up and grabbed my
hand, pulling me toward her.

"Come here and sit by me, Roger," she said. "And squeeze my
hand. I can't take all this stuff this guy's handing out and I may say
something rude."

My mother's good manners took over. I didn't want Charlotte to
say anything rude, so I squeezed her hand and said, "Shhh, Charlotte,
he can't be saying anything quite that bad."

But, then I began listening to Kissinger and I couldn't believe my
ears.

"You have to understand," the National Security Adviser was saying, "these are highly classified documents and they have to be read in context."

What a load of bullshit, I thought. "Tilt toward Pakistan" meant exactly what it said.

"Squeeze my hand again, Roger," Charlotte said. "This is not what people are interested in."

I hadn't let her hand go, but I squeezed it again, because I thought an unseemly outburst should be avoided. If others were troubled by Kissinger's bland assurances that the government knew best, they didn't show it.

Kissinger continued talking. The cadences of his speech, the inflection and the steady flow of sonorous vowel groupings had almost a hypnotic effect on me. If you didn't pay attention to the meaning of the words, the rich flow of sounds was pleasant, almost comforting.

"Cut it out, Mr. Kissinger," Charlotte's voice suddenly interrupted, sharp and clear. It cut across Kissinger's mellifluent diction and pinned him to the couch. Though I was still gripping her hand, Charlotte continued.

"Why don't you just cut that out and tell us when you are going to stop the bombing. That's what the people want to know. The murdering should stop. When are you going to stop it?"

Charlotte had thrust reality into the middle of that elegant sitting room. People just looked straight ahead, and the silence was thick. Charlotte sat there waiting for an answer, expectant. And I sat there holding her hand.

George Weidenfeld began whispering urgently to Marion Javits. It was a hoarse whisper and I could catch its meaning across the room. Because he thought it would be too demeaning for the National Security Adviser to have to respond to such a crude onslaught, Weidenfeld was suggesting that Javits should answer. Marion motioned to Jack and the Senator dutifully cleared his throat and began.

"Well, while I don't fully agree with the President in these matters, and, of course, I have expressed my disagreement to him, I think I am familiar with his thinking about Vietnam," Javits began. Then in trying to explain Nixon's position, Javits began to contradict himself.

By the time he had finished, it was clear that nobody else was going to take up Charlotte's cause, and it was also clear that Javits had made a lousy case for the war.

"That's baloney, Jack," I said at last. "The argument you made doesn't even hang together. . . ."

As I talked on, cutting away at what I saw as inconsistencies in what my host had said, I heard Weidenfeld *humph*ing and growling disapproval.

"Scurrilous," he was saying. "Disgraceful. Treasonous. Here the President is trying his best to settle this war in delicate international negotiations and here these people are attacking him."

I finished with Javits and turned toward Charlotte, and we smiled at each other, but Weidenfeld wouldn't subside. I became furious.

"Mr. Weidenfeld," I spat out. "I don't know how it is in England, but here, one of the great services a citizen can render is to offer reasoned dissent on public policy. That is the only way we have to test the wisdom and the utility of our public policies.

"We in this country have been seared by this war. We have been lied to. Some of our young people have died and lost limbs fighting for purposes which have never been explained to them. Our society is being ripped apart by this war and we are not being given answers to our questions. So, we—or, that is, some of us—will continue to ask questions until we get good answers or until this war is stopped. Here, that is not treason. It is good citizenship."

The party stopped at that point. People just got up and shifted from foot to foot as they lined up to say their goodnights to Kissinger and to their host and hostess. In the general shuffling toward the door, Kissinger and I came face to face. We smiled at each other and shook hands.

"Would you take the President a message for me?" I asked.

"Yes," Kissinger replied tentatively.

"Would you tell him that there are some of us who wish he would tilt toward busing."

Kissinger reddened and looked down toward his shoes. "Oh," he said and moved away.

I heard more about that evening a few weeks later from Barbara Walters. She said that when she, Kissinger and Maginnes had settled into their cab, Kissinger remarked:

"That Julian Bond is sure a fiery guy, isn't he?"

"That's not Julian Bond," Barbara told him. "You've got bigger problems than that. That man is Roy Wilkins' nephew Roger, and he is about to join the editorial board of *The Washington Post*."

She could see Kissinger's face pale as he absorbed the new information.

Another Barbara, Howar, the noted Washington hostess, writer and television personality, conveyed some more reverberations from that evening. Katharine Graham, who was to become my new boss, attended her party for Kissinger and Yevtushenko. Kissinger, according to Howar, went up to Mrs. Graham and said:

"You're hiring dangerous people these days."

"What do you mean, Henry?" Mrs. Graham inquired.

"One of your people, Roger Wilkins, attacked me viciously in New York the other day."

Mrs. Graham laughed and said, "Well, Henry, that's what we hire people for, their independence."

For me, that exchange was an example of Mrs. Graham's character, a forecast of her brave stand during the time of *The Post*'s Watergate disclosures, when the Nixon Administration was bringing extraordinary pressures on her to pull her staff up short. Kissinger's casual knife in the ribs of a man he did not know but whose career he could have been strangling in its cradle was quite in harmony with the character of the man who could order the tapping of the phones of members of his own staff, and acquiesce in the Christmas bombings of North Vietnam while telling the press that he disagreed with the policy.

The final piece of the story fell into place on my first day at *The Post* in early February. I had not heard the Walters and Howar stories when my old friend Liz Drew decided that she wanted to take me to lunch on my first day back in town. Liz decided that we should go to Sans Souci, the lunch place which had become one of the central power rituals in Washington. The Washington lions— Kissinger; Edward Bennett Williams, the lawyer and sportsman; Art Buchwald, the columnist; Ben Bradlee; and a revolving cast that had its hands on the instruments of power and influence in the city— would come to eat, greet each other, gossip and be gawked at by others.

Liz had enough of a name by then to get us in on short notice. We sat at a small table near the front of the restaurant, by a railing that overlooked the sunken middle section in which the lions had their favorite tables. Liz and I were catching up on our own gossip when Kissinger entered, followed by his luncheon guest, David Frost.

Kissinger was at the height of his influence by then. His secret Paris peace negotiations had been revealed, and just that week his picture had appeared on the cover of *Newsweek* and *Time*. He was being called Super K. I had seen him just two weeks earlier in New

York, and it had been a week since he had talked to Mrs. Graha·ı about me. He spotted me as soon as he came in the door and as he came toward me, his face lit up in a gracious and friendly grin. I stood and accepted his hand.

"How are you, Mr. Wilkins. It's good to see you," he said. Frost was behind him and couldn't hear what Kissinger was saying, able only to note the warmth of the greeting.

"It's nice to see you, Dr. Kissinger," I replied.

"Welcome to Washington," he said. "I hope you enjoy the *Post*."

"Thank you very much," I said; then Kissinger moved on by me to greet Liz. Frost came forward then.

"Hello, Julian," he said to me. "It's nice to see you again."

27 Newspaper people had always been heroes to me. They seemed larger than life, and the places where they worked were like magic. Though I was aware that very few people took note of bylines, I always did, and on my first day, I was thrilled, walking through the *Post*'s gray and jumbled newsroom to come upon a young, dark-haired man working at his typewriter. I looked over his shoulder as I passed by. At the top of the pink-rimmed, six-copy paper the *Post* then used, he wrote:

By Sanford J. Ungar
WPSW

I had read Sanford J. Ungar's byline with the legend, "Washington Post Staff Writer" under it in the paper. Now I had actually seen him write it. And I was his colleague in this journalistic enterprise. It was a thrill beyond my power to express.

In those days at the *Post*, the editorial-staff offices were outside the newsroom and ran along a corridor at the front of the building. I arrived on my first day after the morning editorial meeting had ended, so Phil led me down to my office, which was the last one on the aisle, just opposite the back elevator. Ward Just, the novelist, had once composed an editorial in that office suggesting that Nixon's choice of Agnew as Vice-President was as curious as the choice of Caligula's horse as proconsul of Rome. Now it was my office.

Phil opened the door and led me in. I knew from the loss of income that I had moved down the scale substantially by picking journalism over philanthropy. But this contrast was ridiculous. At

Ford there were the polished dark woods, the matching chairs and sofa, the credenza, the silver water pitcher, a sliding glass wall and a view of the garden. Here there was a bare beige room with a linoleum floor, a small empty gray metal book shelf, a dented gray desk, a typewriter, some blank paper and a view of a parking garage across L Street. Newspaper executives like to say that journalists get a lot of psychic income from participating as observers in great events, and from seeing their names in the paper. Looking at this room and thinking about my paycheck, I figured the *Post* was putting a pretty large stock in psychic income.

"Well," Phil said, "there it is. If you need anything, let me know," and he retreated toward the door.

There I was, in a room with a typewriter and a pile of blank paper. I looked at the typewriter and the blank paper. This was my job. I was supposed to do something with these unpretentious tools, write something, make something. I was alone. I tried to think of somebody to call on the telephone. Then Phil's secretary came in with a pile of personnel forms. She was a pleasant and attractive Irish woman named Pat O'Shea, with flaming-red hair and bright-blue eyes. O'Shea made me feel better.

But, after she left, the typewriter was still there. The blank paper was still there. The typewriter seemed to be a little bigger. I turned away and spent the rest of the day on forms.

But the next morning, the typewriter was still there. It had grown some more. And there was still all that blank paper. So, I took a couple of sheets and I wheeled the chair around to the typewriter and rolled the paper into it just like a real writer, and then I wrote a letter to Jean. That helped. The typewriter was back down to size.

I thought that day about being near the top of the heap in a white institution one more time. At least I didn't anticipate racial problems at the paper—its liberal credentials seemed impeccable. Bradlee was a Kennedy person, exuberant, joyous and full of roguish charm. Geyelin, considerably more restrained, had fine manners and quick wit, and he was an extraordinarily pleasant man. Then there were two members of the editorial-page staff who, for me, seemed to anchor and guarantee the decency of the place. The first was Alan Barth, who for twenty-nine years had written editorials for the *Post*. Alan had been close to all the great liberal forces in Washington during his time. He had known Alger Hiss and had been a great friend of Felix Frankfurter. He had also been one of the major voices for decency during the McCarthy time. Donald Graham, who is now publisher of the *Post*, told me that Alan Barth was "everything this paper has stood for over the last few decades."

Alan was a gentle man of great passion and exquisite charm and wit. I had admired him since I, as a college student, had read his *The Loyalty of Free Men*. Now I was to work with him. To be his associate was and is one of the great honors of my life. And, there was a younger man of passion and decency whose elegant touch on the typewriter I had admired for many years. The man was Colman McCarthy, a former golf pro and former speech writer for Sargent Shriver. He didn't talk much, because he stuttered, but Colman exuded an intolerance for bullshit whether it was packed into the construction of an automobile, larded into a school curriculum, or flying around the room during an editorial conference. In the latter case, he would simply go to sleep.

I finally wrote an editorial and then another and then another. Though every major editorial page operates on the assumption that the entire universe is covered by the range of expertise possessed by its writers, I began to see niches and cracks in the *Post*'s pattern of editorial coverage that I began to fill. After I had been there a week or so, I wrote a column for the Op-ed page of the paper to be run under my name. It attacked Vice-President Agnew for his attacks on the legal-services program. It wasn't a great work of art, but it was my first professional byline. Jean was in town on the day it went to press; so, that night at about eleven, we went down to L Street and picked up a first edition, which we read together under a street lamp. At that moment I loved journalism and *The Washington Post* and all of the people in it.

But something was at work at the paper when I got there, something that I had known nothing about. Nine young black reporters in the newsroom had written a letter to Ben Bradlee complaining that the paper discriminated against blacks in hiring, promotion and assignments. They were young reporters who worked for Bradlee. I was a middle-aged editorial writer who worked for Geyelin. The editorial and news functions at the *Post* were scrupulously separated. I didn't understand the newspaper business yet, and their complaint had its basis in events that had preceded my coming to the paper. So, their problems had nothing to do with me. But, of course, they were black and so was I.

Bradlee talked to me about their complaint. I told him that it was important for him and the rest of the *Post*'s management to listen carefully to what the young reporters were saying; that white people were so used to doing things their ways, so unused to listening to black people seriously, so impressed with the fact that there were now some black people at work in the organization where there had been none before, that they found it difficult to hear what the blacks were trying to tell them.

A few days later, Robert C. Maynard, who was the *Post*'s senior black reporter, on leave in California, came through town. Hollie West, the music critic, Bill Raspberry, the columnist, and I took Maynard out for drinks. Eventually conversation turned to the question of the complaint of the younger black writers. There was general agreement that the complaint had merit. We also agreed that we ought to find some way to express our support for them. Raspberry was the only one who had some hesitation about the idea. But that was squelched when Maynard turned to him and said, "Look! If your little brother was down the street and you saw him getting his ass kicked by some big son of a bitch, wouldn't you go down there and help your little brother out?"

That sealed it. Maynard drafted a letter, which was posted on the bulletin board with a general invitation to the staff to sign it. It was clear to me that liberal or not, *The Washington Post*, like the Ford Foundation, was very much a part of white America.

Shortly after I got to the paper, I was invited to appear on a panel at a "counter convention" run by a new journalism review called *More*. It was held in New York and was counter to the American Newspaper Publisher's Convention, which also was being held in the city. The publishers were meeting at the Waldorf. The writers were meeting at the Martin Luther King Center, headquarters of Hospital Workers Union local 1199. I was on a panel called racism, elitism and sexism in the newsroom. There were two feminists, two blacks, and a fellow who had been drinking a lot.

Before I got to speak, Susan Brownmiller set out in powerful and uncompromising terms a feminist manifesto that included the assertion that the blacks had had their decade and it was now time for them to step aside because the seventies was to be the decade of the women. It was clear that a lot of the white women in the audience agreed with her. I was uncomfortable, because I had to follow Brownmiller, but I think I managed to say some useful things, one of which was that I didn't intend to tangle with Ms. Brownmiller.

But, she had tangled with my head. She had said more clearly than anybody I had yet heard that many people who had been the traditional allies of the black movement from the Montgomery bus boycott on, were now interested in other things. Not only was the President of the United States clearly an enemy of the things that had just been started in those fifteen years, but others had wearied of the effort or had found new things to do.

I left that platform with an empty feeling in my stomach. As I was moving slowly away, a young man who had the distinct look of the counter culture—long hair, corduroy pants stuffed into high laced boots and a sort of wild look in his soft brown eyes—came up and greeted me. Journalists on establishment papers, even young ones, would not look like this much longer. The time of the counter culture was running out. The sixties, which had begun to end with the murders in 1968 and the election of Richard Nixon, really ended for me at the first journalists' counter convention as I shook Carl Bernstein's hand on my way out of the Martin Luther King Center in 1972.

By early June, I was getting to be comfortable with my new job though the loss of all the bureaucratic trappings that had provided psychological support at Justice and at Ford was still unsettling. At Justice I had one secretary and a claim on the time of another as well as a personal assistant. At Ford, I had had a secretary and a personal assistant. At the *Post*, I took and placed my own calls and if I wanted to send letters, I typed them myself. I had hated the fraudulence of bureaucracy and especially the opulent ways in which the Ford Foundation propped up the egos of its employees. I had wanted more truth and less bullshit, but working conditions at the *Post* took things down closer to bare essentials than I had been prepared to face.

Yet, with all its psychological deprivations, I thought the environment was wonderful. I began to catch the rhythm of the paper, and I loved it. I would get the *Post* at home in the morning and read it thoroughly at breakfast in the coffee shop of the Madison Hotel across 15th Street from the grand new building that the paper had just completed. Then I'd pick up a *New York Times* and a *Wall Street Journal* and scan them for stories about domestic politics, social welfare programs, civil rights, prisons, legal issues and civil liberties, the issues I generally wrote about. I always had some kind of idea on what I wanted to write by the time Phil convened the editorial meeting at about ten-thirty.

The meetings were informal rituals. Phil, often with his feet on his desk, would start us talking about the day's top news story. These were good discussions. We all liked one another well enough, and if there were any ancient grudges or wounds being nursed, I didn't notice them. Each of us was expected to be prepared and intelligent about the areas about which we wrote, but comment on any subject was acceptable. These meetings were informed, good-humored and often witty. The tone and direction was due, in large measure, to Phil's light hand with us. We rarely left the meeting until eleven-thirty and were often there until a quarter to twelve and with a deadline of about five o'clock and lunch in between, what had seemed like a long day with time to move around in would begin to be a little cramped.

Normally, after the meeting, I would try to call people who knew something about the subject I had agreed to take on. Or I would talk to Bob Asher and Herb Block. Bob was an enormously good-spirited former reporter, who wrote editorials about the District of Columbia, taught part time at the Howard University School of Journalism and was one of the truly nonracial white people I had ever met. He was also very funny. Bob was probably closer to Herb Block, the *Post*'s triple Pulitzer Prize-winning cartoonist, than anybody on the paper. Block is an extraordinarily intelligent man who devours all the news presentations he can find. He keeps an all-news radio station going at all times in his cluttered inner sanctum at the far end of the editorial corridor.

After he had gotten as much news as he could handle, Herb would seek out somebody on the staff to talk over the subject that interested him that day. Often he would seek out an expert—J. W. Anderson, for instance, if the subject was economics. But sometimes, he would look for Asher or me or both of us. I think he sought us out because our political views coincided with his own and we laughed a lot.

By some wondrous and mysterious process, Herb's reactions and our conversation would be transformed over the next several hours into several penciled sketches, which he would bring out and show to us and others. If I thought the drawing was cluttered or unclear, I would say so, but most often, I would roar with delight to see the ideas and attitudes that we had exchanged earlier transformed with wit and intelligence into a graphic and often powerful political statement.

The editorial and news functions were separate. Bradlee had no authority over the editorial page, could not order an editorial in or out of the paper or even shape or shade one. By the same token, Phil couldn't influence the news side of the paper. Church and state, Phil used to call that separation.

But the practice of trying to make sure that the official opinions of the paper didn't slant or shape the news did not mean that we didn't talk to reporters. We did, because they were among the most knowledgeable people about the things we were writing about. Often, in the time between the editorial meeting and lunch, I would go out into the newsroom and pull up a chair by a reporter and ask her or him whether they knew more about the story from which I was taking my editorial than they had been able to put in the paper and ask them about whom I might call. The reporters were always helpful, though I had the impression that most of them thought the editorial page was a waste of time. They said, genially enough, that writing editorials was like peeing in your pants in a blue serge suit—it felt nice and nobody noticed.

After lunch, things became more serious. I would make telephone calls to sources, look in the clippings from the morgue, go through my own files or look in a book for material. I was by then seriously engaged in filling myself up with something to write. If it wasn't going well or if my material was sketchy, the thing I would hand in at five would be pretty splotchy. Or, worse yet, maybe there wouldn't be anything to hand in at five and I would have to explain it the next morning.

By three-thirty it was time to start putting things on paper, and in the early days it was a time of high anxiety or even terror. The one thing that helped to make this period of the day less traumatic for me was that there were a lot of other people around with grim looks on their faces and a tightening in the way they carried their bodies. The casual, even pleasant morning was being paid for now, and in my case, the cost was high. I could feel for Phil as he walked up and down the hall in the late afternoon seeing us all bent over our typewriters and wondering if anything printable would be turned in to him in time to put a page out for the day. But I worried more about myself, because it wasn't clear in those early days that anything of value would come out.

But, incredibly, on each of the five days of every week something came out that I could place in Phil's "In" basket. The payoff, of course, came in the morning when I would pick up the paper and see my words in print as the opinion of *The Washington Post*—an opinion that had a good chance of being read by, or called to the attention of, a substantial portion of the nation's most powerful politicians and important policy makers, an opinion that, just twenty-four hours earlier, had been nothing more than an inchoate response in my head to something I had just read elsewhere.

Phil and I rarely had disagreements in those days about editorials. He might change a line here or a word there—and he generally lopped off my last sentence because he said I had a tendency to "go cosmic at the end." I remember just one editorial I wrote in the early days that did not see the light of day. I had seen a story about a House subcommittee report criticizing the Administration for permitting the White House staff to grow so large. It had increased by some 14 percent since Nixon's inaugural and, according to the committee, no end was in sight. I ran off a little piece decrying the tendency of modern Presidents—especially this one—to insulate themselves with staff members who almost had to become sycophants and competitors for the President's time and attention. I suggested that the practice wasn't good for any President's sense of reality.

The first time Phil and I really clashed over an editorial was when Adam Clayton Powell died. Many white people didn't think much of Adam. They viewed him as a gaudy, swashbuckling, uppity, crooked nigger; a disgrace to his people and to the Congress. I didn't see it that way. Adam had certainly played fast and loose with House expense accounts and airplane tickets, but compared to some of the outright thievery that we knew went on unpursued on Capitol Hill, blacks couldn't get too excited about what it was proved that Adam had done.

What we saw, instead, was a nigger who wouldn't bow low to white folks. We saw a nigger who in the early days had cared enough to walk a picket line to get blacks hired in the stores on 125th Street in Harlem where they spent their money. We saw a man who, in the lonely days before there was a sixteen-member Black Caucus in the Congress, was brave enough to stand virtually alone in the well of the House and try to attach the Powell amendment, prohibiting federal funds from providing segregated services or purchasing materials fabricated in discriminating companies. We saw a man who was smart enough to accumulate the seniority necessary to become Chairman of the Education and Labor Committee and to use the power of that office for the benefit of poor people.

Lyndon Johnson had seen him more as the blacks saw him. Cliff

Alexander, who worked for Johnson in the White House, told me one time that Johnson had had Powell into the Oval Office to discuss a number of bills that he wanted to go through Powell's committee. All during their talk, the President toyed with a gold cigarette lighter with the Presidential seal on it. Powell kept staring at the lighter, so the President toyed with it some more.

Finally, the President said, "You like this lighter, Adam?"

"Yes, Mr. President," Adam replied.

"Well here. You can have it," Johnson said, tossing the lighter to Powell.

Adam thanked the President for the gift, and the two men continued their political conversation. When Adam was leaving the office after they had finished their talk, Johnson called after him, "Adam!"

"Yes, Mr. President?" Adam replied, pausing at the door.

"Don't go losin' mah lighter in some whorehouse."

The two men roared at the joke and then, when Adam was gone, Johnson said to Clifford. "That is one hell of a politician. One of the best on the Hill. And he's straight."

That's what blacks thought too, so when Adam died, I proposed that the paper run an obituary editorial, and I volunteered to write it. Phil wasn't so sure we wanted to glorify such a man. I argued that the man had been an authentic black hero, albeit one with human frailties, some of them as outsized as the talents of the man who carried them. Phil finally agreed to the editorial, but said that it would have to carry a denunciation of Adam's venality. I said I'd see what I could do.

I decided to use Powell's legislative record to make the point that despite the way his career had ended, he had been one of the most significant political figures of his time. I called the clerk of the Education and Labor Committee and asked her for a listing of the significant pieces of legislation Powell had gotten through the Congress. The woman had been put in her job by Adam when he was chairman, and she loved him so much that she was delighted to comply. The list turned out to be hugely impressive. After opening the editorial into a description of how Harlemites had viewed Adam, his early civil-rights struggles in New York and his lonely battles for the Powell Amendment, I put in the whole list the clerk had given me. Then, I made a passing reference to the legal and ethical problems Adam had made for himself at the end of his career and suggested that though those things were bad, the whole of the man was far greater than that.

Phil thought the condemnation should be much stronger, and I tried to defend the piece as I had written it. Phil insisted on something much stronger—something that would have asserted that Powell had disgraced himself, his people and the Congress. I disagreed strongly and said that with all the drunks and unpunished crooks that we knew on the Hill, we would be perpetuating the double standard that Congress had applied to Powell. I would rather we ran nothing if we had to run it with Phil's formulation. I said I wanted my copy back, that I didn't want my work to be the frame for what I would consider to be the unwarranted defamation of a man's life. Phil was angry and so was I. Then I said something that I shouldn't have said.

"Every black person who reads this will know that I wrote it," I said, "and I'll be damned if I'm going to take the heat for views that I don't hold. I think this kind of editorial should weigh the whole of a man's life, not prosecute him for part of it."

The second sentence was all right, but the first enraged Phil. His face got red and his lips were tight.

"We all have to take the heat from our readers for what goes on in this page," he said.

That was certainly true enough, and it was also true that I shouldn't have put my personal concerns into a conversation about the substance of an editorial. But it was also true that this editorial sounded like me, and that, coupled with its subject, was as good as a signature at the bottom of the piece. When people jumped on me for editorials that were conservative about welfare reform or busing, I could always duck by saying, as I often did, "Look, I don't write that shit, and I don't agree with it either." But this was different. I would have to admit that I'd had crap poured into my own editorial, an admission of impotence that I wasn't prepared to make.

Phil and I stared at each other for a tense moment and then he said, "Okay, let's see if we can work out some language that we both can agree on." So he wrote a sentence and I softened it and then he stiffened it a little, and then I softened it a little, and then we let it go, both dissatisfied. The piece ran and I had to admit that it wasn't too horrible, though not exactly what I would have wanted. Phil had to admit about the same thing.

Black friends of mine told me they were pleased that the *Post* had noted Adam's death and were glad that it had taken such a balanced view of him. They told me they were sure that I had enlightened the place and that they were glad that I was there. I took solace in their reaction and in the fact that our editorial was wiser and more human by far than the crabbed and ugly denunciation of Adam that ran on *The New York Times* editorial page.

The struggle over the editorial and the difference between the *Times* piece and the one we ran put my professional reasons for coming into the newspaper business into sharp focus. They also suggested pretty graphically the complexity of the task I had set for myself. The stock in trade of the news side of newspapers is the presentation of as large a slice of contemporary reality as the staff can wrap its mind around. The stock in trade of editorial boards is taking that reality and formulating opinions designed to shape a new and more promising reality.

Both enterprises are based on journalists' perceptions of reality. Throughout the history of the United States, decisions on what ought to be presented to readers of the newspapers, what is important and what is not, and suggestions about how to think about all of that had largely been made by middle-aged and middle-class white males. People's visions of the world are surely shaped by what they have been and have become. A woman's perception of the world has to differ from that of a man and a black's perception has to differ from that of a white. The introduction of a black into a previously all-white environment where the business involves interpretation of current issues cannot help but create profound disagreements.

This is particularly true when some of the issues to be addressed involve race. The bulk of the fight between blacks and their friends and the rest of the country has been about perceptions of reality. The reality that white slaveholders held was that blacks were a lower order of human being whom it was perfectly appropriate to enslave and oppress. The black perception, of course, was that blacks were people just like anybody else and deserved to be free. After slavery, the white perception was that blacks were lazy, shiftless, childlike and in need of the paternalistic system that whites had created. By the seventies, the debate over reality had evolved to a dispute over the view, firmly held by some whites, that too much had been done for blacks, that the racial problems had been solved in the sixties and that it was probably time, for the good of the nation, for the pendulum to swing back some. Much of the business of the NAACP and the Urban League had been centered on chipping away at white perceptions that limited black opportunities and effectively bottled up needed remedial action.

Blacks brought their views of what was important and what the world looked like to their newspaper jobs. Few whites were conditioned to see the world that way; so, in a microcosm, the essence of the civil-rights struggle was played out in newsrooms and on editorial boards, wherever blacks were given writing and editing jobs. Had a black been on the editorial board of the *Times* when Powell died, she or he would undoubtedly have had a struggle similar to the one I had with Phil. I was sure that the Powell episode was only the beginning of my part in the black journalists' struggle to get the press "to see America through a wider lens," as Bob Maynard once put it.

It was quite clear that such struggles could easily be both ugly and soul-searing. The challenges to white people on issues of race would trouble them at least as deeply as my challenges to the whites at the Ford Foundation. Those confrontations were bound to be charged with emotion. I had always found it difficult to contain my anger or my contempt for views and attitudes that were either blatantly racist or the product of an intellectual sloppiness that simply failed to examine racist assumptions and values. On the other hand, the sixties had made racism unacceptable in polite circles, particularly among Northern liberals. To charge them with racism or to suggest that as supervisors they had accommodated racially biased practices seemed to challenge something that was close to the core of their idea of their own decency. In the end, the fights would be about words, shadings and things that should or should not appear in print. The readers would rarely know about the battles.

But, at the *Post*, racial attitudes among those who led the paper seemed enlightened enough. I didn't take Phil's views of Adam Powell as indicative of his whole racial outlook, because I understood that Adam, with his flamboyant behavior and his defiant attitude toward the Congress, cut at white people very hard. Phil, I knew, was a clever man and generally seemed fair and open. It was only through his deputy, Meg Greenfield, that I began to sense something that was at first encounter no more than a troubling, almost subliminal vibration; but it was, in fact, a clue to the intellectual ethos of the *Post*. It came up over lunch in a single sentence—a quicksilver streak through the sky that was gone as soon as it had appeared. Meg and I were at the Madison coffee shop shortly after my encounter with Susan Brownmiller at the MORE convention, and I was beginning to explore the women's movement. I asked Meg about it.

"I don't know much," she said. "I'm like you. I've never been a 'cause' person."

That was either a serious misreading of me or Meg was gently instructing me in the preferred approach to the work at hand. Other things she mentioned at other times confirmed the latter suspicion. High passions were tolerable foibles in minor associates, but not appropriate for more serious members of the staff, the principal shapers of the *Post*'s opinions. We would scream, of course, at outrages, but we would judge each day's events as they were presented to us on a rational case-by-case basis in a framework of intellectualism that favored the credibility and stability of our institutions. Thus, after the May Day anti-Vietnam War demonstration in 1970, there was considerably more concern expressed at high levels on the editorial staff about the disorder and apparent carelessness by some of the demonstrators than there was about the wholesale lawlessness of the roundups carried out by the D.C. police under the leadership of the Department of Justice. The editorial board distrusted general political frameworks, no matter how firmly rooted in actual experience they might be. And, if you looked at the results of this approach on a case-by-case basis, it would be appropriate to call the pragmatic philosophy of the page *drifting right*.

It is true that on straight racial issues—as opposed to mixed public-policy questions such as welfare reform—the members of the board were quite clear and decent. But the elimination of racism was not at the core of their interests, and no matter how easily seduced I was by the personal and social exchanges, my values and my assumptions about American society were not to change. Unfortunately, for everybody, there was no evidence of that time bomb ticking away on both sides of the new relationship in which camaraderie, high spirits and respect sloshed around like champagne in the winning World Series locker room.

Although I expected that there would be disagreements from time to time on racial and social issues, I didn't fully understand the chemistry that attended the addition of a black to a staff like the one that produced the *Post*'s editorials. I understood that white people were deceived when they hired me. I was Roy Wilkins' nephew. I had sparkling credentials to go with a pedigree that suggested that I would be the kind of moderate, reasonable person Meg thought I might be. The degree of my passions about race were not apparent in my appearance and demeanor, as Mike Sviridoff had learned to his dismay.

Though I understood that part of my side of the equation, I didn't understand theirs at all. Although whites who bring blacks into formerly all-white workplaces talk a lot about integration, they seem at bottom to want the *appearance* of change without its substance. The blacks who are deemed qualified for "white" jobs are usually the most whitelike in the population. The expectation—often unconscious, I am sure—is that though the color in the class picture will look different, nothing in fact will have been changed. That may work where people are installing telephone lines or figuring out how to sell shock absorbers. But when it comes to making, shaping or analyzing public policy, that white hope is either fools' gold or a black's nightmare.

The black person who behaves as most whites would have him act in a job that can affect the welfare of blacks forfeits a chunk of his soul—that chunk that makes it possible to respect himself. But, the black who insists on change, no matter how diplomatically, runs the risk of betraying the expectations of the people who hired him.

I loved the ambience of the newspaper and my new relationships. One day when one of my young black colleagues was complaining about the treatment that blacks received on the paper, I told him that I couldn't believe what he was describing could have come from any conscious or unconscious policy developed by my friends at the top. We were drinking after work in a bar near the paper.

"Conscious or not, man," my young friend said, "the paper is fucking blacks. They need a few of us in the newsroom and they need you on the editorial staff, but basically, they don't give a shit."

"I don't believe that," I said. "I love Bradlee and Geyelin. I think they're really straight people."

"You're an asshole," my young friend replied.

"Well, shit," I replied. "I've had fights with white people for as long as I can remember. I'm tired of fighting with white people. And, if I start out thinking they're shits, I'll start seeing shits."

"I don't know nothin' about all that, man," my friend replied. "All I can tell you is that these people ain't no angels. They'll treat *you* good, but they'll fuck *us*."

I couldn't tell him about the conversations I had been having with Ben Bradlee, which gave me hope that the *Post* really wanted to

correct problems like those the young people had pointed out. Bradlee was trying to find a black to appoint as city editor. He thought,
and I agreed, that if a black were there to make critical decisions
about our coverage in the city, a better sense of the life as it was
actually lived in that 60 percent black city would emerge in our
pages. Ben had approached a black editor in Portland, Oregon, but
the guy declined. I suggested that he offer the job to Bob Maynard,
who was the *Post*'s senior black journalist. Ben agreed and made
the offer, but Maynard turned it down on the grounds that he didn't
want to be the ingredients of a "shit sandwich," with a group of white
reporters under him and white editors over him.

After Bob turned that job down I suggested to Bradlee and to
Katharine that he be offered the job of Ombudsman of the paper,
which had just become vacant with Ben Bagdikian's forced resignation. They agreed and Bob agreed. I thought Ben's search had been
sincere, and I expected that the Maynard appointment was the beginning of a serious effort to change things in the newsroom.

But on the Fourth of July I was forced to think back on my
conversations with my young friend and begin readjusting my views
not only of the top people at the *Post*, but of Washington's entire
white liberal establishment as well. Jean was in town, and she asked
if I wanted to go with her to a fireworks display to which she had
been invited on the campus of Mount Vernon Junior College, over in
Wesley Heights, an affluent residential section tucked away far west
of the black sections of the city.

We encountered large crowds of people walking through the dusk
as we approached the playing field of the college. One of them was
Dino Bradlee, Ben's bright and handsome thirteen-year-old son. "I
don't have a ticket, but I can get in with a parent. You be my father
for the night, okay, Mr. Wilkins?" Dino asked with a light laugh.

"Sure Dino," I said.

As I walked through the gate with my hand on Dino's shoulder,
playing out the ridiculous charade that Dino was my kid, I looked
around and realized there weren't any other black people in view and
yet the crowd would run to several thousand.

There were clean-cut families. Women were dressed in Peck and
Peck casuals, and some men had red vests, white shirts and blue ties.
There were large groups of children wearing straw boaters with red-
white-and-blue ribbons on them. The crowd was somehow more
formal and formidable than the tens of thousands of less affluent

people, both black and white, who sprawled casually on blankets in the Mall to see the public fireworks display in front of the Washington Monument.

Jean and I got to the rim of the bowl and headed up the side of the hill, through the people who were already gathered there. When we gained some height, we turned, and the whole panorama was spread out below us. There were at least five thousand people in the sports area of Mount Vernon Junior College, and as far as I could see, everybody who had been gathered there to celebrate the nation's birthday was white.

As it got dark, groups of clean children, decorated in red, white and blue, began to perform on the field. And then several District of Columbia hook-and-ladder trucks with firemen on them came racing onto the field, led by D.C. police cars with lights flashing and sirens screaming. After that, the Marine Corps band marched out on the field, its brass blazing away. It was an ecumenical Democratic evening with Charles Bartlett—John F. Kennedy's old friend—and Jack Valenti—Lyndon Johnson's amanuensis in the White House— sharing the master-of-ceremonies job. Jean and I located our friends, George and Liz Stevens, and as we approached them, they saw us looking around the place and they began looking at it through our eyes.

We didn't have to say anything. They understood.

"I don't believe this," George said.

Liz made her eyes big and shrugged her shoulders when I asked how come nobody on the black side of Rock Creek Park knew about this celebration, and how come the Marines and the fire and police departments were here entertaining at what was essentially a private party? Nobody knew. There was no answer to those questions. George and Liz were embarrassed by it all—for themselves and for us. For Jean and me, everything was compounded by the sight of the children parading to martial music played by a military band. It was the fourth summer of the Nixon Presidency and in that 65 percent black city, the white people—mainly liberals—seemed to be celebrating a country that I didn't live in and I didn't even know about. It was chilling.

The experience was also unsettling for a lot of people who knew me. They all knew of the piece I had done about the Gridiron dinner. Now, when Phil Geyelin or Ben Bradlee or Joe Califano looked at me, my brown face exaggerating the whiteness of the sea around me, they could visualize a new gridiron piece forming in my head. They could see their names in it. The white people of the Northwest of Washington had probably had these innocent semiprivate celebrations with a little help from tax-supported agencies for years without noticing that anything or anybody was missing and without pondering whether it was proper for the police and firemen and Marines to be there performing in the pageant. But now my mere presence raised all the questions. The people I knew there had a hard time thinking about them and talking to me at the same time. I would get the briefest greetings from them and then they would turn away, embarrassed. And, of course, their discomfort compounded my own. It was as if I had sneaked up on them and peeked into their heads to glimpse the kind of America they inhabited when their public faces were off. Walking out of that field that night after the last burst in the fireworks display had faded from sight, I remembered the words of my young friend: "You're an asshole."

But a train of events had been set in motion that was to push race from the home front of any thoughts for several months. It had begun in New York on a Sunday afternoon in June. I was reading the paper after Jean and I had come back from a long aimless stroll through Central Park when I came across a strange little story. It had a Washington dateline and reported that several men had broken into the headquarters of the Democratic National Committee in the Watergate office building on Virginia Avenue. It was thought that the men were Cubans and that one of them was the chief of security for the Committee to Re-elect the President. I showed it to Jean, and we both laughed about it in a puzzled way. We couldn't figure out whether the burglars had been Castro's Cubans or the CIA's Cubans or whether they were Nixon's Cubans. We did a little light speculation and I concluded with a guess:

"I'll bet it's CREEP (formally known as the Committee to Re-elect the President)," I said. "It's probably another one of Nixon's sleazy tricks."

That was nothing more than a guess based on my enormous disdain for the President. The next day Phil wrote a clever editorial entitled Mission Improbable, poking fun at the whole enterprise. John Mitchell, chairman of CREEP, denied that his organization had had anything to do with it and Ron Ziegler, the President's press secretary, declined to give a White House comment on a "third-rate burglary." The Democrats fussed and fumed, but nothing much came of their sound and fury. Larry O'Brien, the chairman of the Democratic National Committee, brought a lawsuit against CREEP and that was pretty much it until the first week in July.

Jean came down for the Fourth of July and one night before the holiday, a bunch of us from the *Post* went out to dinner together at Chez Camille, a French restaurant on L Street, where a lot of *Post* people hung out. Nixon was having a press conference that night, so some of us went back to the paper to watch it on the television set in Ben's office. Ben, Phil, Jean and I and some others watched a strange performance by the President. Nixon, who should have been on top of the world, seemed almost terminally nervous. I couldn't understand why. George McGovern was sure to be the Democratic candidate, the weakest possible challenger, I thought. The polls showed Nixon to be in no trouble in the country, but here he was, sweating and fumbling questions like a man with a problem.

John Mitchell had just resigned from CREEP. The reason given was that his wife's health was bad and he needed to spend time with her. I didn't believe that. Mitchell didn't seem like the loving homebody to me, and from the stories around town about Martha, well or sick, she would have driven any man into acute workaholism. So why did he resign? Why was Nixon so nervous? I couldn't make anything out of it. There were just a lot of questions that I thought ought to be answered.

A few weeks later, when both Phil and Meg were down at the Republican National Convention in Miami and Jim Clayton was in charge of the page, I saw a little story that I thought deserved comment. It described the answer given by the lawyers for CREEP to a request by Larry O'Brien's lawyers for the commencement of pretrial discovery procedures in his Watergate lawsuit. CREEP's lawyers asked the judge to put off that discovery until after the election, claiming that answers given now could embarrass the President in his campaign. That was an astonishing admission, I thought. What was it that could be so embarrassing? I thought the admission deserved comment that might spark more curiosity.

I proposed the editorial to Clayton. He was not impressed with the idea; he discouraged me from writing the piece. I pressed him on it, and he finally agreed to raise it with Phil when he called from Miami. Later, after they had talked, Clayton reported that Phil hadn't been any more impressed with the suggestion than he had been. That was the end of that editorial, but it was not the end of my curiosity about the subject. Something stank there, I was sure of it. Despite the fact that it was clear that the CREEP man had been a former CIA operative, I was pretty sure that the burglary had to do with CREEP and Mitchell's resignation and ultimately Nixon. If there was dirt there, I wanted to get it out. I really hoped that story wouldn't die.

Finally, about a month later, there was a story in the *Post* reporting that Wright Patman wanted to use his banking committee to hold an inquiry into the whole matter, including the report that CREEP had a "slush fund" of several hundred thousand dollars. Phil was on vacation, but Meg thought it was a promising editorial subject, so I went after it. There were a couple of things about the story that I didn't understand, so I went out to look for Carl Bernstein and Bob Woodward, the reporters who had worked on it. I didn't see Bernstein in the newsroom, so I asked someone to point Woodward out to me. It was August 1972, and I had never met him. I didn't even know what he looked like.

Woodward was a broad-shouldered fellow with dark hair and a serious demeanor. What struck me about him right away was that he wore a white shirt with a tie knotted right up to the collar. He was the squarest guy I had met since I had come into journalism.

"Mr. Woodward?" I inquired.

"Yes," he said, rising and extending his hand to meet mine.

"I'm Roger Wilkins from the editorial page," I said.

"Yes," he said, "I know who you are. Nice to meet you."

It was the most formal meeting that I ever had with anybody in the *Post*'s newsroom.

I was as interested in getting some sense of the character of this young reporter as I was about specific questions concerning the story.

"In your story, you said that there are allegations that the CREEP had a 'slush fund,' " I said. "What exactly do you mean by slush fund?"

"I mean they have a great deal of cash on hand that they use for a lot of different purposes," Woodward said.

"You mean cash that is unbudgeted and unaccounted for?" I asked.

"That's right. That's what I mean," Woodward said.

"Do you know where they get it?"

"No, not yet," he said, "but I can guess."

"From corporations and big-businessmen they're holding up," I said.

"That would be my guess," Woodward said.

336 ROGER WILKINS

"But we don't know that yet, huh?" I asked. "We don't know that
well enough to print it?"

"That's right," Woodward replied. "Not yet we don't." He smiled
softly when he said it. Woodward was a very straightforward young
man. He looked me in the eye as we talked, and he was clear about
what he knew and what he couldn't print. He was cool and calm. We
could have been talking about mortgage interest rates. I trusted him.

I went back and whipped up an editorial that summarized what we
knew and asked a lot of questions about what we didn't know. Why
should the President's campaign let clouds form over it? Why didn't
Maurice Stans, the treasurer of the campaign, come out and tell us
about the so-called slush fund? Where had it come from? What was it
to have been used for? And what was going on over at CREEP
anyway? Mitchell was gone. G. Gordon Liddy was gone. Hugh Sloan
was gone. Why were all these people gone? Had they been booted out
for bad behavior? Had they been shunted away so people couldn't
find and talk to them? What had these people to do with the burglars
from Miami? But, beyond all that, if the Republicans had nothing to
hide, why were they permitting all these barnacles to accumulate
around the base of the President's campaign? Why didn't they just
come out and answer the questions?

I thought I knew why. They couldn't, because the answers were
more embarrassing than the unanswered questions. But, the unanswered questions could make them pretty uncomfortable. If I kept
pegging the questions at them, others might take them up as well. If I
could find ways to keep on writing editorials like this one, it would be
like turning up the heat, day by day. Somebody inside the fortress
down there on Pennsylvania Avenue might crack.

I loved my job that day. I surely wasn't writing about mortgage
interest rates.

When I got through with the piece, I showed it to Woodward. It
was the first time I had showed an editorial to anybody in the news
department. But the subject was important. And it was complicated. I
had written with a great deal of heat, and I was going for a terribly
vulnerable spot in the President's campaign. I would get him in the
jugular, if I could. So I had to be accurate. I didn't ask Woodward for
his opinion about my opinion. I just asked him if the facts were
right.

He read the piece carefully and then he handed it back with a smile and said, "It's fine, but there's just one problem. You're awfully rough on Hugh Sloan and you shouldn't be."

"Why not?" I asked. "He's one of the guys they chucked overboard hoping that by getting rid of the hand they could hide the cookie jar, isn't he?"

"No," Woodward said calmly. "He's not a bad guy. He's a good guy and it would be nice if you didn't rough him up."

So I took the stuff about Sloan out of the piece, and it ran as I handed it in. That was the first in a long line of Watergate editorials I was to write in 1972, and I loved doing every one of them. What I couldn't have known then was that after only six months at the paper, that editorial was my first step down a road that led directly out the front door of the *Post*.

I didn't know that then, though, because I thought I was putting my life back together. Our renters' lease on our house on M Street expired, and Eve and the children moved back from New York. Eve and I decided to attempt one more reconciliation, so I ended my relationship with Jean, moved out of the Georgetown townhouse that Tom Wicker and I had shared for a few months and went home again. But it didn't work. In February 1973, after almost seventeen years of marriage, I left again. This time it was for good.

28 Now let me step back a moment and say something about editorial writers. We are true journalists in the sense that we have an obligation to our readers to get our facts straight and to make arguments honest. But, unlike reporters, we can—it is our job to—form opinions. Our task is to enliven and inform public debate on important issues. I had an opinion about Richard Nixon. I didn't like him one bit. My views about Nixon were well settled by the time he took office in January 1969. I had read and heard about his anti-civil libertarian zeal on the House Un-American Affairs Committee and his scurrilous campaign against Jerry Voorhis and Helen Gahagan Douglas. I had seen the Checkers speech on television. I watched how easily he traveled the low road for Eisenhower in the 1956 campaign. I remembered the You-won't-have-Richard-Nixon-to-kick-around-anymore speech to reporters after his 1962 gubernatorial defeat.

By the summer of 1972, enough evidence had accumulated during his three and a half years in the White House to convince me that it was time for him to pack up and go home. In some aspects of foreign affairs, Nixon was shrewd and brilliant, and I think the nation owes him a great debt for his successes. For a time, I believe, he helped make the world a safer and saner place.

But other landscapes were shadowed with horror. He had widened the war in Vietnam, marching us further into the grossest military and political disaster this country has ever known. He had retreated on civil rights, had tried to trim back the Voting Rights Act of 1965, the most successful constitutional legislation in this century. He turned loose the meanest dogs in Justice and the FBI on war resisters and apparently considered using Teamster goons on them. I remember watching Nixon on television announcing before a union convention that Americans constituted one sixth of the world's population, and consumed one third of its energy, and that he wanted to keep it that way.

People have asked me whether I was out to "get" Nixon when I wrote my Watergate editorials. I think no more than my former *New York Times* colleague, Bill Safire, was out to "get" Jimmy Carter when he harped on "Billygate" for months on end. I don't think any journalist, except a fool, thinks that she or he can "get" a President. If it is your honest opinion that he is bad for the Republic or that something that he is doing is bad for the Republic, then it is your obligation as a "professional citizen"—a phrase my *Post* colleague J.W. Anderson once used to describe those of us whose job it is to think carefully about things that other citizens don't have the time to ponder—to point those things out as clearly, honestly and skillfully as you can. You know you can't "get" him—you only maybe can change his course a little bit.

And I was out to change Nixon—no question about that. But it was my conviction then, and it is my conviction now, that *The Washington Post* was not out to destroy the Nixon Presidency or the man himself. During all the months that I worked on Watergate—from August 1972 through early January 1974, I never heard any news-side person who was involved in the story utter one word that indicated that he was out to get Nixon or that he was doing anything other than pursuing the hottest domestic political story he had ever seen—not Woodward, not Bernstein, not their editor Barry Sussman, not the Managing Editor Howard Simons, not the Executive Editor Ben Bradlee. And I never heard the Publisher, Katharine Graham, utter one false note either.

Two of us smelled blood in the water early in the story. My pal Herb Block, the great political cartoonist, had views on Richard Nixon that were, to put it gently, even more firmly held than my own. We figured old Tricky was hiding something—we didn't know what —and we went after it with zeal.

I wrote about twelve Watergate editorials that fall, all based on reporting that Woodward and Bernstein did. Some days, Herb Block and I would have the same idea and the cartoon and the editorial would complement each other. I loved our collaboration, because Herb had been one of my journalistic heroes from the time when my

political consciousness was forming. The editorials I liked best were
those that commented on the judicial proceedings and in which I
would try to urge the "Judicial Officers of the United States" and the
Congress to cut through the sleaziness with which Nixon had surrounded the White House. Also, when it became clear that Nixon
campaign operatives were collecting dirty cash from corporations and
stuffing it into suitcases for delivery at CREEP headquarters, I
thought they were straining our political process beyond tolerable
limits. That day I sat down and wrote an editorial that began:
"There's something to be said about corruption. It stinks."

Sometime into the fall, I realized that the rest of the press was
hesitating about following the *Post* into the Watergate swamp, but I
figured that we were onto such a helluva story that one day they'd
want to play catch-up. I tried to put the complicated facts, as we
knew them, into neat, easily understandable packages that they could
pull from their morgues when their editors said "Go." After the
election, the story floundered. Bob and Carl seemed stymied and
didn't print much, except for one story in which they had one fact
half wrong. The Nixon camp jumped on that and tried to pound us to
death. Congress was just lolling about in the water, as far as I could
tell. But then came James McCord's confession and John J. Sirica
became *the* judicial officer of the United States, and we were off and
running again.

After the beginning of 1973, an ever so subtle change in how we
dealt with Watergate editorials was initiated. We weren't calling it
Watergate anymore, Phil Geyelin said, the subject was too big for
that. The message was clear. I was to participate in the writing of the
Watergate editorials, but I was not to write all of them anymore.
Strangely enough, I wasn't too upset about that, because I was beginning to drown in the subject. I would study the latest Watergate story
over morning coffee, discuss it at the editorial conference, tackle it in
my editorial, and continue living Watergate right through dinner when
it was always, it seemed, the primary topic of conversation. There
were days when I would have preferred being a sports writer.

But, as days passed, pressures on the *Post* began to build. The
White House was preparing to play hardball with the company's
television licenses when they came up for renewal around the country, it was said. A very high Nixon Administration official was said to
have threatened Katharine that unless the paper lightened up, he
would put out the sad facts of her late husband's last illness. That was

all wind above my head, but there is one story about Katharine Graham at her best:

Clare Boothe Luce made a major speech to the newspaper publisher's convention in Washington. She said that she had prepared a speech, but was uneasy about it the night before, when she went to bed. Then, in the night, the spirit of Henry Luce came to her and told her to tell the truth. Whereupon, she launched into a full-scale attack on the *Post* about Watergate and for hiring "enemies" of the President. After the speech, according to my informant, who was at the table with her, Katharine summoned someone who was a mutual friend. According to my informant, Katharine sent Mrs. Luce the following message:

"Phil Graham appeared to me in the night and said to tell you, 'Shove it.' "

Bob and Carl and I became very close during those months. I had written almost all of my Watergate editorials off their stories: That is, I would read one of their stories and then go talk to them to clarify any facts that puzzled me. When I finished the editorial, I would show it to one of them, not for editorial slant, but to make sure that I hadn't gotten any of the facts wrong. They appreciated my work, because as Bob told me once, the fact that the editorial page was backing them up made it easier for them to persuade their editors to print their stories. The way the *Post* worked was that the news side did not suggest editorial policy and we didn't tell them what to put in the paper. But on Watergate, we surely read each other's work with care, and a warm mutual respect developed between "Woodstein" and me.

In the spring of 1973 Bradlee, then a member of the Pulitzer Prize Board, called the whole staff together a few days before the official announcment of the prizes and stood on a desk and announced that we had won the medal for public service. He named us all, including Barry Sussman, the man who edited Bob and Carl during the hard days. I was standing just behind the two young reporters when Ben made his announcement. It was a fine moment.

One last thing ought to be said about that prize. When it was awarded, the work of Bernstein, Woodward, Block and Wilkins was cited. There was no mention of Barry Sussman, Bob and Carl's quarterback, without whom, less would have occurred. Barry deserved a share of that prize.

But, good things happened to me. Years later, when I called Herb

Block to congratulate him on winning his third Pulitzer in his own right, that wonderful man said to me, "Thank you, Roger, but the one I loved the best was the one we won together."

The pressures of time, journalism, the legal and Congressional processes were beginning to pull out the strands near the core of the Nixon Administration by now. John Dean began talking, Jeb Magruder began talking. H. R. Haldeman, John Ehrlichman and Dick Kleindienst were tossed overboard. It was a real mess and about that time I composed a short bittersweet editorial about the Department of Justice, which, in my way, I had loved. I wrote that for reasons that were largely out of its control, the Department was probably past the point where it could conduct investigations and prosecutions that would have much credibility with the American people. It was essential to have such credibility, the editorial argued, because it was imperative that faith in our institutions be restored as quickly as possible. The editorial concluded by calling for the appointment of a special prosecutor. I checked the facts with Woodward, as I always did, and then I gave it to Phil. He said it was too shrill.

That editorial never ran. But weeks later when Phil was out of town, Meg Greenfield, his deputy, came into my office and said that she had been talking with former Justice Arthur Goldberg and that he thought the only way out was the appointment of a special prosecutor. She asked me what I thought of that idea and I said I thought it was a fine one. She asked me if I would come in the next day—a Saturday—and help her write it as the Sunday lead. I asked her if she thought Phil would agree to the position, and she said that was no problem; so I helped her write the editorial and it ran. Months later, after Archibald Cox was in place as special prosecutor, I heard Geyelin brag to somebody that the *Post* had been the first to call for a special prosecutor.

One evening that spring I visited a friend who was dying of cancer and then met with Eve about a problem with one of the children and then headed off to see a woman. But I cracked up the car and destroyed my left elbow on the way. Some splendid doctors in George Washington University Hospital reconstructed the elbow as best they could and saved my hand from paralysis. The four-week stay in the hospital did me a lot of good. I got to watch all of Sam Ervin's Watergate Hearings, for instance, and the rest slowed me down. People at the *Post* and the institution itself were very good to me during that time, but the accident did nothing to detract from my growing reputation inside the *Post* building as an unstable fellow. My friend died while my arm was healing.

A few months later, I learned that the brilliant and beautiful Sheila Okpaku had been separated from her husband, Joe, for some months. So, I contacted her and began seeing her. Since she was firmly rooted in New York and I was finding Watergate and the jealousies it was spawning inside the paper totally oppressive, I decided it was time to give up the *Post* and to leave Washington.

29 Shortly after I left *The Washington Post*, I joined the editorial board of *The New York Times*.

As the idea of returning to New York had formed in my mind, getting on the *Times* was no problem. Abe Rosenthal, who is now Executive Editor of the *Times*, had been shocked two years earlier when it had been announced that I was going to the *Post*.

"Why did you decide to go there and not come here?" he asked. "You are known here. You have friends here."

Abe was right about that. He was a friend. When I was at Ford, I would often spend an evening with him in the little Japanese sitting room that he had fixed up behind his office. We would drink, talk about our childhoods and our insecurities and sometimes I would advise him about his racial situation on the *Times*. Now and then he would take my advice. Harrison E. Salisbury was a friend, Tom Wicker was a friend, Charlayne Hunter-Gault was a friend. And I had met Arthur Ochs (Punch) Sulzberger, publisher of the paper. So, I answered Abe's question.

"Two reasons," I said. "First, they asked me. Second, you didn't."

So, when I was through with the *Post*, I called Harrison and told him that I had a new love, that I was leaving the *Post* and returning to New York. "Would you consider working for the *Times*?" he asked. "Sure," I said. And in due course I got a job offer.

As I was walking out of the private club on Massachusetts Avenue, where my interview with John B. Oakes, the editor of the *Times* editorial page, had taken place, a city bus stopped and a little mass of

blue jeans, green knapsack, unruly hair and golden-brown face came
hurtling out of the door at me. "Daddy," the mass screamed; then
David and I walked down Massachusetts Avenue toward Du Pont
Circle with my arm draped around his shoulder and I felt sad.
Though Amy, who was then fourteen and a brooding, silent teen-
ager, clearly loved me, David's love was like a raw and open wound.
And, once more, I was going away from him and his sister to live and
work in a different city. I would see them regularly as I always had
done, but they would get less of me and I would get less of them. We
would need more than regular visits, I knew.

They seemed to be doing all right in the Georgetown Day School
where race didn't seem to be a problem. They had black schoolmates
and white schoolmates, and Georgetown Day had been the first private school in the District of Columbia to integrate. But I had heard
about one racial story there.

On a field day at the end of the school year, when the children
would play games and compete in front of their parents, a white
woman I knew, who was married to a black man, came up to me and
pointed her son out to me. He was a golden-brown kid and looked very
much like David. He had been in the school just one year, so I asked
the woman how he liked it.

"Okay," she said, "but he has been called nigger here."

"Here at Georgetown Day!" I exclaimed, astonished.

She said yes and that her child had come home hurt and crying and
that her husband had gotten upset and had called the school. The
school authorities, after a little investigation, confirmed to the child's
father that the incident had happened and the father demanded to see
the offending child and the child's teacher.

"What happened when your husband got to the school?" I asked.

"They brought out the boy who called our child nigger," she said.
"It was David Wilkins."

I doubled up with laughter and asked what her husband had done
then.

"He took our son home and gave him a lecture about not being so
sensitive," she said.

Later, I asked David whether he sometimes called people nigger.
His eyes got big, as they always did in those days when he was about
to lie. "Don't lie to me," I demanded.

"Yes, Daddy, sometimes," David said.

I laughed then and rubbed my hand through his hair. "Well, don't call no nigger a nigger until you're sure he's *your* nigger," I told him.

Well, I was going to the *Times* and I was going to subdue my sensitivity too. I had been the lead black in white institutions for sixteen years. At the law firm in New York, at AID, at Commerce, at Justice, at Ford and at the *Post*, I had been close to the most powerful people and never failed to confront them when social unrest rocked their organizations. I had taken out the cudgels and had gone belly to belly with them. I hadn't always won, but I had taken scars and given some. It had taken its toll. I was almost forty-two years old. I had paid my dues and I was tired in my spirit. The *Times* would be my resting place. I would fight for my people with my words and my ideas, but I wouldn't get involved with internal politics.

Shortly before I was to go to the *Times*, I learned that the publisher had told a meeting of the minority caucus on the paper that they shouldn't be so upset about how things were going there. One of the things he had just done was to hire me. As soon as I heard that, I went to Deputy Managing Editor Seymour Topping and told him that if the publisher thought he was going to get me in between the company and the minorities, he could forget it, because I wasn't playing. If I couldn't just come as professional journalist and not as the lead black, there would be no deal. A couple of days later, Top called me back to say that the publisher was delighted with my attitude, because that's just what he thought he had hired, a professional journalist.

John Oakes's operation at the *Times* was very different from Phil's at the *Post*. It always seemed ironic to me that the group at the *Times* was called an editorial board while that at the *Post* was called the editorial page staff. It should have been the other way around. There was a collegial atmosphere at the *Post*. We all talked. We all influenced one another. Even Phil, when he wrote, would take our views into account and Katharine, when she came to our meetings, was simply one of the voices. At the *Times*, we were John's staff, no question about that.

Instead of meeting as a group, John would visit each of us personally to discuss editorial ideas. If he had an idea, we would discuss that and if I had an idea, we would discuss that. The end product of our bilateral conversation was an agreement about what I would work on that day and how it would be shaped. Nobody else had any influence on it.

John and I worked well together, although we had little in common. He is an old-school Princeton liberal who believes in enlightenment as the way to progress. I was twenty-one years younger and believed by then in groin fights as the way to progress. One time when we were arguing about my unalloyed support of the extension of the Voting Rights Act of 1965, John wasn't sure about its absolute ban on literacy tests.

"I'm not sure illiterate people can cast an informed vote," he said.

"They can hear and they can talk, can't they?" I said.

"Yes, but you take in a lot of information reading," he replied.

"Okay, John," I said. "If you'll write an editorial arguing that illiterates shouldn't have to pay taxes or have their sons go off to war, I'll write an editorial supporting literacy tests for voting."

He made a wry face and then said, "Okay, go ahead and write the editorial your way."

John Oakes is a wonderful and principled man. He brought the *Times* out against the Vietnam War very early. He was infuriated when Ford granted Nixon a pardon. He was four square for civil rights as he understood the issue, though he couldn't quite comprehend that genteel and upright New York religious and philanthropic child-care organizations could be screwing little black foster kids. We'd wrangle over such issues and invariably, when he would let me write one of my contested editorials my way, he would come in sheepishly the next day and tell me that his wife, Margery, or one of his daughters had thought the piece was wonderful. One time after he had told me about Margery's approval, I said, "The trouble with you, John, is that you hear this stuff, but think that's only the way women, blacks and kids think." He just chuckled and chuckled. Despite our fights, John and I respected each other, and we are fast friends today.

At about the same time, I was beginning to learn about gay political and civil-rights problems from my friends David Rothenberg and the late Robert Livingston, prominent New York gay activists. I thought the *Times* needed to take a more enlightened attitude on those issues, and I began writing editorials that changed its positions, but it was unfamiliar territory to me, so I had to talk to a lot of people.

One day, I had lunch with the head of the Lesbian Feminist Liberation organization. In due course, the cost of that lunch appeared on my monthly expense voucher and John called me.

"Roger, you don't really think Mr. Sulzberger ought to pay for you to have lunch with a lesbian, do you?"

"Well, think of it this way, John," I said. "Sulzberger has a better chance of getting his money's worth when I'm having lunch with a lesbian than with a heterosexual woman." John laughed and approved the voucher.

I changed the *Times* editorial page. I was the black, the feminist, the gay activist, the civil libertarian as well as a person who often wrote on national politics and occasionally on international affairs. If I had only been dealing with John, the *Times* would have been a piece of cake. But, there were other people there too—like Leonard Silk, the fine economics journalist. I realized after I had been there about six weeks that Silk never talked to me about anything but sports. Now I love sports, but not as a steady diet. Finally after about six weeks of sports with Silk—when it was clear that he was just trying to be friendly, but didn't quite know how with a black—he started another sports conversation.

"What the fuck's wrong with you, Silk, you got a jock strap for a brain?" I asked. We talked about other things, even economics, after that, and our respect for one another grew.

Not every racial incident ended happily. There was a party at which the wife of an editorial board member told me that her husband had been very annoyed when it was announced that I was coming to the board.

"It's a shame," her husband had said to her, "that even on the *Times* editorial board we have to take on unqualified people just to fill some numerical quotas."

As the woman paused to freshen her drink I thought about that. The *Times* had run a bio of me when it announced that I was coming. It had reported that I was a lawyer, had served in AID, had been an Assistant Attorney General and an officer at the Ford Foundation. In addition it mentioned that I had written editorials for *The Washington Post*, though it didn't mention the Pulitzer. Nobody on the board had broad credentials like that. And this woman's husband, though a nice enough guy, whom I liked, was in my estimation a very ordinary fellow.

The woman returned and continued: "But, you know, after you'd been here a while, he came home and told me, 'Honey, Roger's all right. He's a real guy.' "

Then she punched me softly in the arm and winked. She thought she had paid me a fine compliment by telling me that her dreary husband had validated my quality.

Sometimes in the three and a half years that I wrote editorials for *The New York Times*, my friend Kenneth Clark called me the most turbulent man he knew. Whatever truth there may have been in that, my personal life was surely turbulent. My relationship with Sheila wasn't working out. She was learning to be a law professor at Hofstra University on Long Island while I was learning to be a "Timesman" (as *Time* magazine would say). She would come home with her racial horror stories from the Hempstead campus and I would come home with mine from 43rd Street. We would exchange our stories and console each other. Every night it was as if we were standing in the kitchen ankle deep in our own blood.

Sheila and I were very much alike in a number of respects. We had both grown up in a largely white world, each of us had been racial pioneers of a sort, and at the time we were together, each of us was pushing ever deeper into the white world. Neither of us had completed our search for a comfortable racial or occupational identity and all of our pressures were too much for our relationship. We were together for about a year and a half and then we went our separate ways. She is a wonderful woman and we are still very good friends.

The breakup with Sheila was a turning point of sorts. Eve, who knows me as well as anybody, once described me as a "romantic puritan." That's true enough, I think, and I had always believed that in this life I would find "one true love." I knew she had to be strong and accomplished and somebody who could command my respect and not be overwhelmed by me. Though I had known some white women well and had loved Jean, I hoped that the woman would be black. It would be better for my psyche, I knew. Sheila had been my best hope, and it hadn't worked.

There were other women after Sheila. One was a lawyer, the third lawyer I had been involved with. When I told my friend, Carl Holman, about her, he exclaimed:

"Another lawyer! Well, even Picasso had his blue period."

During the years after 1970 Mary and I had occasionally exchanged cards and once or twice had talked on the phone. She had learned to work in stained glass and had set up a business in Santa Fe, New Mexico. In early 1977, after participating in a program at the L.B.J. School at the University of Texas, I went to Santa Fe to see her. We had a wonderful time in her little house on Otero Street and around the town. I stopped by and spent a fine afternoon with John Ehrlichman, who was writing a novel there and awaiting his Watergate trial.

John, whom I had met once in the White House before the Watergate time, was great company. We were like two generals from opposite sides in an old war. The conversation went like this: "How was it when I lobbed in that artillery shell that day?" "Well, how was it when I sent my light infantry out after you?" I had long believed that the course of American history would have been different if Ehlichman and H.R. (Bob) Haldeman and their wives had hit the Washington social circuit and had gone to some of Katharine Graham's parties. That sounds silly unless you've lived in Washington. Washington journalists are just like other people. Many of us are suckers for people who have fame and power. I remember all the days when Phil would sit with his foot on the edge of his desk and tell us what Elliott Richardson had told him at a party the night before.

If Haldeman and Ehrlichman had gone around to the parties, they would have been good old John and brilliant Bob instead of some cartoon-sized Prussians guarding Nixon's door. It's pretty easy to splatter a caricature, but it's harder to splatter a real human being. If powerful people in the press had known those two, it would have been harder to believe that Haldeman controlled a slush fund or that Ehrlichman had told John Dean to "deep six" an FBI report. The reason Henry Kissinger came out of the Nixon Administration relatively unscathed, I thought, was because of his masterful personal manipulation of the powers of the Washington press corps.

When I tried the theory on him, John said, "I think that's right, Roger. I always did."

"Then why didn't you go to the parties?" I asked.

"I asked Nixon and he said no," John replied.

Mary came to New York in late March 1977 to help me celebrate my forty-fifth birthday. We had dinner at a wonderful little Italian restaurant in Greenwich Village with Charlotte Curtis, editor of the *Times* Op-Ed page, David Schneiderman, her deputy, and David's girl friend, Peggy Rosenthal. Charlotte and David and their secretary,

Muriel Stokes, had come into my office at the end of my first day at the *Times* with a bottle of wine and four glasses to welcome me to the paper. Their office was a place of joy and laughter in that sea of middle-aged, middle-sized, white males who were on the editorial board.

Mary and I had a good time at that dinner and at lunch with Ramsey and Georgia Clark the next day. She decided to extend her visit, and we decided that we wanted to try living together one more time. Mary said that she didn't want to take the risk of closing up her business and moving to New York with no guarantees. She wanted to get married. Since my divorce from Eve had come through in January, I said okay. We decided that neither her parents nor my children were ready for this marriage, so we kept it a secret.

On a beautiful Sunday early in April, we were married by Dave Dinkins, a black friend who is City Clerk in New York, at Pam and Tom Wicker's townhouse on East 80th Street. The only people there besides the Wickers were Ron and Charlayne Gault and Ramsey and Georgia Clark. It was a lovely day, we were happy and we had our little secret. A couple of days later, I ran into Judah Gribitz, Governor Carey's counsel, at a restaurant. We greeted each other warmly and then Judah said, "I hear you got married Sunday, congratulations." Some secret!

Mary went back to New Mexico, closed her business and got back to New York in early May. In November she was packed up and heading back to Tucson, where she was raised. The oppressive East and my high-powered life were too much for her. In addition, she was a Western woman, used to horses and the desert; the fumes and canyons of New York oppressed her. She felt she was losing her identity, and my preoccupation with my career at the *Times* didn't help any. We were divorced in January. We had lived together with benefit of clergy and had ended our fantasy.

30 John Oakes's departure from *The New York Times* proved an unsettling shock to me and all who admired him. For reasons that I will probably never fully know, Arthur Ochs Sulzberger—the publisher and John's younger cousin—forced him to retire a year and a quarter before his sixty-fifth birthday, the *Times*'s mandatory retirement age.

Though John's replacement, Max Frankel, is a fine journalist and a highly intelligent man, I decided that I didn't want to write editorials any longer. One of the main reasons was that I, like many writers, am egotistical enough to want my name on my product. While it is clear that the editorial pages of the *Times* and the *Post* are two of the most powerful public-policy megaphones in the country, five years of writing for them had exhausted their possibilities for ego satisfaction. I told Punch that I thought writing anonymously was "an unnatural act" and that I wanted a column. He asked me to stay with Max for his first six months. I did, and then Punch gave me an urban-affairs column in the news department, under the editorship of Abe Rosenthal.

My columns were not to be straight opinion columns. They were to be "news analysis"—a journalistic form that Abe said he had invented. It was supposed to take a regular news story and expand upon it so that the reader got a fuller and deeper sense of what the facts had meant. In *Times* jargon, they were called Q Heads. It was a new form for me and not an easy one to master. My first attempts were flops. I had proved myself over and over again, but obviously I was going to have to do it one more time at the age of forty-five.

There would come a time when I could make a Q Head sing, but it was to take a while.

Judith Cummings, a talented and beautiful black reporter, and I tried living together a couple of times during this period. It didn't work out, but she was a wonderful friend and had a strong influence on me. For instance, she convinced me that my early columns weren't very good. She said that I kept on recycling my own head. She said that even when I quoted some of the leading blacks, like Kenneth Clark, Marian Edelman, Vernon Jordan, Carl Holman, Lisle Carter and Eleanor Holmes Norton, it was still recycling, because we were all close friends and we all thought alike. She said that I had to go out into a broader world and do some interviewing of strangers to make the column come alive. I didn't like to hear it, but she was right; so, I took her advice, and the column became better after that.

Despite my decision to stay out of the racial politics at the *Times* when I first went to the place, there was a tiny cloud on the horizon that I could barely see when I settled into my seat on the editorial board. A suit had been brought under Title VII of the Civil Rights Act of 1964 against the *Times* on behalf of all its minority employees, by people who worked in the commercial departments of the paper. Under my self-imposed rule of refraining from such things because I was too old and too tired, I shied away from it. When Scott Brown, the chair of the minority caucus, invited me to have lunch with her to discuss the problem, I would always say yes, but somehow, I never found the time to have that lunch. When Mary O'Melveny, the lawyer who was doing most of the work on our case, would send me questionnaires about it, I would pitch them into the wastebasket.

But then, Rudy Johnson, a man whose name is little known, but who should forever be a hero to black journalists, began to push the black writers on the paper to become involved in the suit. Rudy had become convinced, from his talks with the lawyers, that the *Times* would not take the suit seriously until the writers, people whose names were familiar to the public, became involved. But newspapers, like other institutions, have their class systems. Writers rarely spend time with classified-ad takers, so the writers were slow to understand that they too had interests at stake in the suit. I was among the slowest.

Finally, because of Rudy, I began to listen. And then I saw some

figures that indicated that on the average, a white high-school graduate who worked at the *Times* made exactly what a black college
graduate who worked there earned. I was like the mule who had just
been hit in the head with a two by four: I began to pay attention.
And, the more I thought about it, the less I liked what I saw around
the place. There was no doubt in my mind that Max Frankel had
tried to hire blacks in the Sunday Department when he had run it and
that he had hired two blacks after I left the editorial page. But there
were few minorities covering New York, a city that was fast becoming half minority. That was one whale of a story, and the paper
wasn't doing it justice. Nor, as I listened to my minority colleagues,
was it doing justice to them. There was something inexorable about
my involvement by then, because I was like my mother and had
learned from her. I couldn't sit on the sidelines.

My decision to get into the suit was complicated because my relationship with the paper was complicated. In many ways, the *Times*
had been very good to me. It had, after all, invited me to become the
first black to work on its editorial board. I was the first black to whom
the paper had given any kind of column and though I felt I was under-
paid in comparison to people of similar background and experience,
I was paid very well, according to the standards of the paper. And
Punch was always very nice to me. If there was something serious to
talk about, I could always go up to his office at the end of the day and
he'd fix me a martini and we'd sit and talk.

But those good things could turn into bad things, not just at the
Times, but at other institutions where I had worked as well. Because
I was viewed as the *different* and the high black, I was afforded opportunities to socialize with the brass. That had been no problem at
Justice because Ramsey and Georgia and Eve and I were truly friends
and the Clarks are very plain people. At other places where I worked
I was admitted to the social circles of the powerful people and I enjoyed it. It often seemed that they also enjoyed me. But sometimes a
transaction was expected to occur, even when my superiors were not
conscious of it. In a subtle way, I was being told that I was different
from the other blacks who worked around the place. I was being told
I was like the white people who owned or ran things. It was the
gentlest seduction in the world because, by and large, they were all
nice and enjoyable people to be with.

Whether they knew what was happening or not, I could see it. But
what can you say: "No, boss, I'm not coming to your house tonight

because I'm afraid you're seducing me into white values"? Or, once there, can you say: "Say, look, boss, I know we're having a good time tonight, but we've got a time bomb here—one of these days there's going to be a racial problem and you'll be on one side and I'll be on the other and then you'll think I'm a wretched ingrate"? You don't do any of those things and you just muddle through because there are no rules. Whites and blacks have rarely met at this level before and people in this generation are making up the rules as they go along. But, in the end, the black either has to give up a little bit of himself that is valuable or, at some point, there is a fight and he does indeed become a wretched ingrate in the eyes of the people who have feted him.

That happened to me at the *Times*, as it had happened before. But this time there was a real zinger. Abe Rosenthal asked me into the circle of editors at the *Times* and I said no. Before I was given the urban affairs column, he asked me to edit the Sunday Week in Review. It would have been a real breakthrough and would also have been a linchpin in the *Times* defense against the discrimination suit. I didn't say no because of the suit, but because I had given up being a boss and a bureaucrat years before when I wanted to be a writer. I loved writing and I didn't want to go back to that old life. So I said no and Abe was angry and I think I became an ingrate at that moment. But the record should be clear. The *Times* did make the offer.

It should also be clear that after I took the column in the news department of the paper, I experienced, in a variety of forms and from a number of people, the racial hostilities that my black colleagues who had worked in the newsroom had described to me while I was on the editorial board. Some of it was almost funny and some of it was almost brutal. All of it made my life unpleasant, and so I was ready, because of my own experiences, to hear what Rudy had to say.

I got into the discrimination suit with fervor. Apart from the encouragement that I gave to others, my most significant participation in the case was the day-long pretrial testimony I gave to the *Times*'s lawyers about what I saw as the paper's deficiencies in its coverage of minority issues, its treatment of me and its handling of black talent. As the most favored black on the paper—though at times the "favoring" was rough—I hoped that my frank testimony would serve as a pre-emptive strike that would induce the paper to enter into a reasonable settlement that would include a good affirmative-action agreement, without a trial that would injure a lot of decent minority journalists. Though I testified only to what I saw and what I believed, I knew life at the *Times* would be difficult for me after that. I showed the transcript of the testimony to Mac Bundy, and he agreed with me that the time for me to move on would come soon.

"You can do a lot of things very well," Mac said to me, "but one of them is not working for white people."

We both laughed at that, and I decided that I would stay until the suit was settled or tried, and then I would leave. But, as pretrial preparations dragged on and the hostility of some of the executives at the paper was manifested, my desire to be out of that place grew by leaps and bounds. Once more I sank into a deep depression, one that wouldn't stop.

In the early fall of 1979, while I was still in that frame of mind, I went up to see the Pope's visit to Harlem, because I knew I'd never see such an event again. I was so deeply moved that I asked Abe, who was surely no friend by then, if I could write about it. He told me to write it, that he would decide whether to print it. I wrote it and it sang. Abe came all the way back to the back of the newsroom, where I sat, to tell me so. He printed it, and the reaction was enormous. Colleagues shook my hand or wrote notes of appreciation. Editors who hadn't spoken to me in months congratulated me. A lot of fan letters came in. I even got a fine one from Mike O'Neill, the editor of the rival morning paper, the *Daily News*.

But I was still depressed, so I went up and had lunch with Kenneth Clark, as I always did when I knew I was in trouble. Though depressed, I was manic and all my feelings about the *Times* came pouring out. Kenneth was worried and tried to calm me. And then he had to go off to a meeting. I had had two martinis before lunch, wine with it, and now I ordered a postlunch scotch. George, my friendly waiter at that restaurant, looked sad and troubled when he brought it to me.

Nursing my scotch, I kept on thinking about the *Times*. I had written editorials, columns and book reviews, for both the daily and Sunday editions. I had written front-page stories, and I had written for the Week in Review, the Travel section, the sports page and the Sunday Magazine. And I had learned how to make a Q Head sing. There was nothing left for me to prove, except that I could take more punishment or watch it.

I also thought about my father, who, because of the color of his skin, the time of his birth and the time of his death, had never been able to do in journalism the things that clearly he had the talent to do. My father had written a column about me in the paper he worked for on the day I was born, just as I was later to write about my Uncle Roy on the day when he died. And, so I sipped the scotch and thought about Daddy and about what I had written about him in *The New York Times*:

> The man believed in the word. He lived by it. He read dictionaries just for the pleasure of it. The first present he gave the boy when he got home from the hospital was a child's dictionary. The boy would be assigned a certain number of pages to read every day. Then he and the man would discuss the new words the boy had learned.
>
> And there were other good times. The night, for instance, when the women in the house were out, and the man and the boy sat quietly by the fireplace reading. The boy was reading about King Arthur and the man was reading *Hamlet*. The boy didn't know then how unusual it was for a grown man to read Shakespeare just for fun. The man read his favorite soliloquy for the boy—"Oh! that this too too solid flesh would melt,/Thaw and resolve itself into a dew; . . ." The boy understood none of it, except that the man loved it, so it was special.
>
> When he became very ill, the man would sit in his bed with a portable typewriter on his lap, trying to write things that would help earn the family living. The boy in later years would abandon the law and take up the typewriter because that, he had come to believe at an early age, was what serious grown men did.

I had written that piece in 1978 when I was visiting Kansas City for only the second time since 1941. While I was there, I went to my father's grave for the first time since his funeral. I thought about him, then summarized those thoughts as I concluded the piece:

> The stranger hunched in his soiled trench coat against the January cold and remembered the boy who had shed one tear that January many years ago. And he tried to remember the man as best he could. The boy is gone now—the years are in his face; and his memory is long, full of woe and joy. He guessed that the man was in him. He hoped so.

I had climbed my daddy's highest mountain, so I took a dime and called 556-1771 and told Nancy Finn, the publisher's secretary, that I was coming in to quit and asked her to arrange appointments for me with both Punch and Abe.

One of the unhealthy things about the *Times* is that a lot of editors resent it when people walk away. They want to say that you were no good anyway. The best thing to do is to get some honor when you're walking out the door. One day when I was cleaning out my desk, William McGill, President of Columbia University, called to inform me that I had been elected to the Pulitzer Prize Board. I could hardly believe it. That was the place for the eminences of the profession. Bradlee had been on it, for instance, and Scotty Reston and Arthur Krock before that. Now, as I was leaving journalism, I was being informed that I was one of the first two blacks to be asked to join the board—William Raspberry of *The Washington Post* was the other. But, I had to tell Dr. McGill that I had quit the *Times* and was going out to be a freelance. He said that didn't matter and that if I would say yes, the deed would be done. I said yes.

There was only one more thing to do before I left. Punch's mother, Iphegene Ochs Sulzberger, had been a warm and kind friend to my daughter Amy and to me. In her eighties now, Mrs. Sulzberger is still an extraordinarily intelligent, warm, witty and wise woman, and like just about everybody who knows her, I loved her. When I called, she had already heard my news and she said, "Roger, you must come up here and tell me what is the matter with you." I laughed and we made a date for me to go to her Fifth Avenue apartment; then she asked, "Will it be tea or cocktails?" I said, "Oh Mrs. Sulzberger, don't be silly." So she said, "Okay, it'll be cocktails then." And I told her why I and a lot of other people with big bylines were leaving the paper and then she gave me a copy of her autobiography, which she autographed, "To my good friend, Roger Wilkins." And when I took that book, kissed her goodbye and left her apartment, I was through with the *Times*.

The newspaper jobs had given me a feeling of connection with the world. Yet I had also had the feeling that my life was slipping from me and that the books I wanted to write wouldn't get written because of the dailiness of newspaper life. The effort that was going into the racial and bureaucratic struggles was sapping and consuming me. My work product was slim and, in my view, of limited consequence. My dissatisfaction grew, and so did my thirst.

My relationship with Judith Cummings had suffered from all of this. When we went out, we were Judith and Roger of *The New York*

Times—a handsome black couple earning regular paychecks at a place where blacks hadn't performed such tasks a mere fifteen years earlier. But that was not enough to sustain us through my unhappiness.

I left Judith and the *Times* simultaneously, and my friends thought I had gone mad again. I wasn't so sure they were wrong. I borrowed an apartment from a friend and comforted myself with Scotch whisky, wondering how long I could continue to support Amy at Barnard and David at his private school in Washington. I had done rash things before, but this time I thought I had been absolutely foolhardy and, despite the concern and affection of dear friends like Richard Harris, Lisle Carter, Ramsey Clark, Kenneth Clark and Mac Bundy, I was terribly alone. I was terrified, and I could not sleep.

One Friday I felt especially desolate. I couldn't even read, and the television set in the apartment didn't work. So I drank. The next morning I was in terrible shape, so I began drinking to steady myself. After three drinks I didn't want to look at the typewriter or the stack of blank paper next to it. I went for a walk in Central Park. People were walking two-by-two, and children were with their parents, and young adults were playing volleyball. The only solitary people were the runners and they were displaying a self-discipline for which I had always yearned. My eyes were red from my solitary drinking, my hair was not well combed, and I had not shaved.

I could not bring myself to attend a party that night given by an old friend from the *Times*. I couldn't let everyone see my ravaged face, couldn't deal with questions about how I was and what I was doing. The truth is that I thought I was becoming a drunk for sure, so I clasped the bottle of Bell's Scotch closer to ward off that fear.

But even with a lot of Scotch that night, sleep wouldn't come. I tossed in bed and sweated with terror. Finally, sometime around four in the morning, a crazy memory touched my mind. It was my grandmother telling me that breakfast was the most important meal of the day. I set the clock for eight-thirty then and went right to sleep.

When the alarm went off, I got out of bed, walked past the bottle of Scotch on the bedside table and got into the shower. Then I shaved and dressed, bought the Sunday paper and found the cleanest eating place I could. I enjoyed a hearty breakfast of soft scrambled eggs, sausage, coffee and toast. It was ten o'clock when I got back to my typewriter on that golden, crisp fall morning. By one, when I was to go over to a friend's house to watch football, I had written fifteen hundred words for my first freelance piece since leaving the *Times*.

A few weeks later I went to South Africa for a conference and up to Zimbabwe to see what it would look like after independence. South Africa was probably the most beautiful country I had ever seen but with the most vicious political system I had ever encountered. Zimbabwe, though devastated by its war of independence, was sadly hopeful. I came back and wrote three pieces about South Africa and one about Zimbabwe and sold them all.

After that, I moved into Bobby Clark's apartment in the Village. Bobby is Ramsey's cousin, and he was on an extended visit to Paris and wanted someone in his place to take care of it. Except for the few months that I had spent with Mary in our picturesque little flat in the West Village, I had had no real home since I had left Eve. I hung onto sanity and self through work and hacked away everything else. I was neither Roger Wilkins, the first black Assistant Attorney General, nor was I Roger Wilkins of *The Washington Post* or *The New York Times*. Nor was there a woman to comfort me. I had honed it down to the bone. I invented myself each day, mainly by sitting down and doing my work on a little Olympia portable typewriter. It was the challenge that I had always feared and sought: Define yourself, nigger, in terms that you can respect. And in that funny little apartment on Tenth Street, I began to be the long distance runner—alone with himself and his fears and pain—that I had always yearned to be.

I knew that I had been obsessive in fighting racial battles and in slamming back at racial insults. Should I have compromised, if not to spare myself the anxiety that I felt each day, then for security and comfort for my family? I knew to a moral certainty that I had hurt my children. Amy, who was by now a junior in college and living in Brooklyn, seemed fine. And so did David, although he was struggling with dyslexia. They would have scars from me, I was sure, but perhaps no worse than those they would have suffered had I attempted to forge myself into a more conventional man. Later, each child would tell me how much hurt I had caused. Amy would say, on Christmas eve in her twenty-second year, "Everybody knows Daddy is a fuck-up," and that would make me cry inconsolably. Ten months later David would stand in my kitchen and explode with a rage that was almost uncontrollable and then dissolve into tears as he told me about his childhood. "I would lie there in bed and wait for you to come home—even before I could tell what time it was—and you were never there. You were never there!"

I was a man living in a never-never land somewhere far beyond the constraints my grandparents had known but far short of true freedom. I knew no black people—young or old, rich or poor—who didn't feel injured by the experience of being black in America. Though some went mad, most coped with the special problems that race presented to them. I had coped by translating my anguish into words, by trying to change the minds and the hearts of people. I believed it was possible to communicate with white people about race and thereby make things better. But there was always the need to write through their denial, which was near the core of racism. White people had been denying the truth from the beginning.

During those days when I was pounding out this book in Bobby Clark's apartment, I was approached by Murray Gart, the editor of *The Washington Star*. Murray was engaged in a stubborn struggle to keep that great old paper alive, and he wanted to know if I would come and help him. Though he never said it, I understood that he was searching for greater credibility and readership in Washington's large black community, and he thought I might be able to help. I knew that I loved the freedom that I had achieved and that I didn't have the strength for yet another bitter internal struggle.

So we negotiated. I would write long pieces for the paper and, aside from him, would have only one editor, my good and respected friend, Eileen Shanahan, a fine journalist and one of the toughest feminists in the business. I would be called associate editor, but I would be more like a writer in residence. I thought the capital needed two papers and that the struggle to keep a good newspaper alive was a noble one.

I surely must have seemed like a mystery to the people in the newsroom, because though my name soon appeared on the masthead, I wasn't around very much. I made a new friend, a young black reporter named Kenny Walker, who was amused at the reactions of some of the whites there to me. "They ain't never seen no blue-chip nigger like you before," he would say with a laugh.

When I moved back to Washington, I got an apartment in Anacostia, a poor black section of town. After so many years of a thoroughly integrated life, it was curious but comforting to get up in the morning and see only black people in my building and at the places where I went to have my clothes cleaned or shoes repaired. Some people thought my living there was something of a gimmick or a conceit, but it wasn't. The rent was cheap, the view was fabulous, and the constant proximity to ordinary black people was psychologically nourishing.

I wrote some things in the *Star* that I liked—about the city and about black people—and was really warming to my tasks when Time Incorporated, the *Star*'s parent company, decided to cut its losses and close the paper down. I was thoroughly depressed, because the *Star* was a fine paper with many fine journalists working on it. Weak though we were, *The Washington Post* had to keep an eye on us, and I am convinced that the competition made the *Post* a better paper. I was also depressed because there was a lot that I had intended to pour into the pages of the *Star*, and now that would never happen.

A few months after the *Star* folded, Kenny and I had lunch at Mel Crupin's restaurant on Connecticut Avenue. When we finished, I went to get a taxi on the southbound side of the avenue. Kenny told me I ought to go over to the northbound side because cabs didn't often pick up blacks going south for fear they were heading toward the ghetto.

"Aw, man, you're crazy," I said.

"No, I'm not," Kenny said. "An awful lot of cabs have passed me by on this side of the street."

"Well, I'll try this one," I said, throwing up my hand as an empty cab came down the street. It slowed and stopped. As I opened the door and stepped in, I turned and grinned at Kenny and said, "Blue-chip." Kenny was still breaking up as the cab pulled away.

EPILOGUE

"My mother is a fish." That is the splendid sentence that opens William Faulkner's *As I Lay Dying*. I didn't know, when I read it, that the fish was a symbol for Jesus. And as I sit working in the summer house on a beautiful lake in Michigan that my stepfather built for his family to enjoy, there are fish symbols all over the place. My mother is a deeply religious woman, and she wanted a few fish around the house because of that. Friends saw that and decided that it had something to do with the lake and all the fishing that people do around here. So they gave her fish things. We have paintings of fish in this house, fish-shaped ash trays, fish dangling from mobiles, fish platters, fish salt shakers; fish all around.

But my sister Judy got it right when she gave my mother a little wall hanging that says, "God couldn't be everywhere, so He invented mothers." I am not a religious man, but I have come to understand lately that I am a Christian to my marrow. I got that from my mother, just as I got from her the notion that my life should be forged into an instrument to be used to make things better for people whose lives are made miserable by the unfairness of our country. My mother is a fish, and so is my stepfather, and so were my father and my Gram. They shaped me and sent me out into a world toward places where there were forms of cruelty they never knew. They never told me what to do out there and certainly never asked me to prove myself by piling up money. They simply expected me to try to be decent and to do decent things.

The family is gathering now for our Fourth of July celebration— Momma and Poppa have come in from Grand Rapids; Judy flew in from Washington; Poppa's niece, Margaret, and her family drove up

363

from Ann Arbor; and Sharon and her husband, Melvin Peters, and their son Troy drove up from Lansing. I have been here all month finishing this book, while my wife, Patricia King, has been grading freshman law exams and preparing a new course she's going to teach at the Georgetown University Law Center next fall.

Patricia and I were married in February 1981, a month shy of my forty-ninth birthday and four months shy of her thirty-ninth. We met in December, I proposed in January and we were in Jamaica on our honeymoon before February was over. It was fast, but it was right. Patricia grew up in the public housing projects of Norfolk, Virginia, and went to the segregated schools there. Then she got a scholarship to Wheaton College in Massachusetts and was stunned, at seventeen, to find herself in what was an almost total sea of whiteness. Before she was through, she was student body president. She went to work at the State Department as a budget analyst and rose to be a GS 11 by the time she was twenty-four.

But she decided that she didn't want to make a career at State, and so, much to her mother's consternation, she quit and went to Harvard Law School. After Harvard, she turned down offers from major law firms to work in civil rights in the government, first at the Equal Employment Opportunity Commission and then at HEW. Instead of taking a promotion that Caspar Weinberger, who was Secretary, offered her, she went to Georgetown to teach. She has done that ever since, except for a sixteen month leave when she served in the Department of Justice as a Deputy Assistant Attorney General, directing the defense of all tort claims brought against the United States. Patricia and I both took great risks with our psyches and our careers before we met. We each ran some of the toughest gauntlets white people can construct. We each sustained massive injuries—some self-inflicted, some not—and we both had numerous relationships on the long roads on which we defined ourselves and which ultimately brought us together—matured, hardened and loving. My time with her has been extraordinary. I have never been happier.

Amy and David are not here. David is seventeen now—big and handsome—and he is spending this summer working as a counselor in a summer program at an Episcopal church where my sister Judy is active. He is in high school and is having a lot of the struggles that seventeen-year-old boys have. But, his racial identity is clear and he is a warm, funny, loving and intelligent person. He isn't cuddly anymore, but he is splendid.

Amy, now grown and beautiful, is in Springfield, Massachusetts, working at her first real job. She graduated from Barnard this spring and decided on her own that she wanted to help working class black people organize themselves so that they could handle their problems better. Nobody told her to do that, and she got her job with Massachusetts Fair Share on her own. Her boy friend is still in New York and she's on her own in Springfield, making her own way. Once when she was a little girl trying to do something hard, I offered to help her. She recoiled and said with great dignity, "My can do it by herself." I'm very proud of old My.

I have set up my writing table on the side porch, so that I can look down at the lake. In the evening, I can watch the sun go down and see its reflection through the white birch trees that are in front of the house. I love this spot better than any other place in America. I am home here—I have come home here—and I know, more clearly than I ever did when I was growing up, that I am an American. But, I do not love my country as I did when I was younger; then I often felt that I was only here at white folks' sufferance. I have seen too much to be able to retain the blind patriotism of my youth.

In a sense, I have been an explorer and I sailed as far out into the white world as a black man of my generation could sail. A New York law firm, State, Commerce, Justice, Ford, *The Washington Post*, *The New York Times*, the Hamptons, Johannesburg and Paris were some of my ports of call along with a number of beds, some warm, some luxurious, some both. I could not stand white people shutting doors in my face, so I pushed through plenty of them. My life wasn't always neat and tidy, and I didn't always do the right thing, but because the fish were guiding me, even when I didn't know it or want it, there were some good things.

After I left and they put some more blacks, some women and some young people on the board of the Ford Foundation, Mac Bundy told Kenneth Clark, "I didn't know one man could change an institution as much as Roger did, but he did it." Warren Christopher, when he was Deputy Attorney General, once told my staff that I was the conscience of the Department of Justice. I liked that, and I like the fact that Ben Bradlee gives me credit for helping him learn better the need for more racial openness at the *Post*. Once, at the *Times*, I was told that a column of mine had convinced President Carter to add $667 million to his budget request for education aid to disadvantaged children. I told that to Uncle Roy when he was very sick in the hospital, and he just smiled and smiled. The *Times* settled our suit with an affirmative-action plan that I thought was pretty good. Our lawyers, Mary O'Melveny and Jonathan Lubell, were wonderful. We even got a little money too. I paid for our honeymoon with part of it.

But in my explorings, I caught some diseases too—not malaria, such as the old explorers got, but depression, divorce and what people call in a genteel fashion, a drinking problem. And I found out that I surely didn't want to live "out there." I met some wonderful people, some of whom will be friends for life. But by and large, I found out that a lot of white folks "just aren't ready," as we used to say about ourselves. A lot of them aren't ready for decency and some of them aren't even ready to be polite.

The neoconservatives are spending a lot of time these days trying to convince us that America's racial problems are over, and that, therefore, we don't need remedies like affirmative action or comprehensive job training anymore. Even up here in the north woods of Michigan, you can tell that that just isn't true. A nice young white fellow named Brian Staley is caretaker of Poppa's house, and when he was over here doing some work the other day, he told me that a lot of white workmen won't work on the "black side of the lake." He also said that the township provided the black families out here with inferior services for our tax money and wouldn't even fix the potholes in the little road that runs behind our properties. I think of those miserable people being mean to Poppa—who at the age of seventy-nine, was elected Michigan Family Physician of the Year—and it turns my stomach.

Of course, you couldn't prove to the poor black people who live in the public housing across the street from Patricia and me, whose children go to terrible schools and for whom there are few jobs, that they live in a fair America. And you couldn't prove to my childhood friends from Harlem, who didn't survive—Ronnie, Sawyer and Andy are dead from drugs, and some others have lived since late adolescence in and out of prisons—that we live in anything but moral squalor.

You can still see it in some white people's faces. Patricia and I drove down to Harbor Springs, a watering spot for the affluent, to have dinner at the best restaurant in the area the other night. There were no other blacks in the dining room when we walked in, and we were dressed as nicely as the best-dressed diners. But some people dropped their forks and others dropped their jaws. Others stared at us with open hostility as we enjoyed our dinner. There were times when I was younger, when that behavior would have made me feel terrible, made me feel like an impolite person who had intruded into a place where he shouldn't have been. America has improved enough so that I don't feel like that any longer. But, I did feel bad that night. I felt bad for my country, because it demonstrated once more how far away so many white people still are from that fair America that I once thought was sure to come.

Ronald Reagan and David Stockman are building those ugly looks into national policy. They are telling poor blacks, Hispanic Americans, native Americans, and a lot of poor white folks too, that there is precious little comfort or decency for them in America these days. Nevertheless, neither the dirty looks nor the marble-hearted program ideas of David Stockman will convince me that I am not an American; that I have no place here. When the going used to get tough in earlier days, I used to dream of going off to Paris or some other place to write. But I knew I would have no bite there and that I had to breathe the air and absorb the feelings of America to be alive as a writer. And, of course, I have to stay to fight for my three-year-old nephew, Troy, for the child Patricia and I hope soon to have and for my grandchildren when they come. So, I know that I will be around to help clean up the rubble Ronald Reagan is creating.

It is a wonder to me that anyone who, in the days of segregation, when he felt like an unwelcome visitor in America, was so blindly patriotic, could now be so depressed about the international and racial future of his country and still draw so much strength from the conviction that he is an American and nothing but an American.

Part of it is simple. I don't believe in the perfectibility of white people anymore. I used to think that there was no more thrilling story in all of human history than that by virtue of the American Constitution, the decency of some whites and the valor of blacks that a people were being raised out of slavery into equality in the greatest nation the world had ever seen. God, how I loved America in 1950, when that was the essence of my understanding of this place! I thought then that prejudice was an individual thing that would die in heart after heart after the Constitution and the true humanity of black people were demonstrated to the people of our country.

I didn't know about the pervasive nature of racism then or about the bitterness of competition, about the genocide practiced on native

Americans or about how the worst aspects of Calvinism had come to influence the worst instincts of a whole people.

And, I hadn't the faintest inkling of the essence of racism, which is the evasion of individual responsibility by finding scapegoats for disappointment, failure and bad behavior and is also the imposition of a white fantasy upon peoples who look different and who have a different culture. For instance, even I thought for a long time that all Mexicans, with big sombreros on their heads, sat in the sun, cuddling their knees and saying "Mañana." I was an American before I knew it.

White people in this country insist on telling those of us who are not white exactly who we are, though they don't have a clue about what they are talking about. One of the great Justices, Roger Taney, told blacks that the Constitution said we couldn't be citizens. The American government told us in World War II that we weren't good enough to fight for democracy, except in segregated units and usually behind the lines. White Americans told us that we were shiftless, unclean and licentious. In the heyday of affirmative action they told us that we were unqualified. And now, the neoconservatives are telling us that we are free. All of that is bullshit. The clearest thing I was ever told by an outsider was by that stewardess on the Air India flight—that I was a man and an American. And I have fought off the fantasies that white people have tried to impose on me ever since.

And, there was one man outside the circle of my own family who helped me to do that more than any other. There were lots of beacons of course. W.E.B. DuBois, Martin Luther King, Jr., Malcolm X, Mary McLeod Bethune, Joe Louis and Adam Clayton Powell were among them. But, Jack Roosevelt Robinson was my main man.

Now, Satchel Paige is my main model. A baseball historian once told me that in one of those inter-color all-star games that they had before organized baseball decided that black men were good enough to play a children's game with white men, that a newcomer slammed a home run off Paige. Paige asked his shortstop who the newcomer was and was told that the man's name was Ralph Kiner, and that he had been rookie of the year and had led the National League in home runs. "Remember, Satch," the shortstop said, "he can hit the fast ball." The next time Kiner came up, Paige, against the advice of his catcher, threw three fast balls past Kiner and then said to his shortstop, "Nobody can hit Satch's fast ball."

That's the game I know. Two guys take turns on the mound firing their best blazers. The one who's still out there firing when the sun goes down wins. That's my game.

But, if it hadn't been for Jackie Robinson, I probably wouldn't have gotten a chance to play my game. Jackie changed the way we all think of ourselves. As an American, I grew up believing in heroes—the Lone Ranger, for instance.

Jackie put human dimensions on heroism. He was as fiercely competitive a man as ever lived, as far as I can tell. But when conditions for the race called for it, he reined in his fire under the most severe provocations—as when he couldn't stay with the Dodgers in segregated St. Louis, or when some "bush" ball players put black cats on the field to taunt him—and just played superb baseball. He was humble and quiet that year, as the needs of his people required him to be. But after he had proved himself in his rookie year and had paved the way for others to come, he became his full competitive, slashing self and he seemed to be saying, "No white folks going to cut me down ever again."

There were others after that. Bill Russell of the Celtics, for instance, who was proud, fierce, superb and a winner. And there was Jimmy Brown, a runner unlike any we have ever seen, who was proud enough to walk away at the top of his game. But, Jackie was the first and the fullest human being. He and the other black athletes engaged white people on fields and courts where there were rules and umpires and where white people had to play fair. Fields of play became human proving grounds where blacks had a reasonable shot at disproving the white fantasy about their inferiority. Watching Jackie, somehow I decided that I would do that on the sloping grounds of government, philanthropy and journalism, where there are no umpires and where white people cheat and demean blacks every day. I took my fast ball to those fields because Jackie had taught me that a black man need never again submit his psyche to the cruelties of white people's racist fantasies. Jackie also helped teach me that I was an American. Jackie was a fish.

President Ronald Reagan called me up here at the lake one day to complain about something I had written in the *Star*. If I were he, I would have complained too. Any fair reading of that column would reveal that I had called him an ignorant bigot and any fair reading of my mind would reveal that that is exactly what I think. Blacks used to laugh at white people who would deny bigotry by asserting, "One

of my best friends is a Negro." But people haven't been that crude
for years. But Ronald Reagan called to say that he knew about bigotry,
because he had had a black teammate in college; he and his white
teammates had been so offended by racial epithets thrown at the black
by the other team that they had turned a 14–14 half-time tie into a
43–14 rout. He also talked about his Catholic father, who wouldn't
sleep in a place that wouldn't admit Jews.

Well, "Pretty is as pretty does," as Gram used to say, so I argued
with the President about his policies, which are sure to hurt the poor
and the minorities. I was polite to the President, but I didn't back off.
We had no more agreement at the end of our civil conversation than
when we started talking.

When I got off the phone, Patricia said: "I'm so proud of you.
There you are, talking to the President of the United States and you
didn't give up one inch of your honor."

I thought about that last night when I read something else I wrote
in the *Star* arguing, on the basis of a trip to Mississippi, that the
Voting Rights Act shouldn't be gutted, as Senator Strom Thurmond
and a lot of other politicians seem to want to do—

> A few days after I got back from Mississippi, I took my daughter,
> Amy, to visit with Uncle Roy before she goes off on her first real job. . . .
> Uncle Roy is old now and he bends over in his chair. He sees best to
> his left and Amy sat on the floor holding his hand and kissing his arm.
> He loves her so. When she would move away, he would put out his left
> hand, looking for her and she would come back and that fine old man
> would smile at her and that splendid young woman would smile at him.
> Looking at them, loving them, I realized something. Because some
> white people are so resistant to change and some powerful white people
> dissemble and misuse power so, Uncle Roy believes that we will achieve
> America's constitutional promises more than I do and I believe more
> than Amy does.
> That is not a promising trend, so I would say to Senator Thurmond
> and others who would destroy the Voting Rights Act: Let my people
> vote or there is apt to be great American sorrow in the time of my
> grandchildren and also yours.

But, gut away though they will, there will always be honorable
black people to come back and to fight another day. I've always
thought that if I have fifteen lucid moments before I die, I'll want to
look back and see that I tried to act with honor, fifteen minutes by

fifteen minutes throughout my life. The struggle of life is not won with one glorious moment like Reggie Jackson's five straight home runs in a recent World Series—wonderful and thrilling though that was—but a continual struggle in which you keep your dignity intact and your powers at work, over the long course of a lifetime.

And that's my answer to David's question about whether he should be a football player or a writer and to Amy's unasked questions as well. It doesn't matter, writer or community organizer or football player. The answer is simply to learn the lessons of all the fish, to follow their paths of decency, and to have courage, because it is hard to do. That's all I know.

INDEX